THE CASE OF RICHARD SORGE

The case of
RICHARD SORGE

F. W. DEAKIN
AND
G. R. STORRY

HARPER & ROW, PUBLISHERS
New York

To
Those unnamed in the text

CONTENTS

CONTENTS

ILLUSTRATIONS

The illustrations appear between pages 192 *and* 193

Richard Sorge in October 1933 at the outset of his mission in Japan

Sorge in hospital during World War I

Sorge on his 23rd birthday, October 1918

Sorge in Oslo, April 1928

Ozaki Hotsumi

Branko Vukelic

Max Klausen

Mrs. Kitayabashi

Sorge in his Tokyo home

Sorge in Mongolia, September 1936

Procurator Yoshikawa with one of the authors (G.R.S.)

Hanako-san with her bust of Sorge

Hanako-san at Sorge's grave

The frozen Sea of Okhotsk at Abashiri, where Vukelic died in prison in January 1945

Mrs. Vukelic receiving the Patriotic War Order (First Degree) awarded to her husband, January 1965

ACKNOWLEDGEMENTS

The authors wish to express their particular thanks to Mr. Kawai Hidekazu. They are also under special obligations to Dr. Tsuzuki Chushichi, to Professor Richard Lowenthal, Dr. Wolfgang Leonhard, Dr. Hermann Weber, Miss Hede Massing and Dr. Margret Boveri.

The following present or past colleagues of the authors at St. Antony's College, Oxford, have contributed expert criticism of the early drafts of this book: Mr. David Footman, Mr. Max Hayward, Mr. H. T. Willetts, Dr. George Katkov, Sir Colin Crowe, Dr. Conrad Brandt, Dr. John Erickson and Mr. John Chapman.

The authors also wish to thank all those persons, notably in Japan and Germany, some of whom have preferred not to be mentioned by name, who have consented either to be interviewed or have provided valuable information by correspondence.

The authors are also indebted for assistance in translating to Mr. M. Matthews, Mrs. Neal Blewett, Mrs. Valerie Jensen and Mrs. Anne Shukman; and to Miss Anne Abley, Librarian of St. Antony's College, for her tireless search for rare publications. The main task of preparing the text of the book for publication has been undertaken with unsparing generosity of time and effort by Mrs. Patricia Kirkpatrick, with the efficient and helpful assistance of Miss Jennifer Rodger.

The illustration of the frozen Sea of Okhotsk is reproduced, with his kind permission, from a photograph by Dr. Fosco Maraini.

Note: The authors have followed the accepted practice in the use of Japanese names in giving the surname first, and the personal name second.

PREFACE

This book is based on all available material published on the Japanese side, dealing with the judicial proceedings against Dr. Sorge; on unpublished evidence of the German official enquiry at the time; and on interviews with many important surviving figures in the drama.

This documentation throws a unique light on the special characteristics of ideological espionage as well as on the history of this particular case. But a substantial part of this material is testimony given in the shadow of prison and court-room in time of war. The correct interpretation of such evidence has been challenging and tantalizing.

The quest for Sorge has led the authors from Japan to Germany; from France to the United States. This task has taken three years, seeking those with direct knowledge of the affair. But this would be yet another story.

Prologue

THE AMBASSADOR AND THE
CORRESPONDENT

AT five o'clock on the morning of Thursday, October 23, 1941, the German Ambassador in Tokyo, Major-General Eugen Ott, dispatched a top secret telegram to Berlin informing the Foreign Office of the arrests of Dr. Richard Sorge, the special correspondent in Japan of the leading newspaper in western Germany the *Frankfurter Zeitung*, and another German national, Max Klausen. The two men had been detained by the Japanese police six days previously on a charge of 'maintaining treasonable connections'.

This disquieting news had reached the German Embassy in the form of rumours, which were only confirmed on enquiry being made at the Japanese Foreign Ministry, who merely stated that the arrests had taken place and that this information should be treated as confidential.

In reply to persistent questioning, the Japanese Foreign Ministry stated that Sorge and Klausen were suspected of being in touch with a third party through the intermediary of Japanese middlemen. I have asked for the results of the interrogation to date to be communicated, but, as enquiries are still pending, this was not granted.

Dr. Richard Sorge was a well-established if controversial figure in the German colony in Tokyo. He had arrived in Japan in September 1933, with a solid reputation as a specialist on Chinese affairs, having worked previously for German newspapers in Shanghai, and with impressive introductions from senior German diplomats in Berlin to members of the Tokyo Embassy and to the Japanese Foreign Ministry.

In the confined and oppressive climate of a European community in an Asiatic capital, the newcomer was quickly accepted. His expert knowledge of China was welcomed in Embassy circles; his military record in the First World War—he had served at one time in a smart

regiment, and was the holder of the Iron Cross (Second Class)—
helped to ingratiate him in particular with the Ambassador and his
service attachés. Impeccably established as the correspondent of the
Frankfurter Zeitung he approached his professional work with a
thoroughness which won the respect of his journalist colleagues, and
he rapidly acquired an enviable reputation as an expert on the subtle
and alien world of Japanese politics. Visiting German officials and
newspapermen would call on him, often with the same introductions
from Germany with which he himself had arrived.

Richard Sorge was quite a figure in the Tokyo world. If his
bohemian exhibitionism, his arrogance and intolerance, particularly
when drunk, which happened frequently, shocked some of his compatriots, he was generally regarded as a serious and talented character
with a natural charm, especially for women.

The German colony in Tokyo, isolated at the other end of the world
from events in Germany, was still a microcosm of a society existing
prior to Hitler's take-over of power in January 1933. Anti-Nazi views
could still be cautiously expressed. A number of German families of
Jewish origin had settled unmolested in Japan. There was an absence
of a dominating and fanatical Nazi tone in the community. The
Ambassador himself was known for his moderate attitude.

Sorge often affected the heretical radicalism of an outsider, but this
was taken in good part as a typical German expression of the temperament of the ex-serviceman from the fighting fronts of the First World
War. Sorge had also prudently joined the overseas branch of the Nazi
party in 1934, shortly after his arrival in Japan, and became a member
of the Nazi Press Association three years later.

The news of the arrest of this distinguished journalist was greeted with
stunned disbelief in German circles in Tokyo. His fellow German
correspondents immediately wrote a joint letter to the Ambassador
expressing their unanimous support of Sorge and their incredulity at
the charges against him. They sent him parcels in prison and sought
permission to visit him. This latter request was refused, but the
Ambassador, accompanied by his counsellor, was reluctantly allowed
to have a formal interview with Sorge lasting a few minutes 'as a
special and unique favour', and only after a firm protest to the new
Japanese Prime Minister, General Tojo.

General Ott, like his compatriots in the Japanese capital, was unable to accept the bald official version that Sorge was suspected of treasonable activities. He had known him since 1934 when Ott had been military attaché in Japan. Sorge was a constant visitor to the Embassy, and a member of the Ambassador's circle of friends. The two men often played chess together, dined in the same houses, breakfasted together in the Embassy compound, and travelled in the Japanese countryside.

Sorge's views, and sources of information, were received and discussed regularly with the Ambassador and his advisers. He was treated and accepted as a personal friend and a reliable compatriot.

After the outbreak of the European war, Sorge was invited to edit a German Embassy news bulletin, and occupied an office for this purpose, where he read the official press telegrams from Berlin. He received a formal payment for this service. As an enterprising newspaperman, and as a former soldier with a brilliant war record, he established close relations with the successive military and naval attachés, and exchanged with them material and opinions on technical problems.

It seemed inconceivable that a man with this reputation and social connections could be the subject of the present accusations. His companion in misfortune, Max Klausen, was unknown to the German Embassy in Tokyo.

General Ott's first reaction to these arrests was that the men were victims of some anti-German intrigues in high Japanese circles. As Ott wrote in his telegram, 'The concensus of opinion among Embassy staff and local German nationals is that suspicion would be misplaced. Sorge, to the best of my knowledge, maintained contact with an informant who had access to the circle of Prince Konoye', the Prime Minister of Japan whose government had just fallen. Crucial negotiations between Japan and the United States were in progress during those October days of 1941, which would decide the balance of peace or war in the Far East. Certain confidential information on the progress of these talks

known to be regarded as a state secret, had reached Sorge. There is thus the possibility of an act of political vengeance or intrigue in which Sorge has become involved. As is recognized here, the group inimical to us still exercises much influence in the police and among officials of the Ministries of the Interior and of Justice; we cannot therefore exclude the possibility of anti-German sentiment being the motive power behind the proceedings against Sorge.

Elements engaged in this struggle behind the scenes of Japanese political life might well have engineered a dramatic and scandalous provocation.

The German Ambassador's telegram to Berlin reached the political department of the Foreign Office in the small hours of October 24 (European time). The official in charge of the desk, who had served in the Tokyo Embassy, minuted:

Richard Sorge belongs to the closest circles of Ambassador Ott's friends. It is well known in leading Japanese circles that Sorge had already formed close connections with the Ambassador when the latter was military attaché. Sorge is regarded as one of the best experts on Japan, though his critical attitude towards his host country has often raised considerable displeasure in official Japanese quarters. . . . As stated in the attached telegram, the arrest could be explained by the influence of anglophile groups . . . who are angered at the fall of the Konoye Cabinet, and attribute it, among other things, to German influence. . . . An approach to Prime Minister Tojo, who as Minister of the Interior controls the police, should clear up the affair as soon as possible.

The first move by the German Foreign Office was to sound out cautiously the Japanese Ambassador in Berlin, General Oshima, who was a friend of Tojo's and the architect, on the Japanese side, of a close and militant German-Japanese alliance, and a violent protagonist in favour of Japan's entry into the war on the side of Germany.

Whatever his personal feelings, Oshima and his staff in Berlin gave little away. It was true that he had received

a background telegram from Tokyo on the affair. This was purely a matter for the judiciary and the police, and in keeping with Japanese custom would be kept free from political influences. Sorge's arrest had no importance, naturally, from the point of view of foreign policy. On the contrary, the Japanese police would not have decided to arrest Sorge had there not been certain definite reasons for suspecting him.

It was possible that he might have been accused of assisting the Japanese Communist movement.

This formal attitude on the part of the Japanese Embassy in Berlin was disquieting and unsatisfactory. The German Foreign Office official thought that this charge was 'highly unlikely. Ambassador Ott and his Embassy staff were agreed in doubting that Sorge – who denied all guilt – could have committed the offence ascribed to him.' Berlin regarded it as a matter of urgency that the affair be fully clarified and Sorge released. Oshima was asked to use his influence in this sense.

On October 31 the Japanese Ambassador was more communicative. In a chance meeting with the member of the German Foreign Office dealing with the case, he said that

it appeared from the telegram which he had received for information from the Foreign Minister that the Japanese investigating authorities had written evidence of Sorge's connections with Japanese Communists. It was well-nigh impossible to intervene in proceedings which were pending before the Japanese courts, since the latter were politically independent and responsible only to the Emperor direct.

Oshima thought it possible that Sorge might have made use of Communists to obtain political information on current trends in the Japanese government and in the population at large. The German official to whom the Ambassador was speaking thought this most improbable. He had served in Tokyo and knew Sorge very well personally, 'but had never been able to perceive any Communist tendencies in him'.

But both Oshima and the German Foreign Office were deeply concerned that this affair should not prejudice, at such a delicate moment, the course of German-Japanese relations in the direction of a full military and political accord, and Oshima's first reaction was similar to that of his German colleagues. He now stressed that 'the best solution might be to let Sorge leave Japan unobtrusively so that the enemy could not make political capital out of the case. He would in any event intervene on Sorge's behalf.'

In Tokyo there were as yet no signs of clarification. On November 13 the German Ambassador telegraphed that, in spite of constant prompting, the Japanese Foreign Ministry had produced no evidence of the charges against the accused and could make 'no headway' with the Ministry of Justice. The necessary enquiries had not yet been made. Nor could the two men receive any further visits.

It appeared that, although the affair was being treated in strict secrecy, the German Embassy had learned of numerous arrests of Japanese subjects. 'A high official informed me under seal of secrecy that more than three hundred persons have so far been apprehended.'

Max Klausen had by now been identified through the records of the German Consulate in Yokohama as an import-export merchant, resident in Japan since 1935. 'The Consulate had not so far heard anything to the detriment of Klausen or his wife as regards their political views.'

On November 25, however, General Ott was able to telegraph to Berlin the contents of a brief note in German, prepared for the Embassy by the Public Prosecutor's Office on the basis of the preliminary investigation of Richard Sorge, and the document had been transmitted by the Japanese Foreign Ministry 'with the request that it be treated in the strictest confidence'. This memorandum lifted the edge of the sinister curtain which had concealed Sorge since his arrest, and was the first laconic indication that he had now begun to co-operate with the Japanese authorities in revealing the real nature of his mission to Japan and of his past antecedents.

The summary, which was now passed to Berlin without comment, contained the elements of the early pages of his 'confession':

The accused, Richard Sorge, after experiencing the horrors of the last war, came to the realization that certain self-evident contradictions are inherent in the capitalist system of the present day, joined the workers' movement towards the end of the war, studied Communist literature and gradually became a believer in Communism. He was admitted to membership of the German Communist Party in November 1919 in Hamburg, and here and elsewhere engaged in clandestine propaganda, agitation and educational work. When, in January 1925, he attended a congress convened in Moscow by Comintern Headquarters in the capacity of a delegate of the Central Committee of the German Communist Party Central Secretariat, he received instructions to join the Comintern Information Department and to continue his work under its aegis. In the spring of 1930, having received instructions to concentrate on espionage, he went to China and carried out his assignment in various localities. On receiving further instructions to carry out parallel activities in Japan, he applied in Berlin for membership of the German National Socialist Party. By way of camouflage, he simultaneously took up the post of correspondent of the *Frankfurter Zeitung*. In September 1933 he arrived in Japan from America in this capacity. From that time until his arrest he concealed his illegal activities by posing as a Party man and newspaper correspondent; in reality, however, he established a clandestine spy network under Comintern guidance with the aid of a

Yugoslav national, Vukelic, of Japanese citizens and of other foreigners; amassed information (again in collaboration with the Comintern) on military, political, economic and various other matters relative to Japan, and sent it to the Comintern by means of a radio transmitter and in various other ways.

General Ott added that he had asked the Japanese Foreign Minister to let him see the evidence on which this startling memorandum was based, and that the latter 'agreed to put in a word about it personally with the Minister of Justice'.

Ott ended his telegram by requesting that the charges levelled by the Japanese prosecution against Sorge should be verified by the authorities in Germany. Certain enquiries would also be taken up by the German Embassy in Japan.

In Berlin, as already in Tokyo, the case of Richard Sorge was opened.

PART I

<hr/>

Chapter 1

THE EARLY LIFE OF RICHARD SORGE

'I was plunged into an intense confusion of the soul.' SORGE

THE life of a spy is by definition undocumented. In the case of Sorge, the very fact that he was arrested in Japan, and in time of war in Europe, made the task of his Japanese interrogators in checking directly his version of his past in Germany a delicate one; and in the Soviet Union, clearly no enquiries could be made. In psychological terms, a European interrogator with a wider knowledge of national characteristics and traditions would probably have been able to provoke a more complete and plausible image of the man, but even the police enquiry conducted in Germany after Sorge's detention in Tokyo in October 1941 reveals grave and startling inadequacies and confirms the technical efficiency of the fabrication of one Communist intelligence agent.

It has been possible to catch a glimpse from time to time of Sorge's life and actions from persons who had known him, and from brief recorded references, and above all from the official enquiry initiated through the German Foreign Office by the security services in Berlin between December 1941 and November 1942.

Richard Sorge was born on October 4, 1895, in the small town of Adjikend near Baku in the Caucasian oilfields. His father, Wilhelm Richard Sorge, was a German mining engineer working for an oil company associated with the Swedish Nobel interests. His mother, who was much younger than her husband, was Russian.*

The family moved to Germany when Richard was three years old, and settled finally in a large house in the Berlin suburb of Lichterfelde. He was the youngest of nine children, and the fourth

* Sorge's father was born on April 5, 1851, at Wettin a. Saale in Saxony. His mother, Nina Kobeleff, was born in Baku on April 20, 1867.

son.* He was close to his mother, and he remained so throughout his life, always sending her presents or a telegram on her birthday.

Sorge grew up a sensitive and nervous child. He always liked to have a light burning in his bedroom at night. He had a happy temperament, and was popular with his brothers and sisters. The Sorge household was a united one, and his boyhood passed uneventfully in a typical wealthy Berlin middle-class background. Richard's father had made and lost considerable sums since his retirement to Berlin, where he had become a banker. He died in 1907, and each of his children inherited a private income from property.

Richard went to the local high school in Lichterfelde, where he displayed no special aptitudes or interests. He had grown into a balanced and healthy boy of outstanding physique. He was, and remained, inordinately proud of his sporting achievements, but apart from a marked interest in history and literature, revealed no special intellectual talents. Like his father and his school contemporaries, he was uncritically patriotic and Pan-German, a cheerful member of the sentimentally national Youth Organization, the Wandervogel, with whom he travelled and camped during the holidays. He was an average and undistinguished member of a comfortable and stable society. As he told his Japanese interrogators, 'I neither desired nor was able to adopt a definite attitude of my own'.

At the beginning of August 1914 Richard Sorge was about to leave school. He was nearly nineteen. On August 11 he reported as a volunteer at one of the military recruiting centres in Berlin and, after a brief training period, was posted to a student battalion of the Third Guards Field Artillery Regiment, and within a month found himself in action in Flanders. On November 11 he underwent the tragic and historic baptism of fire of the German student units at Dixemude where, singing patriotic songs, the young volunteers overran the French machine-gun posts with shattering losses.

The initial war of movement in Flanders halted along the line of the Yser, and the contending armies settled in for the winter of

---

* Like almost every 'fact' about Sorge's early life, even the size and composition of his family is open to contradiction. His own version, as stated to the Examining Judge, was that he had three brothers, two of whom were killed in the First World War. In 1942 one brother and two sisters were living. His former wife, Christiane, states that Richard was one of 'nine children' (*Die Weltwoche*, December 11, 1964). Independent evidence shows that the brother, Dr. Hermann Sorge, was a chemist, and lived for many years in Munich. (Richard described him as 'an engineer'.) He died in Toulouse in 1958. One of the sisters married a leading German eye specialist, and seems to have severed all connections with her brother Richard.

1914 to learn the grim and untried experience of trench warfare. In June 1915 Sorge's unit was transferred to the Eastern Front to take part in the Galician battle for the Austrian fortresses. The following month he received a shrapnel wound in his right leg and was evacuated to a military hospital in Berlin.

During his convalescence he passed his school leaving certificate, after a concentrated period of study, and with the highest marks. He volunteered immediately to return to his regiment, and in March 1916 was posted back to the Eastern Front. Within three weeks he was wounded again, this time severely. Both his legs were broken by shrapnel, and he was left with a permanent limp. After an agonizing journey across 'occupied Russia' he was brought to the University Hospital at Königsberg. For his gallantry in the field he was promoted to non-commissioned rank, and awarded the Iron Cross (Second Class). His military experience and direct contact with the horrors of mass warfare were over, but with them the illusions of his generation, of the student volunteers of 1914. From the initial baptism of fire to the routine nightmare of the trenches on two war fronts Sorge, like many of his contemporaries, had undergone a mystical re-birth, isolating him in an inner world, divorced from his family and class background, and placing in tormented doubt the postulates of the society in which he was still alive.

None of my simple soldier friends knew the real purpose of the war, not to speak of its deep-seated significance. Most of the soldiers were middle-aged men, workers and craftsmen by profession. Almost all of them belonged to industrial unions, and many were Social Democrats. There was one real leftist, an old stonemason from Hamburg, who refused to talk to anybody about his political beliefs. We became firm friends, and he told me of his life in Hamburg and of the persecution and unemployment he had gone through. He was the first pacifist I had come across. He died in action in the early days of 1915, just before I was wounded for the first time.

From 1916 onwards the personality of the young Sorge underwent a revolutionary change, the first in his career. As he expressed it himself, 'I was plunged into an intense confusion of the soul'. For the next two years he was to call in question every element of his previous existence. From the same year onwards, the tracing of his career founders in mystery and contradictions.

In hospital at Königsberg, Sorge had been drawn into a close and warm relationship with one of his nurses, a young Jewish girl whose father was an active Marxist intellectual with connections in the German Social Democrat Party. This episode was the beginning of his self-education, in a climate marked by physical suffering and the stigmata of war. He was just twenty-one years old.

Sorge began to study, feverishly and without plan, the Socialist and Communist classics, both German and Russian.* In spite of his mother's background, he had at the time no knowledge of her native language, and read Russian Marxist writings and the opponents of Marxism in German translation. He also studied on his own the ancient Greek philosophers, and Hegel 'as a ladder to Marxism'.

In October 1916 he enrolled as a student in the Economics Faculty at Berlin University, and lived at home. During this period, at lectures and mixing with his fellow students, he now came in contact with and secretly joined the left socialist organizations in the University. 'I decided not only to study, but also to take part in the organized revolutionary movement.' In January 1918 Sorge was formally released from the army and transferred his studies to the University of Kiel.

It was here that Sorge's intellectual curiosity was decisively aroused and his revolutionary convictions strengthened. The first marked influence on the young student—he was now twenty-three years old —was that of his professor at Kiel University, Dr. Kurt Gerlach, the son of a very prosperous family of strong left-wing sentiments originating from years of study in England, where he had come under the influence of the Fabians. Gerlach was an inspiring teacher, febrile and restless, and searching for a political cause. In his house in Kiel frequent study groups assembled in eager discussion of Socialist and Communist doctrine, in the apocalyptic atmosphere of the imminent defeat of Imperial Germany. The magnificent party machine of the German Social Democrats, whose official leadership—with few exceptions—had supported the war, was already losing the allegiance of many members of the younger generation who turned in the direction of a more extremist and anti-war political opposition, which had founded a separate party in April 1917 under the name of the Independent Social Democratic Party of Germany. It was this latter formation that Sorge had joined, probably even before his arrival in Kiel, and with whose local organizations he was involved during the early months of 1918. He seems to have established the student

* These included Marx's *Capital*, Engels' *Anti-Dühring*, and Hilferding's *Finance Capital*.

section of the party 'with two or three other students', and became its leader. He also acted as 'head of the training group in the district where I lived', teaching and lecturing on the history of the Labour movement, and recruiting new party members. After the mutiny of the German fleet, and the rising of the workers in Kiel, in October 1918, Sorge delivered

secret lectures on socialism before groups of sailors and harbour and dock workers. One of these lectures I can recall even today. I was called for early one morning, secretly led to an unknown destination which proved to be sailors' underground barracks, and there asked to conduct a secret meeting behind closed doors.

With the collapse of the German armies on the Western Front and the abdication of the Kaiser following on the events in Kiel, spontaneous revolutionary outbreaks took place throughout northern Germany, and particularly in Berlin where the extreme left-wing groups attempted to seize power from the official Social Democrat government which was treating with the Western allies. Sorge describes how

with two of my comrades I went to Berlin on official party business to work at party headquarters there . . . It was already too late to do anything when I arrived in Berlin . . . We were forced to halt at the station and searched for arms, but fortunately my weapon was not discovered. Any person who was carrying a weapon, and refused to turn it over, was shot. After being detained for several days inside the station, my comrades and I were sent back to Kiel. One could hardly call it a triumphant return.

Shortly afterwards, he joined the newly formed German Communist Party.

Early in 1919 Sorge moved from Kiel to Hamburg to complete the last stages of his doctoral thesis in political science, which he submitted successfully in August of that year, with the mention *summa cum laude*.*

In the spring of 1919 Professor Gerlach had moved from Kiel to Aachen where he had been appointed to the chair in economics at the College of Technology. He invited Sorge to join him as his assistant.

---

* This date is established from a copy of the certificate from Hamburg University found among Sorge's papers.

Sorge was in Hamburg working for his doctoral thesis, and increasingly involved in conspiratorial activities. But Aachen was in the heart of the Rhineland and of key strategic importance in the revolutionary struggle for power in Germany. Before accepting Gerlach's offer, Sorge was ordered to Berlin by his superiors—the central committee of the Communist party. He first reported on conditions in Hamburg and his work there and was then instructed 'to carry out various political activities for the party in the Aachen area'. His post as Gerlach's assistant was a deliberate cover for illegal work, and he was concerned with the organization of the local cadre section of the regional leadership of the Communist party. His teaching activities at the College of Technology were light, and his immediate interest was in building up youth study groups on Marxist literature, and the formation of a future party élite in the area. All party work after 1919 was in effect conducted underground, and in a climate of feverish dedication. Sorge henceforth devoted himself to such activities with increasing intellectual and emotional satisfaction. He found himself to be a gifted instructor, both eager and patient with the young, who listened to his interpretation of Marxist texts in secret meetings in Gerlach's house and elsewhere in the Aachen area. He retained his post at the College for not more than two or three terms (semesters) and by March 1920 he was no longer employed there.

Significantly his departure coincided with the Kapp *putsch*—an attempt by military elements of the German army to seize political power, which was countered by a general strike throughout the country and armed clashes in the industrial areas, particularly the Ruhr. The German Communist Party had, since its foundation, been recruiting secret military cadres—known as the 'M' Apparat—and organized on a regional basis. With his war record, Sorge was an ideal recruit for such work, and it is more than probable he was implicated in such activities at this time. This seems to be in part confirmed, both by recent Soviet references to his connection with the breaking of the Kapp affair, and his own silence on the subject in his later interrogations by the Japanese.*

At some time after this military episode Sorge began illegal work in the mining districts of the Ruhr. During these months of industrial

* While under arrest in Tokyo, Sorge was deeply concerned at concealing any military aspects of his mission, see p. 273. For the 'M' Apparat, see in particular Eric Wollenberg, *Der Apparat*, and Werner Angress, *Stillborn Revolution: The Communist Bid for Power in Germany* (1921–3) (Princeton University Press, 1963).

unrest he was at least on one occasion a member of a miners' strike committee and active in propaganda work among them.

According to his 'confession', he spent most of this year (1920) in Hamburg employed on organizing party cadres and advising a local Communist paper, and on 'other general duties'.* Sorge also stated that he did not go to Aachen until the following year, but in supplicating for his doctor's degree at Hamburg University, which he received on August 8, 1919, he describes himself as an assistant at the College of Technology in Aachen.

Sorge had been a full-time conspirator since 1919, and it is probable that his confused account of his German years was deliberately contrived to conceal his real activities.

His work in the Ruhr mines must have taken place during the first half of 1920. He was employed for a time as a miner, and himself describes these experiences as 'just as valuable to me as those I gained on the battlefield and my new vocation was equally significant, to the party'. Sorge created party cells in a series of pits in the coal-mining districts of the Rhineland and in the Dutch province of Limburg.† It is significant that the shafts and galleries in the mines on the German-Dutch border were used as a smuggling route for party couriers—and that he may have been connected with such activities. In those early days of German Communism, members of the various sections were frequently ordered to take on different functions.

Firm evidence is, however, available for the next stage in Sorge's activities. His cover had vanished with his leaving the Aachen College of Technology.‡ His work among the miners—which almost certainly had a direct connection with the 'M' Apparat of the party,§ who were ever seeking recruits for eventual action such as street fighting—had attracted the attention of the German police. Sorge's superiors now ordered him to join the staff of a local party newspaper *The Voice of the Mineworkers* and on February 28, 1921, the name of Dr. Richard Sorge appears in the local police records as resident in the small Ruhr town of Solingen.

* No trace of Sorge's membership of any Hamburg section of the German Communist Party during this time (1919–20) has as yet come to light.

† Sorge claims that he was caught and deported from Holland.

‡ In his confession, Sorge wrote that he left 'after a heated political controversy' in 1922. Other evidence invalidates without question this date.

§ One of the leaders of the Soviet military intelligence in Europe, Ignace Reiss alias 'Ludwig' was on secret missions to the Ruhr and Rhineland at this time (1919–20), and was in contact with Sorge.

Sorge's own description of his new functions is bizarre. 'Once, during a school vacation, I edited the Communist newspaper of Solingen for two months while its editor was in prison.' The files of the paper still exist, and show that Sorge was not the editor but, listed by name, he appears as the political leader writer. He made regular contributions, signed 'R.S.' between August 1921 and June 1922.

He was also active in the local training cadres of the party organization, and published in 1921 his first book on the presses of the newspaper. It was a short commentary on Rosa Luxemburg's 'Accumulation of Capital'—a classic but controversial Marxist text. Sorge refers to this pamphlet as 'clumsy and immature' but does not mention that it was published in Solingen.

In May 1921 Sorge married Christiane, the divorced wife of his Professor from Kiel and Aachen, Kurt Gerlach. The two men had been drawn together in frequent political discussions on Socialist and Communist themes since 'Ika'—as Sorge was known among his intimates—had become a frequent visitor to the Gerlach house in Kiel. An emotional attachment between Christiane Gerlach and Richard Sorge strengthened over the following two years. He does not seem to have been precipitate in this relationship. Christiane has written of him: 'Ika was never importunate; he did not need to pay court to people. They flocked to him: men and women.'*

But the affair came to a head in the autumn of 1919 when the two met again in Aachen. 'Ika' rang the door-bell one evening. Christiane realized that she must now face her husband. There was amicable and high-minded talk of divorce, and Christiane left while legal proceedings, lasting nine months, were pending, to stay with her stepmother in Bavaria.

After their marriage, 'Ika' and Christiane set up house in Solingen. She was studying for a doctor's degree, which she received in Cologne in July 1922, and he was ostensibly writing for *The Voice of the Mineworkers*. Christiane never visited the office of the paper and knew nothing of her husband's other interests and activities. And very few of his friends and party comrades from those days who have survived were even aware of his marriage.

* See Christiane Sorge, 'My Husband, Richard Sorge' published in *Die Weltwoche* (Zürich), December 1, 1964.

During these months in Solingen, Sorge's name can be identified on one occasion, apart from his party activities as a journalist, at the Seventh Congress of the German Communist Party held at Jena between August 22–26, 1921. He was listed as one of the forty-one delegates from the regional organization in Rhine-Westphalia.* He also reported on the proceedings in *The Voice of the Mineworkers*.

No other trace of his movements had been found until the local Solingen police records show that Dr. Sorge left the town on September 28, 1922.

Sorge (his party name at this time was 'Robert') was already a trained illegal 'apparatchnik', combining overt propaganda work as a journalist with underground assignments. During the final months in the Ruhr and based on Solingen, he was closely involved, as in Aachen, with organizing work among the miners, and for a time was an instructor at the party training school at nearby Wuppertal.†

Sorge had clearly by now been actively listed by the German police as a Communist agitator. The Rhineland had been under Allied military occupation since the end of the war, and Sorge claims, and perhaps accurately, that the local German authorities threatened to hand him over to the Allied military government and that, for this reason, he was forced to leave the region.

According to his own account, he went to Berlin to discuss with the party central committee his next assignment—and cover. He claims that he was offered a salaried position, but preferred 'to gain more practical experience and to complete my academic training'. It was agreed, therefore, that he should accept a position 'as assistant in the social science department at the University of Frankfurt', at the same time 'engaging in positive activities with the party organization in Frankfurt'.

According to the records of the city police, Sorge was registered as arriving there on October 30, 1922. There is no evidence that, at any stage, he held a post in the University. His new cover was organized in a separate and now identifiable manner.

Earlier in the year Professor Gerlach had moved from Aachen to take up the post of assistant professor of economics at the University of Frankfurt. He had always been an academic wanderer, never content to settle permanently in any university town, but seeking new circles of like-minded intellectuals and prepared for fresh adventures.

* The authors are obliged to Dr. Hermann Weber for this communication.
† This 'fact' appeared recently and exclusively in the Soviet press.

He had been an active Socialist, and it is probable that, like Sorge, he was at this time a member of the Communist party. It was either on instructions, or spontaneously, that he now invited Sorge to come to Frankfurt. The episode of the divorce does not seem to have impaired in any way the personal relations between the two men.

Frankfurt of the 1920s was the commercial and intellectual capital of West Germany and a centre of exciting experiments and experience in politics, literature and the arts. It was also strategically important in Communist terms, in particular to win the allegiance of its powerful middle class to the cause of revolution. Gerlach was in his element. Together with a group of like-minded professors and intellectuals, he established relations with one of the leading Frankfurt Jewish millionaires, Hermann Weil, who had made a fortune in the grain trade with Latin America. In the tradition of the city patricians, and in particular under the influence of his son Felix, he showed a marked and enthusiastic interest in setting up a private foundation*—in this case for social and economic research. The underlying stimulus of the group initiating such an Institute was the experience of the Russian Revolution and its application to German conditions, and to a radical desire to reconsider in academic terms the political, social and economic foundations of society.

In the early stages of planning the new Institute, there was no question of a formal constitutional link with the University. In November 1922 a 'Society for Social Research' was founded with Hermann Weil (and shortly afterwards his son Felix) as President. Among the list of members appear the names of Professor Gerlach† and Dr. Sorge. This body was the committee, which after prolonged negotiations with the University and the local government authorities, promoted the creation of the Institute for Social Research, formally opened in May 1924 with the Professor of Economics in the University as its first director.

Sorge's connection with this institution since the setting up of the original 'Society of Social Research' must have been nominal, and a cover.

Christiane now joined him and found accommodation in a converted cottage, which had originally been a coachman's flat over an

---

* The University of Frankfurt itself had been originally founded through private benefactions. The authors are indebted to Professor Paul Kluke for his assistance in supplying details of the history of the University at this period.,

† Gerlach died shortly afterwards of diabetes in a Berlin clinic. If he had lived, he would have been the first director of this Institute.

empty stable in a patrician town dwelling. The rooms had been painted in gay colours by an artist friend. Here frequent bohemian gatherings of artists, like the savage and brilliant caricaturist George Grosz, musicians such as Hindemith, and other artists and writers were held, particularly on Saturday nights when they usually continued until dawn. Christiane, who came from a prosperous middle-class family and a conventional background, with no marked political interests, found this atmosphere uncongenial—'without light or lustre'.

She was employed at some stage as a librarian at the Institute, where her husband, apart from associating with Felix Weil, seems to have had no precise functions or contacts.

The new body established an early reputation as a centre of research and study, stimulated in particular by the experience of the October Revolution. This was the very climate which Sorge was seeking in order to extend his academic knowledge of politics and economics. He was now able to broaden his intellectual horizon. The staff and students of the Institute formed an active part of the progressive climate of the intellectual salons of the Frankfurt of the 1920s; of the circle round Alfons Paquet, the veteran Quaker journalist and writer whose house Sorge frequented; and Paquet's vivid eye-witness accounts of the Russian Revolution rival those of the American John Reed, and the Englishmen Arthur Ransome and Philips Price, in capturing the enthusiasms and illusions of these days. As one of them described it, 'the new face of Russia excited all alert minds'. Leader writers and literary critics of the independent German newspaper the *Frankfurter Zeitung*, together with the new generation of the German Impressionist painters and writers formed the local intelligentsia of this post-war revolutionary world, Liberal-Communist, and as yet uncommitted to the discipline of party responsibilities.

The group round the Institute also formed an apparently harmless front for the more technical activities of the local Communist party organization. Sorge's rôle in this connection has not been clarified.

He claimed that after his arrival in Frankfurt he became a member of the 'guidance department', handled training matters and was adviser to a Communist paper. His underground party activity was also particularly concerned with 'secret liaison between the central committee in Berlin and the organization in Frankfurt', and he was responsible for keeping party funds and propaganda material, either in his study or the social science library in the Institute, 'concealing large bundles in the coal-bin in the classroom'.

Equally, Sorge's references to his underground work in Saxony at this time remain unsupported by other evidence. He claimed that the party organization in Frankfurt was 'in constant secret communication with the workers' republic there which had been set up by armed rebellion, and that he frequently visited Saxony on special missions', i.e. probably as a courier. The Saxon government, which was officially Social Democrat in composition, accepted on October 10, 1923, as members of the Cabinet, three leading Communists: Heinrich Brandler, Paul Böttcher and Fritz Heckert. Brandler had just returned from Moscow where he had most reluctantly agreed to initiate—backed by Russian financial and clandestine military aid—armed rebellion throughout Germany, starting in Saxony. In the event the Reich government reacted promptly and Saxony, together with its capital Dresden, was occupied almost without bloodshed by the regular army. The Communist leaders retired hastily to Berlin.

The fiasco of the Communist rising in Germany in October, which had been ordered from Moscow, precipitated a major crisis within the party, and was to transform out of all recognition the relations between the Russian and German party leaders.

These issues were the subject of discussion, as elsewhere in Germany, among countless individuals and groups on the fringe of the Communist party, and one such encounter took place at Sorge's flat in Frankfurt, according to the reminiscences of a witness, Frau Meyer, the wife of the leader of the 'Middle Group' of the party Ernst Meyer, who had bitterly opposed Brandler's Saxon venture. 'I afterwards apologized to Mrs. Sorge for boring her with so much politics. We never had any discussions with Sorge himself.'

It is during these months that, according to his own account, Sorge first came in contact with the Russians.

Late in 1923 the leading Soviet Marxist scholar, and head of the Marx-Engels Institute in Moscow, D. B. Riazanov, came to Germany, ostensibly in search of original manuscripts relating to the intellectual history of Marxism. Sorge claimed to have met him in Berlin and in Frankfurt, and for a remarkable reason.

One of the close associates of Karl Marx during the days of the First International was Friedrich Albert Sorge, who emigrated to the United States in 1852 where he was active in the German section of the Labour movement. In 1872 Albert Sorge returned to Europe and was appointed secretary of the First International. He conducted a voluminous correspondence with Marx and Engels after 1870, which was a primary text and source for the study of the whole movement, and was known in such circles in Germany. These letters were published in Stuttgart in 1906. In a preface to the Russian edition, Lenin referred to them as 'an indispensable addition to our progressive Marxist literature'.

Richard Sorge, in the isolation of his prison cell, made the statement that this father figure of Marxism was his own grandfather, and that he was able to hand over to Riazanov 'two or three letters from Marx to Sorge . . . My grandfather was Secretary of the First International. I have heard of him in connection with the Marx-Sorge correspondence. I do not know when he died; but probably in America in the 1870s.' Albert Sorge died in New York in 1906—a fact apparently unknown to his 'grandson'.

Without exception all the articles written between September and November 1964 in the Soviet and East German press underline this relationship between the companion of Karl Marx and the Hero of the Soviet Union (since November 1964), Richard Sorge. One writer even states that Richard's father was educated at the Steffens Politechnic High School near New York, and that in December 1894 Albert Sorge wrote to Engels, 'Our son is working in Chicago'.

It is curious that Richard, who was born in Baku in October 1895 where according to every other evidence his father was at the time working as an engineer, should claim Albert Sorge as his grandfather and make no reference to his father's educational background in the United States, where he could hardly have been in December 1894.

Among the papers found on Sorge after his arrest by the Japanese, however, is the marriage certificate of his paternal grandfather's brother, Georg Wilhelm Sorge, who was born in Torgau in Saxony, the same province whence Marx's companion, Friedrich Albert, had come. Why had Richard Sorge acquired this document, and retained it among his private papers? In 1933 he was considering applying for membership of the Nazi party in order to complete his intelligence cover for his mission to Japan. For this purpose he needed documentary proof of his Aryan ancestry. Genuine papers of his immediate family would have proved this, but the revelation that his mother was Russian might have caused complications with the new German authorities, and, most decisive of all, such documents might well reveal to police specialists Sorge's own true identity, of which there would be records from his life in Germany before 1924. Sorge therefore created a modestly fictitious identity, using the family documents of the maternal side of his father's family. Friedrich Albert Sorge was thus the great uncle of Richard, and the brother of his paternal grandfather. Upon this very indirect but genuine family link—there was hardly any contact between the two branches of the Sorge family— Richard built up his own myth of his Marxist ancestry, and with deliberate ideological intent.

The meetings of Riazanov and Richard Sorge had also another significance. This fleeting contact between the most distinguished Marxist scholar of the founding generation of the Russian Revolution and the eager young German Communist journalist must have engendered in Richard Sorge a deep and flattering intellectual excitement.

Riazanov is said to have invited Richard to the Marx-Engels Institute in Moscow as a collaborator in editing the new standard edition of Marx's works. According to Sorge, however, 'the German party leaders would not release me'. Behind the façade of this 'cultural mission' to Germany there may well have been a more technical purpose. In any event, this may have been the first Russian approach to Sorge, and it is of interest that when the Sorges did move to Moscow, Christiane was employed by Riazanov in his Institute.

The second and decisive known contact between Sorge and Soviet representatives followed shortly after this incident.

The Ninth Congress of the German Communist Party, outlawed by Weimar authorities in the previous November, was held in Frankfurt in April 1924. The meetings were disguised as a Sports Club and elaborate precautions were taken against police raids. Strong arm squads were organized to protect the sessions and the delegates.*

* Although the Communist party had been outlawed after the revolutionary events of October 1923, the ban had been lifted on March 1, 1924, and the romantic bravado of these precautions may have been excessive.

The central theme of the discussions was the responsibility for the fiasco of October 1923, when the Weimar authorities had forestalled any armed revolt in Saxony and Thuringia, and only a sporadic and brief rising took place in Hamburg.* It was on categorical directives from Moscow that orders for an armed rising, planned by the secret military apparatus of the German party trained by Soviet intelligence officers, had been given. This failure to launch a German revolution was the centre of an agonizing debate not only within the factions of the German party, but also in Moscow. The future relations of the Soviet leadership with the Germans was at stake.

A high-level fraternal delegation from the Comintern was therefore sent to Frankfurt to bring every influence to bear in a pro-Soviet sense on the forthcoming elections for a new and united Central Committee of the German party.

This Russian mission consisted of six delegates and was led by Zacharovitch Dimitri Manuilsky, an old guard Bolshevik, one of the most powerful members of the Executive Committee of the Comintern and in special charge of German affairs. Another member was Solomon Losovsky, the representative on the same committee of the Profintern, the Soviet-organized World Federation of Red Trades Unions. The delegation also included three members of the Central Committee of the Russian party.

Sorge records that he was invited 'to help find accommodation' for the Soviet delegates and that at least one or two of them were billeted in his flat. He also 'acted as body-guard', and there is no doubt that he was a kind of guide to the Russians.

Sorge named—in addition to Manuilsky and Lozovsky—two other Soviet delegates, Piatnitsky and Kuusinen, both leading members of the Comintern Executive. There is no confirmatory proof of the presence of these other two men in Frankfurt at this time, and it is unlikely that what would have been in effect the whole Comintern leadership would have travelled to Germany for this occasion. Sorge was to exploit all these names at frequent intervals in his future statements.

Sorge took no direct part in the discussions at the Frankfurt party congress, but his personal charm and attractive personality, irrespective

* One unconfirmed source suggests that Sorge played an active part in this abortive affair.

of his ill-defined illegal status, attracted the attention of Manuilsky and his advisers.

In Sorge's own words:

> At the close of the session they [the Soviet delegates] asked me to come to Comintern headquarters in Moscow that year to work for them. I could not go at once because I had to attend several organizational and intelligence committees immediately after the Frankfurt congress, but the proposal of the Comintern delegation, which was to get me to set up an intelligence bureau for the Comintern, was approved by the party leaders in Berlin and I left Berlin for Moscow at the end of 1924, to begin work in 1925.

In a later interrogation Sorge amended this statement as follows: 'Negotiations for my transfer began in January 1925 . . . A formal request for my services was sent to Berlin from the Comintern.'

The mission of the Soviet delegation to Frankfurt failed, and the majority of the new central committee of the German party initiated a critical line towards the control by the Comintern of developments in Germany.

Ruth Fischer, who was one of the representatives of this 'Left' attitude, gave the following interpretation in later years of Sorge's relations with the Russians.

> Manuilsky did have more success in another important task, which was part of his German mission. In the company of GPU experts he used to seek out certain German Communists, who were suitable for the Russian Intelligence Service. Sorge was introduced to Manuilsky as a man who had already been entrusted with small bits of intelligence work for the German Communist Party. We in the Central Committee knew that German Communists were being enlisted into the Russian service, but we had no influence in this matter—which was a constant source of friction between us and Manuilsky.

The Frankfurt meeting represented the collapse of official Comintern policy towards Germany, but apart from Ruth Fischer's statement there are several sources which reveal the exploitation of this failure by the Soviet Intelligence services. One of their leading agents in Western Europe, W. G. Krivitsky, who later defected, boasted that

> when we saw the collapse of the Comintern's efforts we said, 'Let us save

what we can of the German revolution'. We took the best men developed by
our Party Intelligence and the Zersetzungdienst (literally: Disruption
Service), and incorporated them in the Soviet Military Intelligence [the
Fourth Bureau of the Red Army].

Sorge himself admitted later that agents of the Fourth Bureau had
visited him in the Rhineland and in Frankfurt 'and had attempted to
interest me in joining the Bureau'.

On the assumption that Sorge was in some way connected with the
secret military organization of the German Communist Party since
1919, he would have been inevitably in touch with Soviet officers sent
into Germany to organize and strengthen this 'M' Apparat in
anticipation of a decisive revolutionary uprising in 1923. It is of
interest that one of the senior Russian experts sent to Germany for this
operation was August Guralski alias 'Kleine'. This man now appeared
as a member of the Soviet delegation to the April Congress in Frankfurt in 1924, and it was Sorge who approached one of the active
workers in the local party organization to find a billet for Guralski.

It seems therefore plausible that Sorge had been known for some
time to the Soviet Military Intelligence, and that along with other
German comrades with war experience he was invited to Moscow
during the Frankfurt meeting as part of an operation to salvage such
experts for the service of the Soviet Union after the fiasco of October
1923, and the end of the prospects of early revolution in Germany.

By some pre-arrangement with the German party, Sorge and his wife
left via Berlin for Moscow in October 1924.* They travelled as
students on legal German passports. A new adventure lay ahead, and a
further step was taken away from the personality of the military cadet
of 1914.

---

* Christiane was consulted by her husband about this decision to go to Moscow, which
seems to have been exercising him for some time. In relating their arrival in Frankfurt in
1922 she wrote: '*Had Ika already orders to go to Russia?*' She agreed to accompany him.
See Christiane Sorge in *Die Weltwoche*, December 11, 1964.

Chapter 2

APPRENTICESHIP IN MOSCOW

'I did not want to make clear my organizational links.' SORGE

RICHARD and Christiane Sorge, like all foreign Communists arriving in Moscow, were housed in the Lux Hotel which was run by the administrative machine of the Comintern and under strict police surveillance. According to his 'confession' he appeared in Moscow in April 1925, but recent evidence published in the Russian press shows that he was admitted to membership of the Soviet Communist Party in March, with the party card No. 0049927 issued by the Khamovniki District of the Moscow organization. He was described as an intellectual and party worker, and a member of the Union of Workers in Public Education.

Sorge had now automatically ceased to be a member of the German Communist Party, but this action did not imply any shift in his personal loyalties. The prompt admission of Sorge to membership of the Soviet party implied powerful backing from high quarters.

Sorge stated that he was posted to

the Comintern Intelligence* Division, one of the three major departments, which laid the groundwork for the concrete organizational and political decisions by means of which leadership was exerted over the International Communist Party [*sic*] and was already in existence in early 1925. The passing of time brought the need for expansion on the largest possible scale. I assisted actively in that expansion.

The duties of this department were 'to handle special party problems', to compile reports on national labour movements, and political and economic problems in various countries, and on occasions on exceptional matters of international importance. The head of this

---

* This could also be translated from the Japanese as 'Information'.

'Information Division' was always 'a party comrade with years of international experience, such as the Finnish Communist, Kuusinen.' Like most of the statements, on his European past, made by Sorge in prison, this description of the department in which he worked in Moscow is deliberately obscure and misleading.

Since its foundation in 1919, the Comintern had undergone a series of administrative changes. Its internal structure was essentially that of a party machine on the Soviet model. It was a world party with national sections—the local Communist parties—created according to its original statutes 'to fight for the overthrow of the international middle class and for the creation of an international Soviet republic'. The supreme organ was the World Congress, corresponding to a national party congress, and in principle summoned annually. This body elected formally an executive committee, corresponding to a national party central committee, which in its turn appointed a Praesidium. The first President of this body, and titular head of the Comintern, was Grigori Zinoviev. He was replaced in 1926 by Nicolai Bukharin.

This executive committee had at its disposal a political secretariat to implement its decisions. Among its members since 1922 were Otto Kuusinen the Finnish Communist, and Ossip Piatnitsky, both of whose names were frequently underlined by Sorge. It was here that supreme power lay. Since its inception this group steadily usurped the functions of the World Congress as a policy-making body, and in its turn was subordinated increasingly to the Politburo of the Soviet party.

The most operative of the divisions, directly subordinate to the central committee, was the Organization Bureau (the ORG-buro) headed by Ossip Piatnitsky, an old Bolshevik with a reputation for truculent independence, who began his career smuggling the clandestine paper of the group of Lenin from Switzerland to Russia before 1905. He jealously guarded control of his empire. He was, in addition, a member of the General Secretariat.

The Organization Bureau was established at the Fourth Comintern Congress in 1922, and the central executive of the Comintern transferred to this new section responsibility for all illegal activities abroad, which included the organization of underground cells to promote civil war through the machinery of local Communist parties. This administrative decision led to the creation of a special sub-section of the Organization Bureau—the International Communications Section (the OMS)—to handle these clandestine activities. The OMS was probably also established in 1922 at the same time as the Organization Bureau itself. Its existence is briefly mentioned in Comintern documents in 1923 and the following year, and then shrouded in official silence.

The prime function of this International Communications Section was to provide the connecting link between the executive committee of the Comintern and its leading regional sections, i.e. the Communist parties abroad. The OMS was in essence a secret 'apparat', which sent special agents abroad to convey funds and instructions to the leadership of the local parties. It was the clandestine life-line of the Comintern, and as such an underground body, not openly mentioned even in Moscow. Its agents communicated by courier, and the reports on their missions provided the essential intelligence material on the state of world Communism. The very existence of the national parties depended upon this channel.*

It was into this section that Sorge was almost certainly recruited by Manuilsky's mission in Frankfurt, and it is possible that, even without being conscious of the link, he had been even earlier in touch with the OMS through its main European bureau in Berlin as a local recipient of Comintern funds for the Rhine-Westphalia branch of the German Communist Party.

Apart from his work in such an office in Moscow, Sorge appears to have been intermittently engaged in writing for *Inprecorr*, the journal of the Comintern. The German police enquiry lists eight articles or pamphlets written either by 'I. K. Sorge' or under the pseudonym of 'R. Sonter' between 1925–29. An early brochure appeared in Germany in 1925 under the former signature on 'The Dawes Plan and its consequences', and in 1928 a book was published in Hamburg and Berlin under this latter pseudonym with the title 'The New German Imperialism'.† According to these German sources, Sorge was in this context identical with 'Sonter'. Sorge himself confirmed to the Japanese in his first deposition that he did use in Moscow this code-name in his work in the 'Information Division'. One aspect of Sorge's activities was therefore that of a publicist and research worker employed by this section of the Comintern machine.

---

* The most lucid and authoritative account of the structure of the Comintern appears in E. H. Carr, *A History of Soviet Russia: Socialism in One Country*. Volume 3.

† A copy of this book exists in the Amsterdam Institute. It is not without interest that this work appeared the following year in a Japanese translation.

There are few traces of Sorge and his wife during these early Moscow days. He was no longer a member of the German Communist Party but of the Comintern apparat, and he did not frequent, probably on instructions, the German Communist group in the Russian capital. One of the German leaders, Heinrich Brandler, knew him after 1927 as active in the German Club, the social centre of German exiles in Moscow and of the German-speaking employees of the Comintern. He is described in recent articles in the Soviet Press as being engaged during the years 1925–29 'on party work', and as the chairman of the German Club where 'he actively opposed the Trotskyists'.

In 1926 Sorge travelled on holiday to the Caucasus to visit his father's house where he had been born. It had been converted into a convalescent home. Sorge was delighted with this experience, and described it happily in letters to his mother and family in Germany. Christiane had gone with a girl friend to the resort of Sotchi on the Black Sea, where her husband paid her a brief visit.

Christiane Sorge had found a job as an assistant at the Marx-Lenin Institute working on Marx's manuscripts. But she had not readjusted to her new Soviet environment, which she found frustrating and oppressive. There were incipient signs in her husband of restlessness and drinking, and affairs with women. Her loyalties lay exclusively with him and were harnessed lightly to a political creed. The bohemian fringe of the foreign colony in Moscow in the middle 1920s provided her with inadequate compensation. She was nicknamed 'Burgeoika'—the little bourgeoise—and, increasingly neglected by Sorge, of whose work she knew nothing except that it was 'in an office' which she never saw, Christiane spent her time between the Institute and going alone to museums and theatres, or to borrow books from the meagre library of the German Club. Unlike her husband, who never referred in any statement to the vicissitudes of the political climate of Moscow, Christiane was sharply aware— especially after the middle of 1925—of the acceleration of Stalinist oppression and control. Both at the Marx-Lenin Institute and in the Lux Hotel, she noted a growing intolerance and reluctance of people to speak. Christiane sensed a growing isolation around her, and former friends avoided her company.

In October 1926 she decided to leave Moscow and her husband and return to Germany. Her German passport was returned to her, and late one evening Richard Sorge accompanied her to the railway station to take leave of her. There is no reference to her by him at any stage in his later life. Another loyalty and a further bond with the past seemed to have been broken.

In February 1927 Sorge claimed that he was ordered on a mission to Scandinavia under the party name 'Johann', and that this was a joint operation organized by the Information Division and the Org-buro. His task was to 'engage in intelligence activities concerning the Scandinavian Communist Parties, their economic and political problems and any important issues which might arise'. In later interrogations in Japan, Sorge added that he had the further task of comparing the relative influence of the Scandinavian Communists with that of the Social Democrats in each country.

Between February and March he attended four briefing meetings in Moscow with representatives of the relevant Comintern agencies, including the political secretariat, before his departure. He then seems to have left for Berlin, where he spent a month on 'research'. This consisted, according to Sorge, of working on Scandinavian languages and obtaining the cover of an unidentified sociological review. It is more likely that he was establishing contact with the OMS section of the Comintern there, in order to set up courier communications for his mission.

According to his account, he met the leaders of the Danish Communist Party in the summer of 1927, and went on to Sweden where he spent three months studying local conditions, advising the Swedish Communist Party on propaganda problems and the creation of party cells in the factories. He passed through Copenhagen again on his way to Norway, where he undertook similar work, remaining there until June 1928. He then returned to Berlin in order to 'forward a number of reports'.

Kai Moltke, a member of the Danish Communist Party at the time, wrote a recent article which throws some light on the Scandinavian mission, though like all other sources it adds to the confusion of chronology. According to Moltke, Sorge arrived in Copenhagen early in 1928. His mission had 'nothing to do with intelligence service or espionage, although he had been sent out as instructor for the Comintern'. He gave lectures to party cells, emphasizing that the Danish Communists could only survive if they established connections with extreme left elements within the Trades Unions.

Richard Sorge's sense for detailed organization was extraordinary. His behaviour was not at all illegal or conspiratorial. In his visits to the tough areas of the ports and factories of Copenhagen he had to show that 'he could guzzle as many beers as a sailor, docker, or cement worker, or show his physical prowess as a wrestler.

Surviving former members of the Swedish Communist Party are convinced that Sorge was not in Sweden at all in 1927. The German police records show that a Dr. Richard Sorge was in Frankfurt between August and October 1927 and then left ostensibly for Berlin. This piece of evidence, which comes out of the German enquiry held in 1942, raises two suppositions which at this stage can only be tentative queries. Whatever Sorge's true functions in Moscow were at this period, it is probable that he would be sufficiently aware of the general structure of the Comintern to produce a plausible mention of leading figures such as Kuusinen and Piatnitsky, and of the general structure of the different bureaux. Was the Scandinavian mission an invention to cover what might have been in fact a quite separate undercover operation in Germany, and even possibly under the control of another agency such as the Soviet Military Intelligence, with whom Sorge admitted that he had been in touch before his arrival in Moscow in 1925? He admitted being in Berlin in March/April 1927, where the central office of all Soviet confidential activities in Germany was centred under the orders of a leading Comintern functionary, Mirov Abramov. This functionary worked as press attaché from an office in the Soviet Embassy under Piatnitsky's orders, as the representative of the OMS—the nerve centre of Comintern clandestine operations and concerned mainly with technical problems such as passports, arranging safe houses (as Sorge had done in Frankfurt for the Soviet delegation at the German Communist Party Congress in April 1924), and transferring funds to Western European Communist parties. Sorge was probably under the orders of Mirov Abramov during his own stay in Frankfurt, and possibly the whole account of his Scandinavian mission was merely a blind to conceal a quite separate mission in Germany in 1927–28.

The second query which it is tantalizing to raise and impossible to answer is the possibility that the Dr. Richard Sorge identified by the German police as being in Frankfurt in 1927 was a different man from the Soviet functionary now working in Moscow and on mysterious missions abroad. Even more strange is the note in the same Frankfurt records showing that a Dr. Richard Sorge left for America on February 2, 1926. It is also a vague and uncontrolled hint that Sorge was at one time in California and worked briefly in the film studios. But the only admission by him of a visit to the United States was on his way to Japan in 1933.

In any event, his alleged visit to Norway is equally uncorroborated from other sources, at least in the terms outlined by him. Recent Norwegian evidence is categorical that, if Sorge came on any mission at all, it would have to have been before 1925–26 and at the latest in 1927. There is evidence to show that a delicate operational mission to Scandinavia was sent about this time to promote the 'peaceful separation' between the Norwegian Communist Party and the Mot Dag organization—a left-wing but not Communist-aligned group of Norwegian intellectuals. These negotiations were conducted in the spring of 1928 by Kuusinen himself and continued by a leading German Comintern special functionary, Richard Gyptner,* who was at that time the organizational secretary of the Western European Bureau in Berlin with which Sorge had certainly been in touch on several occasions as well as with the OMS office. Sorge must, however, have accompanied Gyptner to Norway at this time or been engaged on a separate mission. We have a photograph of him, dated in his handwriting: 'Oslo April 1928'.†

Following Sorge's own account, he returned to Moscow in time to be present at the Sixth World Congress of the Comintern which opened in July 1928.

The statutes of that organization laid down that the World Congress of its representatives should be summoned each year. The tide of battle between the Soviet leaders for control of Lenin's succession distorted every timetable. Since Lenin's death in January 1924 the Moscow scene was a battleground for the succession to supreme power and the struggle was not confined to the central machinery of government, but extended to the Comintern and every Communist party outside Russia—also against the background of the October 1923 fiasco in Germany and the receding of world revolution. There is no reference in any of Sorge's later statements, or in the recent 'revelations' in Moscow, to these historic issues.

One of the results of this ruthless fight was the decision to withdraw

---

* After 1945 Gyptner was East German Ambassador in Peking and Cairo, and later deputy Foreign Minister of the East German Republic.
† See illustrations.

from a short-term planning of Communist revolution in Western and Central Europe, and to concentrate on building up the foundations of a united Europe based on the trades unions through Communist factory cells in each country, tightly controlled by the national Communist parties to the exclusion of the Social Democrats as 'social fascists', and bound to the Soviet Union.

By 1928 Stalin's victory was consolidated, and in July the World Congress of the Comintern met in Moscow, the first time since 1924. Not only was Stalin by now in control of the Soviet machine, but also the process of 'bolshevising' the national parties abroad was advanced. The 'Left' opposition to total subservience to Soviet policy and interests had fought and lost its battle within the ranks of the most powerful of the parties outside the Soviet Union: the German. As Sorge put it, in one of his interrogations, 'hopes of imminent World Revolution were put aside'. Stalin was preparing to abandon the planning of a world revolutionary movement, and to concentrate on the building of 'Socialism in One Country'. The immediate activities of the Comintern, now essentially the agent of Soviet policy abroad in regard to the national parties wherever they were actively established, were confined to administrative tasks of organization, of relations with the unions, of disciplining the leadership, and studying relations now deliberately hostile with the Social Democrat groups in Western Europe.

These objectives are those which formed the basis of Sorge's alleged brief for his secret Scandinavian mission. Indeed he claimed that he was now present at the Congress 'as a member of the Scandinavian secretariat' and expert on the affairs of Northern Europe, under the party name of 'Sonter'.

Even more important, however, than the 'New Course' laid down in Western Europe, was the emphasis during the 1928 debates of the Comintern Congress, which dragged through July to September, on the major threat to the security of the Soviet Union which the Imperialist powers—Great Britain and the United States—represented in Asia and the Far East. One of the main theses adopted by the Congress was on 'The Revolutionary Movement in the Colonies and Semi-Colonies'. There is very slight reason to believe that Sorge had a hand in drafting this document, which was presented by Bukharin. According to one unconfirmed witness, Sorge had also been travelling in Soviet Central Asia and Persia the previous year, and it may be that his ultimate interest in Far Eastern and Asian affairs dates from this time.

There was no immediate outward change in Sorge's work. After the conclusion of the Comintern Congress, in September 1928, he told the Japanese police that he returned to Scandinavia. He first went to Norway, where 'party problems of various descriptions seriously impeded intelligence work in the fields of economics and politics'.

Evidence from former Swedish Communist Party circles confirms that Sorge was in Stockholm at this time, and not in 1927 as he stated in his 'confession'. The Swedish party was torn between 'Left' and 'Right' factions, which finally split early in 1929. Sorge was known to his Swedish colleagues 'as a member of the Org-buro, and his business was exclusively with organizational problems'. His own attitude was one of moderate compromise between extreme 'Right' and 'Left' points of view in the national parties. He is described as 'an intellectual type, silent and a little withdrawn, although he was sent out by Moscow'.

It is at least likely therefore that he came to Sweden on one mission after the autumn split in 1929 when the weakened Communist Party needed instructions and aid in questions of organization. One Swedish witness suggests that Sorge may have paid two visits, but doubts whether the first trip could have been before 1929, but there is no question of his having gone later.

Another recent statement in the Danish press published by Richard Jensen, a redoubtable former stoker and ex-member of the Danish Communist Party, throws some light on Sorge's second Scandinavian mission. 'I remember Sorge as if it were yesterday—now I know that he was identical with "Johann".' The Danish leaders at the time seemed to think that Sorge's mission was from Germany, 'but when he had carried out his assignment in this country we (Sorge and Jensen) travelled together to Moscow at the end of 1928 or the beginning of 1929'. Jensen's description of Sorge's task corroborates Sorge's own version. It consisted specifically 'of advocating the reorganization of the entire Party apparatus', switching over from small 'street cells' to plant and factory cells. Sorge was a 'tall, slender and very intelligent man'. He and Jensen toured together the port and seamen's clubs.

At some stage during 1929 Sorge was sent on a mission to Britain. His task had been outlined in his previous general briefing in Moscow. The British scene had been studied intermittently by the Soviet authorities. Stalin himself had expressed optimism as to the possibilities of unofficial Anglo-Soviet co-operation in trades union work. An Anglo-Russian Trades Union Unity Committee had been formed in 1926, and there were hopes of swinging the British Labour Movement, the most conservative in Europe, into active collaboration with their Soviet counterparts.

The General Strike of May 1926 caused a temporary revision of the Soviet attitude. But the failure of the Strike embittered both the leadership and rank and file of the unions, and the British Communist Party suffered a sharp decline. The Party Conference in January 1929 recorded a membership of only 3,500. The economic crisis of that year, however, seemed to offer a new opening for Soviet activity in Britain, and called for special investigation on the spot.

Sorge seems to have received instructions while in Scandinavia* to go to England

> to study the labour movements, the status of the Communist Party and political and economic conditions in Britain in 1929. My instructions to remain strictly aloof from internal party disputes fitted in perfectly with my personal inclinations, and enabled me to devote more attention to political and economic intelligence work than had been possible in Scandinavia.

The record of Soviet espionage in Britain in the 1920s had been a harassed one. The affair of the Zinoviev letter and the police raids on the Soviet Trade Mission in May 1927 had led to the breaking off of diplomatic relations with the Soviet Union by the Baldwin Government. The British security services, experienced in such Soviet activities, were alerted. The work of a Comintern agent in Britain implied greater risks and loneliness than in Scandinavia. It was a heightened and unfamiliar experience for Sorge, and his rare statements to the Japanese reveal little of his English sojourn. His own account is sparse and unilluminating. He had travelled in the mining districts 'and I saw for myself how deep the crisis was'.

He states that he arrived in the spring† of 1929 and stayed about ten weeks. 'My purpose was to study British politics and economics

---

* Sorge also says that he had two briefing meetings at his Moscow hotel on Britain before he left for his Swedish trip after the 1928 Congress.

† He says, however, in one interrogation that he returned to Moscow in May 1929.

but, since the depression had thrown so many people out of work that a general strike seemed imminent, I also undertook investigations—to see whether a general strike might develop.' A strike did break out in the mines and the British Communist Party attempted to collaborate with the Labour Party, but the latter called an early end to the dispute. Sorge 'reported on these matters to the Comintern'. One direct witness believes that part of his mission was 'to work in the Army' collecting military information and spreading subversive propaganda. He described his work as particularly dangerous, and said he was liable to twelve years' imprisonment if caught. He was obliged to lead a secluded life on limited funds and to avoid female company. 'Just think of those slim long-legged English girls.'

It is certain that Sorge never contacted the members of the Politbureau of the British Communist Party while on his English mission, nor did he come as a Comintern emissary. The relevant official who maintained liaison between Moscow and London at this time was a Russian named Petrovsky, known in England as 'Bennett' or 'Brown'. If therefore Sorge came at all it would have been on a separate intelligence assignment, and in such a case he would have clear instructions to avoid the British party.

On his way back to Moscow from Britain Sorge paused in Berlin, isolated and in a depressive state, familiar to his rare intimates. Since 1927 there had been sweeping changes in the offices and bureaux of the Comintern. In a letter written in February, Humbert-Droz, the Swiss Communist and a leading figure in the Comintern hierarchy, wrote to Togliatti in Italy that there were very few non-Russians left in the Moscow offices of the organization. Most of them (like Sorge) had been sent abroad on missions. Kuusinen was withdrawing into 'regional and editorial work' to evade political responsibilities. Bukharin was 'busy with Russian affairs', and although he was opposed to the russification of the Comintern, he was too occupied to attend to its work.*

Sorge now learnt that the reports which he had been sending from Scandinavia and Britain via the Berlin courier service were ignored and left unread. In conversation with another surviving witness in Berlin, he is remembered as saying, 'For a long time—since Bukharin was removed—nobody has looked at my reports.'

He had arrived in Berlin, low in funds, and under strain from the

---

* See Jane Degras: *The Communist International. Selected Documents*, Vol. II, p. 367. A most valuable source for the history of the Comintern.

the hazards of illegal work. He burst out in conversation with one witness who knew him: 'Those swine. How I hate them. This disregard for human suffering and feeling.' He was choking with humiliation and was planning all kinds of revenge. 'At least they must give me proper notice. And they have not paid me for months.'

This period of his stay in Berlin and the manner of his return is clouded—and perhaps deliberately. One source who met him at a private gathering of German party members had the impression that he was '*kaltgestellt*'—a technical jargon for a party member who was 'on ice' between missions or otherwise unemployed. He had been blinded by a savage shock of reality, and something must have broken in him at this time. He found himself one of the army of the disillusioned, an obscure casualty of the consuming power struggles on the Moscow scene.

These accounts of Sorge's state of mind in Berlin in 1929, suggesting that he was going through a fundamental crisis of spirit, are not in any way reflected in his own 'official version' of a break in his career in that year. It is, however, likely that some kind of major breach occurred in Sorge's existence on his return to Moscow in May or June 1929.* It is obscured, with careful deliberation, in his later interrogations.

During the minute interrogation, conducted by Procurator Yoshikawa, I barely managed to cover the complicated changes which occurred in my direct superiors in Moscow. I have detailed herein that prior to 1929 the Comintern was my 'Moscow authorities' (i.e. Centre) and that after 1929 my chain of command underwent a basic change corresponding to that in the world situation. Had I attempted to cover all this complicated material in the early interrogation conducted by the police, it would certainly have caused delay and confusion.

The extent of the confusion thus created invites considerable speculation.

Sorge seems to have antedated his return to Moscow (May or June 1929), possibly to avoid the suspicion of any connection between the complete change in his own position, the dismissal of Bukharin from the Comintern in November and the sackings in the Comintern machine. In one sentence only he seems to confirm his private outbursts in Berlin: 'The Comintern had no interest in my political information'; but throughout all his interrogations by the Japanese he showed

* On separate occasions, Sorge also dates his return to Moscow as 'late in the summer' and 'in September' 1929.

anxious skill in concealing the true nature of the end of his relations with the organization which had begun in the euphoric atmosphere of the Communist salons of Frankfurt in 1924.

His own explanation, apart from the deliberate omissions, is also consciously coloured by that hectic exaggeration of his rôle which he developed in prison.

'Upon my return to Moscow, I presented to the Information Bureau [presumably the OMS] not only my regular report, but also a frank analysis of what was wrong with my information-gathering trips and my investigations in the countries visited. In addition, I submitted the following basic proposals . . .' These were in essence the separation from the OMS of the espionage organizations concerned with political, economic and military problems. 'I further suggested that, at the Moscow end, such espionage agents in foreign countries would have to be more definitely divorced than in the past above all from the Comintern organization, so as to assure a degree of separation adequate for purposes of secrecy.'

In his further interrogation by the Japanese Sorge explained that he had suggested this change to Piatnitsky, 'for I believed that espionage work, which I liked, and for which I think that I am well fitted, would be impossible within the narrow framework of party activities . . . My character, tastes and strong preferences all lead me towards political, economic and military intelligence, and away from the field of party controversies.'

In a massive simplification of the contemporary crisis in the Soviet Union, and in the Comintern, Sorge went on:

There occurred, in fact, a shift in the centre of gravity: from the Comintern to the Soviet Union. Piatnitsky believed that I might not be fitted for party work, that imminent world revolution was an illusion, and that we must concentrate on the defence of the Soviet Union. This is why I left the Comintern.

As head of the Org-buro and its ancillary sections, Ossip Piatnitsky was a central figure in the Comintern organization. Sorge's 'advice' to him, if ever given, was both naïve and superfluous.

It was true that in the 1920s the functions of the Comintern were expanding and ill-defined, and its relations with the Soviet State authorities unclarified. Much depended on the personality, energy and ambition of individuals. Of all the Comintern sections the Org-buro, and with it the OMS, was in the closest touch with the Soviet State Security authorities and the Red Army Intelligence. Even Sorge gives one brief mention of joint conferences between these organs.

After the crisis of 1929, and the establishment by Stalin of absolute control over the Soviet apparatus of government, the security services intensified this penetration of the Comintern machine which had begun in April 1925, and it would be logical that Piatnitsky's organization would be the first target. For whatever motive, the transfer of Sorge to the Red Army Intelligence may well have been either initiated by Piatnitsky or carried out through his connections and with his assistance.

A summary of Sorge's description of his activities between 1925 and 1929 was passed reluctantly by the Japanese authorities to the German Embassy in Tokyo, shortly after the first stages of Sorge's interrogation had been completed. On January 2, 1942, this information was cabled by Ott to Berlin, with the comments of Colonel Meisinger, the Gestapo attaché and a police expert by training in Communist affairs. Meisinger had been on a visit to Shanghai at the time of the arrests of Sorge and Klausen. He was recalled urgently by Ott to Tokyo to investigate the affair, and made an unsuccessful attempt both to secure their immediate release and, failing this, to interview Sorge himself in prison.

His analysis of the two depositions, now reluctantly transmitted by the Japanese authorities to the German Embassy, revealed the professional scepticism of a police specialist. Meisinger thought that the documents were forged, and in any event they were incomplete and unsigned. He drew up a list of some forty questions for submission to the Japanese Foreign Ministry. They were never answered.

In his view, Sorge's deposition contained

certain inaccuracies and inconsistencies, and Meisinger emphasized that it failed to give any concrete details, particularly of dates, names, place-names, methods of communication, and remuneration. The depositions were in part crudely drafted and in part contained mistakes on matters of fact and organization. He considers it doubtful that the author is familiar with the Comintern intelligence service.

The German security services in Berlin were asked to check

these statements. At the end of January they reported, as far as the Moscow years were concerned, that

nothing is known here about Sorge's having worked for the Comintern Information Department under the code name of 'Sonter' from 1925–1929. Nor was it known that he travelled on Comintern business to Scandinavia in 1927 and attended 'the International Congress in Moscow'. This should read 'the *Sixth* [not the Second, as mentioned in the deposition] World Congress of the Comintern' which was held in Moscow from 17.7 to 1.9.28.

According to 'confidential sources' Sorge

who is described as being in strong opposition to Stalin, worked from 1925 to 1929 as private secretary to a leading Soviet official of the Communist opposition in Russia . . . [He] is also said to have exercised certain functions in the Soviet Communist Party, but to have been relieved of them as a result of the dispute with the Bukharin group in the Comintern.*

In the collection of Comintern publications belonging to the German police, it had been possible to identify certain articles written by 'I. K. Sorge'† and 'R. Sonter'.

It is quite possible that Dr. Richard Sorge operated under these two pseudonyms, especially as he himself stated that he worked for the Information Department under these names. If Sorge's depositions contain lacunae and are not expressed in the usual Comintern language, this is probably due to the way the report has been drafted.

Such was the meagre result of the German police enquiry on Sorge's Moscow period, but it contains one significant theory, namely that Sorge may have been in some way connected with Bukharin and the 'Right' opposition. Indeed, Sorge himself on one occasion only described himself as 'a sort of private secretary to Bukharin', and how he, Sorge, 'argued political problems with Trotsky, Zinoviev and Kamenev, who broke decisively with the Comintern at that time'. This masterly misstatement of the misfortunes of the Trotsky group, in the losing battle with Stalin for supreme power in the Soviet machine of government, at the same time conceals the nature of any political relationship, if it ever existed, between Bukharin and Sorge. A further abrupt reference to 'the expulsion of the Trotskyist faction'

---

* The statements were presumably compiled from informers working for the Weimar authorities among the German colony in Moscow. They are not confirmed from any other sources.

† 'Ika' was his family nickname.

produces no further clarification of Sorge's own position in these controversies. But Sorge's departure from his alleged assignment to the Comintern does coincide with the removal of Bukharin as Chairman of the Executive Committee of the Comintern in July 1929, and his final disgrace and expulsion from the Politburo in November of that year.

Behind the turgid outline of his activities written for the Japanese, Sorge concealed any trace of this crisis in his life. He gives no personal explanation of his 'voluntary' transfer but only one significant allusive hint at the pressures and fears engendered in Moscow, which followed the victory of Stalin. In an oblique and cautious aside written in amended notes to his original confession, Sorge speaks of those many foreigners in Moscow who had formerly worked in the Comintern 'or similar apparate', and who had now gone over [like himself] to 'the Soviet apparate or economic agencies'. Many of these foreign Communists now thought 'that the Comintern *has become unimportant and unnecessary*'.

On another occasion, Sorge's language is a model of further calculated distortion.

A radical re-shuffling in key personnel in other (non-Russian Communist) parties, due to inter-party disputes and persecution, have brought about violent fluctuations, and frequent deterioration in the quality and experience of national leaders; with the result that the leading men in the Soviet Union have been forced to concern themselves more with Comintern policy.

The Russian Communist Party 'has successfully carried out its major assignment from the Comintern—the formation of a socialist state'. The wave of world revolution has been receding 'as early as 1928-9, especially in China'. The International Labour Movement was on the defensive. The vital mission now was to defend the construction of socialism in the Soviet Union. 'Trotskyism, forgotten for all practical purposes, was relegated to the status of an empty topic for intellectuals.' The Comintern had no more independent leadership which could defy the Russian Communist Party 'as when Zinoviev was at the helm', but it was a fallacy which did prevail 'among a small minority of Communists' that the Comintern was obsolete. The leading position of the Soviet party was 'of course neither permanent nor constant'. Other national parties would in due course take over power and 'the present domination of the Communist Party of the Soviet Union must be regarded as temporary'.

Such an analysis of the political climate in Moscow in 1928–29 could well have been dictated by the Stalinist police to a member of the Russian opposition. Did Sorge react in this manner while in Moscow at that time; did he come to believe in the official version under the stresses of his secret work abroad and cling to it in lonely isolation; or did he invent his involvement in the Stalinist thesis in the hope of being exchanged?

Any attempt to analyse, in valid historical terms, the true nature of the revolutionary switch in Sorge's organizational links and loyalties is further confused by the recent statements in various articles in the Soviet press. According to this careful synchronized version Sorge, after his admission to the Soviet Communist Party in Moscow in March 1925, was cheerfully employed for the next few years 'in scientific activities' – i.e. writing articles and books on German affairs – and as President of the German Club, loyally expelling suspected followers of Trotsky among the German colony in Moscow.

Richard Sorge is alleged in another recent Soviet account to have made a personal statement about his past life to the party cell in Moscow, to which he belonged, *in 1929*, 'the year in which he wrote his autobiography and filled out the questionnaire'. The latter document would normally have been completed in 1925 at the time of his admission to the party and, strangely, all other documentary evidence about him which is now available to the Soviet journalists in Moscow is dated 1929, 'the year which was a summing up of everything that had gone before'.

In other words, there is no hint whatsoever of any link between Sorge and the Comintern, or any clue as to his activities during the previous four years, which he outlines in prolific and deliberate confusion to his Japanese interrogators. The Comintern interlude is expunged from the record, and Richard Sorge moves out from the shadows of Moscow, in that fateful year 1929, straight into the office of General Jan Karlovich Berzin, the all-seeing head of the Fourth Bureau of the Red Army Intelligence.

This contrived explanation, or lack of explanation, of the background of Sorge's recruitment as a Soviet Intelligence Officer, excites speculation. Perhaps Meisinger's hunch was right after all, and Sorge had never belonged to the Comintern apparat; perhaps Sorge himself told more than a half-truth when he stated that he had already been contacted by Fourth Bureau agents in Germany in the early twenties. It may be that he was recruited as a Soviet Intelligence Officer at this time, and that his subsequent work in Moscow and missions to Scandinavia, Britain, and very probably to Germany, were carried out only under the cover of Comintern agencies. At the time of his arrival in Moscow in 1925 he would certainly have filled out the routine questionnaire and produced his autobiography, prior to his admission to the Soviet party cell, and copies of these documents would have gone to the Fourth Bureau. It is therefore likely that Sorge's 'case' was reviewed by Berzin's office in 1929, either because of an intervention by Piatnitsky, or as part of a known procedure at that moment of political crisis and disturbance in the Soviet machine, whereby the military intelligence authorities extended a protecting arm to rescue valuable and trained foreign Communists who were being expelled by the Stalinist controlled police—the GPU—from the Comintern apparatus 'and other agencies'.*

In any event, Sorge was now to be assigned, after carefully planned technical preparation, to a new and specially difficult and challenging mission, under the direct control of the Fourth Bureau, to China, as one part of a major intelligence offensive in the Far East.

The Fourth Bureau had already recruited numbers of members of the German party after the collapse of plans for armed revolt in Germany in 1923, and brought them to Russia for training. After the central decision to transfer the major effort of the information, intelligence and propaganda services from Europe to the Far East, many of the Soviet missions and espionage groups were headed or staffed precisely by men recruited in Germany and originally trained for similar work in Western Europe. A number of them were to cross Sorge's path in China and were recognized by him 'from German days'.

The major shift of attention by the Soviet leaders from Europe to the Far East represented a supreme gamble to change the balance of world power in their favour. A successful revolution in China, spreading throughout Asia, would destroy the supremacy of the Western

---

* A comment of the former Danish Communist, Richard Jensen, has a certain relevance. 'The fact that I discovered that Sorge later became a spy does not surprise me very much. When the Russians discovered a capable man in the political apparatus, he was frequently tossed over into the GPU or the military intelligence service.' (Article already cited.)

capitalist powers in Europe by annihilating their colonial position, and in its turn threaten the economy of the United States.

Sorge's new assignment was an episode in this operation which, both from the political and intelligence point of view, was initiated against a background of blunders and failure.

He seems to have viewed his China mission 'which was tremendously important to me personally' with relief and intellectual excitement. There were only a 'few political observers' who realized the importance of developments in the Far East, 'and very few indeed were able to adapt themselves unreservedly'.

'At my first meeting with General Berzin, our talk centred on the question as to how far the Fourth Bureau, as a military organization, was concerned with political espionage; for Berzin had heard from Piatnitsky that I was interested in this kind of work. After repeated talks with Berzin I was finally assigned to China.' After this simple discussion, Sorge 'decided to leave the Comintern. I received a formal document officially relieving me of further duties so far as the Comintern was concerned'. He claims that he remained however a member of the Soviet party, and continued to pay dues, 'but my contact as a party member with party cells ceased'.

'I had conversations with Piatnitsky and Kuusinen, in personal terms, about the project.' He also saw Manuilsky. 'These Comintern leaders were old associates of mine, and personal friends of long standing.' Sorge's 'far-flung spy activities in the Far East were something completely new, and were regarded with special interest by my old friends.'

Sorge's constant reference to this trio of senior Comintern functionaries and officials of the Soviet party, and to his close relations with them, was not only a display of his sense of self-importance but was also probably designed to gloss over the shifts in the balance of political power in Moscow, and to conceal his total commitment to the Fourth Bureau, of which he at first insisted that he was not a permanent member but only in contact 'with special individuals'.

In the early phases of his interrogations, Sorge was deliberately ambiguous 'for reasons of my own' in referring to his superiors in Moscow, and mentioned vaguely the 'Moscow authorities' or 'the Moscow Centre'* and at times the Central Committee of the Soviet party.

* The 'Moscow Centre' was in fact a technical term, used in privileged circles, to denote the Fourth Bureau.

In his later examination by the Japanese preliminary judge, Sorge admitted to the real nature of his work:

To be precise, my orders did not come from the 'Moscow Centre' but from the Fourth Bureau of the Red Army. I did not want, in my statement, to make clear my organizational links. So I made things appear ambiguous, camouflaging them in general terms.

He went on to explain the real reason for this deception.

I was afraid that, if I admitted that I was working for the Fourth Bureau, I would be handed over to the Kempei (the Japanese Military Police). I had heard that the Englishman, Redman, had been handed over to them.* Moreover, I felt that the police would not understand what I said about the relationship between the Comintern and the Soviet Union and the Soviet Communist Party. Finally, when the Procurator began his examination in December 1941 he would not believe that I had been working for a military organization.

The Fourth Bureau of the Red Army was dependent, through the Information Department (from 1930–34 the Secret Department, and after 1934 the Special Section) on the Central Committee of the Soviet party. It was one of six sections of the Soviet Military Intelligence, and its prime task was the setting up of a network of agents, espionage groups and communications outside the borders of the Soviet Union. The Bureau had its own training schools for codes, ciphers and sabotage, independently of other Soviet agencies, in particular of the Comintern and the GPU. It was, however, not unusual in practice for personnel and training arrangements to be pooled.

General Jan Karlovich Berzin, the Director of the Fourth Bureau, was a legendary figure of the Revolution, symbolizing the social and ideological background of many senior officers of the Red Army. His real name was Peter Kyuzis, the son of poor Latvian peasants. He was born in 1890 and started life as a farm worker. Having worked his way through a teachers' training college, he early took a militant rôle in the ranks of the Social Democrat Party. He was arrested by the Tsarist police, and sentenced to death. Because of his youth he was re-tried and spent two years in prison. On his release, Berzin sought to educate himself and seems to have followed courses in political economy in Riga. With the outbreak of the February revolution, his activities

* Mr. Vere Redman, an official of the British Embassy in Tokyo, who was arrested on charges of espionage in Tokyo in December 1941. See p. 296 below.

follow a dual political and military pattern. He was a member of the Petrograd organization of the Bolshevik party in October 1917; Deputy Minister of Internal Affairs in Soviet Latvia in the spring of 1919 when the military successes of the White armies led him into commanding a Latvian Rifle Division. Berzin then became chief political commissar of another Red Army unit, where his career in the Soviet security services was launched.

In November 1920 Berzin was made Director of the Fourth Bureau of the Red Army.* Berzin was a remarkable man, and by the time that Sorge met him he was a master of intelligence operations and with personal experience of clandestine missions abroad.

Berzin probably had a file on Sorge dating back to Germany, and certainly since his arrival in Moscow. Sorge's experience as a journalist was of particular interest to the Fourth Bureau both as an excellent cover for operations abroad and as a trained political observer. His undoubted and varied military experience was perhaps of even greater significance.

Sorge's own assignment took shape in a series of briefing meetings. All links with the immediate past were severed. He received a new code name 'Ramsay' from the Fourth Bureau. 'I began to conduct my intelligence operations in my hotel room, and at houses in various locations'. He was then living at the New Europe Hotel and Berzin or his subordinates would call on him there and privately. In his confession, his preliminary briefing assumes a pathetic importance. Series of meetings were held with key Comintern officials, representatives of 'other Communist bodies' and of the Soviet Communist Party and the Central Committee, and military intelligence officers. 'On one occasion two members of the Soviet People's Commissariat for Foreign Affairs attended one meeting to discuss the political side of my intelligence activities.'

During one interrogation in Tokyo Sorge was asked: 'Did you

---

* These biographical details are taken from a recent laudatory article in *Komsomolskaya Pravda*, November 13, 1964, where Berzin is described as 'the founder and head of the Military Intelligence of the Red Army'. His party name was 'Pavel Ivanovich' and another alias or nickname by which he was often known was 'Starik'.

Jan Karlovich Berzin is not to be confused with Jan Antonovich Berzin alias 'Vinter', a companion of Lenin at Zimmerwald and member of the Central Committee of the Bolshevik Party in 1917. He died as Soviet Ambassador in Vienna in 1925.

attend meetings of a preparatory committee in the lobby of the Hotel
New Europe or in an ordinary private house in Moscow?' Sorge
replied that there was no preparatory committee. Berzin and a few
others took part in the talks. He was briefed in the main by officials of
the Far Eastern Section of the organization. General Berzin himself
consulted 'other quarters on the details of my political and economic
mission. He had known all the leaders through the party movement,
and I knew that he kept in touch by telephone with the military heads
and key men in the Central Committee.'

Sorge's final briefing included discussions with the Political and
Code Sections of the Fourth Bureau in order to settle respectively his
basic directions, and technical details of the communications of the
mission. Later events show that Sorge, though no radio expert, had
received a basic training in codes and ciphers.

Sorge was careful not to disclose the names of any officials, other than
Berzin, with whom he now came in contact. Recent articles in the
Soviet press reveal however, as if for the first time, that the member of
the Fourth Bureau directly responsible for Sorge's Far Eastern
mission was 'Alex', whose real name was Borovich and who was in the
Far Eastern section of the Bureau. He was apparently 'a dedicated
Leninist Communist, and a commissar during the Civil War'. Colonel
Borovich entered Soviet service from the military apparat of the
Polish Communist Party. He was Sorge's immediate superior for the
China operation.*

Sorge's terms of reference are described in the following manner.
He was to concentrate his enquiries on the social and political structure of the Nanking government of Chiang Kai-shek, in particular on
its military strength; on the various regional groups and factions in
China opposing Nanking; on the China policy of Great Britain and
the United States; and, generally, on Chinese agriculture and
industry. In other words, Sorge's task was essentially that of a trained
political and economic observer whose prime mission was to study in
detail the resources and policy of the Chiang government. On the
basis of such data the Soviet authorities would be better placed in

---

* Klausen also refers in his prison notes to Borovich, by his real name, as 'a Soviet Jew
who I think led a spy ring in Canada in charge of Japan [sic]'. When Klausen went to
Japan in 1935 he travelled via the United States as far as France on a Canadian passport
originally issued to Borovich.

assessing the balance of power in China between Chiang and the Communists. The Fourth Bureau clearly had no sources of intelligence on the Nanking government. Indeed, there is evidence to show that their network of communications and agents had completely broken down, and that Sorge's mission was part of a general attempt to re-establish links in China.

They were also out of touch with the Chinese Red Army, and the interior regions controlled by the Communists; and the decimation of the Chinese Communist and Trades Union leadership in the coastal cities, especially Shanghai and Canton, after the disasters of 1927 had probably disrupted similar contacts, although these had been hitherto primarily the responsibility of the Comintern and its agencies. In April 1929 the Soviet Consulates had been closed throughout the vital areas of Manchuria on charges of espionage, and diplomatic relations between Nanking and Moscow had been formally severed as a result of this affair.

Apart from the requirements of political intelligence, an even more urgent need was the re-establishment of radio communications without which no espionage net, however limited in scope, could operate. Sorge had no previous experience in this field, having relied in his European missions on the facilities of the Comintern OMS liaison office in Berlin.

The Fourth Bureau also intended to re-establish their network of military intelligence and for this purpose, and also to set up the technical side of a new espionage ring to be based on Shanghai, they assigned an experienced agent to head this China mission with seniority over Sorge.

This man was only known by the code name of 'Alex', and Sorge merely refers to him as 'an old veteran of the Fourth Bureau'. This man had been recruited by Borovich in Berlin, and, like him, was a Pole.

The 'Ramsay' mission was to be joined by a W/T operator to handle communications. There was a radio school run by the Fourth Bureau, but Sorge did not visit it as the man assigned to him was to meet him in Berlin. Sorge identified him as Seber Weingarten, or 'Weingart'.

It now remained to establish Sorge's cover. He was to travel on a legal passport in his own name issued by the German government. His occupation was given as a writer. In November 1929 he left Moscow for Berlin on the first stage of his journey to the Far East.

Here he signed two contracts, which established him overtly as a free-lance journalist. One arrangement was with a publishing house which produced a sociological magazine. The other contract was with an agricultural paper—the *Getreide Zeitung*. Sorge was planning to study agricultural conditions in China, and hoped to use his articles for the agricultural paper as material for a book. Through the editor of this paper, Dr. Justus Schloss, who had been a friend of Felix Weil the patron of the Frankfurt Institute of Social Research where Sorge had worked in 1924, he obtained an introduction from the Press Department of the German Foreign Office dated 28 November 1929, to the Consul-General in Shanghai.

Sorge left Berlin and travelled alone via Paris to Marseilles. Here 'Alex' joined him, and they boarded a Japanese ship. The W/T operator Weingarten, who had been on a Fourth Bureau assignment in Germany, had already joined the ship in Hamburg. The party travelled via Suez, Colombo* and Hong Kong to Shanghai, where they landed in January 1930.

* Sorge sent a postcard from Colombo to one of his childhood friends in Germany.

Chapter 3

THE CHINA MISSION

'The Japanese are a disease of the skin; the Communists are a disease
of the heart.' CHIANG KAI-SHEK

THE city of Shanghai, the main port serving the Yangtse valley and
the industrial centre of China, contained in 1930 the Chinese city,
the International Settlement governed as an extra-territorial enclave
by a Municipal Council elected by the United States, Great Britain,
France and Japan and policed by these powers, and the separate
French Concession. It was a place of vivid contrasts and overlapping
jurisdictions.

Through this port passed the bulk of the overseas trade of China,
and here was the centre of foreign and Chinese investments in the
country. Apart from the foreign community and the Chinese merchants and bankers, the dockers and the factory workers, lay a world
of refugees and conspirators mutually protected within an international enclave. Some 25,000 White Russians had settled here after
the Revolution of 1917 eking out a precarious and obscure existence,
living as small artisans, running restaurants and dance halls. Among
their number were inevitable recruits for the Intelligence Services of
all the leading powers.

Shanghai had also been designated by the Communists as the
centre of the Chinese urban revolution, and the headquarters of the
underground central committee of the Chinese Communist Party,
with its fragile links with the recently 'liberated' Red areas of the
interior. With the collapse of hopes for an immediate revolution in the
West in the late 1920s, Shanghai had been the fashionable magnet for
an international invasion of progressive specialists and advisers from
Europe and the United States, obsessed with the compensating mirage
of an Asian revolutionary triumph.

With the journalists and free-lance writers, the import-export
businessmen, the arms merchants, and the military adventurers, were
mingled the professional Moscow-trained agents, many of them experienced in the abortive experiments of the Comintern and of the

allied Soviet agencies in Germany and Western Europe, whose task it now was to organize the cadres of the Chinese revolution linked to the control centre in the Soviet Union.

Such was the background into which Richard Sorge and his associates were expected to carry their assignment unobserved.

On January 10, 1930, two German nationals arrived in Shanghai in a Japanese ship. They were travelling on passports in their own names, Dr. Richard Sorge and Mr. Weingarten, and their presence was at once known to the Shanghai Municipal Police. The latter were, however, not immediately aware of the existence of the third man and leader of the party, and even now his real identity is unknown.

'Alex', the senior member of the group, was to take over a previous mission of Red Army men operating from Shanghai and, with the help of Weingarten as a radio technician, to re-establish regular radio communications with Russia, which had been severed in recent years. Although Sorge and Weingarten were quickly identified by the Shanghai police as suspected Soviet agents, the real tasks of this new Chinese mission of the Fourth Bureau were never discovered.

During the first six months of his stay in China, Sorge was engaged in preparing the early stages of setting up an organized ring based on Shanghai and extending into central China, and in working his cover as a journalist. His first step was to call at the German Consulate-General in Shanghai, where he reported on January 17, exactly a week after his arrival. He presented a letter of introduction from the Press Department of the German Foreign Office in Berlin dated November 28, 1929, which had been written at the recommendation of the editor of the German agricultural newspaper, Dr. Justus Schloss, who had obtained the backing of the German Food and Agriculture Ministry.

Sorge explained to the German consular officials that he wished to study agricultural conditions in China, and was to write a series of articles for Dr. Schloss's paper. He was accepted without question, and given a series of introductions to leading German businessmen in Shanghai and to other German consular authorities in China.

According to the later account of the German consular official who received Sorge, he was given introductions in particular to the German Dyestuffs and Nitrogen Corporations as being the best placed to possess material on agrarian conditions in China. 'Sorge was then occupying a furnished room in one of the humbler apartment houses and evidently led a rather retired life. His address, according to the address book for Germans in the Far East, was: Dr. Richard Sorge, P.O. 1062, Shanghai.' This latter fact was also known to the Shanghai police.

The German Consulate knew nothing further of Sorge's way of life except that he made long journeys into the Chinese hinterland, and that a vague impression circulated in time that he was connected with 'leftist' circles.

It would appear quite natural, in view of his open journalistic connections established while in Berlin, that Sorge would have made little attempt to conceal his left-wing opinions in conversations with German residents in China. Indeed, an opposite attitude could have caused suspicion.

During these early months there is little trace of Sorge's activities and movements. Fellow European journalists and German businessmen, particularly arms merchants, in the Treaty Ports were obvious preliminary sources of information such as any professional journalist would cultivate.

On May 9, 1930, as noted in the Shanghai Municipal Police records, Sorge left for Canton, where he stayed for six months. He lived in a boarding-house in the International settlement run by a Dutch woman, and unobtrusively widened his knowledge and connections. From this base he went on 'research trips' in southern China, and made contacts in the city itself similar to those which he had established in Shanghai. An introduction to the German Consulate brought him into touch with the German community, and the Consul-General proved helpful to him.

Canton was second in importance only to Shanghai as a Treaty Port and industrial centre, and its proximity to the British Crown Colony of Hong Kong made the city a valuable listening post. It was also the obvious centre from which to study the ruling war lord factions in the provinces of south China, and their relations with the Chiang Kai-shek régime in Nanking.

During these early months Sorge's cover as a journalist specializing in Chinese affairs was securely established. In mid-November, however, he received word from his 'friends' that his presence was urgently required in Shanghai and the first period of apprenticeship was over.

The other members of the mission in Shanghai had been concerned more directly with technical problems. 'Alex' had been instructed either to assist or take over from an existing Fourth Bureau group which had arrived shortly before his own. The first group to be sent to Shanghai for this purpose was led by a member of the Fourth Bureau known under the name of 'Jim' or 'Lehmann'. His main task was to re-establish radio communications between Shanghai and the Soviet Union, and in addition—if he were able to obtain useful intelligence—to transmit the details to his superiors.

'Jim', whose real identity remains hidden,* was a senior radio expert and probably head of the wireless school operated by the Red Army at an establishment just outside Moscow. His mission was strengthened by another specialist from the same W/T school, Max Klausen, who had travelled separately to Shanghai.

Klausen's previous career illustrates the pattern of recruitment of the whole group of technicians selected through clandestine Comintern channels for military or political intelligence. On the network of communications which these men were trained to establish depended the functioning of the whole system of Soviet espionage.

He was the son of a poor shopkeeper from an island off the coast of Schleswig-Holstein. He was conscripted into a signals unit in the German army in 1917 and received a general training in wireless telegraphy. On his discharge in 1919 he became a sailor. As the German Seamen's Union and its international counterpart based on Amsterdam and Hamburg formed part of the Communist system of communications, sending couriers and also using seamen for this purpose on ships throughout the world, it was not long before Klausen was caught up in this machine. In August 1927 he joined the Hamburg seamen's cell of the German Communist Party. The secretary of this unit was Karl Lesse, who was a high-ranking figure in the International Seamen's Union and the Comintern apparatus.

Shortly afterwards Klausen signed on a three-masted schooner bound for Murmansk and engaged in catching seals. His next trip was on a German freighter, the *Eva Rickmers*, belonging to the East Asia Line.

* Also known as 'Willie', alias 'Grevitch'. Klausen describes him as an American Jew.

Through Lesse, Klausen was approached in September 1928 after months of careful observation by an agent of the Soviet military intelligence 'Georg', and asked on the basis of his previous radio experience in the German army whether he would go to Moscow 'to work for an intelligence organization'. Klausen accepted 'Georg's' invitation and left Berlin with a first-class ticket and a Thomas Mann novel. He was told, 'Your destination is in this book.' A simple letter code inside when deciphered contained an address in Moscow.

On arrival in Moscow Klausen was met in this fashion, and taken to the office of the Fourth Bureau of the General Staff. He was thus recruited direct by the Soviet military intelligence.

After a month's intensive course at the Red Army wireless school, Klausen was sent to join 'Jim' in Shanghai and left Moscow in March,* travelling via Harbin. He had been shown in Moscow the photograph of a man who would wait for him every Thursday at 5 p.m. at the Palace Hotel in Shanghai. He was to carry a copy of the *Shanghai Times* in his left hand and a pipe in his right, and a brief exchange of agreed phrases was arranged. This contact led Klausen to a White Russian named Konstantin Mishin, who was 'Jim's' assistant and had been recruited by him locally from the White Russian colony in Shanghai. He had apparently at one time been a wandering street minstrel. After cautious delays, Mishin led Klausen to 'Jim'.

Klausen's first task was to train Mishin as a radio operator, and to endeavour to establish communications with the nearest Soviet W/T relay station at Vladivostok.

In July 1929, after arranging communications between Shanghai and Vladivostok, Klausen was instructed by his leader to travel to Harbin to install another set there for the use of a Red Army group in Manchuria. His radio equipment was obligingly and unknowingly transported for him by a French diplomat. Operating conditions in Harbin were complicated by the watchfulness of the Chinese police. Chinese-Soviet relations on the border were acute, and the raids by

---

* There is a grave discrepancy of dates here. According to his own account, Klausen left Moscow in March 1929, but the German police records show that he sailed from Hamburg for Shanghai in October 1928, and was reported as being domiciled in China and Manchuria by the end of the year. The latter details are presumably correct in view of the chronology of Klausen's movements. It is not clear why he should have post-dated his departure from Moscow by six months.

Chinese police on the Soviet consulate in April of that year had been a standing warning.

One of the unwitting or conscious sources of information for the group appears to have been the American Vice-Consul, Lilliestrom, and it was in his house that Klausen installed his radio set. In October 1929 Klausen returned to Shanghai and found work in a car repair shop as cover for his activity as radio technician of the 'Lehmann' group.

In the New Year of 1930 the arrival of a new mission from Moscow was indicated to Lehmann, and Klausen was ordered to contact one of its members. He turned out to be Weingarten, his colleague from the Fourth Bureau wireless school. The two men had been members of the same Communist party cell in Hamburg and their training had followed an identical pattern. As frequently occurred in these circles, the fraternity of the Moscow-trained W/T operators also served as a means of preliminary contact between missions and individual agents in foreign countries. The two groups now pooled their technical resources, fitting into a general plan for setting up radio communications throughout China and in contact with Moscow via Vladivostok.

Klausen was now introduced to 'Alex' and to Sorge by Weingarten, and was instructed to settle down in Shanghai and find accommodation. He took a one-room flat on the first floor of a house in the Hongkew district. It proved difficult to work the radio set without an outside aerial, and on making enquiries Klausen discovered that in the garret above him was living a Finnish lady. He suggested that they might switch apartments, but she refused and there was a slight unpleasantness. Sorge finally offered to meet the difference in rent between the two flats, and this was agreed. Klausen and his neighbour then began to meet frequently.

This Finnish girl was Anna Wallenius, a refugee in Shanghai from the Russian Revolution. She was the widow of a merchant of the same national origin, whom she had married in the small town of Semipalatinsk in Kazakstan at the age of sixteen. They had escaped together at the time of the Revolution and settled in Shanghai, where he died in 1927. When she met Klausen she was earning her living as a seamstress and a part-time nurse.

In her loneliness she came very soon to depend on her association with her jovial and good-hearted neighbour in the dingy apartment house. She was, of course, unaware at this time of Klausen's clandestine activities. A love affair developed which led Klausen to raise the question of the association, on security grounds, with Sorge himself. One evening Klausen took Anna to meet Sorge at a dance hall. In his interrogation by the Japanese police, Klausen stated that Sorge warned him: 'It is all right for you to marry the girl, but be careful of our secret work. If your marriage threatens our activities you will be recalled by Moscow.'* In any event, Max and Anna settled down together in her original flat under the roof and set up a joint household.

About April 1930 Lehmann left for Europe and his group was absorbed by his successors.† Klausen and Mishin now came under 'Alex's' orders and worked together as a technical team with Weingarten, now disguised as a sales agent for a German patent automatic cooker.

Early attempts to re-establish an intelligence ring in Shanghai moved slowly. 'Alex', whose cover was that of a sales agent for a Czech armaments firm, opened up business with Nationalist Chinese leaders and their local agents and also, according to Klausen, 'surreptitiously with gangsters and Chinese Communist Party members'. But the Shanghai police were on his tracks. 'Alex' and his wife left hastily by ship for Europe. Sorge was now in charge of the Fourth Bureau group in that city.

Among the European journalists working in China at this time was Agnes Smedley, a well-known left-wing American who was officially the correspondent of the *Frankfurter Zeitung* in Shanghai. She was born in 1894 in Colorado. Her father worked as an unskilled labourer, and her mother kept a boarding-house. She had never attended high school, but made brief and disjointed attempts to educate herself; night lectures at New York University, summer school in California, alternated with a brief and disastrous marriage and, towards the end

* In an article already mentioned in the East German newspaper *Neues Deutschland* on October 30, 1964, in an interview with Klausen the latter stated that Sorge's words were: 'This woman is all right and you can have her.'

† Another member of the 'Lehmann' group was a young American woman, known to Klausen as Miss Reh Bennett. She was employed on coding and cipher. Her attachment was brief and she left for Moscow in November 1929. Klausen thought that she was a member of the Communist Party of the United States.

of the First World War, evangelizing work with nationalist Indian groups operating in the United States. In 1918 she was arrested for this activity, and the following year sailed to Europe as stewardess on a freighter. She jumped ship in Danzig and moved to Berlin, where she resumed activity in the cause of Indian nationalism, and began an affair with one of the leaders which lasted for eight years. In 1931 Agnes Smedley was in Moscow at a meeting of Indian revolutionaries and then, ostensibly as a journalist, travelled widely in Germany and Scandinavia. In 1928 she broke off the liaison with the Indian leader, and negotiated a contract with the *Frankfurter Zeitung* to go to the Far East as their correspondent. She travelled via Moscow and was present at meetings of the Sixth Comintern Congress. She had battered her way breathlessly across the world, a rebel seeking a cause, a militant who never paused to equip herself for the battle, the embodiment of the resentments and frustrations of her kind.

In May 1929 Miss Smedley turned up in Shanghai on a false American passport and aroused the immediate suspicions of the Municipal Police. She rapidly became prominent in the progressive circles of the European colony there, the incongruous, minority world of moral and political refugees that existed alongside the respectable business community: writers and journalists awaiting the great Chinese Revolution as a release from their private frustrations, and as a compensation for the collapse of the mirage of revolution in the West. These transient settlers came mostly from Germany and Central Europe, the scenes of the recent defeats of the Comintern; even before 1933 many were of Jewish origin. Others, forming perhaps the largest single group, arrived from the United States, individuals disillusioned with the fading Wilsonian dreams of 1917 and with the impotence of minority left-wing factions in America.

These European elements in Shanghai gravitated naturally to the haven of the local branches of Soviet-sponsored front organizations set up by the Comintern in the '20s to mobilize progressive opinion as an added propaganda weapon in forwarding its revolutionary policies. Such 'independent' bodies were International Red Help, the civil liberties lobby of the Comintern, used, as in the Sacco and Vanzetti case, to rouse and channel sympathy for prisoners in leading political cases in capitalist countries; the Society for Cultural Relations with Foreign Countries, which disseminated from its own publishing-houses Soviet cultural propaganda to local branches throughout the world; the International Union of Revolutionary Writers, and its ingenious publishing syndicate run by Willi Münzenberg.

Miss Smedley was superbly at home in this world and also beyond it, among the groups of Chinese left-wing activists, the successors for her of the Indian revolutionaries of California and Berlin, to whom Shanghai was the main conspiratorial base in China, and where the International Settlement provided a haven from the Nationalist Chinese police of Nanking, though liable to brusque raids from the latter's European counterparts in the Settlement.

Such a circle was a natural target for Sorge as he began to build up and organize his channels of information. He seems to have met Miss Smedley shortly after the departure of 'Alex' for Europe in November 1930. How the contact was made is not known. In one interrogation Sorge hinted that he had an introduction to her from the *Frankfurter Zeitung*. It is possible that they had already met in Frankfurt or Berlin in the 1920s. They were both in Moscow at the same time in 1928.

Sorge was careful in not disclosing this episode. 'I had heard of her while in Europe', he told the Japanese procurator. In his confession he stated:

I knew that I could depend on her. . . . I solicited her aid in establishing my group in Shanghai, and particularly in selecting Chinese co-workers. I met as many of her young Chinese friends as possible, making special efforts to become acquainted with those who volunteered to co-operate and work with foreigners for leftist causes.

Miss Smedley served as a means of introduction, and a small group of Chinese 'helpers and supporters' was cautiously enlisted. Their shadowy cover-names flit across the pages of Sorge's confession. He told the Japanese procurator, 'It is very difficult to remember Chinese names, and many years have passed since then.' But there was also a more realistic explanation. The long arm of the Japanese police could reach out into occupied China. Sorge was protecting his former helpers.

During the autumn of 1930 a decisive addition was made to the circle of Sorge's sources, and the way in which this was done uncovers a fragment of the obscure workings of Communist intelligence activities in China. He was anxious to obtain regular and reliable information on Japanese policy in China, and to have some general material on the Japanese attitude to Far Eastern developments.

As when seeking local Chinese links, Sorge turned to Miss Smedley. Some months previously she had met a Japanese journalist named Ozaki Hotsumi, the China correspondent of the leading newspaper in Japan, the *Asahi* of Osaka. The introduction had been arranged by a certain Mrs. Irene Wiedemeyer who ran the Zeitgeist Bookshop on Soochow Creek. This establishment was ostensibly a European bookshop specializing in left-wing literature and political publications, but in fact it was a local outpost of the world-wide Comintern publishing syndicate set up by Willi Münzenberg and an integral part of their propaganda apparatus based on Berlin. The shop was not only the meeting place of European and Asian sympathizers with left-wing causes, but also a technical link in the chain of communications. The proprietress, Mrs. Wiedemeyer, was a German who had married a young Chinese student in Berlin and had gone with him to Moscow about 1926. She had then been instructed to set up the Shanghai bookshop both for open 'cultural' purposes, and as a safe cover address for personal contacts and a clandestine depository for mail and documents—an integral if modest segment of the Comintern organization in Shanghai.

Even in her capacity as correspondent of the *Frankfurter Zeitung*, Miss Smedley must have regarded her introduction to Ozaki as a Japanese specialist on Chinese affairs as of particular value. But in any case their emotional attitude to world events coincided.

Ozaki Hotsumi was the son of a Tokyo journalist who, at the time of his son's birth in May 1901, had been employed on a newspaper in Taihoku (Taipeh) on Formosa, the Chinese island colony of Imperial Japan. As a schoolboy the young Ozaki had been influenced by the winds of change sweeping the Far East in the wake of the First World War, and after 1919 as a student in Tokyo he was caught up in the post-war social ferment of his generation.

The arrests of the early leaders of the Japanese Communist Party in 1923 made a profound impression on him, and he began to take an active part in Marxist study groups at Tokyo Imperial University, where he took his degree in 1925. After a year's work as a postgraduate student he joined the staff of the Tokyo newspaper *Asahi Shimbun* to obtain, as he put it later, 'a vantage point for interim observations'. The climate of this office, with its cautious conservatism, was dull in comparison with the excited debates of the university study groups which had hitherto been the main intellectual influence on the young Ozaki.

The revolutionary events in China in 1927 provided the spur. In November of that year he was assigned to the China department of the newspaper, and in November of the following year he went as special correspondent to Shanghai. This formal assignment was a personal liberation, an escape from the surreptitious Marxist study groups in university circles, and from the conventional newspaper office of the *Asahi*, and the continuous and successful pressures of the Japanese authorities to circumvent the formation of a left-wing opposition.

Ozaki's contact with Miss Smedley developed into a continuous association and exchange of ideas and information, to their mutual advantage, professional and otherwise. They used to meet in the lobby of the Palace Hotel, or in her apartment, where Ozaki would supply her with news of the Nanking government of Chiang Kai-shek and of the situation in Japan. How far this contact exceeded the bounds of professional journalistic activity is uncertain. Ozaki seems to have been content and rewarded to feel at last that he was a member of a larger company of devoted missionaries, and the extent and precise nature of Miss Smedley's interests did not arouse his curiosity.

About November 1930 Ozaki received a visit in his office from a Japanese living in Shanghai named Kito Ginichi, who told him that he had just arrived from the United States via Indo-China. As Ozaki told his Japanese police interrogator after his arrest, 'I assumed therefore that Kito was connected with the American Communist Party' — or rather its active Japanese section. But he was wary of this visitor, who was in fact, as Ozaki was later to realize, a veteran Comintern agent connected with the Japanese section of the American Communist Party. Shortly afterwards Kito proposed to Ozaki that he should meet 'a brilliant American newspaper reporter'. His name was 'Johnson', and he was a 'good man'.

Ozaki sensed some trap and even feared that Kito might be a police spy. He decided to consult Miss Smedley, who also seemed alarmed and asked whether he had mentioned the proposal to anyone; to which Ozaki replied that he had not. 'She then said that she had heard of him, but warned me strongly against mentioning the subject to anyone else.'

It seems that Sorge also had special and unclarified reasons for being evasive about Kito, who was certainly connected with the Party. 'I state definitely that he was not a member of my group and that I never worked with him. I heard of him several times from Smedley and Ozaki, but never met him, and I have not the slightest recollection of him.' Sorge denied with particular emphasis that it was Kito who had introduced him to Ozaki. 'My guess is that Smedley had some direct or indirect liaison with Kito, and relayed to him my desire to obtain a Japanese who could be trusted.' Finally and mysteriously, 'Moreover, I was prohibited by Moscow from dealing with famous people like Kito.'

A few days later Miss Smedley told Ozaki that 'Johnson' was a 'fine man' and herself introduced Ozaki to him at a Chinese restaurant on Nanking Road. The atmosphere was one of immediate and mutual confidence. Before the end of the discussion 'Johnson' had asked Ozaki to investigate for him details of the internal situation in China, and Japanese policy towards the different Chinese political groups. The fact that 'Johnson' was Richard Sorge was unknown to Ozaki for several years, although the two men were henceforward to meet at least once a month in Miss Smedley's flat or in Chinese restaurants outside the city.

Sorge had found his most valuable collaborator, 'my first and most important associate'.

Since his arrival in Shanghai at the end of 1928, Ozaki had established himself in certain Chinese circles closely connected with the Communist Party, and with whom, as a Japanese sympathizer, he worked without hesitation in a political rôle, subscribing to the funds of such bodies as the Anti-Imperialist League. With some pride he attended meetings of a political advisory group* of five or six members of the Chinese Communist Party, giving lectures on the current international situation. 'The members of the group were not very sophisticated politically and were ignorant of international affairs. So my contribution must have been helpful.'

But apart from a feeling of intellectual superiority, there was the elation of active conspiracy. Ozaki refers to his attendance, as an observer, at two 'flying meetings' held by the Chinese Communists

* This was probably not an 'official' body, but a group set up to attract foreigners of left-wing tendencies.

in Shanghai parks. This was a local invention, 'a type of gathering that could meet and disperse very quickly, like the wind'.

Although he was not formally a member of the Chinese Communist Party, much of Ozaki's time was taken up in working for its organizations or allied groups.

The interest of the Chinese Communist leadership in Japanese affairs was specially concentrated on the Toa Dobun Shoin, or East Asia Common Script School, an establishment of higher education founded for Japanese and Chinese students by the father of the liberal-minded Japanese statesman, Prince Konoye, as a contribution towards Japanese-Chinese understanding. Both the teaching and student bodies at this school were shaken by the wave of revolutionary fervour lapping around them after the revolutionary events in Canton and Shanghai in 1927, and they had a sense of being a progressive outpost of Japanese intellectual life far removed from the oppressive restrictions in their own country. It was indeed through these students that Ozaki originally met some of the Chinese leaders with whom he associated.

This cell within the East Asia Common Script School seems to have been originally set up by the Chinese Communist Party itself, and to have joined up with another group of left-wing Japanese journalists and temporary 'visitors' from Japan, who had gathered in Shanghai for the meeting of the Pan-Pacific Trades Unions in February 1928—a Far Eastern offshoot of the Profintern, the International Red Syndicates based on Moscow. This study circle met regularly and its members were now incorporated in the Shanghai section of the Chinese Communist Party. Ozaki often attended these gatherings, and at one of them he met a Japanese journalist named Kawai Teikichi, who had come to Peking in 1928 and was now working for the *Shanghai Weekly*.

The Japanese attack on Manchuria in September 1931 transformed the Far Eastern scene. Would this 'incident' be a prelude to further advance by Japan into the provinces of northern China? What would be the impact of Japanese aggression on the contending political forces elsewhere on Chinese soil? And above all, what were the risks of a Russo-Japanese war? As Sorge announced one day in Shanghai to Klausen, 'The Japanese Army have captured Mukden, which will complicate our work in China.'

Although Sorge expressly denied that his mission included intelligence work in Manchuria—where there was already a Red Army ring based on Harbin—his original briefing had been extended to include a study of Japanese intentions towards China, and information on recent events in Manchuria was essential to this task. 'Sorge, Smedley and I talked things over,' Ozaki told his interrogators later. He then approached Kawai. The meeting took place in one of the usual haunts—a Chinese restaurant in Nanking Road. Ozaki acted as interpreter and presumably had prepared Kawai for the interview. Sorge briefed Kawai to undertake a mission to north China and Manchuria and to report on four questions: the progress of the new 'independent' Japanese-controlled Manchurian state, now termed Manchukuo; the attitude after the Manchurian Incident of the semi-autonomous Japanese garrison of the area, known as the Kwantung Army; the political reactions of the White Russian, Moslem and Mongolian minorities; and, above all, the state of opinion in these northern border areas towards the Soviet Union.

On his return several meetings took place to go over his written report, one of them in Miss Smedley's flat. Sorge never asked precise questions of detail, but sought to form an impression from Kawai of the general situation. 'I have other sources,' he said. Shortly afterwards Kawai was arrested by the Japanese police in Shanghai, who questioned him but failed to uncover these activities. He was released three weeks later.

The fighting which broke out in Shanghai on January 28, 1932, between a Japanese naval garrison and the 19th Chinese route army, revealed in dramatic and concentrated form the strength and weakness of the Nanking régime, the attitudes of the British and American governments towards Chiang Kai-shek and the objectives of Japanese expansionist policies towards China—indeed, Sorge's main targets assigned by Moscow.

As Sorge wrote in his 'confession':

The outbreak of the battle of Shanghai in 1932 indicated a new trend in Japanese diplomatic policy, although of course at the time we did not definitely know whether it was simply an unexpected skirmish, or whether it represented a Japanese effort to conquer China following the acquisition of Manchuria. It was likewise impossible to tell whether Japan would push northwards towards Siberia or southward towards China. My work became much more important during the Shanghai Incident. I had to try to discover Japan's true purpose, and to study in detail the fighting methods of the Japanese army in the battle of Shanghai.

His own direct experiences of the battle brought back memories as a soldier of the First World War, this time with the increased exaltation of a revolutionary enthusiasm. The Chinese troops in action were directly committed neither to Nanking nor to the Chinese Communists, and to Sorge they symbolized the first real resistance to Japanese aggression. 'I saw the Chinese defensive positions, and I saw Japanese aircraft and marines in action. The Chinese soldiers were very young, but their discipline was very good, although most of them were equipped only with grenades.' In his excitement, with a Teutonic nostalgia for the trenches, Sorge himself handed out grenades to these troops. He visited the fighting in different sectors of the city and then acquired further information on Japanese tactics from the German military instructors attached to the Chinese.

On the general direction of Japanese policy, Sorge received 'very useful information' from Ozaki, who wrote a special report immediately after the Incident, based mainly on interviews with the Japanese service attachés in their Shanghai consulate. This showed the high morale of the Chinese troops, the anti-Japanese sentiments of the Chinese merchant community, and confirmed the deliberate provocation of the Japanese. According to Ozaki's sources, as he told Sorge after the fighting, the Japanese were impressed by Chinese reactions and hoped to localize the affair. The Incident was followed by the setting up of a new coalition government in Nanking, broadening and strengthening the basis of Chiang Kai-shek's régime, on which Ozaki was also able to produce inside information.

Such intelligence, which formed the basis of the long report which Sorge himself wrote and took to Harbin in the spring of 1932 for transmission to Moscow, was of special interest to the Russians. Soviet policy towards China depended on an assessment of the relative strengths of Chiang and the Communists, and if the correct interpretation of the Shanghai Incident was that Chiang might assume the leadership of resistance to Japanese penetration of Chinese territory, the Soviet attitude to the Chinese Communist Party would be affected.

The later view of the Japanese police was that the main achievement of Sorge in China was in furnishing Moscow with important basic information 'which helped to decide Comintern policy towards the Chinese Communist Party'.

In February 1932 Ozaki's newspaper instructed him to return to the Osaka office in Japan. 'I was at a crossroads. I could either continue my collaboration with "Johnson" or accept the *Asahi* appointment. At the time I felt that to go on helping "Johnson" in Shanghai would be too heavy a burden.' Ozaki also wanted to study the Japanese situation at home, and as his *Asahi* connections were an invaluable long-term investment, Sorge accepted the inevitable. 'In that case it cannot be helped.'

It proved to be only a temporary break.

Apart from his Chinese and Japanese informants, Sorge depended for his sources of information on European contacts. These were primarily German businessmen, consular officials, and members of the military advisory group in Nanking. As a reputable journalist, he mixed with ease in this circle, which revolved socially round the Consulate-General. He claimed that he selected as contacts certain members of the military mission and observers attached to the Nanking government, such as Colonel (later General) von Kriebel, who was subsequently Consul-General in Shanghai. 'The military advisers frequently invited me to Nanking and came to Shanghai to visit me.'

Sorge travelled into the interior, to Hankow and other cities, with some of these men. The Germans were also at that time experimenting with new types of civil aircraft in China, and had set up an internal airline—Eurasia—whose pilots were cultivated by Sorge, and from them he claimed to have learnt about conditions in remote districts of China, on occasion flying on trips with them. None of these connections implied the recruitment of agents; these sources were the normal working contacts of a professional journalist.

There was one possible exception: Dr. H. 'Voigt' or 'Woidt'. He was one of the representatives in Shanghai of the German electrical firm of Siemens. Sorge knew him well, and passed on to Moscow economic information received from him even after the China period. Klausen was once told by Sorge that in the event of his being arrested or being forced abruptly to change his address, Klausen was to look up Woidt's telephone number and re-establish contact through him.

There is evidence to show that Woidt worked for the German Military Intelligence while in China. He was certainly a frequent companion of Sorge's in Shanghai, and the mystery remains.

Another German and fellow journalist with whom Sorge exchanged information was Wolfgang Sorge, China correspondent of the Berlin paper *Lokalanzeiger*, with whom Richard Sorge was sometimes confused. Wolfgang Sorge was an old China hand, well connected with the Chinese authorities, an expert on Manchuria, where Richard first met him in Harbin, and the White Russian groups and the Chinese secret gangs, speaking fluent Russian and making frequent trips as a correspondent to the Soviet Union. Richard Sorge told Klausen that he was always careful with this journalist colleague because of the latter's anti-Communism. The Shanghai Police noted him as probably working for the German Intelligence Service.

Some time during the spring of 1931 Weingarten handed to Sorge a message from Moscow informing him that two new agents were in Shanghai on attachment to the group, and that one—'Paul'—was staying at the Palace Hotel and the other—'John'— at the Hotel France. Sorge arranged to meet them by telephone. They were both registered under the names in their passports, 'but I do not recall what the names were'.

'Paul' appears to have been a Balt, like so many of the Soviet agents of this period. He held the rank of Colonel in the Red Army and was an expert on military matters. It is probable that his main assignment was to take over the military liaison with the Chinese Communists, and develop the work which Lehmann and 'Alex' seemed to have had difficulties in establishing. He was also designated as Sorge's successor at some later stage. The two men worked closely together, but on parallel lines. Klausen, who met him with Weingarten at the time, 'thought that he outranked Sorge in Shanghai'.

The other new arrival, 'John', was directly a member of Sorge's inner circle. He was, according to Sorge, a former member of the Polish Communist Party. His present function was to undertake cipher and photographic work. He took a house on Avenue Joffre in the French Concession, which became one of the main meeting places of the group, usually at night after his Chinese servant had gone. Photographs of documents required for transmission to Moscow were developed by 'John' in his bathroom, and turned over to Sorge. He opened a small photographic establishment on North Szechuan Road as a cover.

The meetings at 'John's' house are described by Klausen. Drinks were always served, and Sorge often boasted of his experiences on his trips outside Shanghai. On one occasion he told how he had seduced a beautiful Chinese girl in Nanking and persuaded her to give him a map and blueprints of the Chinese military arsenal, which he photographed and sent to Moscow.

Klausen saw on occasions both Miss Smedley and Woidt at these gatherings. In one note he defined the group as consisting of Sorge, Weingarten, Woidt, 'Paul', Smedley and himself. His impression of Smedley was sharp. 'Intellectually, we were too far apart; the only impression I have of her is that she was a hysterical, conceited woman.'

According to his own account, Sorge left Shanghai for Moscow in December 1932. His original plan had been to return after two years, but 'his duties were too many to be completed' in that time and he had extended his stay by another year.

The identity of his successor 'Paul' remains hidden, and the subsequent activities of his ring can be traced only in fragmentary statements. Of the original Lehmann-'Alex' group, Klausen had been sent by Sorge, on instructions from Moscow, to take over the radio communications of the Fourth Bureau group in Harbin in October 1931.

By early 1934 contact with Shanghai seems to have been cut. It seems that, most probably due to increasing operating difficulties in Shanghai after the 1932 Incident, the Fourth Bureau closed down—at least temporarily—its operations in Shanghai some time in 1933. 'Paul' himself was seen by Klausen in the headquarters in Moscow at some date during that year, dressed in the uniform of a Major-General in the Red Army.

Richard Sorge had spent three years on this China assignment for the Fourth Bureau of the Red Army. He had not only established himself as a reputable journalist, specializing in Far Eastern affairs, but also as an expert on agrarian conditions in China, a subject indispensable to the study of the future of Chinese Communism and also one of his covert tasks. As he told the Japanese procurator, 'because of my articles . . . sent from China, I became well-known in the world of German journalism'. He also acquired invaluable experience of undercover activities under Far Eastern conditions.

The evidence for this side of his work comes almost exclusively from his 'confession' and interrogations when under arrest after October 1941, from Japanese sources and from similar statements of other members of his group in prison in Japan. The story of the China mission has therefore to be reconstructed in fragments against the background of close confinement, isolation and intensive questioning over a period of many months. Sorge himself was aware of the danger to any German nationals who might be implicated, in the event of any liaison between the Nazi and Japanese authorities over the case; and he was also at pains to conceal as far as he was able information as to the structure of Soviet intelligence operations in general. There was always the possibility that he might in the end find his way back to the Soviet Union.

Some picture does emerge, however, of the nature and extent of Sorge's work in China, albeit blurred and at times contradictory, incomplete and misleading.

The terms of his original briefing show indirectly, by their comprehensive vagueness, the lack of accurate and continuous information on China at the disposal of the Russian Military Intelligence, and the experimental nature of the mission on which he was sent. Of the original intelligence targets assigned to him, the main one was the assessment of the political, social and military strength of the Nanking government of Chiang Kai-shek.

His achievements in this field seem to have been primarily those of an expert political analyst, though the means of acquiring his material and the method of the transmission of his reports in themselves label him as a spy. Through his Chinese 'assistants' in Canton the network spread to Nanking and Hong Kong. From these sources Sorge pieced together a coherent picture of the Chiang régime and its ruling élite.

From the German military advisory group in Nanking Sorge was able to report, at least in general terms, on the location and equipment of the Nanking army, the structure of its 'shock' divisions, and the relations of the leading commanders with Chiang Kai-shek. From these German instructors and with the added help of his Chinese 'assistants', Sorge assembled material on the armament industry and in particular obtained blueprints of the arsenal in Nanking.

An assessment of Chiang's military chances in an eventual clash with the Japanese was vital. Equally important was his ability to exploit the rising wave of Chinese nationalism and its hostility to the European powers and their extra-territorial privileges in the Treaty

Ports, especially in Shanghai. His prestige depended to a large degree on reaching a settlement of these issues. The United States, in particular, were favourable to making concessions. A confidential American memorandum on these lines—known as the Fessenden report—was obtained by Sorge before publication 'from the American side'. His exact source is not known.

The Sorge ring never established reliable radio communications between Shanghai and Moscow, and most of their material which they assembled must have been dispatched by courier via Harbin. Sorge mentions that two special and lengthy reports were sent to Moscow, one in late 1930 and the other in June 1932, after the Shanghai Incident.

There is no record of any wireless messages that may have been sent over Klausen's radio set from Shanghai or Canton, and indeed on internal evidence it seems that for technical reasons very little traffic passed. Nor are there any surviving reports which were sent on the courier route to Vladivostok.

For Sorge himself it was a period of invaluable training both in working under open cover as a journalist under the special conditions of Shanghai and the inland areas of China, and also in day-to-day acquaintanceship with the perils and rewards of the life of a Soviet Intelligence Officer abroad. Perhaps, however, the main interest of the China interlude is that during these years two of his main collaborators later in Japan appeared on the scene: Ozaki Hotsumi and Max Klausen, whose fate was from now on to be linked closely with that of Sorge to the end. And the services rendered to Sorge by Agnes Smedley in the creation of the Chinese ring lead directly to the intertwining of her fate with his. During the immediate post-war years it was the attack by the head of the American Military Intelligence in Japan, General Willoughby, on the political record of Agnes Smedley, and her threat to bring a libel action, which was to force into public view the whole Sorge case and its ramifications.

Chapter 4

THE NOULENS AFFAIR

'Noulens pretended to be Swiss. His real nationality I do not know;
I suppose that he was a Balt.' SORGE

SORGE'S China mission was only one link in a chain of Soviet rings operating in the Far East under the instructions of different Soviet agencies. In so far as they can be dimly identified from Sorge's statements, these groups seem to have arrived in China about the same period, and to have been withdrawn almost simultaneously. They had a common overall purpose, with varying specialist functions.

Apart from Lehmann's group in Shanghai, which was replaced by the 'Alex'-Sorge mission, the Fourth Bureau of the Red Army had set up another ring in the same city, referred to by Sorge as the Frölich-Feldmann group. 'Its duty was to make contact with the Chinese Red Army, and gather intelligence concerning it.' These men had their own radio links with Moscow set up by Feldmann who was the radio technician of the party.* Frölich (who also went by the name of 'Teo' or 'Theo') was a Major-General in the Red Army. According to Sorge, this group were unable to fulfil their mission and left Shanghai in 1931.

As Frölich was later seen by Klausen in Harbin, it seems probable that he was sent expressly to strengthen the Red Army group in Manchuria, a key area after the Japanese invasion, and one where, apart from urgent intelligence requirements regarding Japanese military activities on the Siberian border, Frölich was also concerned, according to Klausen, with organizing eventual sabotage groups to cut the Chinese Eastern Railway in the event of hostilities.

Sorge stressed that during the Shanghai period he had no working relationship with this mission, and had no instructions to contact them. 'Shanghai is such a small city that it was difficult to avoid chance encounters.' Sorge went out occasionally with members of this group to discuss general problems, 'but we had no working relationship whatsoever'. It is most likely that the members of these groups had

* In 1935 Klausen met him at the Moscow radio school.

met previously, particularly the radio operators who had all been trained at the same Moscow establishment.

On one occasion Sorge referred to the Frölich-Feldmann group as 'neighbours'—a technical intelligence term to denote a separate ring controlled by another agency.

The Harbin group to which Klausen was attached for a time had as its primary function the collection of military intelligence in Manchuria, but they also had a subsidiary but essential service to perform in connection with Sorge's group in Shanghai. Harbin was the communications centre on the sea-rail route between Shanghai and Moscow on which the Soviet couriers travelled. 'The Harbin group acted as a mail box for me: I forwarded letters and documents to Moscow, and it sent them on.' Funds were transmitted to Sorge through the same channel.* Members of both missions, taking it in turns, established a two-way courier service between Harbin and Shanghai. The Harbin ring seems to have been dissolved in 1932.

Apart from these ephemeral Red Army missions to China, and of far greater significance, was the Far Eastern Bureau of the Comintern itself, the main target of the police forces of the International Settlement and of the French Concession in Shanghai.

The vague existence of a Far Eastern Bureau in Shanghai had first come to light when in April 1931 the French Sûreté in Saigon arrested certain Indo-Chinese Communists who revealed their connection with such a body, but it was a more sensational chain of circumstances which uncovered the organization in detail.

On June 1, 1931, the British police in Singapore arrested a French Comintern agent engaged in clandestine transactions with the Malayan Communist Party. Among his papers was found a telegraphic address and post-box in Shanghai: 'Hilanoul, Box 208'. This discovery was followed up by the Settlement Police, and led to a certain Hilaire Noulens, a teacher of French and German. He was arrested on June 15, 1931. A search of his apartment was fruitless, but one of his latchkeys belonged to a flat at 49 Nanking Road, where three large steel boxes were discovered. They proved to contain the accounts over a period of a year (1930–31) of the Far Eastern Bureau of the

* Remittances also reached Sorge in Shanghai through an account with the National City Bank of New York.

Comintern, together with those of the local branch of the Pan Pacific Trades Union Secretariat.

Although the British and French police were already aware of the existence of a Far Eastern Bureau, a study of these documents revealed for the first time details of their organization and threw invaluable light on the extent and nature of their activities.

The Comintern, with its headquarters in Moscow, had long established as part of its apparatus a series of regional secretariats or permanent departments, each under the control of a member of the Central Executive, to deal with the support and supervision of Communist parties in various parts of the world, and for preparing Soviet missions to them.

The Eastern Department was established publicly as a regional secretariat at the Fifth Congress of the Comintern in 1924. It had its own organization, including propaganda, responsible to the Central Executive and divided into Near, Middle and Far Eastern Sections. A local Far Eastern branch existed in Vladivostok, and it was presumably this office which was moved in secret to Shanghai in 1930 — the year of the general offensive by all Soviet agencies to return to the China field after the disasters of 1927.

The Pan Pacific Trades Unions Secretariat was the Far Eastern branch of the Profintern, the Comintern-controlled organization of International Red Trades Unions, and was set up as a permanent body with headquarters in Vladivostok, alongside the Far Eastern Bureau, after a conference held in Hankow in 1927. This meeting was attended by Lozovsky, the head of the Profintern, and leading members of the Chinese, American, British, French, Indo-Chinese Communist and other parties.* It was a gathering of senior Comintern agents and the purpose of the new secretariat was to finance, organize and support the All-China Labour Federation and to mobilize the Chinese urban proletariat as the spearhead of the new Chinese revolution.

The Secretariat must have moved from Vladivostok simultaneously with the Far Eastern Bureau. Although its existence and propaganda activities were publicly known, the extent of its clandestine work was

---

* Li Li-san (China, representing the All-China Labour Federation); Earl Browder (U.S.A.) the first secretary of the Pan Pacific Trades Unions Secretariat; Ho Chi-minh (Indo-China); Tom Mann represented the British, Jacques Doriot the French, and M. N. Roy the Indian parties respectively.

only revealed by the Noulens affair. It seems to have been a relatively new body, as its regular accounts begin only in February 1931. Its staff was smaller than that of the Bureau—two men and one woman. Their main work lay in organizing and financing the All-China Labour Federation which, though nominally under the control of the Chinese Communist Party, was closely supervised by Moscow.

The results of the police investigation after the arrest of Hilaire Noulens, whose identity was the subject of lengthy international enquiries, showed that he was the head of the Comintern organization in Shanghai, with a staff of nine Europeans.

The work of the Bureau was primarily concerned with China, transferring funds to the Chinese Communist Party and its organizations such as the Youth League, recruiting students and arranging for their travel to the Lenin School in Moscow and the University of the Toilers of the East, thus performing the key task of training future party cadres. An equally important, but separate, function was to establish and maintain liaison with the Chinese Red Armies and Soviet districts in central and north China.

In addition to these tasks in China, this body performed similar tasks in transmitting funds and recruiting students for training in the Soviet Union, and maintaining liaison with the Communist parties of Japan, Indo-China, the Philippines and Korea.

The Far Eastern Bureau and the Secretariat worked in the closest collaboration and may even have operated jointly. Although their accounts were kept formally separate, they were found in the same flat. Both bodies shared a highly developed courier service with Europe and with the Asian Communist parties; cipher and telegraphic correspondence were shared, and also local post-boxes in Shanghai (of which eight were identified). Costs of special missions were shared and members of either body would on occasion carry out assignments for the other.

Funds arrived from the same source, the Western European Bureau of the Comintern in Berlin, and were banked in seven separate Chinese banks. The accounts revealed the extent of the work in Shanghai in 1931: the Far Eastern Bureau was spending between £120–150,000 a year, of which £95,000 was in China; and the Secretariat £1,000 a month.

Noulens appears to have been in general charge of both offices and apart from the vital business of maintaining communications, he seems also to have been responsible for security and accommodation in Shanghai. The combined group had at their disposal fourteen or fifteen establishments for living accommodation, offices and meeting places.

At the time of Noulens' arrest he was carrying two Belgian and one Canadian passport, and was using twelve cover names. Attempts were made by his defence lawyers to prove that he was a Belgian citizen. Police researches, however, unearthed the owner of the false passport in Belgium, and Noulens' identity was tentatively established as Paul Ruegg, a prominent member of the Swiss Communist Party who had disappeared to Moscow in 1924. The Swiss authorities refused to accord him any protection and in August 1931 Noulens and his wife, who had been arrested with him, were handed over by the Shanghai police for trial to the Nanking government.

The arrest of Noulens and the discovery of the apparatus of the Comintern in the Far East spread alarm and confusion in left-wing circles in Shanghai. Sorge himself appears to have left the city two weeks after the news, according to the British Settlement Police card on him, but was back again the following month.

Was there any connection between him and the Noulens organization? On his arrival in Shanghai he had rented a Post Box No. 1062. One of those at Noulens' disposal was No. 1077. The police, who kept a watch on Noulens' post-boxes, were taking similar precautions in the case of Sorge. This may, however, have been an insignificant coincidence.

The police also suspected Sorge of being a member of the Secretariat, but this is explicable in view of the fact that in September 1931 a local committee was formed in Shanghai for the defence of Noulens, whose defence lawyers were maintaining that he was merely the secretary of this body, which was ostensibly an open organization. Agnes Smedley was prominent on this committee, which was sponsored by International Red Help and which included such prominent and progressive American journalists as Edgar Snow and Harold Isaacs, and Sorge seems to have been openly associated with it as part of a world campaign organized in progressive circles for the release of

Noulens. Indeed, when Ozaki first met him he thought that this was Sorge's professional activity in addition to his work as a journalist.

In his 'confession' Sorge claims that he 'first learned that Noulens was secretly operating in Shanghai when he was arrested', but this statement is by implication contradicted by his description of the 'Comintern group in Shanghai', which adds to the picture of that organization revealed at the time of Noulens' arrest.

Sorge met the Comintern group in Shanghai 'by chance' in 1931. It consisted of two branches: the organization and political sections. 'Through this apparat went the direct personal traffic between Moscow and the Chinese Communist Party.' The section was kept 'specially secret'. It was headed by Noulens 'and one or two assistants'. His main duties were to transmit funds to the Chinese party and maintain liaison with its central committee; to find safe addresses for important conferences between Comintern delegates and the Chinese leaders; to organize courier and radio communications with Moscow and to transmit 'secret materials between Moscow and China'. This section was also in charge of security, and the safety of members of the political branch, whose members might be ordered to restrict their movements.

The political branch was headed by Gerhart Eisler 'and one or two assistants'. Its main task was to convey Comintern directives to the Chinese Communist Party, to be a channel for exchanging information between the Party and Moscow, and to 'submit reports concerning all social problems involved in the labour movement in China'. These reports were forwarded by the organizational branch.

According to the Shanghai police records, Eisler lived in Wongshaw Gardens in the International Settlement. Sorge's address after June 1931 was at No. 23 in the same street.* Perhaps he took over Eisler's house.

In spite of these coincidences, the Shanghai police did not identify Eisler as a member of the Far Eastern Bureau,† nor connect Sorge with the Comintern organization in Shanghai. It is a mark of the security training of the members of the Far Eastern Bureau and the

* In a flat sub-let by a Mr. Alexander von Dunin, suspected by the police of being a Soviet agent.

† The functions allotted to Eisler can be identified in the material captured by the police after the arrest of Noulens, and relate to a certain 'Leon'. The description of this man is similar to the known activities and qualities of Eisler.

Secretariat that the police were not able to make any further arrests after the seizure of Noulens and his wife, nor to identify any of their associates in Shanghai.

After Noulens' arrest, Eisler's position was clearly precarious and, according to Sorge, he returned hastily to Moscow. Both men had met previously in Germany, 'since the days in 1921 when we participated in the German Communist movement together', had worked together in the Comintern organization in Moscow, and had met frequently. Sorge admitted that they had renewed their old acquaintanceship in Shanghai, and 'all in all I met Gerhart only three times'. Eisler's mission in Shanghai was, according to Sorge, similar to his own assignment in Scandinavia: namely, that of a special delegate to the local Communist party.

Since 1930 the Russians were especially concerned that the Chinese leadership in Shanghai might become too independent of Moscow, and it is also probable that Eisler's main task was to impose directives on the Chinese Central Committee. Eisler was later to appear, in 1936, as the Comintern representative to the American Communist Party, and having returned on another mission to Europe escaped to the United States in 1941. He was later arrested in New York at the end of the war on charges of espionage. He made a spectacular escape to England, and was allowed by the British authorities to continue his journey to Poland.

Eisler is now living in East Germany, and recently gave a cautious interview to the press in East Berlin describing his contacts with Sorge.

Like Sorge, he admitted that the two men had met in Germany in the early days, and

somewhere else under most complicated circumstances, under which one could easily literally have lost one's head. Sorge was a very calm, coldblooded man. Our conversations when we met (in Shanghai) had to be short and to the point. The rendezvous could not last long. But he could in a few minutes present a complicated situation which explained the intentions and plans of the enemy, and so help the friend and warn him.

Noulens was replaced from Moscow by another experienced Comintern man, also known to Sorge. He was Karl Lesse, a former leading functionary in the Comintern-controlled International Seamen's Union, and the leader of its cell in the German Communist Party.

It was Lesse who had recruited Klausen into the party in Hamburg in 1927, and, shortly after his arrival in Shanghai, Klausen and Weingarten called on him at his hotel. Lesse told the former that he was an organizer for the Chinese Communists and that he was working for the 'Shanghai branch of the Comintern'.

The Shanghai Police now kept a watch on Sorge after the arrest of Noulens, not only on his post office box No. 1062 but on his flat in Wongshaw Gardens between July 1931 and January 1932, after which date there is no record that he was being watched. He is described as leaving the premises only on rare occasions. 'Spent time playing chess with friends. Received many phone calls . . . and very careful that his conversation was not overheard by any member of his household.'

Sorge was reported to have links with one Oswald Doenitz 'an agent of the Third International'. This man was identified by the Shanghai Police as having arrived from Berlin on August 2, 1931, in the shadow of the Noulens case. He posed as a traveller for a Hamburg quack medicine firm. His movements were furtive. He opened business premises, but closed them almost immediately. He changed his addresses so frequently that remittances of funds sent telegraphically from Comintern sources in Europe never reached him. 'Doenitz' left for the Soviet Union in December 1931 having either completed his mission or having more probably—like 'Alex' before him—found the atmosphere unhealthy.

As Karl Lesse came from Hamburg and as—according to Klausen —his cover was 'peddling leprosy drugs', it is more than probable that 'Doenitz' and Lesse were the same person. The police suspicions of his links with Sorge are another indication both of the perils of the profession and the possible dangers of detection to which the Sorge ring was exposed in the wake of the arrest of Hilaire Noulens.

In spite of Sorge's protestations in his 'confession' that he had no technical links with the Comintern group in Shanghai, there is no doubt that Red Army officers and Comintern officials, in the course of their training and missions abroad, formed a clandestine fraternity and established personal relationships. Sorge even commented that 'these organizations [the Red Army groups in China and the Comintern Far Eastern Bureau in Shanghai after the Noulens Affair] collapsed because their members came to know each other too well. . . . Our group avoided contacts of that nature.'

The Noulens affair had two further repercussions in Communist circles in Asia.

Evidence in the Noulens archives uncovered the existence of a sub-branch or 'Southern Bureau' in Hong Kong recently established to maintaiɴ a more direct and independent liaison with the Communist parties of Indo-China and Malaya. On June 6, 1931, the British police there arrested a certain Annamite, Nguen Ai Quac.

This man was one of the leading Comintern agents in the Far East. He had come to Europe from Saigon as a steward on a French boat, had worked at one time as a dishwasher in London, and then moved to Paris to set up a small photographic shop.

This young Annamite worker gravitated swiftly into extreme left-wing circles, and first attracted public attention at the founding Congress of the French Communist Party at Tours in October 1920, where he made a speech on colonial conditions in his native Indo-China. In their search for potential leaders in the Far East the Comintern apparatus in Paris picked on Nguen Ai Quac, and in 1924 he left France for Moscow. It was the same year as Sorge arrived in the Soviet capital.

In the following year Nguen Ai Quac accompanied Borodin on his China mission as an expert on Asian affairs, and began the establishment in Canton and Southern China of the cadres of the Indo-Chinese Communist Party. In 1927 he was a delegate at the Pan Pacific Trades Union Secretariat Congress in Hankow. By 1930 he was in close and active correspondence with the Far Eastern Bureau in Shanghai, and in charge of its sub-station in Hong Kong.

After his arrest a world-wide campaign was launched by the Soviet front organizations headed by International Red Help, as in the case of Noulens, to prevent his being handed over by the British authorities in Hong Kong to the French Sûreté in Saigon. Nguen Ai Quac disappeared mysteriously from sight for eight years. He emerged again into the open as leader of the Communist party of Indo-China (soon to be known as Vietnam). His name was Ho Chi-minh.

The Noulens case also had repercussions in Japan, which, apart from China, harboured the most important Communist party in the Far East from the Comintern point of view. Liaison between Moscow and Tokyo in these years was maintained through Vladivostok via Shanghai, and reporting on conditions in Japan formed an important section of the work of both the Far Eastern Bureau and Secretariat offices. Lengthy reports found during the Noulens raid made it possible for the Japanese Settlement Police to identify at least some of the 'Japanese collaborators' of these offices.

Among the suspects arrested were some students at the East Asia Common Script School. A more important catch was one of the instructors at the school, Nozawa Fusaji, who was a member of Ozaki's study group and whose house was later to become a meeting place for Agnes Smedley and Mrs. Wiedemeyer. He was arrested by the Japanese police in July 1931, some weeks after Noulens, but only held for a month. In reality Nozawa was the contact of the Far Eastern Bureau with Tokyo, but this was not discovered. Nozawa continued his conspiratorial activities and was later to render active services to Ozaki in Japan.

The Sorge group had been brushed very close by the breath of danger.

Sorge himself was sharply impressed by the Noulens affair and its possible ramifications. It was a classic warning.

In his 'confession' Sorge wrote that the Nanking government 'had arrested the leaders of the Chinese Communist Party, and learned from their confessions of Noulens' existence and activities'. The facts were otherwise. The arrest of Noulens was solely due to the capture of Ducroux, the French Comintern agent, in Singapore. A member of the Politbureau of the Central Committee of the Chinese Communist Party who was head of the 'special affairs unit' (GPU) had been arrested by the Nanking authorities in April 1931, and revealed the addresses of several leading party members as well as the links between the party and the Comintern agencies in China.

This episode led to the arrest and execution of the Secretary-General of the Chinese Communist Party and the complete disruption of the ties between the party and the Far Eastern Bureau—a blow which could not have failed to come to Sorge's attention. He made, however, only one cautious and implied reference: 'I also sent news which I happened to hear about the Chinese Communist Party; for example, concerning the activities of the Red Army in China and the collapse of the party leadership, but I had no organized contacts with party members.'

In revenge for this disaster, it was Chou En-lai as one of the senior survivors of the Chinese Central Committee who ordered at once the murder of all the near relatives of the 'traitor' who had revealed the information.

Noulens and his wife were handed over to the Nanking government and tried by court martial in October 1931, and sentenced to death. In circumstances which have never been clarified, the couple were deported to the Soviet Union in the following June and disappeared from sight. They were presumably exchanged for Nanking agents captured by the Russians.

The fate of Noulens made a deep impression on Sorge in his prison cell in Tokyo. Here was the case of a leading Soviet agent who got away. Would not the Soviet authorities react in a similar way to the plight of Sorge himself, whose satisfaction in having completed a brilliant and outstanding mission on behalf of the Soviet Union was now his main solace? This illusion was to remain with him until the end.

The real identity of Noulens was not settled by the British police in Shanghai, who were content to accept the final version of his Swiss nationality. Sorge knew better. 'The Swiss authorities could tell from his accent that he was not a genuine Swiss. I do not know his real nationality: I presume that he was a Balt.'*

If Noulens were in reality a Soviet national, the special interest in him which the Russian authorities displayed might in part be explained. But then Sorge too possessed Soviet citizenship.

---

* Noulens was in fact a veteran member of the Soviet Intelligence apparat, and had graduated via Vienna and Rome to the Far East. He was a Polish Jew. According to some witnesses, he was seen alive in Moscow in 1940, and to others, he was liquidated in the Stalin purges.

PART II

---◀◆▶---

Chapter 5

DESTINATION TOKYO

'I might be able to do something in Japan.' SORGE

SORGE arrived in Moscow in January 1933. He took a room at the Novaya Moskva Hotel and reported to Berzin at the headquarters of the Fourth Bureau. He was given 'an enthusiastic welcome', and told that his work in China had been most satisfactory. He was asked what he had in mind about the future. He was not anxious, however, to discuss the next assignment at once. He wanted first to finish a book he was writing on Chinese agriculture, and he worked on this every night. From time to time he was summoned to the Fourth Bureau for discussions; but Berzin often saw Sorge at his hotel; or Berzin would invite him to his home.

As a member of the Russian Communist Party returning from abroad, Sorge reported to the Central Committee, 'where I again met Smoliansky, who had handled my affairs back in 1929'. Sorge appeared before a small committee and completed the processing required by the Party. 'Smoliansky said that I had a high standing in the Party.'

Grigori Smoliansky was first secretary of that body, and also deputy head of the Central European secretariat. Recent information released in the Russian press suggests that Sorge was a friend who often visited the Smoliansky household. Grigori is described as 'a professional revolutionary and secretary of the All Union Central Executive Committee'.

His son remembers Sorge. He was 'broad-shouldered, with fair hair, sharply etched eyebrows, a straightforward look and firmly compressed lips. But his appearance in no way gave the impression that he was sullen or introspective'.

Sorge had some meetings too—related to his work in China— with members of the Commissariat of Foreign Affairs and of the GPU;

and he also met again 'Jim' ('Lehmann'),[*] chief of the wireless section of the Fourth Bureau and his previous acquaintance in Shanghai. They had a good many questions to ask him. As Sorge told the Japanese police: 'Every time one of them brought up a new question I had to submit a report; so I was kept busy typing day and night.'

It was in April, about eight weeks after his arrival in Moscow, that Sorge, summoned to the Fourth Bureau, was informed by Berzin that he would not be allowed to finish his book. He was to be assigned to another mission abroad. Had he any preferences in the matter? Sorge said that his choice would be Asia, more particularly north China or Manchukuo. Then, half as a joke, he said he might be able to do something in Japan.[†]

A few days later he was called again to Berzin's office. It appeared that the Central Committee of the Russian Communist Party were directly interested in the Japan proposal.

At subsequent meetings with Berzin it was agreed that Sorge's mission in Japan should be on a tentative basis at first.

One would have to discover [as Sorge put it] whether it was possible for me and my collaborators to enter Japan legally, whether it would be possible for us to contact Japanese and foreigners in Japan, what would be the technical capabilities of W/T or other means of communication, and finally whether it would be feasible to collect information on Japanese policy towards the Soviet Union.

This was the essence of his mission. As he wrote in his 'confession', his general assignment was

to observe most closely Japan's policy towards the Soviet Union following the Manchurian Incident, and at the same time to study very carefully the question of whether or not Japan was planning to attack the Soviet Union. . . . This was for many years the most important duty assigned to me and my group: it would not be far wrong to say that it was the sole object of my mission in Japan.

It was decided that in the first instance Sorge would stay in Japan for a maximum of two years. This would give him time to discover whether or not it would be possible for him to undertake espionage

---

[*] See p. 67.

[†] 'I forgot to mention that, while I was working in China, I visited Tokyo on a holiday and spent three days at the Imperial Hotel. I was so favourably impressed with Japan that after my return to Moscow from China, when I was told that I was to engage in espionage activities elsewhere, I jokingly suggested Tokyo as a possible destination.' (Examination No. 10 by preliminary judge. July 28, 1942.)

in Japan. The Japanese were notoriously spy-conscious; and in the atmosphere of nationalist exultation that had arisen after Japan's breach with the League of Nations all foreigners were objects of suspicion. The very fact that Sorge's first mission in Tokyo was tentative suggests that the Soviet Intelligence Services faced peculiar difficulties in Japan.

Berzin told Sorge that he would be assigned two collaborators, one of them a Japanese, and a wireless operator. Sorge was warned to have no contact with the underground Japanese Communist Party or, indeed, with the Japanese left-wing; and he was told to keep away from the Russian Embassy in Japan.

The use of Soviet Embassies and Consulates abroad for espionage purposes had been severely circumscribed by the raids in Hankow and Harbin in 1927, and by the scandal in England in the same year, when the British police raided the Soviet Trade Agency. It had become therefore immeasurably more important to develop special intelligence techniques on the part of various Soviet agencies operating independently of local official representatives. This confirmed Sorge's previous view of the need for the total separation of intelligence activities even from the machinery of the Comintern.

I was an independent leader of an espionage ring operating in Japan and I was sent to Japan as an independent leader of this ring by the Fourth Bureau. I had a special position in the Fourth Bureau, and I was the only Russian Communist in my ring.

As in the case of his previous missions, Sorge attended at least one general briefing conference. Those present included representatives of the Comintern, the Fourth Bureau of the Red Army, the Commissariat for Foreign Affairs, and the GPU. With Berzin's permission he also sought advice and guidance on a more personal basis. He had a series of talks with Smoliansky of the party central committee on Soviet-Japanese relations. He talked, too, with Radek. Small informal gatherings were held at the offices of the central committee. 'About this time I met an old friend "Alex" at the committee. Radek, "Alex" and I engaged in lengthy discussions of general political and economic problems involving Japan and East Asia.'

'Alex' has recently and firmly been identified by the Russian press as Borovich; he is not to be confused with the 'Alex' of the China mission. Sorge himself describes him as having 'previously worked for the secretariat of the Russian Communist Party in Moscow, but was at this time with the Fourth Bureau'. It was clearly Borovich who was now directly in charge of organizing Sorge's mission in Japan.

The mention by Sorge of Radek is both significant and puzzling. Both Sorge and his wife Christiane seem to have known Radek during their stay in Moscow. But this stormy petrel of the early days of the Comintern, and the German fiasco of 1923, was now in political disgrace and only dimly on the fringe of power.

Among his multifarious gifts, Radek was a specialist on Chinese affairs in the leading circles of the party, and also Rector of the University of the East, to which training cadres of Asian students were sent to form the future leadership of Communist parties in Asia. It seems that Borovich was attached to Radek as a 'military adviser' during this period.

Both the Bukharin–Radek opposition group in the Soviet party, and the directorate of the Soviet Military Intelligence, were already by now under fire from Stalin. Like Smoliansky, both Radek and Borovich were to die in the purges, and their work together in preparing Sorge's mission to Japan symbolized the end of an epoch.

Another useful contact was with two members of the Soviet foreign service who had been stationed in Tokyo. Both spoke Japanese and 'they explained conditions in Japan'. Sorge completed his round of calls by seeing 'my old friends Piatnitsky, Manuilsky, and Kuusinen'.

It remained for Sorge to work out suitable cover for his new mission. It would be that of a German journalist. This cover had served him well in China, and he had indeed already made a reputation for himself as a correspondent. As to Sorge's group in Tokyo, the members would assemble through clandestine contacts once he had reached Japan.

Sorge left Moscow for Germany, on the first stage of his journey to Japan, on May 7, 1933. He had spent some four months in the Soviet capital. It is probable that for at least part of this time he lived with a Russian woman, Katerina, who was employed as an engineer in a concern producing medical supplies. Certainly he was to share a flat with her on his next visit to Moscow in 1935; and acquaintances regarded her as his Russian wife.* It seems likely that he must have

* According to an article published in *Komsomolskaya Pravda* of January 13, 1965, Sorge married a certain Yekaterina Maximova in Moscow in 1933 after his return from Shanghai.

met her in the early months of 1933; but it may be that the association dated back to 1929, if not earlier.

Sorge arrived in Berlin with an established reputation as a journalist with special experience of the Far East. A fellow worker of Sorge's in the Soviet military intelligence has recently published in the Russian press, under the pseudonym of Comrade 'Gorev', a brief description of Sorge in Berlin in June 1933.*

'Gorev' was himself also preparing to leave Berlin on a mission to the Far East when he received instructions from 'the head of the Berlin illegal organization, whom I knew as "Oskar" ' to meet Comrade 'Ramsay'. 'Gorev' was told that he and 'Ramsay'—Sorge's new code name—would be 'neighbours', and that the two men should discuss together 'certain operational questions'.

'Gorev' describes their first meeting in a café in an aristocratic suburb of Berlin, and in reminiscing on Sorge's remarks retails unconsciously the general account of the world situation in 1933 which Sorge himself gave later to the Japanese police: the growing danger of war against the Soviet Union, the line up of opposing forces, Fascist and Soviet, and the difficulties of clandestine work in Japan. The main impression which Sorge made on his companion was 'the sense of purpose of a Soviet military intelligence officer'.

According to 'Gorev', Sorge's mission to Berlin was to obtain a genuine passport, and a newspaper correspondent's card. The files of the Weimar police had fallen into Gestapo hands: Sorge was

---

* In the autumn of 1964 a pamphlet was published in Moscow in a collection issued by the paper 'Komsomolskaya' under the title 'I knew Sorge' by a certain Jan 'Gorev'. From internal evidence it is clear that the author was at some time a colleague of Sorge's in the Fourth Bureau.

It is perhaps not a coincidence that 'Gorev' was also the cover name of Alexander Skoblevski, a senior Soviet functionary sent to Berlin on a special mission in 1923 to advise the German Communist Party on the organization of its military apparat prior to the October rising. It seems clear that Sorge was at some stage also connected with this work.

Skoblevski alias 'Gorev' was arrested by the German police on charges of subversive activities, and tried in a spectacular Treason Trial in Leipzig—the so-called Cheka-Prozess —in 1925. The Soviet authorities promptly staged a counter trial of two German students in Moscow, who were already under arrest for alleged espionage. In due course a suitable exchange of prisoners took place.

Shortly after the recent publication of 'Gorev's' pamphlet on Sorge in 240,000 copies, it was announced that the booklet had been abruptly withdrawn from circulation.

A book published in June 1965 in Paris—Nicole Chatel and Alain Guerin, *Camarade Sorge*, pp. 299–300—which is largely based on Soviet sources, gives a somewhat implausible biography of 'Gorev'. The mystery remains unclarified.

personally known also to many former associates of the German Communist Party. The operation was highly dangerous. Berzin, the head of the Soviet Military Intelligence, whom 'Gorev' claimed was responsible for the plan, was taking a calculated risk, but he was a master of 'the dialectics of intelligence'. The Gestapo machine was not yet a perfected instrument; Sorge was confident, thorough and brave. He had already made a profound study of Nazi literature and phraseology, and had arrived in Berlin 'ideologically qualified'.

Sorge later claimed that he applied for admission to the Nazi party. This idea may have been discussed with his Soviet superiors, but it was improbable that such a move was made.

It was also not essential, at that time, for a German journalist to be a member of the newly founded Nazi Press Association. Sorge did, however, report to the police in Berlin, according to their records on June 1, 1933, and applied for a new German passport, and made it appear in his *curriculum vitae* that he had returned to Germany direct from China and not via Moscow. When doing so he produced respectable character references, believing correctly that these would make it unlikely that searching enquiries would be made into his past history. Even if his past links with the German Communist Party in Hamburg and the Ruhr were to be uncovered that was now old history, and plenty of ex-Communists had joined the Nazi party.

However, it was not until October 1, 1934, that he was formally admitted to the Tokyo branch of the Nazi party. There was ample time, therefore, in which enquiries could have been made into his past career. It has been suggested that there must have been a Soviet agent in a responsible post at Gestapo files. If Schellenberg is to be believed, he examined 'Sorge's file' in 1940 and found that

if it did not prove him to be a member of the German Communist Party one could not help coming to the conclusion that he was at least a sympathizer. He [Sorge] had certainly been in close contact with a large number of people who were known to our Intelligence Service as Comintern agents, but he had close ties with people in influential circles and had always been protected against rumours of this sort.

Be that as it may, Sorge took a calculated risk that spring in Berlin. It was a characteristic piece of insouciance.

According to 'Gorev', his fellow intelligence officer, Sorge sent the following message from Berlin to the Moscow centre on June 9: 'The situation is not very attractive for me here, and I will be glad when I can disappear from this place.'

And on July 3 he wrote again: 'With things livening up in these parts, interest in my person can become much more intensive.'

Sorge stayed in Germany about eight weeks. He was busy establishing his journalist's cover; but he appears to have had at least one meeting with Christiane in Berlin. There is reason to believe that it was at this juncture that he and Christiane, so long separated, obtained an amicable divorce. To his old friends, Sorge was still, as one witness recalls, 'the old Communist idealist'.

'He still wanted to free the world from capitalist imperialism and militarism, and wanted to make wars impossible in the future. All difficulties, shortages and mistakes in the Soviet Union were only regrettable transitional phenomena.'

His friends noticed, at the same time, that he was drinking a good deal.

He secured the agreement of two newspapers—the *Börsen Zeitung* and the *Tägliche Rundschau*—to send them articles from Japan. The latter was a somewhat progressive paper, and it was suppressed in December 1933. Up to that time Sorge sent them regular articles. The leader writer of the *Tägliche Rundschau*, Dr. Zeller, was an ex-soldier; and partly for this reason he and Sorge took to each other. Zeller had a friend in Japan, Lt.-Colonel Eugen Ott of the German Army, an assistant attaché temporarily posted, for liaison and instruction, to a Japanese artillery regiment in the city of Nagoya. Accordingly Zeller gave Sorge a letter of introduction to Ott. In this Sorge was described as completely trustworthy, both politically and personally. In relating this episode to his interrogators nine years later, Sorge remarked: 'Germans abroad at that time were suspicious of each other. So if I were to be trusted by Ott a letter such as Zeller's was indispensable.'

A bolder move was to seek support from a leading National-Socialist theoretical journal—*Geopolitik*—founded by Karl Haushofer, whose conception of geopolitics, the relations of policy and geography, was fashionable in high party circles. Sorge met the editor, Dr. Vorwinckel, in Berlin. Vorwinckel already knew Sorge's name, from contributions that the latter had sent from China to German periodicals. Vorwinckel was obliging enough to provide letters of introduction to two members of the German embassy in Tokyo.

Having collected further introductions from journalist colleagues in Berlin, and from business firms there trading with Japan, Sorge then went to Munich to call on Karl Haushofer. From him he also received further letters to Dr. Voretzch, the German Ambassador in Tokyo and to Mr. Debuchi, the Japanese Ambassador in Washington.

It is worth remembering that the orthodox Marxist view at this time was that the Nazi régime would be short-lived. Moreover Sorge was aware that some Germans in Japan were bound to be anti-Nazi. Therefore, as he was to put it, 'after careful consideration I armed myself in Germany with letters of introduction from both *Geopolitik*, which was pro-Nazi, and from *Tägliche Rundschau* which was anti-Nazi'.

Sorge had also approached the Dutch financial newspaper, the *Algemeen Handelsblad* of Amsterdam, who agreed to accept regular contributions from him in Tokyo.*

The main undercover contact that Sorge made in Berlin was to meet his future radio operator 'Bernhardt'. They arranged to meet again in October in the Imperial Hotel, Tokyo.

Sorge was now ready to leave on his journey, with high-level introductions and secure cover as a foreign correspondent. He travelled under his own name on a genuine German passport. In his last letter from Berlin, dated July 30, he wrote:

I cannot claim to have achieved one hundred per cent, but it was simply impossible to do more, and it would be pointless to stay on here in order to obtain representation agreements with other papers. . . I am sick of being idle. At present I can only say that the prerequisites for my return to work have been more or less created.

As there were practical difficulties and risks of being identified if he were to take the Far Eastern route, either by Siberia or by Suez and Shanghai, it had been decided that he should travel by way of France, to avoid detailed controls in the North German ports, and the United States.

He sailed, therefore, in July from Cherbourg to New York. There is no trace of his leisurely movements during the following weeks, except that he called on the Japanese Ambassador in Washington with Haushofer's letter of introduction, and received a similar document to present to the head of the Information Department of the Foreign Ministry in Tokyo; and in New York and Chicago he contacted two

---

* The authors acknowledge the courtesy of the present editor of this paper, who writes: 'Richard Sorge worked for the *Algemeen Handelsblad* from 1934 to 1940, as correspondent in Tokyo. He was not in our service, but wrote articles for us regularly. In January 1940 we published his last article.'

members of the Comintern apparatus in the United States. One of them was an employee of the *Washington Post*, whom he met at a rendezvous in the Chicago World Fair. From him Sorge learnt that his Japanese collaborator would be joining him from California, and the method of contact in Japan was arranged.

Sailing from Vancouver he arrived in Yokohama on September 6, 1933.

Chapter 6

THE JAPANESE SCENE

'The cherry blossom among flowers;
The warrior among men.'
JAPANESE PROVERB

THE political atmosphere in Tokyo when Sorge arrived was as oppressive as the weather in September, the season of sudden typhoons. Everyone was nervous. For the threat of violence was heavy in the air. Little more than a year had gone by since a Prime Minister, Inukai Tsuyoshi, had been shot down in his official residence by a group of young officers; and in July 1933, just two months before Sorge's arrival, the police had uncovered at the eleventh hour a plot to assassinate the entire Cabinet.

The prospective victims of this murderous conspiracy were Premier Saito Makoto and his twelve colleagues. Admiral Saito was a man of temperate and sanguine disposition. He was unaffected by patriotic hysteria and was therefore a target for nationalist attack. His general outlook is illustrated by a remark he made, as Premier, to the editor of *The Japan Advertiser*: 'Everything will be all right so long as we old men are here to put on the brakes.'

But as a national figure this sagacious sailor was overshadowed by his Minister of War, Araki Sadao. Lt.-General Araki was famous throughout Japan for his advocacy of *Kodo*—the concept of 'The Imperial Way'. Like other elements in the ultra-nationalist mystique of this period, *Kodo* was often sincerely, if conveniently, represented as ineffable by its devotees. The essence of their creed, however, was belief in the virtues of 'direct rule by the Emperor' and in Japan's heaven-sent mission to extend her empire.

'Direct rule by the Emperor' was never precisely defined; doubtless the idea was too lofty to sustain analysis. But to young ultra-nationalist officers it implied a radical reconstruction of Japanese society on state socialist lines. All wealth—in terms of finance, capital equipment and land—above a certain valuation would be surrendered, or (as the *Kodo* myrmidons put it) 'restored', to the Emperor. It is not surprising that among the advocates of *Kodo* were many former Socialists and Communists. For this concept seemed to bring revolutionary action into harmony with the tradition of loyalty to the imperial house. It had a strong appeal for politically conscious, discontented junior officers in the army and navy, who despised the great capitalist combines—the so-called *zaibatsu*—and the parliamentary politicians who operated with and, in many cases, on behalf of these concerns. At the same time such extreme nationalists had a vivid fear of international Marxism as represented by the Comintern and the Soviet Union. The latter was considered to be Japan's outstanding external enemy.

As for the nation's heaven-sent mission, the occupation of Manchuria, which began in September 1931, was but a step in a process that must continue; and it was the contention of General Araki and the *Kodo* school that the next move should be to the north and northwest. To judge from speeches he made in 1933, Araki regarded war with Russia as inevitable and indeed imminent. He set the date for the clash some two years ahead. He referred on many occasions to 'the crisis of 1935–36', when Japan would be compelled to take up arms against the Soviet forces in the Far East.

With Araki as Minister of War and his friend, Lt.-General Masaki, holding another key post as Inspector-General of Military Training, it appeared that the *Kodo* school—the *Kodo-ha*, as it was known—had come to dominate military thinking in Japan. This view seems to have been widely accepted at the time in the circle of military attachés in Tokyo. The American Ambassador, Joseph Grew, noted in his diary for September 7, 1933 (the day after Sorge reached Yokohama), that one of his own assistant attachés, in agreement with his foreign colleagues, supposed a Japanese-Russian war to be 'absolutely inevitable' and had predicted that it would occur in the spring of 1935.

In reality, however, Araki and Masaki, the paladins of *Kodo* and the heroes of the young officers, were already beginning to lose ground by the summer of 1933.

The Japanese army was by no means the rigidly disciplined, monolithic organization that its image presented to the outside world. It was a prey to keen and often very rancorous factional strife. Araki and Masaki had powerful enemies within their own service. In opposition to them there were massed those senior officers who believed it would be unwise to pick a quarrel with Russia and who thought that the voluble Araki was both rash and over-emotional, and a bad example to his juniors. These opponents of the *Kodo-ha* were known, in the jargon of the day, as the *Tosei* school, the *Tosei-ha*, or 'Control Faction'; a title that suggests that this body of opinion was relatively sober and restrained.

It is true that there may have been a more substantial infusion of common sense in the 'Control Faction' than in the *Kodo-ha*. But 'Control' is hardly an appropriate term for the officers who were to plunge Japan into seemingly endless warfare in China. They were less radical than their rivals, less overtly excitable, but they were determined that the political power of the army, much enhanced by success in Manchuria, should be still further enlarged.

In the second half of 1933 the 'Control' school was starting to undermine *Kodo-ha* hegemony. For outside the army it had some important allies in its resistance to Araki's form of extreme nationalism.

At the apex, the Emperor himself was temperamentally averse to militarism in all its forms. An excellent horseman, he was an impressive figure at the annual review on the Yoyogi parade ground of the Guards battalions stationed in the capital. Mounted on his white charger he was the literal embodiment of the Japanese Supreme Command. Nevertheless, in a subtle but unmistakable way, the scene was not reminiscent of the All-Highest at Potsdam. One is bound to suspect that the Emperor of Japan regarded his command of the armed forces as a somewhat unwelcome if inescapable duty.

The Emperor was a reserved, scholarly figure, devoted to his personal hobby, the study of marine biology. Since the murder by Japanese officers of the Manchurian war lord, Chang Tso-lin, in 1928, he was beset by anxieties as to what could be done to check the excesses of his own army. In theory the Emperor was not only sacred and inviolable but also all-powerful, save for the constitutional obligation to legislate with the consent of the Diet. In practice he was not supposed to take action on his own initiative. In matters affecting military and naval operations he acted on the advice of the service chiefs of staff—such affairs were outside the competence of the Cabinet—and in the administration of the army and navy he took the advice of the War and Navy Ministers, who were invariably generals and admirals on the active list. On the ratification of treaties with foreign powers his advisers were the Privy Council. All other policy decisions were made by the Cabinet and formally endorsed by the Emperor, to whom members of the Cabinet were individually responsible.

In addition the Emperor was open to other important sources of influence. The Lord Keeper of the Privy Seal held a position some-what analogous to that of the Private Secretary at Buckingham Palace. The Lord Keeper was the day-to-day adviser of the Emperor on political affairs, and he was present at most audiences granted to civilian ministers. This office in 1933 was occupied by Count Makino, a liberal-minded veteran who had long attracted the enmity of the extreme nationalists. Indeed he had been one of those marked down for assassination in July 1933. Like Premier Saito this old man was there 'to put on the brakes'. The same could be said of the Minister of the Imperial Household and the Grand Chamberlain, both of them close to the Emperor. But the most eminent of these personal advisers was undoubtedly the aged Prince Saionji, the last surviving member of the small but powerful oligarchy known as the *Genro-in*.*

Thanks in large measure to several years spent in republican Paris as a young man during the seventies, Saionji distrusted the influence of military men in politics. He had a rational, sceptical cast of mind and was reputed to be both pro-French and pro-British. He cherished a passionate but reasoned loyalty to the imperial house; and it was his conviction, so far as one can judge, that the English monarchy should be the model for the Japanese. In other words, the Emperor must stay aloof at all costs from contentious issues. The Emperor must not be tempted, save in exceptional circumstances and on the most weighty advice, to take an open stand on any question of high policy. He should be a constitutional monarch as well as a theocratic sovereign.

The behaviour of the Japanese army in Manchuria in 1931 and thereafter incurred Saionji's profound disapproval. But the cautious old man never failed, until his death in 1940, to warn the Emperor against showing his hand too plainly in opposition to the army's moves. No doubt Saionji believed the wave of nationalist hysteria would recede. Meanwhile the Emperor could place a hand tentatively on the brakes; but he must never sit at the wheel.

It was not always clear, in fact, who was occupying the driver's seat in the headlong course that Japan followed during the decade before Pearl Harbour. It was the question to which the Embassies and foreign correspondents in Tokyo were for ever seeking the answer. The structure of power was such that it called for one person or one group to take ultimate control, to direct and co-ordinate at the top the separate and nominally equal functions of the Cabinet and the

* This was an extra-constitutional body composed of the original leaders of Meiji Japan. The word *Genro* means 'original elder'.

Supreme Command. In earlier days this final authority had rested in practice with the *Genro-in*. By the close of the nineteen-twenties it began to look as though the Cabinet—a Cabinet composed, except for the service ministers, of party politicians—might conceivably attain a status and authority superior to that of the armed forces. This trend, however, was sharply checked in 1932; and after Inukai's murder in May 1932 party cabinets had come to an end, the Saito administration being composed almost entirely of officials.

By 1933 the army and navy counted for more than any group of civilians; and of the two services the army was the more powerful. But, as we have seen, the army itself lacked unity, and it was not to resolve its factional differences until after the Tokyo mutiny of February 1936. However, if one can speak in terms of a collective view representative of the army as a whole, the army's position in the nineteen-thirties was that it desired to exercise the reality without incurring the responsibility of power.

The navy, too, suffered from disunity; but factional divisions here were less acute, although the navy was not without its quota of radical young officers. But the really serious rift in naval circles had occurred in 1930, over the matter of the London Disarmament Treaty. By 1933, in response to the growing pretensions of the army, the navy had begun to close its ranks. The thoughts of senior naval officers were concentrated on the prospect of the next disarmament conference, to be held in 1936. There was general agreement that at that assembly Japan must make no concessions to Great Britain and the United States. We may be sure that this conviction was inspired not only by considerations of ocean strategy, but also by the belief that a more powerful navy, in terms of ships and guns, would mean greater influence in Tokyo *vis-à-vis* the army.

For there was little love lost between the two services. Japanese naval officers tended to regard their compatriots in the army as brave but stupid, as narrow-minded zealots with no realistic awareness of the world beyond East Asia. Certainly talk of an imminent clash with the Soviet Union disturbed the navy, to whom the thought of a possible Japanese-Russian war in 1935 or 1936 was most unwelcome. It was the navy's fear that war with Russia might involve Japan in a confrontation with the United States, and this had to be avoided at least until the nineteen-forties. Time must be allowed for a building programme to be planned and completed, and for the stock-piling of oil supplies. In general the navy wholly rejected the idea of a necessary conflict with Russia. Opinion in the navy favoured expansion to the south-west, in the area of China. Accordingly, in the debate between *Kodo-ha* and *Tosei-ha* the latter could be certain of support from the navy.

Indeed the Saito Cabinet, like the succeeding administration under Admiral Okada, was described at the time as a 'navy cabinet'. For it was common gossip that Prince Saionji's motive, in recommending Admiral Saito as premier to succeed Inukai, was to bring the navy in as a counterweight to the Araki faction in the army.

Over these two armed services the Diet exercised virtually no control. It is true that the Diet had the power to amend or turn down the annual budget presented by the government; but in the event of rejection the budget of the previous year came into force. In any case, by 1933, the two Houses of the Diet had lost much of the influence they enjoyed in the twenties.

Moreover, one of the two leading parties—the Seiyukai—contained a strongly nationalist element that welcomed the more positive role of the army in political affairs. Even the Minseito, the Seiyukai's great rival and reputedly the more 'liberal' of the two parties, was by no means unaffected by the wave of patriotic feeling that swept Japan during the Manchurian adventure and the subsequent breach with the League.

As for the Japanese left, this was a minority movement thrown into disarray after 1931. Many Socialists had jumped on the bandwagon of militant nationalism. The growth of Fascism in Europe may have played some part in this; and threats from right-wing fanatics doubtless imposed silence on some Socialists. But of much greater importance was the belief that the exploitation of Manchuria would assuage the economic distress created by the world depression. Araki and the *Kodo* school could be seen as a positively anti-capitalist force. Thus many Socialists and some Communists discovered that they could extol the virtues of 'The Imperial Way'.

Those Socialists who refused to swim with the stream faced a harassing time. They were subjected to unceasing surveillance by the police, and drastic limitations were placed on what they could say or write in public. For newspapers and magazines of every kind existed by favour of press regulations speedily and often arbitrarily enforced by the police. The latter were at pains to expose and eradicate what they called 'dangerous thoughts', and these were not confined to the ideas of Marx and Lenin. Openly uncompromising Christians, pacifists, feminists, advocates of birth control, enthusiasts for Esperanto—

all these, as well as left-wing Socialists, were liable to be arrested without warning. Arrest, of course, did not necessarily mean prosecution. It might involve nothing worse than a few hours' questioning and admonition in the local police station. Or it could mean a week, a month, three months, in police custody, followed by release, no charge having been made. As in most police states, police behaviour in Japan was inclined to be capricious.

The Communist party was outlawed. Active support of Communism or open sympathy with the aims of the Comintern, attracted not only arrest, and stringent interrogation, but also certain prosecution, followed usually by a heavy term of imprisonment—unless the accused was able to convince procurators and judges that he had undergone a genuine change of heart. Adherence to left-wing revolutionary beliefs was the most heinous ideological crime, and it was the invariable aim of the police and legal authorities to secure not only confessions but also proofs of apostasy from the Communists in their hands. In this respect the official attitude recalled that of the Shogun's government during the persecution of the Christians in the first half of the seventeenth century.

To foreign residents in Japan this obsession with the question of 'dangerous thoughts' seemed faintly ridiculous. To all appearances the Japanese people were law-abiding and conformist, united to a man in loyal devotion to Throne and Emperor. But most foreigners in Japan had little direct knowledge of the potentially revolutionary discontent that had arisen as a result of the Depression. The collapse of the silk market in America in 1930 had brought a large proportion of the farming population to the edge of complete destitution. Two years later there was a disastrous crop failure in northern Japan. The only way in which many thousands of farmers' households in that region escaped actual starvation in the winter of 1932–33 was by selling their daughters to the city brokers who descended on the countryside on behalf of tea-houses, cafés, and bordellos. The worst sufferers and those who keenly sympathized with them—notably, young army officers who often came from country homes—focused their resentment on the government of the day, on Big Business and the Diet politicians, and on those remote figures, the Emperor's 'courtiers', such as Saionji or Makino. To have criticized the sovereign himself would have been a form of blasphemy that education and family upbringing made unthinkable. Revolutionary rage, none the less, demanded some outlet. This was found in the ultra-nationalism that erupted in violence at home and abroad during the nineteen-thirties.

At that time a majority of the working population of Japan was still engaged in agriculture, despite all the heavy industrialization that had taken place. The huge rural population provided industry with a continuing supply of cheap labour, both male and female. These worked in a small number of giant concerns—iron foundries, steel works, shipyards, mines and factories—and in a multitude of medium-sized and small workshops, many of the latter employing no more than five or six men. Many of these workshops turned out a varied range of products commissioned by branches of one or other of the great financial-industrial combines, the *zaibatsu*, which dominated the economy and preserved close and traditional links with the government.

Wages might be low and hours of work long, but in those years life was more tolerable in the cities and towns than in the countryside. Paternalism, the accepted tradition in Japanese industry and commerce, had virtues as well as defects. Once a man was an established employee of some factory or mine his employers had an obligation to look after him until his retirement. In the big firms the workers received such benefits as a bonus twice a year, free or greatly reduced housing and medical care. Undoubtedly there were many instances of gross exploitation of labour. Standards laid down by the International Labour Organization in Geneva were more often ignored than observed. Collective bargaining, as understood in Great Britain or America, was in its infancy, and the trade union movement was still frail and unassertive. On the whole the Japanese urban proletariat, the natural soil for the seeds of Marxism, seemed docile, more conscious of duties than of human rights.

The administrative structure of government was in the hands of an often overbearing but generally efficient civil service. An aristocracy of birth still exerted some influence. The House of Peers had powers that made it in many respects at least the equal of the elected House of Representatives. But in terms alike of real power and general prestige the higher ranks of the army and navy and of the civil bureaucracy, including the *noblesse de robe*, overshadowed the descendants of the Kyoto nobility and of the territorial lords of Tokugawa days. Local government was supervised by the Home Ministry, and prefectural governors were Home Ministry officials despatched from Tokyo. There was similar centralization of control throughout the state educational system and at all levels of the judiciary.

For Sorge the respect demanded by and paid to the government official—policeman, headmaster, service officer—was reminiscent of conditions in Germany before 1918. Yet Japan must have impressed him as an unknown land, for which two years in China would be but slight preparation. The atmosphere of Tokyo was radically different from that of Shanghai. Thanks to the Settlement and the French Concession, the tone of Shanghai was largely that of a Western city. Tokyo, on the other hand, was far less international than was apparent at first sight to the visitor from abroad.

It is true that the centre of the city was composed of modern buildings, in piquant juxtaposition to the wide moats and walls surrounding the imperial palace, the site of the Shogun's castle. In this seemingly cosmopolitan district there crouched a long, low building of brown and yellow brickwork, redolent of a Maya altar in Yucatan. This was the Imperial Hotel, famous among Europeans as the last grand hostelry in a chain, on the Suez route to the East, that began with Shepheard's at Cairo.

In the hotel's low-ceilinged lobbies, set at different levels, and in the caverns of the subterranean bar and shopping arcade, there congregated a mixed company of tourists, government guests, journalists, and men from the foreign Embassies and business houses. The Japanese seemed to be in an unobtrusive minority, their good manners rendering their presence at times almost invisible. Such of them as did frequent the hotel were nearly always those who had lived abroad and acquired foreign tastes and friends. On sale at the hotel bookshop were two different Tokyo daily papers in the English language. The ambience of smiles and politeness wrapped the visiting European and American in a floss of well-being that did no harm at all to personal vanity.

But the Imperial Hotel—like the Tokyo Club or the international clubs in Yokohama and Kobe—was a tiny enclave fundamentally alien to the surrounding terrain of Japanese *mores*, Japanese language and Japanese people.

Outside the enclave the foreigner met with almost universal courtesy together with much curiosity. He was never regarded with the aloof indifference that he would often encounter in a Chinese environment. Japanese curiosity might be friendly or hostile. It was rarely absent.

The foreigner was bound to find the Japanese language a daunting barrier to a real understanding of the people. Consequently most foreign residents were more restricted than they suspected in their contacts with the Japanese. In the case of Embassies the language barrier meant that exceptional reliance had to be placed on the two or three members of the diplomatic and consular staff who had specialized in Japanese. For a similar reason correspondents of the foreign press usually depended heavily on the services of their English-speaking Japanese subordinates. The same situation prevailed in most of the foreign shipping offices, banks and export-import houses.

Since English was a compulsory subject throughout secondary and higher education, it might be supposed that all Japanese of any standing would have some command of the language. This was not necessarily so. The educated man—a graduate, perhaps, of one of the imperial universities—might be able to read and write English with some facility. But in a great many cases he felt unable to speak the language and was ill at ease when addressed in English by a foreigner. Perhaps only the British, as a people, are worse linguists than the Japanese.

If to this difficulty of language one adds another—namely the singularity of Japanese psychology—the hazards of communication can be readily understood. Though open and affable in small talk, the Japanese of those days, when conversing with foreigners, were inclined to be guarded and reserved if the talk proceeded in a more serious direction—towards politics, for example. On such matters the Japanese tended to be politely but firmly evasive.

To a certain extent this was due to the nature of colloquial Japanese, which on the whole eschews direct and positive forms of speech. A statement can be so hedged by qualification as to render its meaning obscure to the foreigner. In talking with a compatriot a Japanese knows that in most cases the unexpressed nuance, behind the seeming ambiguities of what is actually said, will be clearly grasped. There is little need, then, to be specific in every instance.

But there was a more important reason for this general evasiveness. The thirties were a peculiarly anxious, disturbing time for most Japanese. 'Dangerous talk', like 'dangerous thoughts', could lead to unpleasantness. Both had frontiers that were undefined. So common prudence alone made the Japanese at that time more than usually reticent in their conversations with foreigners.

Moreover, aggression in Manchuria and the fighting at Shanghai, early in 1932, had alienated sentiment in the United States as well as in much of Europe; and then Japan had flounced out of the League at

Geneva. All this made the Japanese at home feel isolated from the world and introduced, in their relations with foreigners, a further element of self-conscious reserve.

Such, then, was Japan when Sorge arrived in the late summer of 1933. To Western eyes it was indeed a paradoxical country. This was a state ruled in theory by a god-like Emperor, who yet could scarcely exercise direct authority, and governed in practice by a centralized bureaucracy that was obliged, in matters of high policy, to follow the course imposed upon it by one of the fighting services. This was a nation famous for the obedience, the Confucian discipline, and self-sacrifice, of its people. Yet it harboured demons of unrest whose murderous violence was committed always in the Emperor's name. This was a land loved or hated by the few foreigners who came to know it well; and, assuredly, such feelings were reciprocated from the Japanese side.

It was wise of Sorge to perceive that his first two years in Tokyo must be a time for experiment and trial. For by comparison with China, Japan was indeed a closed book.

Chapter 7

THE MUSTER OF THE RING

'To work, comrades!' LENIN. December 31, 1910

ON arrival in Tokyo Sorge took a room at the Sanno Hotel. His first call was at the German Embassy. The new Ambassador, Dr. Herbert von Dirksen, had not yet arrived from Europe. Sorge was well received by the senior staff. He seems indeed from the beginning to have established very cordial relations. According to his own account, the staff were particularly impressed by his introduction from the Japanese Embassy in Washington to Amau Eiji, head of the Foreign Ministry Information Department.

After I got to Japan the German Embassy asked me if I knew anyone in the Foreign Ministry, and I was told I could be given an introduction to officials there. I said rather proudly, with the letter to Amau in my pocket, that an introduction to the Japanese Foreign Ministry was unnecessary.

After visiting the Embassy Sorge, the following day, called on Amau at the Foreign Ministry and was introduced to several Japanese and foreign journalists. Amau was an important figure in those days, as the recognized spokesman of the Foreign Ministry, presiding at a weekly press conference attended by the leading journalists in Tokyo.

One of these—Mitsukado Aritomi of the *Jiji Shimpo*, who was friendly with the German Embassy—went out of his way to show Sorge some kindness. For example, he found him accommodation at the Meguro Hotel, which was more reasonably priced than the Sanno. A little later, when Sorge acquired a home of his own in the Azabu district, Mitsukado helped him to move in. It is indicative of Sorge's caution during these early days that he was suspicious of these gestures of goodwill. He came to the conclusion that Mitsukado was probably working for the Metropolitan Police Board. For Mitsukado introduced him to a Japanese, an ex-Socialist, who spoke to him in Russian. Sorge, as was his invariable custom in Japan, pretended not to know the language.

Whether or not his suspicions were justified in this instance, Sorge was correct in his belief that his movements, like those of all foreign residents, would be watched by the police and their agents. He felt bound to proceed with great circumspection. No serious espionage could be attempted until a working group of collaborators was formed and he himself had obtained some first-hand knowledge of the general situation in Japan. To this end he began building up a collection of books on the country; and this was to grow in time into a library of over a thousand volumes.

In early October he was ready to contact his radio operator 'Bernhardt', whom he had met in Berlin. 'Bernhardt' had arrived in Japan that month and he and his wife (as 'Mr. and Mrs. Wendt') had taken up residence in a suburb of Yokohama, his cover being that of a businessman. When they met in the lobby of the Imperial Hotel, Sorge told 'Bernhardt' that he must lose no time in setting up a wireless transmitter in his house, and he then declared that he must be put in touch with the third member of the ring, the Yugoslav Branko Vukelic.

In his initial interrogation by the Japanese police, Sorge stated that while staying at the Hotel Noailles, Paris, on his way to Cherbourg from Germany, a contact man called on him and told him that 'a certain Vukelic' was already installed at the Bunka Apartments.* This was a block of service flats, about a quarter of an hour's drive by taxi from the Imperial. On Sorge's instructions 'Bernhardt' telephoned the flats, confirmed that Vukelic was staying there, and made his way over to contact Vukelic at the Bunka Apartments on Sorge's behalf. At Vukelic's flat a kind of Zen dialogue took place:

Bernhardt: 'Do you know Johnson?'

Vukelic: 'I know him.'

Bernhardt: 'I myself am not Schmidt, but I was sent by him.'

'Bernhardt' then left.

Next day, Sorge, satisfied that his man had been identified, went to see him. At this, their first encounter, Sorge was disturbed to find Vukelic both unwell and out of funds. It was not an auspicious beginning to their collaboration.

---

* But later Sorge changed this story. He told the Preliminary Judge that details of contacting Vukelic had been arranged before he left Moscow, and that he had been informed in Moscow that Vukelic might be in Japan before he (Sorge) reached Tokyo. (Preliminary Judge's Examination No. 10: July 28, 1942.)

Branko Vukelic was at this time a young man of twenty-nine. A curious course of events had led him and his wife and small son from Europe to the Bunka Apartments in Tokyo. He was born in August 1904 at Osijek in Croatia and was the son of an Austro-Hungarian officer.* His childhood was spent in garrison towns of the Monarchy. In 1918 the family was living in Zagreb, where Vukelic went to high school. The new Yugoslav State was emerging out of the First World War in a climate of intellectual ferment and controversy and, like many of his fellow students, Vukelic came under the influence of both national and left-wing ideologies.† While at school he joined a group called the Progressive Darwinist Club, and went through the growing pains of a teenage revolutionary.

In 1922 the Yugoslav Minister of the Interior was shot by a young Communist, who was subsequently executed. According to the recent reminiscences of Vukelic's mother, this brutal episode had a profound emotional impact on her son. On hearing the news of the death sentence on the young terrorist, Branko contracted a high fever and took to his bed, and a few days later laid a wreath of red carnations on the fresh grave at Zagreb cemetery. He expressed his feelings in a series of sketches depicting the tortures and brutalities of the Yugoslav police inflicted on political prisoners.

On leaving high school Vukelic enrolled in the Zagreb Academy of Art. Here he joined the Communist student faction of the Marxist students' club in the University, and became involved in frequent clashes with the police—much to the alarm of his mother. On at least one occasion he seems to have been placed under arrest.

Branko thought it prudent to leave the country for a brief spell and he spent several months in Brno in Czechoslovakia, where according to his mother he 'continued his underground party activities'. He registered at the Faculty of Architecture at Brno University, but after two terms he returned to Zagreb.

By now Mrs. Vukelic was thoroughly alarmed at the political activities of her son. She had separated from her husband, and in 1926 she moved to Paris with Branko and his two sisters, where he registered as a law student at the Sorbonne. The Yugoslav police must have forwarded

---

* The records of the various interrogations of Vukelic cannot be found. There exists only an incomplete but substantial portion of a statement or confession made by Vukelic to the Procurator in charge of his case. It is largely on this source that the following paragraphs are based. A recent article containing new biographical material on Vukelic appeared in the Yugoslav monthly magazine *Review* in October 1964.

† He was in fact of Orthodox Serb extraction.

his dossier to their French colleagues, as he was arrested again on two occasions in Paris. In his later account to the Japanese, Vukelic claimed that he had, at the instance of his mother, broken with the Yugoslav Communist groups at this time. The party was banned after the assassination of the Minister of the Interior in 1922, and split into warring factions. The political attitudes of the young Yugoslav generation mirror the confused problems of the new unitary State, bringing together for the first time in history the Serbs, Croats and Slovenes. The opposition to the established Belgrade government consisted of elements both Communist and strongly separatist. These groups coalesced in various underground formations, such as the Marxist student club in Zagreb, and several of Vukelic's contemporaries were to end in 1941 as supporters of the Axis-controlled 'Independent State of Croatia'.

According to the recent article on Vukelic in the Yugoslav press, which appeared in October 1964, the turning-point in Vukelic's life in France was his meeting with Colonel de la Roque, the brother of the leader of the Cagoule—an extreme Fascist and terrorist organization. In view of Branko's previous contacts with similar individuals and groups in Yugoslavia, this is not as surprising as it might appear. In his interrogations by the Japanese police, however, he maintained a total silence on this episode. It is alleged that, through de la Roque, whose private secretary he became, Vukelic moved in business circles in Paris. It is possible that it was through the influence of de la Roque that he became an employee of the Compagnie Générale de l'Electricité —a fact which he did admit to the Japanese.

The recent Yugoslav material implies that Vukelic was really acting under Communist instructions in penetrating de la Roque's circle. There is no further evidence to corroborate or refute this suggestion.

In January 1930, while staying at a seaside resort on the French Atlantic coast, he met a Danish girl Edith Olson, with whom he fell in love. They later married and had one child, a boy named Paul.

In August 1931 Vukelic returned to Yugoslavia to serve in the army, resigning his job in Paris at the same time. But his military service was brief, for in November he was discharged because of illness. Together with his mother he went to the south of France for a period of convalescence. Not until the end of January did he rejoin his wife and child in Paris. He now began to look for a job, as his old firm could not take him back.

On his return to Paris at the end of January 1932

he began to lead a strange existence. He never went out except when he had to attend to some business for the Baron [Colonel de la Roque]. Once a month he had a meeting with 'Ivan', with whom he had long confidential talks. He studied photography with singular application and assembled a radio transmitting set at home. He took up journalism and began writing for some newspapers.

In his statement to the Japanese police, Vukelic does not refer to the mysterious figure of 'Ivan', but instead claims that one day, while he was out looking for work, he ran into two old friends from Zagreb in a café in the Latin Quarter frequented by Yugoslav students. One of them, whose name was Klein, had been a senior member of the Zagreb Marxist club. The other, a man called Budak, had also taken part in the club's activities, though Vukelic remembered him best as a Croatian separatist. Moreover both had been in the same class together in the high school at Zagreb.*

Klein and Budak told Vukelic that they had escaped across the mountains into Austria when the Yugoslav government organized its intensive campaign against the Communists in 1929.

Vukelic saw a lot of his two friends in the ensuing days. One suspects that even then his domestic life was not very harmonious. Not once did Klein and Budak come to his home. Invariably he visited them at their lodgings. He told them about his failure to find a job, and about his experiences in the Yugoslav army. They were sympathetic, and they promised to help him find work. To this end they asked him to put in writing his own story, with special reference to his short period of military service.

Accordingly Vukelic produced what was in fact both a piece of autobiography and a political report, amounting to sixty pages in all. Much of it was concerned with an analysis of the situation in the Yugoslav army. Vukelic summed up the report as follows:

I described the demonstrations that we had dared to organize in the army, and I described other incidents that I had witnessed or heard about. In conclusion I described the contradictions of nationality and class that divide the officers. For some officers were Serb, others were Croat. Those officers who had served in the Great War of 1914–18 came from country backgrounds; but many of the younger officers came from the bourgeoisie. I discussed and analysed their psychology.

* It is conceivable that Vukelic's friends may have been Hugo Klein, later a well-known psychoanalyst in Zagreb, and Milo Budak who was later prominent in extreme right-wing Croatian politics and Minister of Education in Pavelic's 'Independent State of Croatia' after 1941.

During the next two or three weeks, while Klein and Budak were reading this document, the Yugoslav press carried reports of trouble in the Zagreb garrison, some of whose officers were arrested on charges of conspiring against the government. Klein praised Vukelic for the perceptiveness of his analysis to which this news bore witness. A man who can write like this, he told Vukelic, has no need to worry about finding a job. In any case he was going to send Vukelic's manuscript to *Inprecorr*, the organ of the Comintern. When Vukelic jokingly protested, Klein assured him that the report was most helpful to 'The Movement'—referring of course to the work of the Comintern.

There was no doubt an element of flattery in Klein's praise; but he was probably genuinely impressed by the report. Vukelic could express himself well both in writing and in speech; and his knowledge of the Yugoslav army was based, after all, not only on his own brief experience of military service, but also on what he had learned from his observations as the child of an officer's household. Vukelic, a tall, thick-set figure, was often, in Japan, taken to be a former regular officer. There was always something vaguely military about his bearing.

Klein now began to press him to become an active worker for the Communist cause, telling Vukelic that the years of inactivity since his break with Communism could be regarded as 'leave of absence' rather than 'desertion'. Vukelic, however, at first rejected Klein's proposition. He said he was no longer a convinced Communist, that he had ceased to believe in the prospect of imminent revolution. He had no wish to take part in the agitation and propaganda work of the Yugoslav or French Communist Parties. He admitted the theoretical possibility of 'Socialism in One Country', but he doubted whether it could succeed; it was more likely that Russia would deteriorate into a society controlled by a system of state capitalism and governed by a ruling class of bureaucrats and generals.

But Klein would not listen to these objections. He forced Vukelic into the position of admitting that there might be a possibility of world revolution, provided peace was maintained for many years and Stalin's Five-Year Plan proved to be a success. He pointed out—and this helped to decide the issue for Vukelic—that the prime task of the Comintern was to help the Soviet Union by maintaining world peace, thus enabling the Russians to develop socialism in their country.

Vukelic shifted the line of his argument, by attacking the Comintern for its intellectual poverty, citing as one example the thesis, expressed in *L'Humanité*, that the German Social Democratic Party was to blame for the rise of Nazism. To this, Klein's rejoinder was that Vukelic's very argument showed that 'the new organization', for which he (Klein) and Budak worked, was in need of fresh blood. It needed someone like Vukelic for a certain specific task. The Comintern was very short of good information. The local Communist parties were too absorbed in electoral tactics, and their members were too exposed, too well-known, to obtain inside information. Furthermore, said Klein, the Comintern had been weakened by factional strife, thanks to Trotskyites and others. So information coming in from Communist parties was sometimes unreliable. This lack of sound information was the reason why *L'Humanité*, for example, could offer only superficial interpretations of what was going on in the world.

These remarks came as a revelation to Vukelic, who had imagined that, as a centre of world-wide intelligence, the Comintern was surpassed only by the Vatican. He was also impressed decisively by Klein's argument that the purpose of 'the organization' was to cooperate in the passive defence of the Soviet Union while that country was engaged in the building of Socialism.

In his confession ten years later Vukelic declared:

It was my belief that if the Soviet Union could be defended for a decade from the onslaught of war, that country would have a socialist culture, economy and system of defence strong enough to resist any capitalist attack. Klein agreed with this opinion of mine.

Even if it was impossible to achieve world revolution in our time we could at least place our hopes in a country that had undergone the invaluable experience of socialism; and thus we could leave the socialist ideal to coming generations. This, I felt, gave me a fresh motive for taking part in the Movement.

Finally, Vukelic agreed to meet another member of 'the organization', hoping thereby to learn more about the work on which he was to engage.

That this would be espionage was probably something that he neither expected nor desired. In those days, at any rate, intellectuals like Vukelic with Marxist sympathies, whether or not they were party members, did not as a rule regard espionage as an acceptable task for a Communist. This was notably true in France at that time. For example, Henri Barbé (a leading figure in the French party), summoned to Moscow in 1931, indignantly refused Berzin's proposal that he should work for Soviet intelligence. Barbé told Berzin that the tradition of the French Labour Movement was against engaging in this kind of activity, and he demanded that Berzin should cease recruiting agents from among militants in the French Communist Party.

The stranger whom Vukelic was to meet turned out to be a woman of around thirty. She used the name 'Olga' and was athletic in her appearance and tastes (she boasted, it seems, of her prowess in skiing). Vukelic judged, from her accent, that she came from a Baltic country, possibly Finland. He met her alone, through a recognition signal arranged in advance. This was in March 1932.

Later evidence from Paris suggests that 'Olga' was of Polish origin, and a member of the apparatus of the OMS (the International Communications Bureau) of the Comintern, the most vital and covert section of the whole machinery of that organization.

In her approach to Vukelic 'Olga' appears to have adopted the same general argument as Klein, pointing out the duty of all good Communists to defend the Soviet Union. She went on to say that the particular work of 'the organization' was to collect information. This seems to have put Vukelic on his guard. For he replied that he had no experience of conspiratorial work and, apart from four months' military service, no knowledge of military affairs.

'But the duties involved,' said 'Olga', 'are not those of a military detective in the Phillips Oppenheim manner. I don't propose to steal secret codes by seducing young officers—though I might not refuse to fall for an attractive young French officer if this was going to help us. I don't expect you to be a safe-breaker. I want you to make use of your experience as a journalist.' (Vukelic had told her he had written two or three articles for the Yugoslav press as a student.)

She emphasized that he must observe and analyse events as a Marxist, that wherever he went there would be 'some experienced comrade' to educate him. 'And there will be sympathizers who will collaborate in the work.'

'Why,' asked Vukelic, 'can't the Comintern use Soviet Embassies to collect information?'

'Every country except Russia can use an Embassy for intelligence as well as propaganda; and they can make use of business firms, missionaries, and students. In our case we have to rely on young Communists like yourself and on other sympathizers. Soviet Embassies are always watched. If a Soviet Embassy gets involved in this the Soviet Union becomes an accomplice of the Comintern; and the Soviet diplomatic service and the Comintern don't always have the same views.'*

When Vukelic pleaded that he lacked experience as a Communist, 'Olga' replied that this was in fact an advantage; his name would mean nothing to the police.

So in the end, possibly without much enthusiasm, he consented to work for 'the organization'. 'Olga', he tells us, instructed him to remain in Paris. She gave him some translation work and 3,000 francs as an allowance.

At their next meeting that spring, about a month later, 'Olga' told Vukelic that he would be assigned either to Roumania or Japan—the likely choice being Roumania. Soon after this she introduced him to 'an elderly white-haired comrade, with the air of a businessman, who probably came from a Baltic country'. This man spoke very little; but he observed Vukelic attentively while asking him a few casual questions about his past career and future plans. Vukelic realized that he was being sized up; but he believed he made a good impression on the stranger.

It seems that Vukelic met 'Olga' several times 'before the summer', and thereafter on only two occasions—in the middle of the summer, and in the early autumn.† Not very long after his meeting with the elderly stranger, Vukelic was informed—presumably by Olga—that his destination was to be Japan, not Roumania. But he was not yet given his marching orders. 'Olga' agreed that his wife Edith and the child should accompany him to the Far East. For he pointed out that Edith was a qualified teacher of Danish gymnastics, which were popular in Japan at that time, and that this could provide one ostensible reason for their journey East. Accordingly, 'Olga' arranged a meeting at which, in Vukelic's words, 'some senior comrade—a woman—should decide whether or not my wife was suitable'. Edith passed the test. ('The comrades paid little attention to the matter of my wife's ideology; for she was merely accompanying me to Japan, and it was not expected that she would do much work for us.') So she

---

* Olga's words have been rendered into direct speech, without embellishment, from the indirect speech in which they appear in the Vukelic Statement.

† Meissner in his book *The Man with Three Faces* suggests that their relationship was amorous; but on this point there is no reliable evidence either way. Meissner also suggests that Olga was a well-known Parisian hostess, an attractive and wealthy young woman. Here again, sound evidence is lacking to support this proposition. It is more likely that she was the sister of 'A. Tilden', the head of the Soviet services in Paris.

began to brush up her skill in gymnastics. Indeed she travelled to Denmark to obtain letters of introduction from well-known Danish schools that had good connections with the Japanese gymnastic world.

In October, at his last meeting with 'Olga'—'actually she was in bed, after an appendicitis operation, but she got up to keep the rendezvous'—Vukelic was told that his assignment to Japan was definitely confirmed. 'Olga' said she envied Vukelic, for Japan was famous for its beauty.

'How long,' asked Vukelic, 'shall I be there?'

'Two years—if you feel uneasy about the idea of going it will be quite all right for you to refuse. But once you have made the decision to go you will have to work faithfully, and you won't be allowed to leave the country when you like.'

Vukelic accepted this. But he admitted that his real ambition was to go to Moscow to study Marxism. He was assured that it might be possible, one day, for this wish to be granted.

At 'Olga's' direction he then met 'another comrade'—a man in his thirties, Jewish, a Southern European, possibly Hungarian. This man, it seems clear, handled the details of Vukelic's departure; and it was this man who told Vukelic that he should stay in the Bunka Apartments, Tokyo, where a contact would visit him and give him further instructions.

Now, after months of waiting, Vukelic suddenly found that he was to sail in six weeks—hardly time in which to secure adequate cover. However, he discovered that the French illustrated weekly, *Vu*, was planning a special number on the Far East.* He approached the magazine and talked his way into an appointment as their correspondent, for he was a competent photographer. At the same time, through an exchange of express letters, he persuaded the Yugoslav newspaper, *Politika*, to take him on as their special correspondent. He was not a complete stranger to the paper, as he had sent them some articles already.

The departure of Vukelic for Japan was known at least to his mother. In their last conversation in Paris he said to her, 'There is nothing dangerous about it. You know I have always had an affinity for that country.'

The family sailed from Marseilles on December 30, 1932, in an Italian ship. It was a long voyage, via Suez and Singapore—while they were on their way Sorge returned to Moscow from China—and it was

---

* This special number in fact never appeared.

not until February 11 that they disembarked at Yokohama. It happened to be the Japanese public holiday of *Kigensetsu*, the commemoration of the traditional foundation of the state by the Emperor Jimmu in 600 B.C.

Almost at once Vukelic realized that he was going to have great difficulty in making ends meet. 'Olga's' friends had provided him with the sum of 1800 Yen before he left France, and he had reckoned that this would keep him going for six months. He had understood that a married couple could live in the Tokyo Imperial Hotel on 10 Yen a day—and the Bunka Apartments, of course, were bound to be cheaper. 300 Yen a month, then, seemed adequate. But he quickly discovered that his calculations were at fault. They were based on information that was out of date.

It was all a glorious failure, and later on I had great hardships.

10 Yen a day covered room, rent, and meals for a couple ten years before that time. In 1933, when we arrived, a married European couple spent more than 10 Yen a day even in the Bunka Apartments. Furthermore, 10 Yen a day did not allow for any extras —sightseeing, for example. 10 Yen a day did not allow for 1 Sen to be spent on things like that.

Regarded by many Japanese at that time as symbolizing—together with the Imperial Hotel—the last word in European luxury and sophistication, the Bunka Apartments (*Bunka* is the Japanese word for 'culture') could be more truthfully described as representing provincial standards of comfort and taste during the late Victorian age. The building faced a busy road and, beyond that, a deep cutting containing a rather gloomy canal (Ochanomizu—'honourable tea water') and a very lively electric railway. The trains rattled by every few minutes from an early hour, all through the day.

To be immured in indigence here was a trying experience for both man and wife; Edith Vukelic, from all accounts, not being renowned for thrift.

It seems clear that Vukelic understood he would have to wait until August, at the earliest, before he could expect a visit from 'Schmidt', the man who was to give him further instructions and guidance in Japan. This at least is the inference to be drawn from Vukelic's remark, in his confession, that he left Marseilles with 1800 Yen 'to cover six months'. Yet 'Schmidt' (Sorge) did not contact him until October.

This raises the question as to why the Vukelic family were packed off so far in advance of Sorge's own arrival in Japan. Neither 'Bern-hardt', the wireless operator, nor the fourth member of the ring, the Japanese from America, came to Tokyo before the autumn. Why should Vukelic have travelled so much earlier?

It may be that he wanted to be on his way as soon as his des-tination had been agreed upon. But this is not what emerges from his later account to the Japanese procurator. It seems more probable that those who were concerned with his movements had a motive for getting Vukelic and his wife off on their journey without further delay.

This motive could have been anxiety about the ultimate con-sequences of the exposure by the Paris Sûreté, in June 1932, of an intelligence apparat headed by the Soviet agent Izaia Bir. The arrest of Bir and six of his associates was followed by the flight from France of Jacques Duclos, one of the members of the present leadership of the French Communist Party, and by intensive police searches and investigations, lasting for months. Nobody could be certain where the hunt would end.

Capital importance was attached by Moscow to the establishment of a new network in Japan. The year 1932, after all, saw Japanese troops stamping their feet on the banks of the Argun, Amur, and Ussuri Rivers along the Manchurian frontiers of the Soviet Far East. Someone like Vukelic, already earmarked for this network, could not be allowed to incur the risk of arrest before his journey had begun.

Having met Vukelic, Sorge came to his rescue. He gave him some money immediately. Later he advanced him a larger sum, sufficient for Vukelic and his wife and child to move from the Bunka Apartments to a rented house in Sanai-cho, Ushigome ward.

This was after Sorge had received funds from a courier at Nikko. This meeting—the first with a Fourth Bureau courier in Japan—had been arranged in Moscow before Sorge's departure for Germany and the Far East. The courier came from Shanghai at the end of 1933, or at the beginning of 1934. On arrival he telephoned the German Em-bassy and also wrote to Sorge there, saying that he had arranged for the doorman at the Imperial Hotel on the morning of a certain day to bring Sorge to his room.

The meeting at the Imperial Hotel took place as planned. Next day Sorge and the stranger went sightseeing at Nikko; where, among the stone lanterns and cryptomerias of Ieyasu's memorial shrine, Sorge was handed a package, 'chiefly containing money'. He was also told the number of a post office box in Shanghai, 'for use in case of need'.

Sorge must have subsidized Vukelic fairly heavily at first. It was through Sorge, also, that Vukelic was introduced to a wider circle that, in the end, was to embrace most of the foreign press corps and some senior members of the French and British Embassies. Sorge, in a word, set Vukelic on his feet. He had to, if his collaborator was to be of use to him.

Meanwhile the fourth member of the ring, a Japanese, Miyagi Yotoku, about the same age as Vukelic, was waiting in the city for a sign from 'Schmidt'. He had arrived in October from California. He made a point of reading the daily English-language newspaper, *Japan Advertiser*. One morning in the middle of December he saw what he was looking for. It was a notice in the 'want' column, reading:

WANTED Ukiyoye prints by old master, also English books on same subject urgently. Apply Box 423, Japan Advertiser, Tokyo.

This had been inserted, on Sorge's instructions, by Vukelic. Miyagi sent a reply to the paper, and he and Vukelic accordingly met in the offlces of *The Japan Advertiser*. Both Miyagi and Vukelic carried in their wallets an American one-dollar note. The dollar notes bore consecutive numbers, thus providing the two men with means of mutual identification.

Some days later, just before the year ended, Sorge met Miyagi in the Ueno Art Gallery, using a recognition signal arranged beforehand. (Sorge, for example, was wearing a black tie.) Miyagi, far from being a hardened and experienced *apparatchnik*, was—like Vukelic—an amateur caught up in a situation designed by and for professionals. It was not until he had met Sorge four or five times that he realized that he was being invited to become a spy. For Sorge now asked him to supply information on political and military matters in Japan.*

Miyagi Yotoku had spent his childhood in the island of Okinawa, where he was born in February 1903, the second son of a farmer. The latter had moved to Davao in the Philippines in 1906. A year's

* Procurator's Examination: Myagi: No. 28, March 30, 1942. In this same session Miyagi remarked: 'Sorge never explicitly told me to carry out espionage.'

experience of farming there had proved a failure, and the elder Miyagi had then crossed to America, where he worked on a farm near Los Angeles. So the boy was brought up in Okinawa by his grandparents. He was moderately gifted, for in 1917 he passed the entrance examination for the prefectural teachers' training school. But before two years had passed illness—incipient tuberculosis—compelled him to leave.

This was in March 1919. In June of that year he joined his father in California.

It was not a good time to arrive in the United States, for it was during the height of the anti-Japanese agitation in California. The sixteen-year-old boy was plunged into a strange society, and the first thing he had to do was to learn English. For this purpose he attended school at Brawley, California, where his father was living.

Miyagi was to discover that he would be the victim of discrimination at three levels. Not only was he made aware of the white American's colour prejudice against Asians in general and against Japanese in particular (specifically political rancour was involved too, so far as Japan was concerned), but he also suffered from the superior airs that Japanese residents in America, especially the *Nisei* (second-generation Japanese), adopted towards more recent immigrants.

Japanese immigrants to the United States were treated with disdain by the Japanese Embassy and by leading *Nisei*. Sometimes the Japanese military attaché actually spied on Japanese immigrants.

But this was not all. Miyagi found that in America, in the Japanese community in California, his Okinawan ancestry marked him out. Early in life he developed, as a native of this island, something of a sense of inferiority *vis-à-vis* Japanese from Honshu and the other main islands. The inhabitants of the Ryukyu archipelago, of which Okinawa is the largest island, have been governed by the Japanese directly or indirectly for generations, and a great measure of assimilation has taken place. Nevertheless differences of custom and culture— not great, but still significant—separate 'pure' Japanese from 'pure' Okinawans. The latter have always been quick to resent instances of discrimination practised against them by *pukka* Japanese.*

This has naturally bred in the Okinawans a certain rebelliousness. The fact, for example, that he was born in Okinawa profoundly

---

* 'I detested,' wrote Miyagi, 'the tyranny of the Japanese bureaucracy in Okinawa.'

influenced the mental development of Tokuda Kyuichi, perhaps the most famous of the Japanese Communist leaders.

Once his English was proficient Miyagi enrolled at an art school in San Francisco; but his infected lung gave him further trouble, and after some months he had to leave. On his recovery he entered the San Diego School of Art. He had genuine talent as a painter, for on graduation, in 1925, he was top of his class. After about a year's work on a farm he moved in the autumn of 1926 to Los Angeles, to a house opposite the main railway station.

On these premises Miyagi with three other Japanese took part in the venture of running a restaurant, which they named the 'Owl'; and in a room at the back of the 'Owl' they formed, with other friends, a small society for weekly discussions on philosophy, art and social questions. This soon became known as the *Reimeikai*, or 'Dawn Society'. The membership increased as time went by; although there were probably never more than about thirty members at any time. They were joined by an anarchist who had once been on close terms with Kotoku Shusui, the Japanese anarchist executed in 1911 for plotting, so it is said, to murder the Emperor Meiji. Another new member, a Communist, had worked with Katayama Sen, the veteran Marxist who had made his home in Moscow. According to Miyagi the 'Dawn Society' was at first liberal-left and undogmatic in character. Miyagi himself started to read the works of Russian writers—notably Tolstoy, Gorky, Bakunin and Kropotkin—and was converted to anarchism.

In the summer of 1927 he began to live with a Japanese girl called Yamaki Chiyo. She plays no part in our story, and virtually nothing is known about her.* But Miyagi and the girl moved as lodgers to the house of a Mr. Kitabayashi, and this is a name that should be remembered. For Mrs. Kitabayashi—a motherly woman then in her forties—becomes, as we shall see, the focus of attention several years later. After the move to the Kitabayashi home Miyagi started to achieve some success as a painter. At all events it seems that from the sale of his pictures he was able to make enough money to pay his way.

Meanwhile, in the back room of the 'Owl' harmony had been destroyed. The 'Dawn Society', in Miyagi's words, 'was veering towards the left', a process that was accelerated when the members, now some thirty in all, were treated to lectures on Marxist theory by

* There is evidence that Yamaki Chiyo later married an Okinawan, Nakandakare Nobuyoshi.

two Europeans who had joined the society—'Fister' (a Swiss) and 'Herbert Harris' (a Russian college professor). This trend was not to the liking of Miyagi and the other anarchist members. Consequently there was a series of rows culminating in a split, which, as Miyagi put it, 'spelled the death of the society'. There was in fact a take-over bid by the Communists, who now formed a majority in the society. When this failed, the Communist members broke away from the 'Owl' and formed their own small but active group in another part of Los Angeles.

Miyagi himself did not become a Communist until about two years later, in 1929; his conversion, according to his own account, being due not so much to the books he read, or to the influence of friends, as to his resentment of 'the inhuman discrimination practised against the Asiatic races' in the United States. Even at this stage he did not join the Communist party itself, but with Yamaki Chiyo and Mrs. Kitabayashi he became a member of an affiliated organization, the Proletarian Arts Society, founded in the summer of 1929. He ran its tiny magazine and gave some lectures to fellow members on the history of fine arts. During this period, as at earlier times in his life, he was often unwell.

It was thanks to the persuasion of a Comintern agent, Yano Tsutomu, that Miyagi eventually joined the party. Yano, who had worked in the New York area before coming to California, was in Moscow in 1930. He returned to America and shortly afterwards was in touch with Miyagi. This was towards the end of 1930. They were in contact during the succeeding months, and in the autumn of 1931 Yano prevailed upon Miyagi to join the party.

Miyagi says that he objected at first, on the grounds that his earlier record provided sufficient reason for him to refuse. It is not clear what this statement implies. Is he referring to his ill-health or to lingering reservations he still had about Marxism-Leninism? Yano at all events overcame Miyagi's resistance, telling him that membership of the party 'would facilitate' his activities.

I then agreed to join and I assumed the party alias of 'Joe'. Since I was not in good health I was excused from party meetings and a number of other activities. My chief tasks were to study the distribution of Japanese farm workers and analyse Chinese problems.

He was relieved of the formality of putting in a written application to join the United States Communist Party; but his alias, 'Joe', was registered by Yano with the Comintern in Moscow, for Yano 'maintained direct connections with the Comintern as the party organizer in the United States'.

A little more than a year later Yano introduced Miyagi to a white American, or European, who was evidently a person of some standing in or with the Comintern. The stranger asked Miyagi to go to Japan. 'It will be for about a month,' he told Miyagi, 'because you are a man of this side'—meaning that Miyagi belonged to the American, not the Japanese, party. Further instructions would be given by a man in Los Angeles, known to Miyagi, called 'Roy'.

It seems that Miyagi accepted this suggestion or order and he saw Roy; but he took no further action. He 'continued,' as he put it, 'to help strikers and to look for suitable subjects to paint', although Roy repeatedly urged him to set off on his journey.

Then, one day in September 1933, Roy and Yano together called on Miyagi and told him he really must leave without further delay. He was to go to Tokyo, where a task awaited him, but he would not have to spend more than about a month in Japan.

When at last, in October, Miyagi was ready to embark, Roy instructed him to return after three months at the latest. So Miyagi travelled light, leaving most of his personal effects in Los Angeles. Roy gave him $200 for expenses and a one-dollar note. Watch for an advertisement for *ukiyoe* in *The Japan Advertiser*, he told Miyagi. Roy went on to explain how the identification with the Tokyo contact would be made, through the comparison of the dollar notes bearing consecutive numbers.

The gaps in this story are tantalizing. Who was the *apparatchnik*, American or European, who called on Miyagi with Yano in the autumn of 1932? Who was Roy? Who indeed was Yano? Why was Miyagi chosen as Sorge's native collaborator in Japan?

If the first question cannot be answered, the second is almost as baffling. But Miyagi had a cousin in Los Angeles called Miyagi Yosaburo, who was a party member and used the name 'Roy' in his business. In the direct interrogation record Yosaburo makes no appearance. But in a note on 'the Communist Party', written by Miyagi at the instigation of the procurator, Yosaburo is among those listed as having been arrested by 'the repressive hand of the American authorities' during a Communist meeting at Long Beach, California.

These arrests took place in January 1932. Those charged were not United States citizens, but Japanese subjects. It was illegal for an alien to advocate the overthrow of American institutions. Other sources, furthermore, do not confirm the atatement that Miyagi Yosaburo was among those arrested and charged.

Miyagi in his testimony referred to Roy as 'an American Communist'. If Yosaburo were a *Nisei*—a second-generation Japanese-American with American citizenship—and assuming that he and Roy were identical, then Miyagi's description of Roy as 'an American Communist' is formally correct. But if Yosaburo had American citizenship he could scarcely have been indicted with the others at Long Beach, for it was not illegal for an American citizen to be a member of the American Communist Party. On the other hand, Yosaburo could have been arrested and then released, without being charged. This could explain the inclusion of his name in Miyagi's list.

All this amounts to surmise so far as the identification of Roy is concerned. But there is one further small clue. Miyagi informed his interrogators that after he had left America he learned from Mrs. Kitabayashi that Roy had often called at the Kitabayashi home in Los Angeles and asked for any news of Miyagi Yutoku in Japan. This behaviour rather suggests that Roy was a Japanese; and one could argue that such personal concern reflects the attitude of a relative or friend rather than that of a business or political associate. There is, then, the possibility that Roy was Miyagi's cousin, Yosaburo; and Miyagi may have been successfully disingenuous when he told the procurator that Roy was a party member in Los Angeles whom he had known personally for some time.

As for Yano, all we know is that he came from New York and had worked for the American Communist Party from the early 1920s, possibly at one time with the mysterious Kito Ginichi, the agent who helped to introduce Ozaki to Sorge's Shanghai group.[*] He had at least one alias (Takeda); and he seems to have been a figure of importance in party circles at the national level. According to Miyagi, 'Yano came to San Francisco from New York party headquarters to act as organizer'. This, so Miyagi says, was late in 1929 and followed the arrest of four leading Japanese Communists in San Francisco and Los Angeles. Yano evidently visited California on several occasions before 1929, for he happens to be among those listed by Miyagi as belonging to the 'Owl' discussion group, as one who joined 'Fister' and 'Harris' in lecturing to the members.

* See p. 74.

It is tempting to believe that while in Moscow in 1930 Yano was encouraged to recruit suitable Japanese in the United States for clandestine work. Certainly his standing with the party in California would not have suffered as a result of his stay in the Soviet Union. We may guess with some assurance that it was Yano who chose Miyagi as a reliable activist for future work in Japan; and Miyagi's admission to the American Communist Party in 1931 can probably be interpreted more correctly as his enlistment, under pressure from Yano, in a Moscow-directed apparat. For, as we have seen, Miyagi was not asked to make written application to join the party. Yano attended to the whole matter, registering Miyagi—as 'Joe'—with Comintern head-quarters.

Yano had plenty of time to assess Miyagi's character and habits before the autumn of 1931. After all, he must have known Miyagi back in the days of the 'Owl'. It looks therefore as though Yano—or those who instructed him—were keeping Miyagi as a 'sleeper', or passive agent, for some unspecified future assignment—at least until the latter half of 1932, when it was first put to Miyagi that he ought to go to Japan. If Miyagi 'was excused from party meetings and a number of other activities', this is explicable not only in terms of some consideration for his weak health but also as a means of ensuring that he did not attract the attention of the Japanese consular authorities. The latter had been known to harass Japanese radicals on the Pacific Coast.* Miyagi's utility as an agent in Japan would have been com-promised from the start had he been on a blacklist in the Los Angeles Consulate. For when he left for Japan this information would assuredly have been passed on to the authorities in Tokyo.

At all events Miyagi was a sound choice. The narrative will show that he carried out his duties in Japan with loyalty, persistence and imagination. His seemingly lackadaisical response to the first prompt-ings to return to the Far East might imply he was happy enough to stay on in California among his friends in the Japanese community there. But Berzin was beginning to move his pieces across the board. Vukelic was already in position, in Tokyo, early in 1933. Sorge was there in September, with 'Bernhardt', the radio operator, due to follow soon after. It is understandable that precisely at this time Yano

---

* Accusations of this nature against Japanese consular officials were made not in-frequently during World War I and later. For an account of the difficulties, arising from alleged consular activities, faced in America by Katayama, see Hyman Kublin: *Asian Revolutionary* (Princeton, 1964), Ch. XII.

and Roy should have put strong pressure on Miyagi to leave for Japan as soon as possible. In this matter, of course, they were simply passing on instructions received—through what channel we cannot say—from Moscow.

After his arrival in Japan Miyagi, unlike Vukelic, was neither without companions nor pressed for money. He lodged at a friend's house and had little difficulty, it seems, in selling his paintings. Indeed, for the next five or six years—until the summer of 1939— he was to earn an adequate income from the sale of his pictures.

Miyagi met Sorge, as we have noted, towards the close of 1933, in the Ueno Art Gallery. In the New Year, after one or two further meetings, Sorge (known to Miyagi as 'Smith' or 'Schmidt') asked him not to return to America. He ought to stay in Japan, where he would be of most use to the cause they both cherished—namely the prevention of war between Japan and the Soviet Union. Not without some hesitation, Miyagi agreed.

Sorge was still feeling his way at this stage. He did not demand a great deal of information from Miyagi; and what he obtained from him, in these early days, was the verbal repetition of news and comments that had already appeared in the Japanese press and magazines. This kind of material was valuable to Sorge, the journalist; but it was not of much immediate use to Sorge, the spy.

In terms of the requirements agreed upon in Moscow, the operating ring was now complete. Sorge (as Berzin had promised) had his wireless technician and his two collaborators, one of them being a Japanese. But from Sorge's point of view Miyagi had his shortcomings; he had been in America since the age of sixteen, so the world of Tokyo was unknown to him. He had, of course, no contacts within the government or among the senior ranks of the armed services. Experience and maturity—Miyagi was thirty when Sorge met him— were still lacking. Miyagi could read and speak Japanese. This, for the time being, was his only qualification as an associate, apart from his native sensibility, intelligence, and goodwill.

It is impossible to say at what moment Sorge decided to resume contact with Ozaki Hotsumi. The intention may have been in his mind from the day his mission was defined by Berzin. For he knew of course that his Shanghai collaborator was with the *Asahi* in Osaka. Sorge understood Japanese habits well enough to know that, in the circumstances, it was best to approach Ozaki through a third party, preferably a Japanese. This would have to be Miyagi. There was really no other choice.

In the spring of 1934, five months after their association began, Sorge sent Miyagi off as an emissary to the Osaka *Asahi*, to see Ozaki Hotsumi. The outcome of this journey was to determine to a great extent the course of Sorge's mission in Japan.

Chapter 8

EARLY DAYS IN TOKYO

'I think I am managing to lead them all by the nose' MESSAGE
FROM SORGE TO MOSCOW, JANUARY 7, 1934

AT the reception desk of the Osaka *Asahi* Miyagi handed in a visiting
card, bearing the name of 'Minami Ryuichi', and asked to see Ozaki.
He told him that he had come on behalf of a foreigner who had been
very friendly with Ozaki in Shanghai. This person was now in Japan
and was eager to renew the friendship.

Ozaki was immediately suspicious. This stranger, 'Minami', could
be a police spy who had learned something to his discredit in Shanghai. Ozaki was very much on his guard. All the same, during what
must have been an uncomfortably stiff conversation, he sensed that
the foreigner who wanted to see him might well prove to be 'Johnson',
the European agent whom he and Agnes Smedley had known in
China.

A newspaper office was clearly no place for a further talk on this
subject; so it was agreed that they should meet again that evening, in a
Chinese restaurant. Here Ozaki's initial fears were dispelled, and his
guess as to the foreigner's identity was confirmed. 'I learned,' he
recalled later, 'that "Minami" was Miyagi Yotoku, a member of the
American Communist Party who had been sent to Japan on the orders
of the Comintern, and that one of his tasks was to bring "Johnson"
and myself together again.'

A few days later Ozaki met Sorge ('Johnson') at an agreed rendezvous in the deer park at Nara. The precise course of their conversation
is not known to us. But at some stage Sorge asked Ozaki to work with
him again. 'Will you help me again?' asked Sorge. 'This time it's
Japan, not China.' He would like to be kept informed of Ozaki's views
on the political, economic, and military situation in Japan. Ozaki did
not disappoint his friend. Years later a judicial document presented
the matter in these terms:

He [Ozaki] met Sorge, who urged him to renew his intelligence activities.
The accused readily agreed to join the ring, although he was fully aware

of the fact that Sorge, together with Miyagi Yotoku and others, had organized an intelligence ring in Japan, with headquarters in Tokyo, to seek and collect various items of information on our military, diplomatic, financial, political, economic, and other affairs, as well as military secrets and secrets relating to our military resources—such information to be transmitted and divulged to the Moscow authorities.

'*The accused readily agreed.*' This suggests that Ozaki responded to Sorge's proposition with little reluctance or hesitation. Indeed, the Japanese term used in the judicial records—*kaidaku*, 'ready consent or acceptance'—has the nuance of 'prompt agreement' or, even, 'hearty consent'. Most Japanese who have looked into the Sorge Case, and in particular those who knew Ozaki, have found it impossible to believe that Ozaki 'readily agreed'.

It may be acknowledged that Ozaki's decision to help Sorge in Japan was logical. But it seems inconceivable that he made it without misgivings. He crossed his Rubicon that day in Nara. That this called for a particular kind of courage is self-evident to anyone who has had first-hand knowledge of Japan in the nineteen-thirties. Most left-wing Japanese intellectuals in Ozaki's position would not have announced any decision then and there. Even a promise to exchange information, as between one journalist and another, would scarcely have been—in those difficult times—a case of *kaidaku*, of 'prompt and ready consent'.

The fact remains that he did accede to Sorge's request. When the Special Higher Police (*Tokko*) came to the end of their interrogations of Ozaki, some five months after his arrest, they stated in their report that he believed 'the mission of divulging inside information on Japan was vitally important and should be regarded as an honourable assignment'. This we can accept. It is also clear that Ozaki's decision is some testimony to the force of Sorge's personality. Between the two men there was great esteem. Collaboration in Shanghai had bred real friendship. Was Ozaki, subjectively at least, under an obligation to 'Johnson' (as Sorge, until 1936, was known to him)? Could it be that he hardly knew how to refuse a claim on this obligation?

The range and quality of the intelligence provided by Ozaki during the next seven years will be apparent in the course of this story. But Sorge had access to another source of equal or greater importance— namely the German Embassy.

Sorge's association with Colonel Eugen Ott was fateful for both men. To Sorge it was to prove his most valuable link with the German colony in Tokyo, and, as their personal relationship developed, his acceptance by Ott and the officials of the Embassy became a cardinal element in his network of sources of information.

Colonel Ott, who had served as an artillery officer in the First World War, had held an important post in the Political Administration Section of the Ministry of Defence during the days of the Weimar Republic. He had been a member of the personal staff of General Kurt Schleicher and was by his side during the latter's ephemeral and last-minute tenure of power, backed by army support, in December 1932 as the last Chancellor of Germany before the advent of Hitler. In June 1934, Schleicher was shot during the Röhm purges, as an act of personal revenge by the Nazi leadership. His protégé, Ott, had been posted in the previous year away from the perilous climate of the new German régime, and was sent as a military observer to Japan.

He was stationed in Nagoya, as special liaison officer with the 3rd Artillery Regiment. In May 1934, when Sorge met Ozaki at Nara, Ott was military attaché, having been appointed to this post in February, though still remaining at Nagoya. It will be recalled that in Berlin Dr. Zeller, of the *Tägliche Rundschau*, had given Sorge a letter of introduction to Ott. This letter, as we have noted in a previous chapter, described Sorge as '*completely trustworthy, both politically and personally*'.

Life for a foreigner in a provincial Japanese city could be very lonely. However interested he might be in his surroundings, however fluent his command of Japanese, there would be moments when the European longed for the presence of a congenial compatriot. Indeed the more diligently he studied Japanese life and the Japanese language, the more sharply he must feel the need for an occasional return to his own environment, for the mental refreshment that only his fellow countrymen could provide. In this respect Colonel Ott was fortunate, for he had his family with him. Nevertheless the foreign community in Nagoya was small, and scattered all over the huge city (then the fourth largest in Japan). The cosmopolitan centres of Tokyo–Yokohama, in the east, and Kobe, in the west, were several hours away by train.

Sorge's arrival must have been welcome. He was an educated man and an ex-soldier; and like Ott he had served at the front. This formed an immediate bond between them. As Sorge himself put it, 'one reason for the friendship can be traced to my career as a German soldier who fought and was wounded in the First European War. Ott took part in that war as a young officer'. Ott and Sorge belonged to the same generation, Ott at this time being in his early forties and Sorge just turned thirty-nine. Another link between them was the fact that they had both served in the same Division. But it is notable that as a rule Sorge was able to establish particularly good relations with German officers, both in China and Japan. The war, after all, was one stretch of his adult experience that he could discuss openly without risk to himself and his secret mission.

It is generally agreed by those who knew him that Sorge could be good company—provocative, amusing, generous, coarse and refined by turns. He could make scathing remarks about dedicated Nazis; and this would do him little harm in the eyes of Ott.

As Sorge was to tell his interrogators, 'Ott thought me to be a man of rare progressive views, neither Nazi nor Communist, a somewhat eccentric person with no partisan commitments.'

The suggestion has been made that while Ott was in Nagoya Sorge was able to supply him with useful information on Japanese military matters, or at least with some new insight into Japanese affairs. Added value would thus have been given to Ott's reports to the military attaché in Tokyo, or through his office, and Ott's professional standing enhanced. This may have been so. But between Sorge's arrival in Japan and Ott's transfer, on promotion, to Tokyo in the early spring of 1934 there cannot have been many meetings between the two. Furthermore, it is doubtful whether Sorge had access to much information of value during his first six months in Japan.

Sorge became a really close friend of the Otts after they had moved to Tokyo, to a house in Shibuya. Frau Ott was a kind-hearted as well as an artistic and perceptive woman. She and her husband provided Sorge with a fireside. He returned the affection they felt for him. It has been remarked that only for Frau Ott would Sorge 'behave'. He had the bohemian's impatience with bourgeois good manners and much disliked the accepted social conventions of the foreign community. Hostesses in Tokyo soon gave up inviting him to their luncheons and dinners. He abhorred formal clothes, and he could not be relied on to fulfil social obligations. The wife of one German resident, for example, remembers inviting Sorge to dinner, but he never turned up, and his excuses afterwards were unconvincing. His hosts were offended and he was not invited again. But in the company of the Otts Sorge did not show his boorish side—or, if he did, Frau Ott scolded him in a maternal way and he would be contrite. Only for Frau Ott, it was remarked, would Sorge consent to wear a dinner jacket in the evening.

It may be correct to interpret Sorge's cultivation of the Otts solely in terms of his secret aims. But at a time when, on this specific point, he had no motive for lying—during his interrogation by Procurator Yoshikawa—Sorge went out of his way to say: 'Ott was a fine man.' Granted that Sorge's entire career was an exercise in sustained duplicity, this remark implies that he had at least some human and strictly 'unprofessional' regard for the friend whose trust he so infamously abused.

At the end of 1933 the new German Ambassador, Dr. Herbert von Dirksen, arrived in Tokyo. He had previously been Ambassador to the Soviet Union. In Sorge's view Dirksen's prime mission was 'to steer German–Japanese relations along a course hostile to the U.S.S.R.' The fact that in 1933 both Japan and Germany had left the League of Nations created a bond between the two countries. This could be greatly strengthened by shared hostility towards the Soviet Union.

Sorge was already on good terms with the Embassy staff. An article on Japan for the *Tägliche Rundschau*, written late in 1933, attracted favourable notice in Germany and enhanced Sorge's standing with Embassy officials.

Sorge's foothold in the Embassy was further consolidated after the arrival in 1934 of a new naval attaché, Captain Paul Wenneker.

> He was a man of noble, martial, character. But he was quite out of his depth in political matters when he arrived; and I was able to be of some help to him here. Like me, Wenneker was a bachelor; and we travelled together to places like Atami and became boon companions.

The genial and indeed convivial association with 'Paulchen' (as Sorge called his friend) was to endure throughout Wenneker's first spell of duty in Japan, from 1934 to 1937, and would be renewed when Wenneker returned to Tokyo in 1940, with the rank of rear-admiral, following his command of the pocket battleship *Deutschland*. This friendship, of much relevance to Sorge's clandestine work, is another illustration of the attraction Sorge's personality had for many, if not most, German officers.

Prince Albrecht von Urach, too, was numbered among the friends whom Sorge made during his first year in Japan. Urach, who arrived in Tokyo in 1934 as correspondent for the *Volkischer Beobachter*, had read some of Sorge's articles before leaving Germany and was interested in meeting him. Sorge, he discovered, was a typical Berliner, shrewd, uproarious, fond of drink and women. The two men, indeed, had at first sight little in common. Urach, a member of the Wurttemberg nobility, was more elegant and less boisterous than Sorge. But he was easy-going and good-natured, and he was younger than Sorge and less experienced as a journalist. Sorge's personality diverted him. Here was a man of refreshingly eccentric views; yet he was obviously sound at heart, since he was well liked by Ott who had served in a division commanded by Urach's father, a distinguished general in the 1914-18 war. Moreover, Sorge had spent much of his front-line service in an infantry regiment (the Berlin 'Mayflies') in which Urach's father had begun his own professional military career. At all events Urach and Sorge took to each other immediately. Although the former represented the main Nazi party newspaper, Sorge made no attempt in his presence to disguise a number of unorthodox views— for example, an open admiration for the Red Army. But then Sorge often seemed outspoken to his German friends; and to none of them, including Urach, did he ever betray by the slightest hint, or slip of the tongue, that he had first-hand knowledge of the Soviet Union.

By the late spring of 1934, when he had his first meeting in Japan with Ozaki, Sorge's reputation in the German community was becoming well defined. He was recognized as an energetic journalist with an uncommon gift for understanding Far Eastern affairs, as an expert for whom evidently both the ambassador and the military attaché had a certain regard. If some were shocked by stories of wild behaviour, most men at least were tolerant. Sorge, after all, had no wife and family; and as for his drinking bouts, these were not alien to the tradition of the foreign correspondent. A French journalist who met him during this period describes Sorge's manner as 'a strange combination of charm and brutality'.* Sorge, in an odd way, was becoming an object of both disapproval and respect.

---

* Letter from M. Paul Mousset. However, Reuter's correspondent in Japan at the time, who knew Sorge during the latter's first weeks in Tokyo, reports that Sorge gave the impression of being 'quiet, unassuming, intelligent'.

Like other correspondents he attended the press conferences held three times a week at the Foreign Ministry. He maintained regular contact with the Rengo (later Domei) News Agency and with the press bureaux of the War and Navy Ministries. He joined the Keihin (Tokyo–Yokohama) German club, making full use of the library as well as the bar, and in due course he became a member of the Tokyo Club, which contained one of the best collections in the world of books in Western languages dealing with Japan. He travelled outside the capital a great deal, taking a particular interest in the farming countryside, at that time economically backward, with many areas still prostrate from the aftermath of crop failures and the collapse of the American silk market. He dined at Lohmeyer's, the excellent German restaurant run by a Tsingtao veteran in a basement, a block away from the Ginza. He was constantly in and out of the Imperial Hotel, gossiping in the lobby or throwing dice in the downstairs bar. He was, of course, a frequent caller at the Embassy, with news and comments to exchange in the chancery and in the officers of the service attachés. If at first his association with Dirksen was spasmodic, it was to become closer as the months went by.

Then as now Tokyo was, if anything, over-stocked with 'Western' cafés, restaurants, and bars—these being additional to purely Japanese-style centres of refreshment and fun. There were French, Italian, Spanish, Russian, Scandinavian, and Latin American café-bars. There was at least one café equipped and decorated in the manner of a resolutely antiquarian English inn, with oak presses, pewter mugs and warming-pans on the walls. In such establishments the waitresses would sit beside the customers after bringing them their drinks, playing a kind of ersatz Geisha rôle, flattering the guest with compliments, rallying to his jokes, and making sure his glass was well filled. (At the 'Blackbird' the girls dyed their hair a strident orange, but in the late thirties this was stopped, on patriotic grounds, by the police.)

It was only fitting that German-style cafés and beer-halls should play their part in this charade. Two of these—the *Fledermaus* and *Rheingold*—were much favoured by Sorge. Both were owned by German nationals and staffed by Japanese waitresses. Both were in the Ginza district of the city. The *Fledermaus* was a rather small, dimly lit, café, with no more than four tables and two or three waitresses. Friedrich Sieburg, the writer, who saw a good deal of Sorge during a visit to Japan, has given us an unflattering description of the *Fledermaus*.

It was a gloomy hole with dirty, threadbare, seating, covered with imitation tapestry. There was nothing Japanese about the place, except for one or two low-class serving-girls, who used to come and sit next to the customers, put their arms round their necks and giggle affectedly. Japanese scarcely ever went to the place. It was a riddle to me how a man of taste like Sorge could frequent such a filthy hole.

Prince Urach, too, recalls the *Fledermaus* as a 'smoky, unattractive bar' where Sorge often got drunk. 'He experienced all the various phases of intoxication: high spirits, tearful misery, aggressiveness, persecution mania, megalomania, delirium, semi-consciousness, and the dreary solitude of a hangover that can only be cleared away by more alcohol.'

The *Rheingold* was quite different, much larger and altogether more cheerful. It was a restaurant as well as a bar, owned and managed by a well-known caterer, Herr Ketel. The waitresses tended to be girls with pretensions to intelligence and culture. Conditions of work and pay were very good. Customers included cosmopolitan Japanese of some standing in the business and political world, as well as members of the German community and other Europeans. In the *Rheingold* Sorge, as we shall see, was to find a faithful inamorata.

Carousing in the bar of the Imperial, at the *Rheingold* and *Fledermaus*, or in the seaside 'hotels' of Hommoku, Yokohama, Sorge and his bachelor friends became known by the censorious as 'the Balkan club'.

Vukelic and 'Bernhardt', the radio operator of the ring, were not of this company. At this time Vukelic's main value to Sorge was that of a photo-technician. It was his function to make photographic copies of reports passed to him by Sorge. The results, usually in the form of microfilms, were then sent to Moscow through infrequent meetings with couriers in Shanghai. Vukelic possibly had more of this photographic work to do in the early days than later. Radio contact with the Fourth Bureau proved to be largely a failure, due in great measure, as Sorge discovered, to 'Bernhardt's' timidity.

After establishing his cover as a businessman, an exporter in Yokohama, 'Bernhardt' had set up, eventually, two transmitting sets, one in his Yokohama home, the other in the Tokyo house occupied by Branko and Edith Vukelic. In operating these sets 'Bernhardt' claimed to be hampered by many technical difficulties. These existed, no doubt. But it is evident that he was beset by fears of sudden exposure and arrest. It is relevant to quote what he is reported to have said, after he returned safely to the Soviet Union in 1935:

I operated as a foreign trader in Yokohama, sending a steady stream of samples of Japanese products to foreign firms, and thus covering my activities. Sorge, seeking recognition by Moscow headquarters, ordered me to send numerous messages, but I did not send many of them because, as a wireless technician, I felt that frequent sending and receiving of messages would be tantamount to inviting discovery by the police.

At about the same time Sorge had this to say about 'Bernhardt':

Bernhardt's radio technique was satisfactory, but he was forever drinking and in many cases he neglected to send out information. A man who engages in espionage work must show some courage; he was extremely timid and did not send half the messages I gave him.

Some time in 1934 Sorge decided that 'Bernhardt' would have to go, and by the beginning of 1935 arrangements had been made for him and his wife to return to Moscow within the year.

Having regard to the exploratory and tentative character of his initial mission, what information of value was Sorge able to collect in 1934 and the first half of 1935 for transmission to the Fourth Bureau? The answer is, not a great deal perhaps, but enough surely to impress the Fourth Bureau, and certainly enough to fortify Sorge in the belief that espionage in Japan was indeed a practical proposition.

In the spring of 1934 the fundamental question that Sorge had been sent to investigate—namely, Japanese intentions towards Russia—assumed particular importance. For during the winter Japanese–Soviet relations had been markedly tense. No progress had been made in the talks between the two countries on the future of the Russian-controlled Chinese Eastern Railway, which bisected the northern part of Manchukuo. It was clear that the Japanese would either buy the line or seize it. If negotiations for purchase dragged on inconclusively there was always the possibility that the Japanese Kwantung Army, the real rulers of Manchukuo, would simply take over the railway, with or without approval from Tokyo.

Most of the foreign military attachés in Tokyo believed that a Japanese-Soviet conflict was probable in 1935. The American Ambassador, Joseph Grew, had a long conversation with his Russian colleague, Yurenev, on March 9, 1934. He alluded to the common opinion among the attachés that the spring of 1935 might see a Japanese attack on the Soviet Far East. But, Grew noted in his diary,

'the Ambassador replied that while nobody could foresee a precise
date, he thought it more likely that such an attack would occur this
spring. . . .'

The early spring of 1934 could have been a time of peculiar un-
easiness for Sorge, only mitigated perhaps by the fact that the Otts
had moved to Tokyo. Ozaki's help was to be enlisted in May. But he
was, after all, in Osaka, not in the capital; and at this time he had
no close contact with the inner circles of the Japanese Government,
least of all with the High Command.

Miyagi was pressed to find out what he could about military plans;
and during the first half of 1934—the date is not known—he produced
for Sorge a report on the army's policy towards the Soviet Union.
Miyagi's report stated that an attack on Russia appeared to be imminent, judging from views expressed by people in the army and from
the character of army personnel postings. He also pointed out that the
Kwantung Army had been reinforced, that certain officers in contact
with the press were agitating for an attack, and that the *Sakurakai*
('The Cherry Society'—an association of nearly a hundred politically
active captains, majors, and lt.-colonels) was becoming more
influential and 'might bring forward the timing of an attack on the
Soviet Union'.

In this report, based on the gossip of acquaintances and a careful
study of newspapers and magazines, the reference to the *Sakurakai*
must have been of considerable interest to Sorge. This was precisely
the kind of information that he could pass on confidentially, and much
to his advantage, to the German Embassy. For although by this time
the *Sakurakai* was not really a secret society, it was nevertheless just
the sort of semi-clandestine association that Japanese officers did not
advertise to civilians, let alone foreigners; and it is most improbable
that any European Embassy had ever heard of it.

However, the war scare died down by the middle of May. During
the summer—probably in July—Miyagi was told by Sorge that 'the
Comintern' wanted information on the Japanese Army based on
military publications. Thereupon Miyagi became a regular subscriber,
through a bookshop in Kanda (Tokyo's Charing Cross Road), to the
monthly magazine, *Gunji to Gijutsu* (*Military Affairs and Technology*).
Beginning with the issue of August 1934 he copied extracts from a
number of articles with such titles as 'New Soviet Weapons', 'An
Analysis of the Red Army', and 'New Weapons of the French, German, and British Armies'.

This could scarcely be classified as intelligence material of the highest grade; and it is not surprising that after a few months Sorge told Miyagi that no further contributions from this source were required. Equally it is no matter for surprise that when Sorge was in Moscow in 1935 he was told that the transmission of extracts from *Military Affairs and Technology* should be resumed.* So Miyagi went back to work on this particular task; though he abandoned it, presumably on Sorge's instructions, in the spring of 1936.

The calibre of Miyagi's information, however, was greatly to improve as he developed his sources. These included a handful of people who might be described as sub-agents of the Sorge ring. It was indeed Miyagi's hope, as he told Sorge in 1934, to build up a national network, with reliable informants in most parts of the country. This he was never able to achieve, 'because there was a dearth of suitable persons'. Nevertheless, in time he could rely, like Ozaki, for information from a circle of unwitting as well as conscious collaborators. But he already had an assistant working for him. This was an acquaintance from the Californian period, Akiyama Koji, who had returned to Japan a few months before Miyagi.

Mrs. Kitabayashi, Miyagi's hospitable landlady in Los Angeles, had introduced him to Akiyama at her home, back in 1931. Akiyama was then employed by a Japanese language newspaper, the Los Angeles *Nichi-Bei Shimbun*. It seems that he was helpful in giving support and publicity to an exhibition of Miyagi's paintings. He was already in his early middle age when he met Miyagi; for he was born in 1889.

Once in Tokyo Akiyama does not appear to have prospered; and Miyagi, soon after coming to Japan himself and mindful no doubt of favours received in California, began helping Akiyama, to the tune of 20 or 30 Yen a week—a modest but by no means despicably small sum in those days. Akiyama may then have asked Miyagi if he could be of service to him in some way. Or it may be that the proposal came from Miyagi. At any rate Akiyama was soon doing written translation work, for Miyagi, from Japanese into English, and he was being paid by the hour for it.

It was Miyagi's practice, when it came to intelligence of a factual nature, to give Sorge a report written in Japanese. When writing his reports Miyagi was careful to use black ink. The reports were

---

* One is reminded of Whittaker Chambers' remark—'Bykov, in the Russian fashion, preferred the dragnet or volumetric production of documents.' Whittaker Chambers, *Witness* (New York, Random House, 1952), p. 426.

photographed by Vukelic for later dispatch 'to the Comintern', and for photographic purposes black ink showed up much better than blue. But often there were reports of immediate interest to Sorge that would have to be translated fairly quickly into accurate English. The translator on most occasions was Akiyama, who used blue ink, Miyagi not caring to reveal that the papers would be photographed. Akiyama, the graduate of a commercial high school in California, was doubtless more at home in English than Miyagi. When translation was required Akiyama settled down to it, working up to four hours at a stretch, depending upon the length and complexity of what was involved. He translated into English, from Miyagi's handwriting and from numerous Japanese texts, a remarkable flow of military, economic and political intelligence.

This was to continue for the best part of eight years, providing Akiyama with a steady, if basically insecure, subsistence. For much of the time, moreover, he lived with Miyagi. He appears to have been quite uninterested either in Communism or in Miyagi's underground activities. He was aware, of course, that they might be arrested and that they would then be heavily punished for treason and espionage. Yet this curious man—whom Willoughby justly calls 'the only mercenary'—was seemingly indifferent to the need for secrecy. 'He was not the kind of person,' Miyagi admitted, 'who could be a serious collaborator in espionage work.' Akiyama in fact was bound to Miyagi by ties of mild friendship and strong economic convenience. Ideological sympathy played a minimal role in the association. This had obvious drawbacks, and in 1939 Miyagi tried to find another skilled translator, but without success, 'and so we had to let Akiyama carry on'. But it is noteworthy that whenever Sorge expressed anxiety about the association with Akiyama, whom Sorge almost certainly never met, Miyagi declared emphatically that the man could be trusted.

Virtually all the intelligence obtained by Sorge in 1934, and in the first six months of 1935, was sent to Russia by courier. For, as we have seen, wireless transmission, with 'Bernhardt' in charge, was almost non-existent. 'I was able to send only very brief messages,' Sorge confessed, 'and these very seldom.'

To send material by courier meant going to Shanghai. Sorge himself made the trip in May 1934, handing over his package to a stranger whom he took to be a Scandinavian. ('I do not know what he did, or where, nor did I ask.') The next trip probably took place—although no date is given—during high summer, after mid-July (following the Cabinet change in Japan when Admiral Okada succeeded Admiral Saito as Prime Minister). The emissary from Tokyo on this occasion was 'Bernhardt's' wife, who met her contact (a woman) in a room at the Palace Hotel, Shanghai. There was one more courier journey to Shanghai that year—in the autumn, when the nervous 'Bernhardt' carried the material from Japan. The arrangements for this trip formed the subject of one of his infrequent communications by W/T. It was 'Bernhardt's' wife once more who went on the next trip, at the beginning of 1935. She seems to have had some of the temper that her husband lacked.

Sorge's visit to Shanghai in the late spring of 1934 was not his only continental journey that year. He accompanied Ott on a tour of Manchukuo during the autumn. There is no reason to suppose that Sorge met a Moscow courier while he was on this tour, about which indeed we know very little. The risks involved would have been too great to ignore. The fact that Sorge was Ott's companion on this Manchurian trip is itself eloquent of the friendship that had grown up between them.

It was at about this time, but probably before the Manchurian tour, that Sorge's status was enhanced by notification of his formal admission to the Nazi party.

Meanwhile there was a turn of events profoundly relevant to Sorge's prospects as an effective spy. In September 1934, Ozaki was invited by the *Asahi* to join their Tokyo staff. His main immediate concern in Tokyo was to be a research organization known as The Society for the Study of East Asian Problems (*Toa Mondai Chosa-kai*). This body had just been set up under the auspices of the Tokyo *Asahi* and was largely staffed by *Asahi* men. The society's principal interest being Chinese affairs, it was appropriate that Ozaki should be associated with the organization. He was already becoming recognized as a promising China expert, and his translation of Agnes Smedley's *Daughter of Earth* was published at this time. In substantial measure thanks to his connection with this research society—in whose activities representatives of the armed services, government departments, and big business took part—Ozaki, after moving to Tokyo, greatly enlarged the range of his personal contacts.

Once Ozaki was settled in Tokyo he began to meet Sorge at regular monthly intervals. They met in restaurants, or occasionally in *machiai* (high-class geisha club-restaurants). Ozaki gave some of their names to his interrogators, and the list reads like a *Guide Michelin* to Tokyo in the thirties (*Gajoen*, Lohmeyer's, *Meigetsu-so* in Ueno, *Kagetsu* in Tsukiji, *Kimi-shiraku* in Akasaka, and many others). At the first few meetings with Sorge he used an alias ('Odake') in his dealings with restaurant staff or geisha. Then he perceived that this could cause difficulties, attracting the very suspicions he was anxious to avoid. 'So after that I said I was Ozaki of the *Asahi*.'

A main recurrent topic of conversation between Sorge and Ozaki, during the winter of 1934–35, seems to have been the alarming growth of ultra-nationalism. This was indeed closely related to the basic issue of Japan's relations with Soviet Russia. Broadly speaking, the nationalist movement, carrying all before it, consisted of two streams —traditionalist and radical. Although the latter favoured a frontal attack on the bastions of capitalism, both were implacably hostile to Communism and regarded the Soviet Union as the natural enemy of the Japanese state. Since the Army was striving to gain absolute control of Japan's destinies, and was promoting and exploiting fanatical nationalism to this end, it followed that a study both of ultra-nationalist manifestations and of any checks whereby these could be restrained was of lively interest to Sorge.

Earlier, in July, at the one meeting the two of them had been able to arrange between their reunion in Nara Park and Ozaki's move to Tokyo, Ozaki had given Sorge a detailed account of the various right-wing and radical, 'fascist', machinations and 'incidents' that had taken place during the immediately preceding years—notably Premier Inukai's assassination on May 15, 1932. They had met at the Heian Shrine, Kyoto. In the famous garden, walking perhaps by the water-lilies, with the cicadas scissoring in the summer heat, they could converse at length without much fear of being overheard.

All such information—including what was purely historical and therefore not transmitted to Moscow—added to the capital of specialized knowledge that Sorge was busily acquiring at this time. It was of great value to him not only as a foundation for conclusions to be reached as a journalist and as a spy, but also as a means of impressing the German Embassy with the promising quality of his insight into current Japanese affairs.

The quest for further intelligence on the extreme nationalist movement led Ozaki once more to utilize the services—inside Japan this time—of his old Shanghai associate, Kawai Teikichi.* The latter cherished a sincere regard for Ozaki, whom he had come to look upon as a kind of patron. Kawai had spent three weeks in the hands of the Japanese police in Shanghai, in May 1932. In July of that year he returned to Japan, losing no time in seeing Ozaki, to get his advice and, no doubt, to reassure him that the police in Shanghai had not been put on the scent of the 'Johnson' ring. Ozaki advised him to lie low for the time being. But at the end of 1932 he had encouraged him to go back to the continent, to north China, to work there on behalf of the Chinese Communists.

Ozaki himself had followed Kawai to Peking within a matter of two or three days. There they had a reunion with Agnes Smedley, and Kawai's future mission in the area was discussed. He was to keep in touch at regular intervals with a certain Chinese (not identified), informing the latter of the activities of the Japanese Army and the attitude of local Chinese leaders. Ozaki had then returned to Japan from what was ostensibly a year-end holiday.

Kawai, with funds given him by his Chinese contact, ran a bookshop in Tientsin. This was opposite the premises of the Japanese Army's 'Special Service Organ' in Tientsin. The 'Special Service Organs' were political operations and intelligence bureaux heavily involved in all manner of manœuvres, licit and otherwise, designed to further Japanese interests on the continent.

Kawai's personal history included a spell of active work as a young man in two strongly nationalist societies sponsored by the conservative Seiyukai party in the Japanese Diet. After he first went to China as a journalist, early in 1928, he became known as a 'China *ronin*', an emotionally loaded term, meaning—for some—a patriotic Japanese always ready, at any cost, to promote his country's influence among the Chinese. For others the term was derogatory; in their eyes the typical 'China *ronin*' was an obstreperous carpet-bagger. The circumstances of his early life, both in Japan and in China, brought Kawai into close touch with various right-wing adventurers; and he did not allow these associations to lapse after his conversion to Communism; although 'conversion' is probably altogether too strong a word to use in the context of Kawai and his mental processes. For he does not seem to have had very positive ideological convictions, although he was wholehearted in his sympathy with the Chinese Communists. It is likely that he recognized, soon after he first arrived in China, that

* See pp. 76–7 above.

they were the wave of the future. But his services to Ozaki both in China, and later in Japan, were probably motivated by instincts of personal loyalty rather than the promptings of a firmly held set of beliefs. He was no intellectual. Yet his emotional commitment to Ozaki was staunch. It is evident that Sorge and, in time, Miyagi considered Kawai to be little more than a brainless sponger—a verdict that ignores the man's courage. This survived a severe test when he was in police custody in Shanghai, and, before long, it was to face an even more trying ordeal.

Kawai's bookshop in Tientsin was well placed, because his reputation and connections as a former right-wing activist and as a 'China *ronin*' made him *persona grata* with the 'Special Service Organ' across the road. This in turn enabled him to gather much information of value to the Chinese Communists. However, his relationship with his Chinese contacts became increasingly tenuous, until it finally ceased; whereupon he returned to Japan again, to see Ozaki, 'to find out,' as he put it, 'what to do next'. This was in February 1934. Ozaki told him to carry on in north China until 'some sort of liaison' could be established. But just over a year later—in March 1935—Kawai came back to Japan, sought out Ozaki at his Tokyo address, and once again asked for instructions.

This time Ozaki advised him to remain in Tokyo. Accordingly, 'in order to comply with Ozaki's instructions and to solve the immediately pressing problem of securing a livelihood', Kawai went to live with a friend of his called Fujita Isamu, who resided in a Tokyo suburb. Kawai had known Fujita in north China. Indeed Fujita had been connected with the Tientsin 'Special Service Organ'. But in the summer of 1933 he was involved in Tokyo in the bizarre right-wing terrorist plot known as 'The Affair of the God-sent Soldiers' (*Shimpeitai Jiken*)—a proposed *coup d'état*, alluded to earlier, that included in its programme the annihilation of the entire Japanese cabinet, at one blow, by aerial bombardment. Fujita's part in all this was peripheral. The Affair of the God-sent Soldiers, however, underlines the fact that Kawai's friend, Fujita, was a myrmidon of the Extreme Right. This meant that Kawai was strategically placed to feed current information on the ultra-nationalist movement to the Sorge ring.

Nevertheless, he was not brought into direct contact with Sorge, and he was not informed that Sorge was now in Japan. But Ozaki introduced him to Miyagi. One day early in May 1935, Ozaki said to Kawai: 'I expect you are pretty bored, so I want to introduce a good friend to you. He has just come back from France, and as he has no friends he tells me he needs companionship. Do come and meet him.'

Ozaki arranged a dinner for the three of them at a Ueno restaurant, and at this first meeting Miyagi and Kawai took to each other at once. Ozaki left for home just before midnight. But the other two stayed on. Kawai got dead drunk, and when he awoke next morning he found to his confusion that he had been brought across town in a taxi to a *machiai* patronized by Miyagi. This was the beginning of an association between Miyagi and Kawai that lasted for the next eight months. For the purposes of the Sorge ring, he became Miyagi's sub-agent.

Under examination by the procurator, seven years later, Miyagi maintained that Kawai supplied little information of value. It is certainly true that as a source of intelligence Kawai was much more useful in China than in Japan. In his own country he appeared to lose his bearings. He was always short of money and he seemed unable to secure regular employment at this period. But his close contact with adventurers like Fujita was not entirely unproductive. For in June 1935 he and Miyagi were able to prepare an elaborate, if roughly drawn, diagrammatic chart showing the leadership, alliances, and enmities of the rival factions in the Japanese Army.

This remarkable chart was given to Sorge by Miyagi and it was found by the police among Sorge's effects, following his arrest. It was an accurate guide to the intricate power structure of the Army. So equipped, Sorge, among foreigners in Japan, was to be uniquely qualified to interpret the insurrection that broke out in the heart of Tokyo in February 1936.

Soon after Miyagi had given him the chart Sorge departed for Moscow, to report to the Fourth Bureau on his mission and its prospects. 'I told Moscow that I wanted to be recalled for consultations, and in order to be given a better wireless operator than Bernhardt. In May 1935 I had instructions from Moscow to return without delay.' He packed off 'Bernhardt' first. The 'Bernhardts' travelled to Moscow via Shanghai and Siberia. Then, at the end of June, Sorge sailed for America—concealing the fact, needless to say, that he was proposing to go on from America to the Soviet Union. He took with him a substantial backlog of documentary intelligence, including, we may be sure, a copy of Miyagi's chart. All this material was in the form of photographic copies, presumably on microfilm.

We have a single vignette of Sorge in America at this time, sketched by a woman who had known him in Berlin in the twenties:

Ika (Sorge), whom we had originally known as a calm, scholarly man, had changed visibly in the few years he had been working for the Soviet Union. When I saw him for the last time in New York in 1935 he had become a violent man, a strong drinker. Little was left of the charm of the romantic, idealist student, although he was still extraordinarily good-looking. But his cold blue, slightly slanting eyes, with their heavy eyebrows, had retained their capacity for self-mockery, even when this was groundless. His hair was still brown and unthinned, but his cheekbones and sad mouth were sunken, and his nose was pointed. He had changed completely.

In New York he was given a forged passport by 'a Communist party contact man'. ('I did not want my real passport to show that I had been in Soviet Russia.') It was an old passport refurbished to fit its new owner, bearing Sorge's photograph and personal description. His nationality was stated to be Austrian, and he was given 'a long and outlandish' name.

From America Sorge sailed for France, although his departure was nearly postponed at the last moment. He forgot to pay his exit tax, and this was discovered by a customs officer on board, just before the vessel left the dock at New York. 'It looked as though he were going to take me off the ship, but I slipped him fifty dollars and the matter was dropped at once. Things are very flexible in the United States.'

Having arrived in France, he travelled to Russia by way of Austria, Czechoslovakia and Poland. At the Soviet Consulate in Paris he had obtained his entry visa by going through the regular procedure 'just like any other traveller'. ('I was not given any special privileges.')

And so, after a long, circuitous, journey by train he reached his destination:

> 'To dreamer and to midnight wanderer
> Moscow is dearer than the whole wide world:
> There he's at home, and at the primal source
> Of all with which the century shall flower.'*

But Sorge was 'home' for barely three weeks; and it was to be for the last time.

---

* Boris Pasternak (1943).

Chapter 9

INTERLUDE IN MOSCOW

'Ah, native place! What a misfit I've become' FROM *Soviet Russia* BY SERGEI.
ESENIN—A POEM WRITTEN IN 1924

WHEN Sorge returned to Moscow in July 1935 he reported directly
to the new head of the Fourth Bureau, General Semyon Petrovich
Uritsky. Sorge described him as 'not greatly interested in purely
military information'.

General Uritsky was born in 1895—the same year as Sorge. His
career bears a striking similarity to that of Berzin, and indeed the two
men had worked closely together for several years. In August 1919
Uritsky was 'Head of Operations of the Red Army staff intelligence',
and later commander of a cavalry brigade. He made his military
reputation in leading the assault on the mutinous fortress of Kronstadt
in March 1921. His subsequent career was that of a senior Red Army
commander until he replaced Berzin as head of the Fourth Bureau in
1935. This appointment was made by 'the Central Committee of the
Party and the chiefs of the People's Commissariat for Defence'.[*]

Sorge was able to state with confidence to Uritsky that, from his
knowledge and contacts, the organization of espionage in Japan was a
feasible proposition. This must have been heartening news to his
superiors. For, if Whittaker Chambers is to be believed, another
Communist spy ring in Japan at this time, led by an American,
achieved precisely no results at all. The American 'had just one
success to report. He had won the baseball championship of Japan at
the Tokyo Y.M.C.A.'.[†]

Sorge sought and obtained recognition of Ozaki as an authorized

---

[*] These biographical details are taken from an article by Geller in the *Red Star*—
the Soviet Red Army newspaper—of March 2, 1965, commemorating Uritsky's rehabilitation. He had been arrested by the GPU on the night of November 1, 1937, and shot
'soon after'.

[†] Summoned to the Fourth Bureau to explain what had happened, the American contrived to talk himself out of his difficulties, and he was sent back to the United States on
a further intelligence mission. There he met Chambers, to whom he made the revealing
declaration: 'I will not work one more *hour* for those murderers.' Whittaker Chambers,
op. cit., pp. 388 and 411.

member of his ring, and he requested that either Weingarten or Klausen be appointed wireless operator in place of the nervous 'Bernhardt'.

At the same time he asked for 'absolute freedom' to develop any relations he deemed necessary with the German Embassy in Tokyo. What was meant by 'absolute freedom' can be appreciated from the following admission to his Japanese interrogators:

During my visit to Moscow in 1935 I was given permission to supply a certain amount of information to the embassy, in order to strengthen my connection there. It was left to my own judgment as to what information I should pass on and as to when it should be given. But I promised Moscow that I would limit such information to the minimum.

As Sorge put it, the simplest way of conducting espionage inside the German Embassy was 'discussion, consultation, and study; to exchange information of minor importance for information of major importance—in other words, to use a sprat to catch a mackerel'.

The Seventh Congress of the Comintern was in session while Sorge was in Moscow, and he wanted to attend it; but he was strictly forbidden to do so. This made sense, for he might have been recognized by some of the foreign delegates or observers at the Congress, and the fact would have leaked through to Germany and Japan.

During his stay in Moscow Sorge lived in Sadovaya Square, in a room previously occupied by one of his friends. Here, for the short time he was in Moscow, Sorge resumed a relatively secluded domestic life with his Russian 'wife', Katerina. After Sorge returned to Japan brief messages for him from Katerina were occasionally included in communications sent him by wireless from the Fourth Bureau; and he is reported to have sent letters and clothing to her from Japan through normal postal channels.*

Kuusinen and Smoliansky called to see him, but Manuilsky—busy perhaps with the Congress—only made a telephone call, partly to tell Sorge that he must on no account attend any of the Congress sessions. Piatnitsky was ill, and out of town. Social life, then, was, as Sorge put it, 'very restricted'. The only person whom he saw at all frequently was the man who had been for a time his wireless operator in China, the German technician Max Klausen. For Max was ordered by the

---

* Some of these letters have been published in *Komsomolskaya Pravda* on January 13, 1965. Katerina died in Krasnoyarsk, Siberia, on August 4, 1943.

Bureau to get ready to join Sorge's Japan group. There was accordingly plenty for the two of them to discuss.

Klausen had been recalled to Russia in August 1933. Before that he had spent some eighteen months in Mukden. There, under the eyes of the Japanese who were in occupation of the city, he had operated, from an upstairs room of his house, a secret wireless transmitter. This sent somewhat infrequent signals to Soviet territory, containing items of intelligence gathered by a local Fourth Bureau ring working under the general direction of an officer based on Harbin. Max Klausen's cover in Mukden was his business—a shop selling motorcycles, bicycles, and motor car accessories. The capital required to set up this enterprise— $2,000 (U.S.)—had been supplied to him by the Fourth Bureau.

Max, and Anna, whom everyone accepted as his wife, were well known in the European community. Max became secretary of the German Club about six months after his arrival in Mukden. In keeping with his background as a North German seaman, he was a tubby, clubbable figure; the reverse of intellectual; rough, coarse, but seemingly generous; devoted, in his fashion, to his companion Anna. It must have tickled his humour that at about the same time a colleague in the Mukden ring, another German, became treasurer of the Club.

But Max Klausen's activities in Mukden, both legal and otherwise, failed to prosper. In the course of one year he transmitted no more than fifteen messages; and the quality of the information was not of a high order. As for the cycle shop, not a cent of the capital sunk in the business was recovered. Later, Max summed it all up in a pardonable understatement: 'Our venture in Manchuria was, on the whole, a failure.' It is not surprising that in the end he was told fairly brusquely to hand over his duties to someone else and return to Moscow.

Max and Anna came back on the Trans-Siberian railway, with tickets made out for Berlin—partly because Max believed that this would make it easier for them to leave Manchukuo, and partly, no doubt, to pacify Anna, who dreaded the thought of entering Soviet territory. She was staunchly anti-Communist; and it is doubtful whether she was really aware, even at this stage, that Max was working for a Soviet apparat.

It would be going too far to say that Max was in disgrace when he called at the Fourth Bureau on his return to Moscow. But he was certainly under a cloud; and his reputation cannot have been enhanced when he had to report that during the night of their arrival, at the Moskva Hotel, he and Anna had been robbed of every kopek they possessed. Anna herself claimed later that she had been doped and robbed of her passport.

However, the Bureau merely recommended that he and Anna leave at once for Odessa, for a spell of rest and recuperation. In fact it was ten days before they set off for this holiday, since Max rather naturally declined to leave until he could have his luggage with him. For some reason he had been unable to take it from the Trans-Siberian train to the Moskva Hotel. The luggage was eventually collected by the Fourth Bureau and there handed over to the Klausens—which suggests that Berzin and his officers may have wished to conduct an unhurried examination of the couple's personal effects.

During the few days of delay Max was taken to the Bureau's wireless school in the southern outskirts of Moscow, and he was told to submit a written report on his work in China and Manchukuo. This amounted to less than four typewritten pages and could only have been regarded as exiguous by his superiors.

At Odessa Max and Anna were lodged in a suburban villa belonging to the Fourth Bureau facing the Black Sea, about an hour by tram from the centre of the city. It contained about ten rooms and could therefore, under Soviet conditions, accommodate fifty or sixty persons. Max went out fishing every day, unaccompanied by Anna, who spent much of her time taking leisurely and, one supposes, lugubrious strolls along the beach. But once or twice he took her to see the opera in Odessa. Max discovered that Weingarten was staying in the villa. So the two of them often went drinking together in the city, since the villa—on Berzin's orders—was strictly 'dry'.

The holiday lasted for six weeks, and then, back in Moscow, Max was posted to the wireless school, his main job being to help design a new portable combination transmitting and receiving set. Max Klausen was a very competent technician, and one would imagine that his presence at the school was helpful to all concerned. Together with others he did in fact succeed in constructing a new set—although he did not use this type in Japan, 'because it was very complicated and hence difficult to repair'. When this project was finished he was given further practical training in the transmission and receipt of wireless messages. This took place on the fourth floor of the school.

Here he worked with Weingarten and a member of the Red Navy. They exchanged messages with clandestine operators in Poland, Roumania and Turkey, as well as with Soviet wireless posts along the Balkan border. Max also gave a course in radio transmitting techniques to young soldiers billeted at the school.

Then, quite suddenly, at the beginning of 1934 he was ordered out of Moscow, to the Volga-German Republic. He was issued with travel documents in the name of Rautmann—his own passport being retained by the Fourth Bureau—and he was informed that he would be employed as a repair hand in a Motor Tractor Station.

Max stated later that this banishment was the penalty he had to pay for unsatisfactory work in Manchukuo; but a more likely explanation is that it was a punishment for his association with Anna. Indeed, before leaving Manchukuo he had courted disfavour by turning down a suggestion from his superiors that he should travel to Russia without his companion.

He departed for the Volga Republic full of rancour against the Fourth Bureau; and at first he and Anna had an uncomfortable time. A tractor repairman's wage was far from adequate for the two of them. But before very long conditions improved. For the supervisor at the station soon came to recognize Max's ability, and put him to work installing wireless sets at farms and on tractors, thus establishing a useful system of two-way farm-to-tractor intercommunication. Max was encouraged, too, to run a course on wireless operating for farm workers, and for a period he even blossomed out as a political propagandist, endeavouring 'to glorify the existing Soviet régime'. This meant a gratifying rise in pay; and prospects seemed even brighter when an official from Engels, the Volga-German capital, offered him a thousand roubles a month to work at a similar station there. This offer impelled Max's own supervisor to compete, so far as he could, by an inducement of his own, although this was less substantial than the Engels offer—being no more than six hundred roubles a month.

So when in the early spring of 1935 Max received a telegram from the Fourth Bureau, instructing him to return to Moscow, he ignored it. He was equally unmoved by a second and a more pressing telegram from the same address.

But he was not to be allowed to go on living in peace by the banks of the Volga. In April the head of the Engels branch of the Communist Party turned up in person at the small town where Max and

Anna lived. Summoning Max into his presence he flourished a telegram from Marshal Voroshilov and told him, in a stern and indeed
rebarbative tone, that he must go to Moscow immediately.

Max had to obey. He left for Moscow, without Anna, armed with
a letter of introduction from the Engels branch of the Communist
Party to the *First* Bureau of the Red Army. Max knew perfectly well
that the document was addressed to the wrong department, and he
was aware that it would lead to confusion and delay once he reached
Moscow. But this in no way disturbed him. On the contrary, his
feeling was one of malicious satisfaction. He harboured a grudge
against the Fourth Bureau for the way in which he had been treated.
In any case he did not, as a rule, incline toward works of super-
erogation, and so he duly reported at the First Bureau. As he had
expected, it was only after several telephone calls by officers of that
department that he was finally identified and claimed by his own
section.

On his eventual arrival there he was conducted to the office of
General Berzin, who asked him why he had taken no notice of two
telegrams recalling him to Moscow. Max replied that it was because he
'had achieved social and economic stability in the Volga', and he took
the opportunity of protesting against his earlier banishment to that
area. Berzin promised to have this matter looked into, and he consented to Max's determined plea that he should be allowed to fetch
Anna from the Volga Republic.

To this end Max was given train tickets and cash. But he stayed in
Moscow about a week before leaving for the south-east. Most of this
time he was sight-seeing; for he had no work to do, although he was
assigned to the West European division of the Bureau and was told
that in due course he would be sent to Germany. Living quarters
were provided for him at the wireless school.

On returning to Moscow with Anna, Max obtained, thanks to help
from the Fourth Bureau, a house in the suburb of Khimki. Having
installed Anna therein he decided to go on living at the wireless
school, visiting the Khimki house only about once a week. Anna
stayed there all the time. But in less than a month—as a result, it
may be, of pressure from the long-suffering but far from spineless
Anna—Max contrived to rent a room for the two of them in the
centre of Moscow which had been vacated by a factory worker who,
according to Max, 'had left Moscow to escape the summer heat'.

The May Day Parade of 1935 saw Max Klausen and Weingarten

trudging across Red Square at the head of a little group of young Chinese men and women. These were trainees on a special course at a branch of the wireless school designed exclusively for Chinese Communists. Max himself was not concerned with their instruction, which was Weingarten's responsibility. This course for Chinese operators—its very existence, according to Weingarten, was a closely guarded secret—had not been started when Max and Anna had left for the Volga Republic, in January 1934. The famous Long March of the Chinese Red Army began in November of that year; and it has been alleged that the decision to transfer the main Red base from the Kiangsi–Fukien border to the north-western region of China was made on instructions from Moscow. In May 1935, the Long March was still in progress—northern Shensi was not reached until August. It is clear that the young aspirants working under Weingarten were destined to report to the Chinese Red Army, after the latter was established in a part of China to which there was direct, if difficult, access from the Soviet Union, through wild but friendly territory. Indeed Weingarten himself was earmarked to go to Red China. This is why Max Klausen, not Weingarten, was allotted to Sorge's mission to Japan.

One day later that summer, Weingarten told Klausen that Sorge was in Moscow and wanted to meet them both, at the end of the day, in a bar near the wireless school. When the three met, Sorge announced over drinks that he wanted one or other of them to join him in Tokyo. But Max pointed out that he was now in the West European divison of the Bureau and was due to leave, sooner or later, for Germany.

'You don't need to worry about that,' Sorge assured him. 'I'll arrange for you to come to Tokyo.'

Max was called soon afterwards to the office of Korin, who was in charge of Far Eastern operations at the Fourth Bureau. He was informed that he was assigned to that division as from that day, and that he would be joining Sorge in Tokyo. Sorge himself was present in the room when Max received his new orders.

At the time, Max was giving a course on the assembly and operation of wireless sets to a Swedish couple, in a Fourth Bureau officers' billet near Smolensk Square. He now relinquished this task and began to prepare himself for what lay ahead.

More than six years later, after his arrest in Tokyo, he prepared a written statement of his views on Japan, for the benefit of the Special

Higher Police. Certain passages warrant quotation, since they illuminate the cast of Max Klausen's thoughts. It should be remembered, however, that he was perhaps writing under duress, and without doubt under conditions of rigorous confinement.

I considered England [wrote Klausen] to be the most tyrannical country in the world, but later I came to feel that Japan, a newcomer to the modern world, was worse than England, because Japan had become a powerful capitalist country by the very simple and cheap method of copying all the inventions originated in other nations. This aroused my indignation.

Since even the other capitalist countries harboured a similar resentment, it was natural that I should have felt highly satisfied when ordered by Moscow to proceed to Japan for espionage work. . . .

Actually I knew nothing of Japan before I came, but I regarded her as an aggressor nation, because she had subjugated Korea some thirty years ago and conquered and occupied Manchuria some ten years ago. I felt a burning indignation, and I intensely desired the overthrow of the Japanese capitalist system. At that time I did not understand the true motives of the Japanese government. . . .

I was very proud when Moscow put me in charge of the wireless operations of the Tokyo spy ring. I came to Japan as an enemy of the Japanese Government and, I thought, as a friend of the Japanese people.

I had always thought that the Japanese were groaning under brutal oppression from the government, and therefore, after I arrived, I believed that in opposing the political system I was working for the welfare of the people. But I was mistaken. I have never seen a country ruled by a more sincere government. Japan is a country of the first rank. In the years I spent here I came to realize that I had made the greatest mistake of my life.

Sorge and Klausen left separately for Japan—the former probably at the end of August 1935, and the latter in September. The two evidently had a joint farewell briefing from General Uritsky. He reminded them that the basic purpose of their espionage, overriding all else, was an accurate analysis of Japan's intentions *vis-à-vis* the Soviet Union. Was Japan planning an attack and, if so, when? In his 'confession' and in oral evidence to the Japanese preliminary judge, Sorge claimed that Uritsky had told Klausen and himself that their ultimate duty was 'to prevent war between Japan and the Soviet Union. This was a matter of extreme concern to all quarters in Moscow.'

Sorge implies that Uritsky warned him to watch very closely the developing pattern of Japanese-German relations. Although in the summer of 1935 'it was still too soon to predict how far the slow improvement in relations would go, Moscow was convinced that a rapprochement was taking place, and, moreover, that it was directed chiefly against the Soviet Union'.

No doubt Moscow was already aware of the fact that the first, very tentative, feelers had been extended from the German side. For in May or June Ribbentrop had asked a German businessman with Far Eastern connections, Dr. Friederich Wilhelm Hack, to approach Major-General Oshima, the Japanese military attaché in Berlin, and convey to him confidentially Ribbentrop's own personal suggestion that Germany and Japan should consider negotiating some kind of defensive alliance against the Soviet Union.

Obscurity surrounds Sorge's journey back to Tokyo. He states that he left Moscow by air. Willoughby reports a story that Sorge travelled to Japan in the first Junkers flight from Germany. But there is no record of Sorge's inclusion among the crew and passengers on that journey.

The evidence suggests that in fact he returned to Japan by way of Europe and the United States. According to his own story he passed through Holland – possibly to see the Amsterdam newspaper which he represented. He says that there he destroyed his false passport (bearing the Austrian name). He recounts, too, how on the return trip he visited a tailor in New York, who had made him a suit before he had sailed from that city earlier in the summer. When he met the man again, after landing in America, Sorge used the Austrian name shown on the false passport. The tailor remembered Sorge and recalled, too, that two or three months earlier his name had been different. However, Sorge observed later, 'people in the United States do not think it strange if the same man uses two different names'.

It is at least certain that Sorge was in Tokyo again before the end of September 1935. It is a curious fact that, so far as available records show, the Japanese judicial authorities seem to have shown little interest in Sorge's journey from Moscow to Tokyo in 1935.

Rather more is known about the movements of Max Klausen. He travelled by sea from Leningrad to Le Havre, where he transferred on to another vessel bound for New York. Anna was left in Moscow, but it was clearly Max's intention to meet her later in Shanghai and take her back with him from there to Japan. The Fourth Bureau supplied Max with the necessary funds and two passports, Italian and

Canadian, in addition to his own. He crossed the Atlantic on the American vessel *Boston*, and he may have worked his passage as a member of the crew, for it appears that at Stockholm he bought a U.S. seaman's certificate. But he had his German passport renewed at the New York Consulate. While in New York he stayed, in accordance with prior instructions, at the Hotel Lincoln. He was visited there by a 'Mr. Jones', an *apparatchnik*, who asked him how he was placed for money. Perhaps surprisingly, Max refused the offer of further funds. Still, he had been given $1,800 (U.S.) by the Fourth Bureau when leaving Moscow, and if he crossed to New York as a paid seaman his expenses so far could not have been very heavy.

It was on November 14 that Max Klausen boarded the *Tatsuta Maru*, as a passenger, at San Francisco. The ship docked at Yokohama a fortnight later, on the 28th. A wireless set was not among Max's effects when he landed. But he smuggled in two tubes for a small set. Other components he would have to obtain in Japan.

Before they parted in Moscow, Sorge had said that he would be in the Blue Ribbon Bar, near Sukiyabashi, Tokyo, between certain times every Tuesday evening. November 28, 1935, the date of Klausen's arrival, was a Thursday. But the following evening Max went to the German Club in Tokyo and there he met Sorge. However, on this occasion they could only exchange a few words, for there were several other men standing by. But they were able to snatch a few minutes' private conversation in the library, when it was arranged that they should meet in the Blue Ribbon at six o'clock the next evening.

Meanwhile in Moscow Anna was entirely on her own. A day or two after Max's departure a woman, who said she had been sent by the Fourth Bureau, called on Anna and told her to keep to herself and not to associate with anybody. To make sure that these instructions were being carried out, this female visited Anna almost every day. From time to time a man from the Bureau appeared and gave Anna money for her living expenses. Under perpetual surveillance, Anna had to endure this lonely existence all through the autumn and winter.

The subsequent fate of Max Klausen's friend and fellow radio-technician, Weingarten, is not clear. No doubt he went to China. But it has been suggested that he was sent at a later stage into Germany, where he enlisted in the army. He was arrested in 1943 at a military intelligence headquarters on the Eastern Front. It was discovered that one of his main tasks was to supervise the arrival of secret agents sent into Germany from the Soviet Union. He was induced to work for the Germans, continuing to operate his set, thus delivering new Soviet agents, as they arrived, into the hands of the Gestapo. The latter, of course, had extracted from Weingarten the key to his code, but they still had need of his services. Every operator has a different touch, and Moscow would have detected any change immediately. If this report is true, it is improbable that he survived to see the end of the war.

Chapter 10

THE REAL MISSION BEGINS

'It was not skill, nor the examinations I had to pass at the Moscow Intelligence School, but my basic study of Japanese problems that counted most.' SORGE

AFTER his return from Moscow Sorge's first concern was to see Klausen established, with a transmitting set in working order. This took some time. In December Sorge introduced Max to Vukelic and suggested that the radio set should be operated from the latter's house. Vukelic was then living alone—Edith had returned home to Denmark for a brief visit—and he and Max chose two rooms upstairs that seemed suitable.

The first transmissions, however, appear to have been made, not from the Vukelic home, but from the house of Gunther Stein, a journalist representing the *News Chronicle* and *Financial News* of London. Max Klausen had been introduced to Stein by Sorge at the latter's home in December. Gunther Stein had arrived in Japan earlier in the year. He later became a naturalized British subject, but he was German by birth. At one stage in his career he had been Moscow correspondent of the *Berliner Tageblatt*. His book, *Made in Japan*, was to win him wide recognition as an expert on Japanese economic affairs.

Under interrrogation by the *Tokko* Police, Max Klausen stated that Gunther Stein was a member of the Sorge ring. Sorge himself described Stein as a 'sympathizer', rather than an actual member of his group. This would seem perhaps the correct interpretation of Stein's position.* Until he left Japan early in 1938 he was of some service to Sorge and his associates.

At their first meeting, in Sorge's house, Max Klausen and Gunther Stein discussed problems of radio transmission, and Stein evidently

---

* In his Statement, as amended by him during the Preliminary Judge's Examination, Sorge declared that Gunther Stein 'was a sympathizer but never an actual member of my group. Actually, however, he did give us positive co-operation'. ('Sorge's Own Story', Part II, Ch. I), also Preliminary Judge's Examination, Sorge, No. 11; July 29, 1942. Sorge had earlier told the police that he had 'manœuvred' Stein gradually 'toward participation in our work'. Police Interrogation of Sorge, No. 10; December 22, 1941.

offered to place his quarters at Max's disposal. For he drew a map to show where he lived, and a few days later Max made his way there and inspected the house. It was from an upstairs room there that he first made contact with 'Wiesbaden' (Vladivostok) in the middle of February 1936.

Meanwhile danger had come very close to the ring. On January 21, 1936, Kawai Teikichi was arrested by the Special Higher Police.

Kawai, it will be recalled, was lodging at the suburban home of a right-wing adventurer, and he was keeping Miyagi and Ozaki supplied with information on the ultra-nationalist movement.

On the morning of January 21 he woke suddenly, noticed the extreme cold, and looked at his watch. It was barely five o'clock. He called to mind that January 21 was the day on which Lenin died, and he remembered that he had a rendezvous that evening with Ozaki and Miyagi in an eating house downtown.

At that moment the sliding partitions were drawn apart and no fewer than eight detectives swarmed into the room. Kawai tells us that his first thought was: 'All is discovered!' The faces of his comrades—in Shanghai, Tientsin, Manchukuo, and Tokyo—passed before his eyes. Had the police uncovered something in Tokyo? Or was it on the continent? If the former were the case, it was very serious; it meant that the authorities had a lead to the main conspiracy. But if the police were acting on information from the continent, then the situation, Kawai felt, was not quite so desperate.

One of the detectives, a *Tokko* officer from Metropolitan Police Headquarters, thrust a document in front of him. It was a warrant for Kawai's arrest issued by the Judicial Consul of the Japanese Consulate in Hsinking, Manchukuo. 'You're going to a cold place,' said the detective. 'Get dressed in ten minutes.'

Kawai declares that when he felt the chill of the handcuffs on his wrists, as he was hustled out of the house, his spirits suddenly revived, and he said to himself: 'Right! I'll lead these dogs a dance!'

There followed a slow journey across Japan to the port of Moji in northern Kyushu. Passed from one police station to another, from one prefectural jurisdiction to the next, Kawai was guarded by ten different escorts. From Tokyo to Kawasaki, to Atami, to Gifu, to Kyoto; then to Kobe, Fukuyama, Iwakuni, Shimonoseki, and finally to Moji—by bus, tram, train and car, the trip took over a week; and at Moji there was a wait of two or three days before the Dairen steamer arrived. On the boat Kawai's handcuffs were at last removed, and he was able to take his first bath for a fortnight. He was even allowed some *saké* with his evening meal. So far the journey, though tedious, had not been unduly distressing. Kawai had been subjected to little or no interrogation. Nobody seemed very clear about the charges against him; and a procurator in Tokyo had actually suggested that the whole affair might be a mistake.

Things were different, however, from the moment he was delivered to the port police at Dairen. The desk officer fairly roared at him: 'Here comes a great rascal! We've been picking up your friends in Mukden, Kaiyuan, Peking, Tientsin, Tsingtao and Shanghai. And you have turned up from Tokyo. You bastard! You see now that justice has long arms.' But at least the Dairen Water Police Station was well heated, and Kawai spent two nights there before being sent on up the railway to Hsinking, where he was locked up in a cell of the city Detention House.

It was not long before he was brought before the judicial consul in the Japanese consular court. He was charged with propaganda activities in Shanghai and with having induced, on orders from 'The International Communist Party', one Soejima Ryuki at Mukden, in October, 1931, to enter the *Kempeitai* (Military Police) for the express purpose of obtaining secret military information. It was alleged that Kawai had passed on such information, received from Soejima, to members of the Chinese Communist Party.

When these charges were read out to him Kawai felt a certain sense of relief. The authorities seemed to have a confused picture of what had been going on; and it looked as though the enquiry would concentrate on his links with the Chinese party. Invited to reply to the charges, he stated that those relating to propaganda activity were true. As for the other charges, he denied them. He had never received such information—a figure of thirty-seven items of secret military intelligence had been mentioned in the charge-sheet—and surely Soejima himself ought to know this very well.

'All right,' declared the consular official, gathering up his papers. 'I shall address further questions to you next time.'

Kawai was taken back to his cell. Almost at once he was called out again, to face two detectives, who started to interrogate him in earnest. One of them was courteous, even soft-spoken at times; the other was rough and abusive. Their questions were directed to the nature of the information Kawai had been given by Soejima, and to the way in which this had been passed on to the Chinese Communists. Kawai denied truthfully all knowledge of this.

Finally, he was removed from the Detention House and conveyed through the snow to the Hsinking Police Station; and here he was dragged down into the icy cellars below the building. From adjoining dungeons came curses and screams in Japanese, in Korean, in Chinese. 'In this place,' said one of the detectives, 'even if you are murdered your death will be put down to natural causes. Why not be co-operative before trouble starts?' Kawai made no answer. Whereupon his clothing was removed and he was beaten into insensibility with a steel rod.

On regaining consciousness he found himself lying on a couch in a warm room. Someone brought him some hot coffee, and he was then sent back to the Detention House cell. After about twenty-four hours he was again taken to the cellars of Hsinking Central Police Station and subjected to further beatings. This torture continued for some five days. It was then abandoned. The police could not make up their mind about Kawai; and he knew that he had won. The name of Ozaki Hotsumi had never passed his lips.

In the consular court Kawai was awarded a suspended sentence of ten months' imprisonment for violating the Peace Preservation Law, and in June 1936, he was released from custody. Later he found out why he had been arrested. It was Soejima Ryuki who had given his name to the police.

His association with Kawai had begun in the spring of 1929, in Peking. Soejima was a clerk in a Japanese government agency. He and Kawai and three or four other Japanese, sympathetically interested in the Chinese Communist movement, had joined forces to make a study of Marxist literature and its application to the situation in China. In course of time, theoretical enquiry giving place to practical work, the study group had grown into the Sino-Japanese Struggle League, an organization for agitation and propaganda directed by the Chinese Communist Party.

Early in 1932 Soejima had entered the Japanese *Kempeitai* in Manchukuo as an interpreter. In February 1933, he was ordered to join in the operations to clear Chinese forces from Jehol Province. Soejima hoped to die in battle, and as a last service to the Chinese Communist cause he stole a number of *Kempei* secret documents, with the purpose of sending them to Kawai, whom he believed to be in Shanghai and who would be responsible for passing the papers on to the Chinese. To this end Soejima entrusted the documents to a courier. But by this time Kawai had left Shanghai for good, and it was through another channel that the papers eventually reached the Chinese party. Of these transactions Kawai knew nothing; and so he could maintain his ignorance of the affair under questioning by his tormentors in Hsinking. Soejima, on the other hand, evidently believed in good faith that the secret papers had passed through Kawai's hands.

The Jehol fighting failed to provide Soejima with a soldier's death but it fired or revived a bourgeois conscience. Soejima began to have agonizing qualms about what he had done. These lasted for many months and were exacerbated by the fact that in 1935 he believed he was under police surveillance. In the end he went voluntarily to Hsinking Central Police Station and confessed all.

One by one, in various cities in China and Manchukuo, the members of the Sino-Japanese Struggle League were seized by the Japanese police. Kawai himself, when he was arrested in Tokyo, was probably one of the last to be taken into custody.

His interrogation at Hsinking, being barbarous, was also clumsy and unintelligent. By confining the scope of their investigations to Kawai's relations with Soejima and the Chinese Communists the police failed to uncover his connections with Ozaki and the Sorge ring in Shanghai. But if Kawai was not asked a single question about Ozaki this does not detract from the fortitude he showed in the cellars at Hsinking. As he observes in his book:

> If under interrogation at Hsinking I had said the faintest word about Ozaki, Sorge, or the work in Japan, then the Sorge ring would have been discovered in 1936. But in that case Sorge and Ozaki would probably have escaped being sentenced to the extreme penalty—death.

After his release Kawai remained on the continent, and for some years his active connection with the Sorge ring ceased. He did not return to Japan permanently until September 1940.

We have no record of how Ozaki and Miyagi reacted to Kawai's sudden disappearance from Tokyo; and there is no evidence that Sorge was informed by them of what had occurred. In any case they were soon busy collecting intelligence for Sorge on an event that electrified Japan and, indeed, the world. This was the mutiny by part of the Tokyo garrison in the early hours of February 26, 1936.

While Sorge was in Moscow dramatic events had been taking place in Japan. On July 16, 1935, General Mazaki, the hero of the radical *Kodo* ('Imperial Way') faction, was forced to retire from the important post of Inspector-General of Military Training. His resignation had been engineered by his enemies and was correctly interpreted as a victory for the more traditionally minded *Tosei-ha* ('Control' faction). The ousting of Mazaki caused a sensation, and Tokyo soon buzzed with rumours of impending violence. The young hotheads of the *Kodo-ha*, it was claimed, would never accept what was happening; for the annual army personnel transfers and promotions, announced on August 1, made it clear that the Ministry of War intended to break the back of the *Kodo* faction by posting trouble-makers overseas.

Among those affected was a certain Lt.-Colonel Aizawa, stationed in a town on the Inland Sea. This officer had made a special journey up to Tokyo to protest against Mazaki's resignation. He had sought out, in the Ministry of War, the chief of the military affairs bureau, Major-General Nagata, in charge of army postings and a known opponent of Mazaki and the *Kodo-ha*. Aizawa had it in mind to kill Nagata if the latter refused to listen to him. But he went no further, in a stormy interview, than to demand Nagata's resignation. In most armies, of course, such insubordination would not have remained unpunished. So it is not surprising that two weeks later Aizawa was informed that he was to be posted forthwith to a unit in Formosa.

Once again Aizawa travelled up to Tokyo. He marched into the Ministry of War, strode along the passage to Nagata's room, opened the door and drew his sword. Aizawa's first stroke failed to dispatch the general. Another officer, who happened to be in the room, tried to protect Nagata and was severely wounded for his pains. Nagata was finally hacked to death. 'I was ashamed,' declared Aizawa at his court martial, 'that I had failed to kill Nagata with a single stroke of my sword.'

Assassination was by no means foreign to Japanese tradition. But the murder of a general by a field officer had not been known for more than fifty years. Everyone realized that the incident was symptomatic of what was termed *gekokujo*—the 'overthrow of seniors by juniors, of the higher by the lower'. This expression, first used to describe the feudal anarchy of the fifteenth century, seemed appropriate to the situation in the Japanese army, with its politically active young officers, whose radical and indeed mutinous temper threatened military and civilian leaders alike.

Thus Sorge returned to a Japan that was even more unsettled by portents of violence than it had been when he had first arrived in the country two years earlier. Both Ozaki and Miyagi interpreted for him the significance of Nagata's murder, and he can have been left in small doubt as to the probability of some further bloodshed.

The famous *Ni Ni Roku Jiken*, or 'February 26 Incident' was related to Aizawa's killing of General Nagata, and to its aftermath, Colonel Aizawa's court martial. This was held in the barracks of the 1st Division in Tokyo. It proved to be a long-drawn-out affair and was accorded ample publicity, day after day, in the newspapers. Aizawa and his lawyer turned the defence case into a sounding board for the half-baked ideas of the *Kodo* faction, expressed with prolonged and polemical vigour. The president of the court let the moral initiative pass to the accused. Aizawa succeeded in presenting himself as a disinterested Japanese patriot, concerned only with the fate of his country and desirous of ridding it of the weakness, corruption and treachery in high places symbolized by the cabinet, senior advisers to the Throne, the great capitalist combines and some of the military leaders, among them his victim, Nagata.

This *cause célèbre* unsettled many young officers of the 1st Division who shared Aizawa's views; and in January the police uncovered an assassination plot by some of these officers.* In fact there were plenty of warning signs of trouble to come. The only action taken by the military authorities was to order the 1st Division to stand by for service in Manchukuo, and to be ready to move at the end of February.

Aizawa's court martial dragged on through February, each day's proceedings inflaming a climate already disturbed by rumours of imminent bloodshed. Both Ozaki and Miyagi kept Sorge well supplied with information on the Aizawa case and its implications. Sorge, then, cannot have been taken wholly by surprise by the armed outbreak that occurred on February 26. According to Sorge, 'the people in the Embassy were at a loss as to how to interpret the event'.

What occurred on the morning of February 26 and during the next three days was decidedly baffling to the uninstructed observer. Some

---

* The main prospective victim was General Watanabe, Mazaki's successor as Inspector-General of Military Education. He was among those murdered, some weeks later, on February 26.

1,400 soldiers left their barracks before dawn, in a heavy snowstorm. They were commanded by junior officers, none of them above the rank of captain. The main body of insurgents took possession of a group of buildings in the government quarter of Tokyo, including the Ministry of War, Metropolitan Police Headquarters, and the Diet. Simultaneously, parties of mutineers carried out attacks on the Prime Minister's residence and on the homes of several public men. Two ex-Premiers were among the victims, the Prime Minister himself having a remarkable escape from death.* The leaders of the *coup*, the young officers, issued a manifesto, couched in vague, idealistic terms. It declared that all had been performed from a sense of duty to the Emperor.

Thenceforward the mutineers were passive. They were waiting, it seemed, for influential generals of the *Kodo* faction to take over direction of state affairs. The government, too, was strangely inactive at first. It was only late in the evening of February 26 that an announcement was put out by the Ministry of War. This did not speak of 'rebels', or even 'insurgents', but merely of 'young regular officers'. The next day was one of parley with rebellion, of meetings between certain generals and the mutinous young officers. But while this was going on, reliable troops were being massed, the First Fleet was concentrated off the city, tanks rumbled through the snow-covered streets, and an armed cordon was thrown round the rebel strongholds—part of it manned by naval ratings. Two days later, on February 29, the rebel officers and men surrendered without a shot being fired.

Sorge was fascinated by this astonishing, abortive *coup d'état*. Throughout the four days that it lasted he tried to see what he could with his own eyes; and he told the members of his ring to investigate the precise nature and consequences of the affair. 'Our espionage group,' said Sorge, 'made the incident one of its special duties.'

In his 'confession' he writes:

The incident had a very typical Japanese character and hence its motivations required particular study. A discerning study of it, and, in particular, a study of the social strains and internal crisis it revealed, was of much greater value to an understanding of Japan's internal structure than mere records of troop strength or secret documents.

* Premier Okada's brother-in-law, who greatly resembled him in appearance, deliberately exposed himself to the assassins, who shot him down, supposing him to be the Prime Minister. The ex-Premiers were Takahashi and Admiral Saito.

Sorge analysed the February 26 Incident in at least three separate reports—one for the German Foreign Office, another for the Bureau in Moscow, and a third for publication as an article in Haushofer's journal, *Zeitschrift für Geopolitik.*

The report for Berlin was written at the instigation of his friends in the German Embassy. How this happened is best conveyed in Sorge's own words:

> To Dirksen, Ott, and Wenneker I stressed again and again the social aspect of the February 26 Incident, telling them that I understood the social problems facing Japan. As a result the Embassy staff turned their attention to this side of the Incident, and they tried to collect as much material as possible about it. Ott himself had a particular channel through which he was able to collect pamphlets and broadsheets.
>
> My espionage ring, of course, amassed a great deal of material on the whole affair. In fact I came to learn a lot from various sides. So my opinions easily coloured the view taken by the Embassy; and both Dirksen and Ott tried to draw even closer to me. This is why I was asked to write a report on the Incident for Berlin.

Sorge claimed that his opinions carried considerable weight in the German Embassy from 1936 onwards. There can be no doubt that his reputation was established by his perceptive interpretation of the February Mutiny—an interpretation that might have been unremarkable and superficial but for the help of Ozaki and Miyagi.

The state of martial law, proclaimed in Tokyo when the February outbreak occurred, remained in force for many weeks. This made matters no easier for foreign diplomats and journalists eager to find out the real significance of the Incident. None of them, it is a fair conjecture, could rely on the advice of Japanese confederates as cooperative as those who fed intelligence to Sorge. Miyagi, for example, was gathering information on the mutiny for a full two months after it was over.

It was of course his report to Moscow that was Sorge's prime concern. Soviet interest in the February Mutiny could be expressed in a series of questions. To what extent did the outbreak reflect deep discontent in the country at large? What were the aims, economic and political, of the young officers? Would the upshot of all this turn out to be a weakening of the power and prestige of the Japanese army? What effect would the affair have on the course of Japanese foreign policy? Would it sharpen or moderate the anti-Soviet stance of Japan?

Sorge provided Moscow with the answers to these questions. In a factual account of what happened he included certain information omitted from his article in *Geopolitik*. The Police Report on Sorge tells us that he transmitted to Moscow information 'on the encirclement of the insurgents by naval units in the area around the Foreign Ministry'. In *Geopolitik* Sorge was careful not to go beyond the statement that the navy 'strongly condemned' the mutiny and that this 'contributed much to preventing the extension of the rebel movement'. For the Japanese authorities were at pains to conceal from foreigners the rancour that existed between the army and navy. One of the most closely guarded secrets was the exact part played by the navy in supporting the Emperor's firm reaction to the mutiny. If Sorge had been as explicit in his press article as he was in his report to Moscow he would have run the risk of being expelled from Japan.

Naturally Sorge discussed with Ozaki and Miyagi the social and ideological meaning of the revolt, and with their help he grasped the essential content of a banned book, *Nihon Kaizo Hoan Taiko* (*An Outline for the Reconstruction of Japan*), the bible of the young officers. Shortly before his arrest Kawai Teikichi had obtained for Miyagi a copy of this book. Its author, Kita Ikki, was actively involved in the February Mutiny and was to be executed, with other ringleaders, for his part in stirring up insurrection. Imperialism, centred on the mystique of the Emperor, and state socialism, formed the main elements of Kita's gospel. His ideas, for all their attachment to Emperor and imperial army, bore clear signs of Marxist influence — this indeed was why the book, in its original form, had been banned for years.

It is not surprising, then, that Sorge, whether he really believed this or not, should have told his friend Urach that the Japanese Communists may have had some connection with the uprising, and that he did not dismiss the possibility of a Communist Japan still ruled by the Emperor. Years later, during the last stages of the Pacific War, Prince Konoye, in private audience at the Palace, told the Emperor that he had come to the conclusion that the radical young officers of the nineteen-thirties were the conscious or unconscious tools of international Communism.

It was Ozaki who clarified for Sorge the connection between the mutiny and the economic woes of the rural areas. But it was a newly arrived assistant military attaché at the Embassy, Major Scholl, who was able to give Sorge the German translation of a clandestine pamphlet on military grievances, written by two cashiered officers, who themselves were subsequently ringleaders of the mutiny.* Scholl, promoted lieutenant-colonel after his arrival in Tokyo in January 1936, quickly became one of Sorge's close friends. For Sorge discovered that Scholl had served on the Western Front, in the ranks, in the same unit as himself.

The pamphlet produced by Scholl rounded out what Sorge knew, thanks to Ozaki and Miyagi, about the background to the factional confrontation—between *Kodo-ha* and *Tosei-ha*—of which the February Mutiny was the climax.

It was evidently Ott's opinion that the mutiny would have the effect of weakening the power of the Japanese army; for he believed that there would be a reduction in the military budget. But Miyagi's conclusion betrayed deeper insight. Granted that the political parties would recover some influence, he judged that nevertheless 'the people in general hated the political parties, and the February 26 Incident would be a turning point, leading to a drastic redirection of Japanese politics, with the army becoming the motive power in political life'. That is just what happened. Japan's military leaders used the lively fear of another insurrection to enforce their will on the government. General Terauchi, the mouthpiece of the now triumphant *Tosei-ha* and Minister of War in the new administration, virtually dictated not only the composition of the Hirota Cabinet but also its basic policies in education and finance, not to mention national defence and diplomacy.

Ozaki's view was that henceforth Japan's foreign policy would become increasingly anti-Russian. Miyagi's prediction was somewhat different. He argued that towards foreign countries a conciliatory policy would be adopted. This would mean that an attack on China rather than Russia was to be expected.

In his report to Moscow Sorge inclined towards Miyagi's opinion. The essence of this document was summed up by Sorge in the following words:

There were two ways in which the Japanese Government could handle

---

* The pamphlet, 'Views on the Housecleaning of the Army', was written in July 1935, by Captain Muranaka and Lieutenant Isobe. For writing this tract, which exposed many secrets about earlier factional rivalries and plots, both officers were dismissed from the army. They donned uniform again on February 26, 1936, to take part in the insurrection. Condemned to death, they were executed in September 1937.

the aftermath of the February 26 Affair. They could either introduce social reforms, at the same time imposing strict discipline on the army, or they could adopt the policy of permanent expansion.

This phrase, *permanent expansion*, is my own invention. It came to me from Trotsky's phrase, 'permanent revolution'.

Japan adopted the second course. Whether the direction of this permanent expansion was to be China or Russia was a question of the greatest importance to the Soviet Union.

I remember that I reported to Moscow that the direction would be China. For I had in mind a tradition of Japanese expansion that went back to the days of the Empress Jingu.

It was a sound analysis. Sorge, it must not be forgotten, was never a 'letter-box'. His 'confession' contains this revealing passage:

It has been my personal desire and delight to learn something about the places in which I have found myself, a fact particularly true with respect to Japan and China. I have never considered such study purely as a means to an end; had I lived under peaceful social conditions and in a peaceful environment of political development, I should perhaps have been a scholar –certainly not an espionage agent.

An observer versed in ancient Japanese history, wrote Sorge, could understand Japan's modern foreign policy; and the passing political scene in Japan could tell him far more than the police suspected.

I took it upon myself to see that our information was screened most carefully, and only what I considered essential and absolutely safe was sent. . . . This ability to select material and present a general appraisal or picture of a given development is a prerequisite for intelligence of genuine value, and it can be acquired only through much serious and careful research.

Again, one must not think that our work ended when our reports had been sent out by radio. Such messages constituted only one of many phases of our intelligence activities, and certainly not the chief one. At irregular intervals I sent great quantities of mail to Moscow, which included not only documents and other materials but also reports written by myself . . . they represented serious and painstaking efforts to present, on the basis of abundant information and research, an accurate and objective long-range picture of new developments and of the general situation during the past several months. Such laborious reports could never have been attempted without comprehensive study and knowledge. Unlike Berlin and Washington, Moscow knew China and Japan too well to be fooled easily. The Soviet level of knowledge of Far Eastern affairs was far above that of the American and German Governments, and Moscow demanded that I send in systematic, soundly based and carefully planned reports at intervals of several months.

Sorge did not transmit an immediate, interim report on the February Mutiny by radio. For although Max Klausen's set had made contact with Siberia its capabilities had not yet been fully tested. Thus Sorge's report on the mutiny was sent out, on microfilm, in April to Shanghai—Klausen acting as courier.

Sorge revealed that for this Moscow report he photocopied all the German Embassy documents used in the preparation of his report for Berlin. It was from this time that he began to photograph papers inside the Embassy, with his Robot camera.

It was probably also from about this time that he was shown at least some of Dirksen's dispatches to his home government. For Sorge told his interrogators: 'The Moscow Centre was interested not so much in whether the Embassy dispatch on the February 26 Incident was correct or not, as in the attitude of responsible Germans to the Incident.'

Therefore I reported to the Moscow Centre not only Dirksen's views on the Incident, but also his assessment of how the Japanese Government was surmounting this crisis. I also sent to Moscow Ott's report to Dirksen on Japanese Army reactions to the Incident.

According to Sorge, Dirksen's assessment was superficial. 'He thought the Incident was a mere reflection of the army's ignorance. . . . Ott's report was a little more profound.' From Wenneker, the naval attaché, Sorge learned that 'tension between navy and army was extremely acute thanks to the Incident'. 'This information, of importance to the Moscow Centre, I transmitted to the Soviet Union.'

The article 'The Army Revolt in Tokyo', by 'R.S.', under the date of March 1936, in *Zeitschrift für Geopolitik* of May that year still reads well. Neither the narrative nor the conclusions require much amendment in the light of later knowledge. It is easy to understand why the article attracted interest at the time. It is perhaps the best published European account of the February Mutiny.

Examining the article today, with the benefit of hindsight, can one detect the ideological convictions of the author? There are a few passages that might be regarded, conceivably, as significant, and even revealing, in this context.

It was not isolated individuals who this time aroused the passion of the rebels. This time, more plainly than before, it was representatives of institutions and of political and economic principles. These institutions and these economic and political principles had to be smitten and destroyed to make room for new ones.

It is no coincidence that the main blow struck by the rebels was concentrated against Finance Minister Takahashi. The attempt on Premier Okada, which failed, was basically of less importance. . . . For the rebels he [Takahashi] was the symbol of all Japan's finance capital, under the domination of which the claims of the army and the social needs of the peasantry remained unanswered.

(Is it fanciful to perceive in that second paragraph, with its references to Takahashi and Okada, the hand of Ozaki Hotsumi?)

The deepest causes of these radical political currents in the army is the social distress of the Japanese peasantry and the lower bourgeoisie of the towns. . . . Given the lack of political organizations of the peasantry and the purely formal interest the two main parties take in them, the army had to become the mouthpiece and organ of the increasing tension among these urban and rural classes. Herein lies the greatest significance of the revolt of the Tokyo Division.

Evidently Sorge felt satisfied that he had not shown his true colours. For an Austrian businessman, then in Tokyo, recalls that Sorge let everyone know that he had written the article and that it had been written with Ott's help and co-operation. 'His uninhibited boasts showed clearly beyond any doubt how pleased he was with this publication. Vanity is the sole proper explanation. And in Sorge's case such reckless vanity was tantamount to plain stupidity.'*

Be that as it may, Sorge was embarrassed—no doubt he was also secretly gratified—when Radek reproduced part of this article in *Pravda* and praised it in an editorial. Radek, says Sorge, had not 'the slightest suspicion that I was the author. . . . I was astonished to see this in *Pravda* at the Embassy, where the article attracted some interest. Through Klausen I immediately asked Moscow not to reproduce, in future, articles signed "R.S." in *Geopolitik* and *Frankfurter Zeitung*.'

* In this context it is worth noting that Karl Haushofer the owner of *Geopolitik*, like Ott, had begun his military career as an artillery officer and, like Ott, had done a tour of duty with the Japanese army (1909–11). In the autumn of 1936, while on a brief visit to Germany, Ott studied Haushofer's plans and ideas relating to Japan at the Geopolitical Institute.

The February 26 Affair was a landmark in Sorge's career, both as a spy and a journalist. It marked the beginning of his real mission in Japan, his first major report to Moscow being his study of the insurrection. It was from this time that he could feel securely established in his close relations with the German Embassy. The publication of the *Geopolitik* article coincided with his début as a regular contributor to the *Frankfurter Zeitung*. Thus at the same time both his cover and the base for his clandestine work were greatly strengthened. The one supplemented the other to mutual advantage for the next five and a half years.

One pendant must be added to the story of Sorge and the February 26 Affair. Weather conditions chanced to give the insurrection a peculiar historic significance in the eyes of many Japanese. The snow that fell early in the morning of February 26, providing the backcloth to the assassinations, could not fail to remind the Japanese of a scene cherished in their hearts and portrayed many a time on stage and screen—namely the revenge, during an Yedo winter in the seventeenth century, of the Forty-Seven *Ronin*.

This episode, one of the most famous in Japanese history, marked the culmination of months of feigned passivity on the part of the avenging warriors—passivity designed to throw their enemy, who had caused their lord's death, off his guard. They attacked his house early one morning, in a snowstorm. Having killed him, they took his head to the temple where their dead lord had been laid to rest. They presented the head of their enemy to the tombstone and then surrendered to the authorities, who after much deliberation decreed that the warriors must commit *hara-kiri* for having disturbed the peace of Yedo (Tokyo).

We may be sure that Sorge, with his knowledge of Japanese history, noted the similarities between that vendetta and the 1936 insurrection.* But of particular relish must have been the masterly deceit practised by the warriors before they carried out their revenge. Their leader, for example, abandoned himself to weeks of drunkenness and debauchery. But behind this camouflage he and his followers were able to spy out the movements and plans of their enemy and so, in the end, vindicate their honour. 'These fellows', Sorge is

---

* No doubt, too, he noticed certain parallels between both these violent dramas and a third, namely the assassination of the shogun's chief minister, Ii Naosuke, one snowy morning in 1860, outside the Cherry Gate in Yedo, by nationalist fanatics from Mito.

quoted as saying, 'laid the bloody head of their master's deadly enemy on their master's grave, and then they slit their own bellies. They knew how to cover up their aims with drinking and restless wandering.'

Chapter 11

THE CONSOLIDATION OF THE RING

'One must not reveal secrets to any outsider, even one's most trusted friends.' SORGE—statement to the *Tokko*

SORGE claimed that in 1936 he obtained 'a recognized position as unofficial secretary to the military attaché', Colonel Ott, and he was given a room in the German Embassy. It is clear that this was an informal and possibly eccentric arrangement. Of course when the Ambassador showed him confidential papers Sorge could not take them to his room—there to photograph or copy them. All he could do was to memorize their salient points and summarize these afterwards in writing. But when his advice was sought by other members of the staff he would often ask to be allowed to take the relevant documents to his room. 'I should like,' he would say, 'to be able to go over this slowly.' Once in his own room he would photograph the more important passages in the material.

If I was unable to take this kind of chance – namely borrowing the actual documents –I waited until the papers were transferred to the archives and then I could borrow them at my leisure. I did my photographing not only in my room but also elsewhere in the Embassy, if I happened to be in a hurry.

But as time went by and the Embassy staff increased, photography became, in Sorge's words, 'really dangerous work'. There was a growing risk that someone might suddenly come into his room. So occasionally, when an official lent him a document, Sorge would ask to be allotted for an hour or so a special room, where he could be certain of being left undisturbed. 'I would tell the man who lent me the document that he might feel embarrassed if other members of the Embassy saw that I had access to confidential material.'

Sorge had also been invited to become leader of the local branch of the Nazi party—an invitation of course that came not from the Embassy but from ardent party members in the Tokyo area. Sorge had no intention of accepting this position. None the less he mentioned the matter to Ott and asked his advice. The very idea of Sorge holding this post amused both Ott and Dirksen; and Ott jokingly told Sorge that he should accept the invitation, because then the Nazi party would include at least one sensible *Führer*.

One day, soon after the February Affair, Ott called Sorge to his office and told him that the Ambassador and himself had learned, from sources in the Japanese Army General Staff, that certain German-Japanese negotiations were in progress in Berlin. The German Foreign Office was not involved in these negotiations, in which the leading participants were Ribbentrop, Oshima, the Japanese military attaché in Berlin, and Admiral Canaris, head of German Military Intelligence. If Sorge is to be believed, Ott asked him for help in encoding a telegram to German Army Headquarters in Berlin, seeking further information on the negotiations.

He asked me to swear not to tell anyone about the matter. I agreed, and I helped him to encode the telegram in his private house. He asked me, rather than a member of the Embassy, to help him, because the matter required the utmost secrecy.

There was no answer from Berlin, and Ott was very annoyed. He spoke to Dirksen, and the latter told him to repeat the request for information, using the army code, but he cautioned him to encode the telegram only with Sorge. So Ott asked me to help him again.

Finally a reply came from German Army Headquarters advising Ott to go to the Japanese General Staff for information. Ott did so, and I heard from him what had transpired. However, I cannot remember the details now. But in general he learned that negotiations were in progress but were highly confidential, since it was important that politicians should not get wind of them.*

If this statement is true it is convincing proof of the trust that Sorge had won for himself. Yet in fairness to Ott and Dirksen, this should be viewed perhaps rather as an indication of Sorge's adamantine deceit than as evidence of gullibility in high places.

Sorge learned more—indirectly at least— about the secret talks in Berlin from Dr. Hack, the German businessman who had been acting as Ribbentrop's unofficial agent in the early stages of the negotiations.†

---

* Sorge is said to have told an acquaintance in the Imperial Hotel one evening in 1936 that he had been helping Ott to encode telegrams to Berlin.
† See p. 162 above.

Hack came on a confidential visit to Tokyo in the spring of 1936, on behalf of Ribbentrop and Admiral Canaris. According to Sorge, Dr. Hack came to Tokyo in order to promote, 'by working outside the Embassy', an atmosphere favourable to the conclusion of a German-Japanese alliance.

Dirksen had gone on leave to Germany when Hack arrived in Japan; and it was probably the Ambassador's absence that made Hack at first reluctant to say much to Colonel Ott about the real purpose of his visit. But he became less guarded, says Sorge, when he learned that Ott had been given some information about the Berlin talks by the Japanese Army General Staff. Dr. Hack then admitted that his basic mission was to discover how far Japan could be regarded as a reliable military partner in an alliance. Hack warned Ott that the whole matter was top secret, pointing out that it would be disconcerting if the Russians came to hear of it. He stressed the fact that as Ribbentrop was not yet Foreign Minister there would be a good deal of opposition within the German Foreign Office to the projected alliance.

Hack's insistence on the need for absolute secrecy was well-founded. He confided to Sorge that Soviet agents were known to have been keeping a watch on the homes of Ribbentrop, Admiral Canaris and General Oshima. It was precisely for this reason, he told Sorge, that he had been acting as a 'go-between', so that communication between the three men might be undetected by Soviet spies.

This was the kind of information that Sorge found droll. In notes that he prepared for the Special Higher Police he claimed that Ribbentrop, Canaris and Oshima were under surveillance as a result of his own report to the Soviet authorities. As soon as Hack told him this story he lost no time in passing it on to the Fourth Bureau. 'I believe', wrote Sorge, 'that Hack, too, was watched thereafter.' Then, for the benefit of the *Tokko* officers if not of posterity, he added, with typical impudence: '*One must carefully refrain from careless talk and not reveal secrets to any outsider, even one's most trusted friends.*'

Meanwhile in Berlin Dirksen found that apparently nobody in the Foreign Office knew anything about the confidential German-Japanese talks. Returning to Japan in the late summer, he told Ott that it was only in the Japanese Embassy at Berlin that one could hear rumours about the progress of the talks. However, while in Berlin Dirksen had called on Ribbentrop, who gave him some details, with permission to pass on the substance of these to the Foreign Office.

Dirksen was more enthusiastic than his military attaché about the prospective Anti-Comintern Pact, which was finally concluded on November 25, 1936. Sorge implies that his own influence played a part in shaping Ott's somewhat lukewarm attitude to the Pact. 'Of course,' said Sorge, 'I was fundamentally opposed to the idea of this alliance; and I did what I could to influence Ambassador von Dirksen and Colonel Ott against it.' He then goes on to outline the arguments he used in this attempt to influence their views. He reminded them of 'Bismarck's policy, the traditional policy of Germany —alliance with Russia against Britain and France'. He pointed out the danger of being allied in a military sense with a Japan caught in the aftermath of the February 26 Affair. The internal state of the Japanese Army was 'quite discreditable'. Moreover, it would be wrong to suppose that the Soviet Government was on the brink of collapse, or that the Red Army was powerless. Finally he declared that the negotiations for a Japanese-German military alliance amounted to 'an adventurous enterprise launched by Oshima and Ribbentrop to further their own personal ambitions'.

My views here did make some effective impression, so far as Ott was concerned; and his attitude was more or less sceptical. But Ambassador von Dirksen was naturally eager for an alliance to be concluded, and on his opinions I could exert no influence.

All this rings true. But it should be remembered that in 1936 Sorge's overt views on a German-Japanese alliance against Russia would have coincided with those to which Colonel Ott in any case inclined, for, like all those strongly sympathetic with Haushofer's geopolitical doctrine, Ott favoured a Berlin-Moscow-Tokyo axis. Sorge is not likely to have done more than to confirm him in his convictions.

In expressing pro-Soviet views, at any date before the outbreak of the German-Russian war, Sorge would by no means have attracted the suspicions of senior officials and service attachés at the German Embassy. For he could remind them of certain facts with which they were all familiar—namely, in Sorge's own words: 'that the German Army, before the advent of Hitler, had obtained great benefits from association with the Soviet Union; that German aircraft and artillery could be said to be the product of Soviet factories'.

The prolonged negotiations in Berlin, transferred late in the day to the official diplomatic level, gave birth at length to an agreement which was little more than a remonstrance and a pledge of mutual co-operation against the activities of the Comintern—a diplomatic counterblast to the proceedings of the Seventh Congress at Moscow in the previous year. There was, however, a secret addendum. Its existence was suspected at the time on all sides, not least the Soviet; and a remarkable volume of international propaganda was pumped out by the Soviet Government and its sympathizers about the villainy of these secret clauses.

It is true that the preamble to these unpublished clauses stated that the Soviet Government (unmentioned in the published text) was furthering the aims of the Comintern and 'intends to employ its army for this purpose'. But the clauses themselves did not go beyond an undertaking by Germany and Japan to consult each other, should one of them become the object of an unprovoked Soviet attack or threat of attack. A commitment of this kind fell far short of a military alliance.* The Russians should have been aware that the secret provisions of the Anti-Comintern Pact were no great menace to Soviet security. This information reached them from Sorge, if from no other quarter.

But a vital if incalculable factor was Stalin's paranoia. In 1936 Berzin—Sorge's former chief—was in disfavour. It would not have been out of character for Stalin, even at this stage, to harbour suspicions of Berzin's protégé in Tokyo.

Thus anxieties in the Kremlin may not have been mitigated, after all, by photocopies from Sorge of two dispatches composed in the German Embassy in Tokyo at about the time that the Anti-Comintern Pact was signed.

One of these, shown to Sorge by Ott, was a detailed report on Japanese military capabilities in the event of a Japanese-Soviet war. It gave particulars of troop strengths in Manchukuo and of defensive positions on the Manchukuo-Soviet border which Ott himself had inspected. Ott reported that these fortifications were incomplete and that in his opinion Japanese forces in Manchukuo were not ready for war. Japanese military equipment was out of date. This rendered

---

* Nevertheless, one authority has pointed out that this commitment 'laid the foundations' for a military alliance, 'and was intended as such by its framers, the Japanese General Staff on the one hand and the Ribbentrop Bureau on the other'. F. C. Jones *Japan's New Order in East Asia* (London, Oxford University Press, 1954), p. 26.

Japan an unreliable partner from a military point of view. Japan required several more years of preparation. It was premature for Japan and Germany to consider hostilities against the Soviet Union.

The other dispatch, prepared by Dirksen and shown by him to Sorge, dealt with the reaction of major personalities in Japan to the agreement with Germany. It explained that the Japanese Government itself was by no means united on the desirability of war with the Soviet Union; and that this was the reason why, on the Japanese side, the negotiations for an alliance culminated merely in a pact against the Comintern. Dirksen admitted that the Pact was not well liked in government circles in Tokyo, but he ended by asserting that this state of affairs would improve in time.

In the matter of the Anti-Comintern Pact, then, the Fourth Bureau —whatever Stalin felt—had good reason to think highly of Sorge's work.

The task of discovering the nature and precise outcome of the German-Japanese negotiations was one that Sorge had to carry out with little help from the members of his ring, although in the autumn of 1936 some useful confirmatory information came from Ozaki, through his contacts on the *Asahi*. Ozaki's standing with the paper was such that, as he put it, he was 'quite free to go into the leader writers' room and editor's office'.

During 1936 Ozaki's position, like Sorge's, was much consolidated. For in the summer he had attended, as a member of the Japanese delegation, the conference of the Institute of Pacific Relations held at Yosemite, California. The fact that he was chosen to join the delegation, led by a former Foreign Minister, Yoshizawa Kenkichi, was in itself recognition of his stature as an authority on Chinese affairs, and of his credentials as a reliable unofficial interpreter, and indeed defender, of Japanese policy towards China.

On the voyage to America Ozaki shared a cabin with a man, younger than himself, with whom he formed a close friendship. This was Saionji Kinkazu, secretary to the Japanese delegation, the grandson of the venerable Prince Saionji, the last *Genro*.* The association with young Saionji and with an old school acquaintance, Ushiba Tomohiko, who was also with the delegation, would have important consequences for Ozaki.

* See p. 107 above.

Not long after he returned from Yosemite Ozaki was invited to a tea party in the Imperial Hotel for the Japanese delegates. Sorge was present. He and Ozaki were formally introduced to each other by a third guest. It was only now that Ozaki discovered that the foreigner whom he knew so well as 'Johnson' was in fact called Dr. Sorge.

This was in September 1936, and Sorge, like Ozaki, had just returned from a trip abroad. In late August he had gone to Peking, ostensibly to attend a conference of foreign journalists; and he had then paid a visit to Inner Mongolia.* His main purpose, however, had been to deliver accumulated material on microfilm to a Soviet courier.

This encounter, arranged beforehand over Klausen's radio, took place at the Temple of Heaven. The courier on this occasion was well known to Sorge:

> This time it was not an ordinary courier whom I met, but my old friend 'Alex' [not the Shanghai 'Alex' of 1930], who had formerly worked for the Secretariat of the Russian Communist Party in Moscow but was then with the Fourth Bureau. At this meeting he was to consult with me about all kinds of problems connected with the work; i.e. about organizational and political problems.

Sorge must have learned from 'Alex' Borovich of the growing terror in Moscow. As for 'the organizational and political problems' to which he refers, speculation does not take one very far. It is probable that finance was discussed. For it was from the autumn of 1936 — after Sorge's visit to Peking — that Klausen, as he confessed, 'was entrusted with full responsibility for the ring's funds, including picking up remittances from Moscow sent through American banks'.

In April, as we have seen, Max Klausen went to Shanghai as Sorge's courier, carrying microfilm material dealing with the February Mutiny among other things. Max had hoped to meet Anna and bring her back with him to Japan. But she was not there, and he had to return alone.

At that moment the unfortunate Anna was in Siberia. It was in March that a man from the Fourth Bureau, who came from time to time to pay her living expenses, told her that she must prepare for a long journey. The destination would be revealed later. She

---

* Sorge stated that in 1937 he wrote for Ott a report on this visit to Inner Mongolia. 'This report contained some confidential material—for example, on the activities in Inner Mongolia of those Japanese who were engaged on military or other special duties.' Procurator's Interrogation of Sorge, No. 35.

was seen off from a Moscow station a few days later by the man from the Bureau and the woman who had kept her under surveillance. They had given her some American currency and told her that her immediate destination was Vladivostok, at the other end of the Trans-Siberian Railway. They explained that the conductor on the train would give her a passport in the name of 'Emma Konig' and that she would be met on her arrival.

It was not an auspicious journey. The train conductor did not supply her with a passport; and the only persons she met on reaching Vladivostok were the Russian security police. They had been questioning her for three days when she was rescued by the man who ought to have met her on the station platform. He gave her some money, the 'Emma Konig' passport, and a steamship ticket to Shanghai. He told her that she must destroy the passport on arrival there. A letter from Max would be awaiting her either in the Central Post Office or at Thomas Cook's.

Anna had to wait for a month before she could board a coastal steamer. When she arrived in Shanghai she discovered that there was nothing for her at the Central Post Office. She went to Thomas Cook's. Yes, she was told, there had been a message for her. But it had been lost. Anna, of course, was no stranger to Shanghai; and she was soon able to rent a room in a friend's home. She gave this address to Cook's and waited for the arrival of Max.

It was not until the second half of July that he found her. Max had come to Shanghai on another courier mission. His pleasure at seeing Anna again can hardly have been greater than his relief, on this occasion, at the fulfilment of his clandestine mission. For on the journey across Japan, to join the Shanghai boat at Nagasaki, he had experienced an unnerving shock. A police detective had boarded the train at Moji, seated himself next to Max and started to ask a great many questions. This was common form in Japan at that time. But Max was much alarmed. Wrapped tightly in a white cloth in his left trouser pocket was a roll of microfilm. He feared that the Tokyo police had sent orders down the line for his arrest. But after about half an hour the detective left the train.

In Shanghai Max finally legitimized his union with Anna by marrying her at the German Consulate. Anna became the wife of a man who, to all appearance, was beginning to launch out on a successful business career. It seems that by now Max had already established the firm of 'M. Klausen & Co.' for the manufacture and sale of printing presses for industrial blue-prints—a profitable concern, employing fourteen men in a small workshop near Shimbashi Station.*

The following year, 1937, was to be fateful—and indeed fatal—for Japan. On July 7 Japanese and Chinese troops exchanged shots near the Marco Polo Bridge outside Peking, and from that date until August 15, 1945, there was to be no peace for either China or Japan.

Most observers, Japanese and European, thought that the clash in north China would be settled, like so many others, by a truce negotiated locally, and no doubt to the disadvantage of the Chinese. But in the summer of 1937 there was a new temper in the Chinese Government. For since the remarkable Sian Affair in the previous year—the kidnapping of Chiang Kai-shek by Chang Hsueh-liang—the Chinese were prepared to put aside their own bitter dissensions in the interest of common resistance to Japan.

Thus, in July 1937, the Chinese turned down Japanese demands for a local settlement, and as the situation grew worse they began to move up reinforcements. The Japanese, on their side, dispatched more troops to north China; and there were signs that, despite announcements from the government that there was to be no extension or aggravation of hostilities, the Japanese army was prepared, if need be, to strike a heavy blow at the Chinese.

The German Embassy in Tokyo, according to Sorge, was taken by surprise, but was not unduly alarmed. Dirksen and Ott (who had now been promoted Major-General) predicted that the fighting would soon come to an end.

Dirksen and Ott were very optimistic, claiming that the Kuomintang were extremely weak. But I maintained that hostilities would last for a long time, that the strength of the Kuomintang should not be underestimated.

Neither Dirksen nor Ott agreed with me. But the course of events turned out to be as I had forecast. So Dirksen and Ott had to admit that I had been right, and my stock in the Embassy rose accordingly.

---

* Max Klausen's first cover was an export-import business; but this was not a success, and he gave it up. The Japanese records do not reveal the exact date at which 'M. Klausen & Co.' was founded. But if an account in an East German newspaper is to be accepted, the firm was in existence before Max brought Anna home from Shanghai. *Neues Deutschland*, November 2, 1964.

Sorge's forecast, of a prolonged Sino-Japanese struggle, was certainly influenced by Ozaki's opinion. But this is not to say that Sorge did not reach his own view independently, partly founded on his conclusion that Japan's national expansion would be towards the south—to China and beyond—rather than the north. But Ozaki's interpretation of events carried immense weight; all the more so because Ozaki was now in close touch with persons in the entourage of Prince Konoye, Prime Minister of Japan since early June.

Ozaki was able to assure Sorge that there was a conflict of views in the Konoye Cabinet as to whether or not the north China operations should be pursued with greater vigour. Ozaki himself was under no illusions about the nature of the fighting. He told Sorge that it would inevitably develop into large-scale war and would not be confined ultimately to Japan and China.

As the fighting in north China spread, in August, to Shanghai, and as local hostilities grew into the war that the Japanese called 'the China Incident', Ozaki and Sorge began to meet more often. They had been meeting once a month. They now tried to see each other once a fortnight, mostly in restaurants. But, in Sorge's words, 'as time passed it was not at all easy to find a new place on each occasion. I rarely went to foreign restaurants, but when I did so it was with Ozaki'.

In Japan there is a myth that Sorge and Ozaki could be seen almost any day, talking together in the lobby of the Imperial Hotel. In reality that was a place that Sorge avoided whenever he wanted to meet Ozaki, for the lobby and bar were always watched by police spies.

Ozaki's association with Prince Konoye's circle arose, in part, from his trip to the conference of the Institute of Pacific Relations at Yosemite. Saionji Kinkazu knew Konoye and indeed often called on him; for at this time, although without any official position, Saionji was on the fringe of the political world. He was interested in politics, and—as he phrased it—he tried 'to help Konoye by encouraging various people to co-operate with him'.

Ushiba, the school acquaintance of Ozaki, who was also at Yosemite, had become one of Konoye's private secretaries. The friendship between Ozaki and Ushiba, formed during the American trip, had been maintained and strengthened after the delegation returned to Japan.

But of more importance, at this period, was Ozaki's association with the Chief Secretary to the Konoye Cabinet, Kazami Akira. Ozaki had come to know Kazami through an organization known as the Showa Research Society (*Showa Kenkyukai*), which was substantially endowed and had its own premises and administrative staff. It was founded in November 1936, by friends and admirers of Prince Konoye. Their general purpose was to study, and recommend action on, problems of Japan's domestic and foreign policy, so that Konoye would have a body of unofficial but instructed opinion to consult when the time came — as his friends believed was inevitable — for him to accept the office of Prime Minister.

Konoye had declined to be Premier after the February Mutiny. This increased, if anything, the popular desire that he should take office. He was a general favourite, for several reasons. The army hoped to use him as a respected figurehead and they believed, too, that he was on their side. Liberals thought he would be some kind of bulwark against fascism. The general public thought of him, since he belonged to the most exalted branch of the ancient Fujiwara house, as disinterested, free from ambition and therefore a refreshing contrast to the generals, admirals, party politicians and bureaucrats who had held the Premiership over the previous ten years. Moreover he was still relatively young. He was forty-six in 1937. His friends and admirers included people of nearly every shade of opinion — from conservatives and right-wing adventurers to socialist intellectuals. He was an opaque, attractive figure, born a thousand years after his time.

The majority of the members of the Showa Research Society, which included some of the best minds in Japan, could be described as sharing a broadly liberal outlook. In the Japanese context this implied an approach to politics not wholly unlike that of many English conservatives between the wars. As patriotic Japanese they esteemed the monarchy and had an instinctive regard for the army and navy. They had developed a certain contempt for many, if not most, of the party politicians. But they feared and resented the overbearing pressures exercised by the two services, especially the army. They were in fact frightened men. It was now both futile and unsafe overtly to oppose the army and its demands. Prudence seemed to dictate a feigned compliance with the drift towards totalitarianism at home and military aggression abroad. Only by this means could the leaders of the Japanese Army be guided back — somehow, some time —

to the path of moderation and common sense. This was an illusion cherished, notably, by Konoye himself.*

Kazami Akira was the leading figure in the China study group of the Showa Research Society, which Ozaki joined in the spring of 1937. Kazami was Ozaki's senior in age—he was born in 1886—and was taking an active interest in Chinese affairs while Ozaki was still a schoolboy. Ozaki felt drawn towards the older man, who clearly reciprocated the friendship. The closeness of the bond between them may be gathered from Ozaki's own words.

Outsiders saw me, I used to feel, as a kind of staff officer to Kazami.

Kazami possessed a wonderful political instinct. He never expressed his own views frankly. He revealed them only in a roundabout way. So it was necessary to understand the way he thought and felt, in order to know what he was really thinking. I developed the ability to judge the general drift of his opinions from his laconic remarks, or from what he left unsaid.

Ozaki goes on:

Sorge often asked me what Kazami's views were on major questions, and I used to give an instant answer. This was because, thanks to my daily contact with Kazami, I was able to imagine what was going on in Kazami's mind.

On the political aspect of the China Incident, then, Ozaki could hardly have been in touch with a better source. And once he had been accepted by Konoye's circle of friends, he was treated virtually as one of themselves.

It was Kazami who invited Ozaki, in the summer of 1938, to become a temporary Cabinet consultant (*naikaku shokutaku*). A *shokutaku* is an expert, or a temporary employee, not carried on the regular pay-roll of the organization which he serves. Thus the term has a very loose meaning. It can refer to a man whose advice may be sought only rarely, on specific subjects. It may also be used for a research assistant who is never consulted on matters of policy. Sorge's position in the German Embassy, long before he was editing the daily news bulletins after the outbreak of the European War, might have been described, without stretching the meaning of the term too far, as that of a *shokutaku*. When Ozaki was appointed Cabinet adviser he received a formal letter containing the phrase: 'Herewith we entrust you with the business of research.'

---

* Some members of the Showa Research Society were nationalists; others were socialists, non-Marxist and Marxist. There is an instructive examination of the society and its membership—including an unsympathetic but able assessment of the 'liberals'—in Chalmers Johnson, *An Instance of Treason* (Stanford University Press, 1964), pp. 114-121.

Richard Sorge in October 1933 at the outset of his mission in Japan

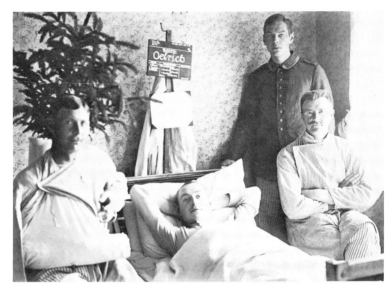

Sorge (rear) in hospital during World War I

Sorge on his 23rd birthday,
October 1918

Sorge in Oslo, April 1928

Ozaki Hotsumi

Branko Vukelic

Max Klausen

Mrs. Kitayabashi

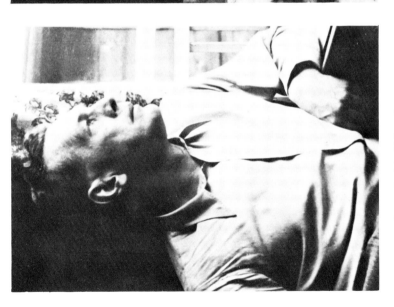

Sorge in Mongolia, September 1936

Sorge in his Tokyo home

Procurator Yoshikawa with one of the authors (G.R.S.)

Hanako-san at Sorge's grave

Hanako-san with her bust of Sorge

The frozen Sea of Okhotsk at Abashiri, where Vukelic died in prison in January 1945

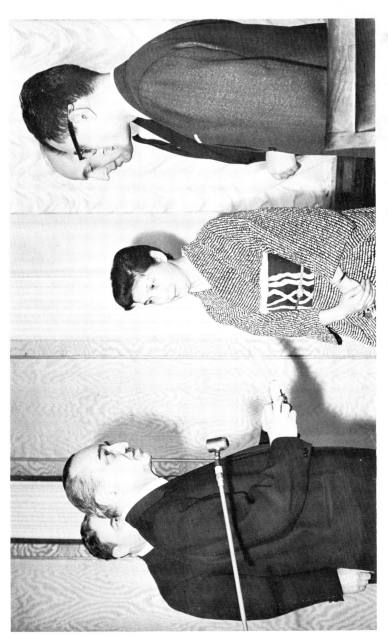

Mrs. Vukelic receiving the Patriotic War Order (First Degree) awarded to her husband, January 1965

But, as Ozaki put it, his actual work 'was to help Kazami; nothing definite was laid down'.

I gave Kazami my views on events in China. . . . It was never my intention to realize my political ideals by exploiting my position as Cabinet consultant. All I did was to offer concrete advice on individual items, while at the same time obtaining accurate and valuable information. Needless to say I passed on such information, acquired in the Cabinet office, to Sorge. I had free access to documents in the office of the Chief Secretary (Kazami) and of the other secretaries.

Throughout the period from the February insurrection of 1936 to the China war in the summer of 1937, Miyagi had not failed to supply Sorge with a flow of information on a great range of subjects, economic and social, as well as political and military. His reports were based on information from sub-agents, on his own observation and reading, and on what he heard from friends or chance acquaintances.

Miyagi could not have the direct access to official secrets that Sorge and Ozaki enjoyed. Nevertheless, he was indefatigable in obtaining intelligence of every kind. If Sorge had been able to start a new life as a scholar in Japan Miyagi would have been his ideal research assistant. The fact that he was an independent artist, with no commitment to the discipline of office hours, may also have meant that he had more time than Sorge and Ozaki to devote to espionage.

After the fighting in China had developed into regular warfare at Shanghai as well as in the north, Miyagi produced for Sorge a lengthy report, covering a number of important subjects. It included, for example, a factual account of the occupation of Peking, as well as a description of what actually occurred at the Marco Polo Bridge. There was a study, too, of a new navy light bomber, and intelligence on the dispatch of reinforcements to Shanghai.

In the first half of 1937 Miyagi gave Sorge a report on military dispositions in the Japanese-Soviet border area of the island of Sakhalin, together with a map showing the location of Japanese camps and barracks. In the summer of that year he was able to hand Sorge a report on the structure of the Japanese Army's Special Service Organs (*Tokumu Kikan*). Of particular interest here to the Fourth Bureau was Miyagi's account of the Special Service Organ at Harbin, Manchukuo. For he was able to describe the training of those recruited by the Harbin office—a training that started with a year's course in such subjects as advanced Russian, demolition techniques, and the art of personal disguise. Potential spies and saboteurs, after this first year, were organized into small groups of three or four men for further training.

During the winter of 1937–38 a Japanese man and woman— Sugimoto Ryokichi and Okada Yoshiko—fled over the border in Sakhalin to the Soviet Union. They belonged to an *avant-garde* theatre group, which was touring Karafuto (the Japanese part of the island). The Japanese-Soviet frontier—a desolate region of block-houses and boundary stones—was a favourite place for tourists to visit, under proper police supervision. In those years no stranger, Western or Japanese, could move a yard in Sakhalin without a policeman at his elbow.

Yet, though accompanied by police, Sugimoto and Okada managed to escape across the snow to Soviet territory. When news of this affair was released it created, naturally enough, a great sensation; and much was said and written about the wickedness and folly of the couple's behaviour. But Sorge's suspicions were aroused. It was odd that Sugimoto and Okada should have been able to outwit the police in this fashion. The episode, as related in the press, seemed so im-probable that Sorge suspected that the fugitives were in fact Japanese spies. So he told Miyagi to look into the affair. Through his sub-agents Miyagi was able to gather enough information to present a fairly exhaustive report. This cleared Sugimoto and Okada, and stated, in Miyagi's words, 'that they were ordinary decent people who had acted out in real life one of their own dramas'.

The movement of prices and wages; the effects of the Kobe flood disaster on local munitions production; the Japanese order of battle at the capture of Wuhan—on these and a host of other subjects Miyagi, in 1937 and 1938, collected important and substantial information.* Some of it may have been available legally, in published form. But from about the beginning of 1938, when it was clear there would be no early end to the war in China, the police did their best to discourage foreigners from buying Japanese books and periodicals

---

* Other subjects included: the design of the special plane (the 'Kamikaze') flown from Tokyo to London in the early spring of 1937; the attack on the U.S.S. *Panay*; the disagreement between General Staff H.Q. and the C.-in-C., Central China (General Matsui), resulting in the latter's recall; the Tokyo visit of Wang Ko-min, head of the puppet régime in Peking; the significance of General Itagaki's appointment as Minister of War; the Japanese left; unemployment; migration of volunteer farmers to Manchukuo. But these are a mere sample of the topics investigated by Miyagi and his sub-agents.

dealing objectively and in detail with the country's economic, political and social problems.* In the background, continually harassing the civil police and pressing them to be ever more vigilant in their surveillance of aliens, were the *Kempeitai* (Military Police), who were always disposed to give the term *gunji himitsu* (military secrets) a wide interpretation.

So, once the China war was well under way, Miyagi was rendering Sorge a service, even when, occasionally, he supplied him with information from open, legitimate sources.

Throughout his years in Tokyo Sorge lived in the same house—No. 30 Nagasaka-cho, Azabu. A middle-aged woman came every day at six in the morning to do the housework and prepare his meals—breakfast and lunch, for he rarely dined at home. She departed in the afternoon, soon after four. When she fell ill and died Sorge engaged another woman of the same type; and she was employed by him up to the time of his arrest. This second maidservant had been a cook at the Soviet Embassy.

The house was what the Japanese in those days called a *bunka jutaku*, or 'an up to date residence'. But by contemporary European or American standards it was rather small. A German writer, who was a frequent caller at the house in 1939, has described it as 'scarcely more than a summer house in a small garden'. But most of the Japanese houses in that secluded district of Azabu—the quarter of the *haute bourgeoisie*—were much the same.

In the upstairs room that Sorge used as his study the untidiness that surrounded him amused or shocked his friends. For there was a seeming chaos of books, maps and papers. One visitor recalls that many of the books were on economics, and notably on Japanese agrarian economics. There was barely space for a couch, a desk and a chair or two. There were one or two fine Japanese prints and some good pieces of bronze and porcelain. The room also contained a gramophone, and a pet owl in a cage.

The house being in the Japanese style, the floors of the rooms were covered from wall to wall with *tatami*, or close-fitted matting. Sorge respected Japanese custom by removing his shoes at the front-door,

---

* For example, from time to time booksellers would be warned not to sell certain books and magazines to foreigners, and they would be asked to report—with a description of the persons concerned—instances of foreigners trying to obtain such publications.

by wearing slippers on the stairs and tiny corridor and by going about in stockinged feet on the matting. He slept in Japanese fashion, on a mattress laid on the *tatami*, with his head on a small round, hard pillow. Prince Urach, in a description of Sorge's bathroom, remembers that 'the fanatically clean Sorge scrubbed himself daily in Japanese fashion and then, drawing up his knees, climbed into the wooden tub filled with hot water'.

Perhaps nobody, apart from Sorge and the cook, saw more of this cramped environment than a girl called Miyake Hanako, whom Sorge met when celebrating his fortieth birthday in October 1935, at the *Rheingold*, where she was employed as a waitress.

Sorge courted Hanako-san with generosity and persistence before she allowed him, several months later, to become her lover. From late in 1936 or early in 1937 Hanako-san spent about half of nearly every week at his house, and they would often leave home together in the early evening— Sorge to the Domei News Agency, Hanako-san to the *Rheingold*.

Hanako had a good voice and was eager to be trained as a singer. Sorge arranged for her to go to a German teacher; and in the early summer of 1937 she left the *Rheingold* and devoted her time to the study of music. She regarded herself as Sorge's common-law wife; and indeed she believes that he regularized the union by registering it at the Azabu ward office. But Sorge, for obvious reasons, could not contemplate married life, and he told Hanako that he must live alone. Nevertheless, for two or three days at a time she came to his house until shortly before his arrest in October 1941. Occasionally they took a holiday together for one or two nights at Atami, the hot-spring seaside resort south-west of Tokyo.

Hanako-san remembers Sorge with devotion; and her loyalty commands respect. She wanted children by him. But he would not hear of it, because, as he told her, his work involved a certain danger. At the time the significance of this remark escaped her. Yet, though she had not the faintest suspicion that he was a Communist agent, she suspected that he might be active in matters outside his work as a journalist.*

---

* Most of the passages in this chapter relating to Hanako-san are based on interviews that one of the authors had with her in Tokyo. Soon after the war she wrote her memories of Sorge, *Ningen Zoruge, Aijin Miyake Hanako no shuki* (The Man Sorge, Memoirs of His Lover Miyake Hanako), Tokyo: Nisshin Shoten, 1949. A later version is Ishii Hanako, *Ai no subete wo Ningen Zoruge* (All My Love for the Man Sorge), Tokyo: Masu Shobo, 1951. (Hanako's mother's name was Miyake, Ishii being the name of her father. Today she is known as Ishii Hanako.)

Hanako-san was a mild Socialist. ('Like many other women I used to read left-wing novels.') And she had been fond of a student who was expelled from his high school, on the eve of graduating, for 'Red' activities. So she was neither shocked nor surprised by the remarks Sorge made on the evils of Japanese militarism, on the miseries suffered by the Japanese working class, or on the detestable nature of the Nazi régime.

Her sympathy with such views was genuine; and it may be that Sorge took care to make sure of this before he allowed himself to become more than fleetingly attached to her.

Hanako-san herself takes a realistic view of the relationships Sorge formed with other women. 'After all,' she remarks, 'he was a bachelor. And it is natural, isn't it, for a famous man to have several mistresses?'

She cannot analyse what his real feelings towards her may have been. But he was unfailingly generous, and indeed gentle, during the six years that she knew him; and he was particularly considerate to her when she was ill. He had a strong will, but he was slow to anger. The only time when she saw him lose control of himself was when he learned of the German attack on the Soviet Union. On that day he wept as though his heart would break.

'Why are you so upset?' she asked.

'Because I am lonely. I have no real friends.'

'But surely you have Ambassador Ott and other good German friends?'

'No, no,' said Sorge. 'They are not my real friends.'

At the end of April, 1938, Major-General Ott was appointed German Ambassador in succession to Dirksen, who had been posted to London. At this time Sorge was about to pay a brief visit to Hong Kong, as he had an accumulation of secret material to be handed to a Soviet agent there. General Ott asked Sorge to act as Embassy courier on this occasion. Sorge, to use his own words, 'was a kind of "double courier" to Manila and then to Hong Kong, with documents from "both sides"'.

He celebrated his return to Japan in his accustomed style, in the *Rheingold* with Urach. At 2 a.m., when the bar finally closed, Sorge mounted his motor-cycle. He had bought the machine from Max Klausen. It had given him much pleasure and his friends some anxiety. For even when he was sober, he rode it at high speed in the narrow, unevenly-surfaced side streets of the city.

With Urach on the pillion Sorge drove to the Imperial Hotel. He asked Urach to join him in raiding the quarters of a resident known to keep a well-stocked bar in his room, but in the event Sorge went up to the room on his own. There he drank a whole bottle of whisky. He then invited his friend to come home with him on the pillion. (This was one of the evenings when Hanako-san was not at Nagasaka-cho.) Urach wisely declined, and Sorge set off alone.

At Toranomon, behind the South Manchurian Railway Building, he turned left off the broad thoroughfare and accelerated up the narrow road that ascends by the wall of the American Embassy — a road that was then little more than a dirt track. He lost control of his machine and crashed head-on into the wall.

Fortunately for Sorge the police box at the gate of the American Embassy was within sound, if not sight, of the accident. Though badly hurt, and bleeding profusely from the injuries to his face, Sorge did not lose consciousness, and he was able to give Urach's name to the police. The latter telephoned the Imperial Hotel, and Urach made his way at once to the scene of the crash. When he arrived, Sorge, who could barely speak, managed to whisper: 'Tell Klausen to come at once.'*

Klausen hastened to St. Luke's Hospital, where Sorge had been taken after the accident. What followed can best be told in Max's own words:

Badly shaken up but undaunted, he handed me the English reports and American currency which he had in his pocket and which outsiders could not be permitted to see, and, as if relieved at last, fainted. From the hospital I went straight to his house to remove all papers relating to our intelligence activities, even taking his diary. A short while later Weise of the DNB (the official German News Service) came to the house to seal all his property so that nobody would touch it. I shuddered when I thought of how our secret work would have been exposed had Weise arrived before I did.

Sorge's jaw had been fractured and he lost most of his front teeth. His face, if not disfigured, bore permanent marks of the accident — perceptible on photographs taken after May 1938. In the words of one observer, 'the scars on Sorge's face made it look like a Japanese theatrical mask — they gave his features an almost demoniacal expression.* When Sorge came out of St. Luke's, the Otts were particularly kind to him, Frau Ott inviting him to stay at their home until he was well again.

In June 1938 — when Sorge had just recovered from his accident — a Soviet general named Lyushkov crossed the Manchurian border and surrendered to the Japanese Kwantung Army with information of the highest importance on the strength of the Soviet military position in the Far East. His revelations might well affect major decisions of Japanese policy towards the Soviet Union.

Lyushkov was sent to Japan and interrogated at the headquarters of the General Staff. He was a senior officer in the GPU, one of whose military functions was the security of the frontiers of the Soviet Union. His defection related to the extensive purge of opposition groups to Stalin, in progress throughout the country, and including the ranks of the GPU itself. Lyushkov had succeeded in arranging for his family to escape to Europe before he fled.

In his first interrogations by the Japanese, Lyushkov explained in detail the structure of the internal opposition in Siberia, and produced a remarkable account of the Soviet internal scene.

This information was passed by the Japanese to Colonel Scholl, who showed it to Sorge. These revelations produced intense excitement in the German Embassy, and Scholl cabled to Berlin with a request for the urgent dispatch of a Soviet specialist to Tokyo to interrogate Lyushkov on matters of particular interest to the German government. At the same time Sorge sent a series of radio messages to Moscow summarizing the preliminary results of Lyushkov's statements to the Japanese.

According to their usual practice, the Moscow Centre maintained a grim silence over the affair.

With the arrival of Admiral Canaris's envoy, Colonel Greiling, from the military counter-intelligence, the second interrogation of Lyushkov began. The results were summarized in a memorandum of about one hundred pages entitled 'Report on a meeting between Lyushkov and the German special envoy, and related information'.

Scholl lent the document to Sorge, who promptly photographed the most significant passages, omitting in particular Lyushkov's

---

* In a letter to his Russian 'wife' Sorge wrote: 'At present I look like a battered knight-bandit.'

description of his own political position, and radioed Moscow tartly for instructions as to whether he should bother to transmit the film. The tone of the reply measures the importance which Moscow felt forced to give to the affair. Dated September 5, 1938, it read as follows:

'Do everything possible and use every available means to get copies of documents to be received by Canaris's special envoy from Japanese army or copies of documents received personally by envoy from Lyushkov. Report at once all such documents obtained.'

The film was duly sent by courier and its contents revealed the extent of the damage which Lyushkov's statements might yet provoke at the highest level.

His main thesis, based on detailed analysis, was that because of wide discontent in the Red Army and the existence of a strong opposition group in Siberia the Soviet military machine in the Far East would collapse in face of a Japanese offensive.

In addition, Lyushkov set out the distribution of the Red Army formations both in Siberia and the Ukraine,* and revealed information of the military wireless codes in use. This technical information was very detailed, especially in regard to the Red Army units in Siberia. The location, organization and equipment of each division — of which Lyushkov stated there were twenty-five — was given in detail.

It must have been clear at once to both the Japanese and German Military Intelligence that the evidence produced by Lyushkov was a reflection of the extent of the purge of the ranks and leadership of the Red Army following the trials of Marshal Tukhachevsky and other senior officers, and was of startling importance in building up an assessment of the impact of these events on the military strength of Russia. Sorge was not exaggerating when he commented later: 'One consequence of Lyushkov's report was a danger of joint Japanese-German military action against the Soviet Union.' It was, within the possibilities of one intelligence mission, Sorge's main task to contribute towards the avoidance of such a disaster.

Sorge's personal reactions to the affair throw a corner of light on the extreme dedication of his own convictions.

I considered that Lyushkov had defected not only because he was discontented with the treatment which he had received from the Soviet

---

* Either Lyushkov had also served previously on the European frontiers of the Soviet Union, or as a senior GPU officer had access to the Soviet order of battle in that region.

authorities, and due to some offence in Siberia, but also because just at that time the purge was being enforced within the ranks of the GPU and he was afraid that he would be among the victims. I assumed that Lyushkov gave a political reason for his defection only because he had friends in the opposition groups in Siberia.

A traitor's statements and activities are always stereotyped, and therefore I did not have much interest in Lyushkov.

Having, however, seen the first revelations of the GPU 'traitor' to the Japanese General Staff, Sorge was immediately aware of the impact which they might have in governing circles in Japan and Germany.

He was alarmed at the first Japanese reactions. The German Embassy was apparently told that 'the Soviet Union was on the verge of disintegration'. Sorge had always considered that his special prestige in Embassy circles should be exploited politically, and in a propaganda sense, in spite of Moscow's cold indifference to this self-appointed and supplementary rôle, and on this occasion he countered the Japanese arguments 'by pointing out that Lyushkov was an unreliable and minor figure'.

It was dangerous to judge Russia's internal situation from statements made by a man like this. Lyushkov's remarks, I said, were just the kind of thing that one found in anti-Nazi books written by German refugees. These often suggested that the Nazi régime faced imminent collapse.

Lyushkov may have been in initial charge of the GPU purge of the Soviet Far Eastern Army, which was under the command of Marshal Blücher who, formerly, under the alias of 'Galen' had been the leading Soviet military expert on Borodin's staff in China in 1923 and adviser to a promising Chinese general, Chiang Kai-shek.*

Between June 1938, when Lyushkov defected, and the end of the year when Sorge had transmitted to Moscow the results of the enquiry in Tokyo into the former's extensive revelations, Blücher had vanished without trace. His disappearance and the massive extermination of the opposition in the ranks of the Soviet army which

---

* It is interesting to note that after handing over the Fourth Bureau to Uritsky, Berzin was posted to the Far Eastern Command as deputy to General Blücher. Subsequently Berzin was sent to Spain as head of the Soviet military mission to the Republican government. He was recalled to Moscow in 1937, and shot. In 1964 General Berzin was officially rehabilitated.

coincided with his secret execution may well be related directly to Lyushkov's defection and the light which Sorge had been able to shed on it.*

In the event of a Japanese attack on the Siberian border, the Japanese estimate of Soviet military forces was, thanks to Sorge, available in Moscow.

There is no direct evidence of the evaluation of the Lyushkov material by Japanese and German military experts, but the following year a large-scale trial of strength on the borders of Manchukuo and Outer Mongolia, in the region of Nomonhan, was mounted, with disastrous results, by the Kwantung Army. There is a tempting hint in a later testimony by a leading procurator in the Sorge case, Yoshikawa Mitsusada, that there was a connection between the failure of this operation, based as it was on Lyushkov's information, and Sorge's transmission to Russia of the Japanese evaluation of Soviet strength. After describing the dispatch by Sorge of the film of the Lyushkov material, this official went on: 'Later the Nomonhan Incident occurred.'

Sorge's activity in connection with the Lyushkov affair was one of the greatest services he rendered to the Fourth Bureau during his Japan mission.†

Other members of the Sorge ring were also able to provide valuable intelligence of Japanese intentions, as well as some purely military information, during this period.

About a month after Lyushkov defected, a sharp Japanese-Soviet clash occurred on a hill known as Changkufeng, south-west of Vladivostok, on the borders of Korea, Manchukuo and Soviet Far Eastern territory. Fighting continued for a month, on a heavy scale. But on the basis of information from Ozaki — now a Cabinet consultant — and Miyagi, who pressed his sub-agents to find out everything possible about troop movements, Sorge was able to assure Moscow that neither the Japanese Government nor the Japanese army would allow the affair to develop into real war.

---

* In an article entitled 'The Far Eastern Red Army' in *Contemporary Japan*, Vol. VIII, No. 8 (October 1939) reprinted from *Kaizo* (September 1939) Lyushkov refers to the sudden disappearance of Blücher 'at the time of Changkufeng'. The Changkufeng clash between the Japanese and the Russians took place between mid-July and mid-August, 1938—in other words soon after Lyushkov's defection. This seems to support the theory that Blücher's 'disappearance' and Lyushkov's flight were not unrelated.

† There are some indications that Lyushkov may have been shot by the Japanese in August 1945.

At the time of the more serious and prolonged hostilities at Nomonhan Ozaki was out of touch with the Cabinet secretariat, Konoye having been succeeded as Premier in January 1939 by Baron Hiranuma. But from the beginning of June 1939 he was employed as consultant to the Investigation Department of the South Manchurian Railway, in their Tokyo branch, and in this new appointment he was well placed so far as intelligence from Manchukuo was concerned. Again he was able to assure Sorge that the government had no wish to risk full-scale war with Russia.

Miyagi, for his part, supplied Sorge with much information on the military reasons for the Japanese defeat at Nomonhan, on the types of weapon and other equipment used in the fighting, and on popular morale.

Vukelic, who was now a correspondent for the French news agency Havas, was invited with other journalists to visit the battlefield. He was able to give Sorge only superficial information about Japanese airfields and military equipment. But it seems that Sorge may have warned him to be most careful not to do anything that might attract attention, since the trip was under official Japanese Army sponsorship.*

In talking with Ott, Sorge made the most of Japan's discomfiture at Nomonhan.

I pointed out that statements by Lyushkov and others, about the supposed weakness of the Red Army, were now exposed as lies. If the Japanese Army wanted to drive the Red Army from its present positions, then 400–500 tanks would be required; and this was beyond Japan's industrial capacity. Germany ought to study the whole Nomonhan Incident more deeply and should reject the old idea that the Red Army was incapable of putting up serious resistance.

Then, in what appears to have been a whimsical aside to the procurator, Sorge remarked: 'However, I suppose Germany accepted Lyushkov's ideas rather than my own.'

---

* This at least is the inference to be drawn from a question by the Preliminary Judge, who asked Sorge whether it was true that he had warned Vukelic in this sense. Sorge's reply was: 'I don't really remember. But it is very probable.' Preliminary Judge's

Chapter 12

TECHNICAL OPERATIONS

'Six dangerous years passed uneventfully.' KLAUSEN

RICHARD SORGE was a highly experienced Soviet Intelligence Officer with long years of training in secret work behind him in Germany, in Moscow, in Scandinavia and, briefly, in England. The establishment of an impeccable cover was a prerequisite for undertaking his missions. Before coming to Japan Sorge had built up with typical thoroughness, and some personal risk to himself, his journalist cover during his underground visit to Berlin in June 1933. During his assignment in Japan, it was as correspondent of the *Frankfurter Zeitung* that he achieved his reputation as a specialist newspaper man on Far Eastern affairs, and his overt work was of central importance in establishing relations with members of the German Embassy in Tokyo, and was his essential cover.

At the time of the official German enquiry into Sorge's antecedents, initiated in November 1941, the German Foreign Office sought to establish the facts leading to the employment of Sorge by the *Frankfurter Zeitung*. The editor of the day was quite firm in his statements, and denied in categorical terms any suggestion that Sorge had been in touch with the paper before his departure for Japan.

Until March 1936 we were entirely ignorant of Mr. Sorge's existence in Tokyo. In March, we received from him a letter dated February 4, 1936, and addressed to Editor-in-Chief Dr. Kirchner in Berlin. In this Mr. Sorge said that various people in the German Embassy in Tokyo had drawn his attention to the fact that we had then no correspondent there; he therefore took the liberty of asking whether we would be interested in receiving occasional articles from him on matters of political, economic or general interest relative to Japan or Manchukuo. Should we wish for personal references, the following would be glad to supply details: Ambassador Dirksen, Tokyo; and Colonel Ott, military attaché of the German Embassy in Tokyo. The letter was accompanied by a preliminary article.

On March 4 Mr. Sorge, who had not yet received a reply, sent a further article with a brief covering letter. In their reply, dated April 4, 1936, the paper stated that they would be pleased if Mr. Sorge continued to work for them; but asked him to send as many descriptive articles on Japan as possible. No other arrangements were entered into. Mr. Sorge dispatched articles from time to time, including some on specific themes especially commissioned by the paper. In a letter dated October 7, 1936, Mr. Sorge said that the signature we had chosen for his articles, 'from a correspondent', did not satisfy him, and he asked us either to omit it or to select some more usual appellation. The paper thereupon replied that they would willingly designate him their correspondent, but could do this only if they were assured that he belonged to the German Press Association. Later, on March 4, 1937, the paper learned from Mr. Sorge that he had applied for membership of the Press Association, but that the long distances involved had delayed the proceedings. There were no objective difficulties, but until all formalities were complete it seemed advisable to describe him as a contributor, not a correspondent. On March 28, 1937, Mr. Sorge added that in order to speed up his enrolment in the Press Association he had asked the German Embassy in Tokyo to help by providing him with certain papers (he was a German domiciled abroad) and that the Embassy had kindly promised its support. A good deal later, on March 14, 1940, the paper learned that Mr. Sorge had been admitted to the German Press Association as a leader writer.

As regards any contractual relationship between the paper and Mr. Sorge, this can be said to have been non-existent. Moreover, the paper took up none of the references cited by Mr. Sorge in February 1936, it being assumed that Mr. Sorge would not have submitted such references unless they had actually been available to him. It also emerged in the course of correspondence with him that he frequently sent articles to Germany through the Embassy. More important, however, was the impression gained both from correspondence with Mr. Sorge and from his journalistic work that he was a most serious and thoughtful person, gifted with both an understanding of a newspaperman's job and political insight. In addition, conversations with persons returning from Japan revealed that Sorge was indeed highly esteemed in the Embassy and was considered one of the best-informed people in Tokyo.

No sort of agreement involving a closer relationship was entered into with Mr. Sorge. In several letters he was given to understand that his work was highly valued by the paper. He drew no fixed salary, but received only honoraria for individual articles and telegrams. Telegraphic reporting only increased in scope after the outbreak of war. In June 1941 we learned that Mr. Sorge had incurred certain expenses while travelling on behalf of the paper; he was therefore given an expense account, enabling him to move about freely in the interests of the paper pending a final settlement.

To sum up, it can be stated that until very recently Mr. Sorge was a contributor to the *Frankfurter Zeitung* in a legal and formal sense; but was not bound to it by any contractual relationship. The close connection that grew up as the years went by could be ascribed solely to the quality of his contributions. In all the years that passed since his earliest letters, the paper never took up a reference about him; but Mr. Sorge cited these references only in those letters. Whatever oral information on Mr. Sorge we later received served only to confirm our own impression of him, as one enjoying the esteem and full confidence of the German Embassy in Tokyo.

This is the evidence as taken from our records; it is exhaustive, since nothing further is contained in them.

After his arrival in Japan Sorge extended his public respectability by applying to join the Nazi party in the autumn of 1933. He was admitted in October of the following year, and such was the casual and superficial attitude of the bureaucrats in the foreign organization of the party in Berlin that his card, which still exists, contains nothing except his bare name and address in Tokyo, China (the latter word deleted in pencil, and 'Japan' inserted). Such was Sorge's official party record.

Finally, he completed his image as a loyal Nazi journalist by joining the Press Association of the party, in 1940.

Of the other chief members of Sorge's ring only Klausen had difficulty in establishing satisfactory 'cover'. Ozaki had been associated from the beginning with *Asahi*, the most reputable paper in Japan. Miyagi, who was among hundreds of his compatriots in returning to Japan after a period in the United States, continued his previous occupation as a painter. Vukelic, like Sorge himself, had arranged to do work for Western newspapers; later he obtained his post in the French Havas News Agency in Tokyo. Bernhardt, the wireless operator, ran an import-export business in Yokohama during his brief and ineffectual stay in Japan. Klausen, however, was slower to find an overt occupation. Sorge 'tried to find a legitimate cover for him', and Klausen eventually set up a joint printing firm and traded in blueprint duplicates. This became a joint stock company with a branch in Mukden and undertook work for large Japanese firms and the armed services. As a business, however, it had the drawback from the point of view of espionage of achieving financial success. It was this, together with the patient resistance of his wife Anna to underground work, which ultimately weakened Klausen's energy and efficiency as a member of the ring.

On arrival in Japan in November 1935 Klausen was instructed by Sorge, as his first task, to build a radio set. Klausen had discussed with his predecessor 'Bernhardt' in Moscow the scope for buying parts in Tokyo. He had brought two tubes from America; he needed another ten. These and other necessary equipment he was able to collect from shops on the Ginza dealing in radio parts. He obtained copper wire from a hardware store to build the tuning coils. As one of the most experienced instructors of the Moscow radio school, and inventor of improved radio sets for clandestine work, Klausen brought great expertise to his work as well as the practical knowledge of operating conditions from his China mission.

He faced cheerfully, at least in the early stages, the practical difficulties of operating. His first task was to dispose of the clumsy transmitter built by 'Bernhardt', and together with Vukelic he took a boat trip on Lake Yamanaka and dumped it in its deep waters. This adventure took place in May 1936. In Klausen's words:

The radio set which my predecessor Bernhardt had left at Vukelic's house was so bulky and conspicuous that we thought we had better get rid of it. Vukelic and I decided to toss it into a nearby lake, and around 0700 hours one day we boarded a train at Shinjuku dressed as hikers, each carrying a stick and a rucksack loaded with a receiver, three transmission transformers and other parts. We were worried about baggage inspection *en route*, but nothing happened, and at Otsuki station we transferred to an electric car which took us to Yoshida. From there we took a taxi to a hotel on Lake Yamanaka. The hotel employees who tried to help us with our rucksacks were surprised by their weight and asked what was in them. We were taken off guard, but managed to save ourselves further embarrassment by replying without hesitation, 'We brought along half a dozen bottles of beer.' 'We have plenty of beer here,' they said, hurrying off to our rooms with our packs. We were afraid that if someone should discover what was inside he might notify the police, so we talked things over, rowed out to the middle of the lake in a rented boat and tossed everything away. We returned to Tokyo relieved of a heavy burden indeed. Later, when I talked to Sorge about it, he commented curtly, 'You should have got rid of it in Tokyo instead of going so far away.'

By the middle of February 1936 Klausen had assembled the set, and was told by Sorge to begin operating from the house of Gunther Stein. He brought the transmitter and receiver in a black bag from his house to Stein's on each occasion. The set was installed, with an inside aerial to obviate attracting notice from the street, on the second floor to avoid interference from earth magnetism. He needed less than ten minutes to prepare the set for transmitting and receiving and less than five minutes to dismantle it. Until August 1938 when Stein left Japan, Klausen worked regularly from this house. Thereafter he worked from his own house, from Vukelic's, and from the house of the latter's former wife Edith, alternating between these addresses to avoid possible detection. His training in Moscow and experience in Shanghai had taught him to choose a location in densely populated sections of the city to confuse direction finding by the Japanese security services, and to operate from the second floor of wooden houses to facilitate transmission and limit magnetic interference, such as had hampered his activities in the early days in Canton and Shanghai.

Klausen's radio operations from Tokyo were a masterly technical achievement, and a valuable experiment and model for the Soviet network as a whole. His superiors indicated their impatient interest in the lessons of his original Japanese experience in a message sent to Klausen in September 1938. 'How and where are you keeping W/T sets? How many and which houses are used for W/T operations? Where can material be purchased? What parts are best? Can sets be operated from Jap houses and farmhouses? How are these operations being camouflaged? This seems to be a very difficult operation. What is being done to overcome it?'

The exact location of the Soviet station which controlled the clandestine missions of the Fourth Bureau abroad was not known to the radio operators themselves, but only referred to under the code name 'Wiesbaden'.

According to the Japanese Ministry of Communications, whose specialist services intercepted some messages between 'Wiesbaden' and an unidentified set in the Tokyo area as early as 1937, the former station was located in the Shanghai area up to 1940. This would have been a relay station, for technical reasons, which passed on the messages to a main radio establishment in the Soviet Far East, probably Vladivostok or Khabarovsk. After 1940 communications were maintained direct between the Vladivostok area and Klausen's set in Tokyo.*

For the first two years the volume of traffic was intermittent and each radio contact was initiated on the Soviet side. In July 1938, however, Klausen received the following message: 'From August 1 we shall be prepared to receive your messages during first fifteen minutes of every hour.'†

The call signals were those assigned to amateur Chinese stations by international convention. Contact was smooth, and usually established within ten minutes of operating. Klausen and his Soviet base were therefore working ostensibly on an amateur basis on illegal wavelengths. Although the existence of this traffic had been detected by the Japanese agencies concerned, they could not decipher those messages which they intercepted or locate the set operating in the Tokyo area. The Japanese lacked mobile equipment for radio patrols; and direction-finding from fixed points in the city could never narrow the radius of detection to less than two kilometres.

In addition to messages sent by radio, the Sorge ring maintained communications with Moscow by courier via Shanghai and Hong Kong. Bulky reports recorded on film were handed over to Soviet agents, and funds transmitted by them to the couriers.

Klausen, for instance, undertook two such journeys. In July 1936 Sorge told him that, under instructions from Moscow, certain films 'which were photographic copies of valuable documents belonging to the German embassy' were to be delivered to a bookshop in Shanghai. Klausen was given prearranged instructions to hand over the material to the woman manager. This rendezvous was unknown to Klausen. It was the Zeitgeist Bookshop run by Mrs. Irene Wiedemeyer, and was the mail drop and contact point for Soviet agents in the Far East.

---

* Sorge's version of these arrangements was that at one time an attempt had been made to set up a permanent radio contact in Shanghai in addition to the Vladivostok link. It was to be a relay station only, and not intended to set up links in China. 'Except for two or three times, attempts to contact Shanghai failed. On orders from Moscow, we tried to make direct contact with Khabarovsk, but this was discontinued by Klausen in order to prevent our communications being monitored.'

† This was the first message of the ring intercepted by the Japanese communications authorities from their listening station in Korea.

It had already been actively used by Sorge in the days of his China mission.

On his second trip in June 1939 Klausen was given elaborate instructions to contact a Soviet courier in the ground floor café of the Palace Hotel in Shanghai. 'For identification, I was to place a green book on the left-hand side of my table and the other person was to put a yellow book and a pair of gloves on the right side of his table.' No contact was to be made, but both men were to memorize each other's faces and meet in the evening on the street in the French Concession. Klausen was to accost the stranger and ask the way to a certain street. A quick exchange then took place—a package of 18 or 19 rolls of film and 6,000 U.S. dollars. Klausen describes the shadowy encounter. 'He was around forty-four or forty-five, broad-shouldered, a Russian or a Balt. He had driven alone to the street where we were to meet, and was awaiting me. He drove off as soon as we had concluded our business. Of course, we did not engage in any personal conversation.'

Klausen's wife, Anna, was also reluctantly employed as a courier on the Shanghai and Hong Kong routes on two occasions in 1937 and 1938.

Representatives of Soviet special agencies working abroad normally received strict routine instructions—to have no contact with the diplomatic missions of the Soviet government in the countries in which they were operating. After the outbreak of the European war in September 1939, however, and the attendant risks of travel to the International Settlement in Shanghai and the British colony of Hong Kong, Sorge was instructed to risk the establishment of contact with Soviet emissaries in Japan.

In January 1940 the following instructions from Moscow were received, addressed to Klausen. 'You will henceforth receive funds from, and maintain liaison with, a comrade in Tokyo. He will send you two tickets for the Imperial Theatre . . . the man seated next to you will be the comrade.' The two tickets appeared shortly afterwards in Klausen's post-box at the Tokyo Central Post Office and, together with his wife, he kept the rendezvous. In the darkness of the theatre Klausen's neighbour passed him a white handkerchief containing banknotes, and left his seat.

A similar contact in another theatre enabled Klausen to hand over seventy rolls of film and receive further funds. On the next occasion, as Klausen was ill, Sorge himself kept the rendezvous. On radio instructions Klausen subsequently went to a restaurant, where two men were awaiting him, and he was told that one of them would henceforth be his contact.

Further meetings took place either at Klausen's house or at his office. The Russian identified himself as 'Serge' and from his conversation Klausen deduced that he was a member of the Soviet Embassy in Tokyo. As the activities of the Sorge ring were intensified by the need for accurate and detailed information on Japanese policy towards the Soviet Union after the outbreak of the European war, the meetings between 'Serge' and Klausen became more frequent.

On one occasion, on August 6, 1941, there was a meeting between 'Serge' and Klausen, in the latter's office, at which Sorge was also present. 'I seem to recall that Sorge and 'Serge' argued about the Russo-German war. The latter said that he knew Sorge from a photograph which he had seen in Moscow.'

Klausen met 'Serge' for the last time on October 10, 1941, and handed over a map of the Tokyo, Kawasaki and Yokohama areas, marked with the anti-aircraft and searchlight positions. This proved to be Klausen's last mission. The two men fixed a rendezvous for November 20 which Klausen never kept. He was arrested on October 18.

During his subsequent interrogation he was shown two photographs by the Japanese investigating officer. The first was of Klausen's original contact in the Imperial Theatre, who had been identified by the Japanese as a Consul at the Soviet Embassy named Vutkevitch. The second contact—'Serge' to Klausen—was the Soviet Second Secretary and Consul, Viktor Sergevitch Zaitsev, a member of the Russian Military Intelligence.*

After the arrests of the Sorge group, he quietly left Japan. In 1943 he appeared as 'Second Secretary' in the Soviet Embassy in Canberra, where one of his colleagues, Petrov, later defected.† In 1947 he was accredited as press attaché to the Soviet Embassy in Washington. It is perhaps significant, however, that by that date

---

* Klausen's memory of his meetings with these Soviet officials was refreshed and clarified when he was confronted with two volumes of his 1941 diary which the Japanese police had confiscated in his house.

† In reality Zaitsev was the first known representative appointed to Australia of the GRU (Chief Military Intelligence Directorate of the Soviet Armed Forces, previously the Fourth Bureau).

American authorities were still in the early stages of investigating the Sorge Case, and it is doubtful whether any connection would have been apparent between the new Soviet press attaché in Washington and Richard Sorge.

'Before I left on my missions to China and Japan,' Sorge confessed, 'the codes which I was to use were explained to me at my hotel by a man from the Fourth Bureau. We spent a full day going over the instructions.'

The work of ciphering and deciphering was the closely guarded secret and the responsibility of the head of each mission abroad. The system adopted by Soviet agents was based on a simple chart substituting single or double figures for the letters of the alphabet for a combination. It was one which could easily be memorized. In order to complicate the breaking of the code an arbitrary list of figures was added to the ciphers of the coded message. These were taken at random from the pages of the German Statistical Year Book, the exact passage being identified in the message.

The ingenuity of this system lay in the infinitive variety of figures available in the Year Book, and also in the fact that this publication was to be found in almost every German household in Japan, so that, provided the copy in use bore no suspicious markings and all messages were burnt after transmission or receipt, a house search by the police would yield no clue of the operation.

As the work, and therefore traffic, of the ring increased, Sorge obtained exceptional permission from Moscow after 1938 to entrust the ciphering work to Klausen.

The system proved to be secure during the period of operations of the group, and there is no evidence to suggest that the Japanese succeeded in breaking the code of those messages at the time.

The Sorge group in Japan was financed from Moscow in the early stages by cash transmitted through Soviet couriers at prearranged meetings in Shanghai or Hong Kong, by drafts through the National City Bank of New York or the American Express to private accounts in Japanese banks,* and after 1940 through clandestine meetings with Soviet Embassy representatives in Tokyo. Klausen was in charge of

* Japanese exchange control became more extensive early in 1940.

the accounts, which were rendered once or twice a year to Moscow in photostat by courier. The total sums received between 1936 and 1941 totalled about $40,000.

Sorge had originally been told by the Fourth Bureau that he must not spend more than $1,000 a month on the expenses of the group. This niggardly sum was mainly spent on rents and current expenses for the main members. Ozaki drew no allowance except when travelling. Small sums were needed to meet repairs to the radio set, and occasional payments to minor informants of Ozaki and Miyagi. Sorge, Vukelic and Ozaki lived on their salaries as journalists, Miyagi as an artist, and Klausen as a businessman.

Sorge was never in possession of sufficient current funds from Moscow to meet the smallest emergency. When it was decided to send Edith Vukelic to Australia after her divorce a special sum of $400 had to be authorized by Moscow and paid over by Zaitsev in Tokyo for this operation.

Even the original estimate of $1,000 a month was successively cut, and Sorge was told to make further economies. Klausen was ordered by cable at the end of 1940 to use the profits from his firm 'as funds for the ring', and this action of the Fourth Bureau accelerated his ideological disenchantment. From this moment he became idle in making up the accounts and, worse still, dilatory in destroying messages already received and sent, and in sending material awaiting radio transmission. The financial meanness of the Soviet agency thus directly created a security risk, and provided key evidence to the Japanese police when Klausen's house was searched at the time of his arrest.

Only Sorge himself and Klausen, who had been recruited directly by the Fourth Bureau in Germany, were aware of the identity of their superiors. Miyagi had been active in the Japanese section of the American Communist Party and assigned 'a brief mission' in Japan by an unidentified Comintern agent. He severed connections with the American party, and had strict instructions not to contact Japanese comrades in Tokyo.

At first Miyagi thought that Sorge and himself were the only members of the group, but as the months passed he identified Vukelic, Ozaki and Klausen as completing the ring.

Like Miyagi, Vukelic assumed that he had been recruited, in Paris, into 'an organization directly belonging to the Comintern' with no connections with any national Communist parties. 'Sorge never revealed the inside story of the precise character of our organization.'

Ozaki's impressions of the work of the group were more explicit. He had already learnt from Agnes Smedley in Shanghai that he had been registered under the code name 'Otto' with the Soviet authorities in Moscow, and that he was working for some section of the Comintern.

For practical reasons of security, Sorge limited contacts between members of the group. Klausen as the radio-operator and treasurer was aware of at least the aliases and code names of each member, but even he did not know the real identity of Ozaki until the last days of the existence of the ring; and he learnt Miyagi's name only after his arrest. Ozaki only met Klausen once and was unaware of his name. He never saw Vukelic.

Sorge's arrangements to meet his assistants were always elaborately planned. He alone was in direct touch with the main members of the group. With Klausen this presented the least difficulty. They were both members of the German Club in Tokyo: it was normal that they should meet as compatriots. The main meetings took place at Sorge's house. The only danger was the handing over of documentary material and the chance of a bureaucratic and routine check by the Japanese police of Klausen's car. Klausen was well trained in using different routes each time that he drove to Sorge's house, and a simple code was arranged for an emergency, which might also imply the presence of a mistress. As Sorge once told Klausen, 'When I have my gate lamp lighted please don't come in because it means I have a visitor.'

In principle, all rendezvous were fixed in advance, and often openly by telephone.

Sorge and Vukelic were fellow European journalists, and they met frequently and openly at the latter's house until his divorce from Edith Vukelic. Indeed, there seemed little point in maintaining strict security rules for routine contacts between the three European members of the group. As Sorge put it, 'Strict adherence over a long period to this theoretical principle was difficult and a waste of time.'

Meetings between the European and Japanese agents presented a more serious risk of detection merely because it was a routine habit of the police to discourage intercourse between foreigners and the local population.

Sorge deliberately kept routine contacts with Ozaki and Miyagi as far as practicably possible in his own hands, and elaborate arrangements were made to meet in discreet restaurants in Tokyo, frequently changing the rendezvous, 'but as time passed it was not at all easy to find a new place on each occasion'.

Sorge and Ozaki used to meet regularly once a month, but as the work increased under the pressure of international events they were obliged to contact each other more often. After the German attack on Russia they met every Monday. Ozaki usually booked a table in his own name, and occasionally they also met at the Asia Restaurant in the South Manchurian Railway building where Ozaki had an office.

After the outbreak of the European war the group decided that, owing to a stricter supervision of foreigners in Tokyo, it would be less risky to meet in Sorge's house. Although this was located almost next door to a police station and was clearly under constant routine surveillance, it was natural for Ozaki as a leading newspaperman to call on a distinguished German colleague, and the risk of conversations being overheard was much less in a private house than in a Japanese restaurant.

Ozaki and Miyagi continued to meet at frequent intervals in restaurants, and after a time invented a cover which enabled Miyagi to call at Ozaki's house to give painting lessons to his daughter.

During the nine years of the ring's operations—except possibly for the last months in the case of Sorge himself—there is no evidence to show that the movements of its chief individual members, and their meetings, were the subject of any special surveillance or suspicion on the part of the Japanese police.

The main and constant danger which overshadowed the daily activities of each member was the discovery of compromising material as the result of an accidental or routine check, either in a car or at one of the houses of the group.

Klausen was perhaps the most exposed. On his frequent journeys by car he carried his transmitter in a black bag to the various private houses from which he operated the set. He had several close shaves.

One such episode took place in the autumn of 1937.

I had taken a taxi from my neighbourhood as usual to radio some messages to Moscow, and upon my arrival at Vukelic's home around 1400 or 1500 hours, I discovered that a large wallet I had put in my left trouser pocket was gone. I darted outside but the taxi had already disappeared. The wallet contained 230 yen in Japanese currency, my driver's licence with photo attached, and Sorge's English text of a financial report that we were to send to Moscow. It was to be photographed at Vukelic's house. The other code messages, fortunately, were safely tucked away in my old black bag. I must have forgotten my wallet in the car because I am certain that I took it out and opened it. Of course, I didn't know the licence number of the car. I didn't know what to do, so I told Vukelic I had lost my wallet and a large sum of money and asked his advice. He was talkative by nature, and I was afraid he would tell Sorge about the financial report, so I kept it secret. The following day, I had the audacity to report my loss to the Lost and Found Department of the Metropolitan Police. I said that I had lost some Japanese currency, my driver's licence and a scrap of paper with English writing on it. The wallet was never recovered. I was in a state of constant anxiety for several days.

Ozaki was passing to Sorge highly sensitive information from Japanese government circles, but insisted on doing so verbally; and the results would be drafted, after discussion between the two men, by Sorge as messages to be radioed direct by Klausen. Materials and documents obtained from time to time by Ozaki were handed by him to Miyagi for translation into English and then brought by the latter to Sorge.

Material obtained by Sorge from the German Embassy would be filmed either by himself in the building, or by Vukelic if the documents were temporarily in his house, and, together with other 'borrowed' documentary material collected by the group, handed from time to time by arrangement to Soviet couriers.

There was no hitch in these arrangements until the arrest of the group, when compromising material was found in each of the houses of the main members. This formed the preliminary basis of the charges and interrogations.

A theoretical security risk to the ring also lay in the varying degrees of complicity in their work of their womenfolk. While in prison Sorge wrote smugly: 'Women are absolutely unfit for espionage work. They have no understanding of political and other affairs, and I have never received satisfactory information from them. Since they were useless to me, I did not employ them in my group.'

It seems true that in Sorge's own extensive relations with women during his stay in Tokyo there was no element of espionage, and his private affairs never touched upon this activity.

The Sorge ring was able to operate with impunity, with the sole exception of the intercepting by the Japanese communications experts of unidentified messages, over a period of eight years. The technical achievement of the ring was masterly. As Sorge wrote later: 'I myself was surprised that I was able to do secret work in Japan for years without being caught by the authorities. I believe that my group [the foreign members] and I escaped because we had legitimate occupations which gave us good social standing and inspired confidence in us. I believe that all members of foreign spy rings should have occupations such as newspaper correspondents, missionaries, business representatives, etc. The police did not pay much attention to us beyond sending plain-clothes men to our houses to question the servants. I was never shadowed. I never feared that our secret work would be exposed by the foreign members in the group, but I worried a good deal over the possibility that we should be discovered through our Japanese agents, and just as I expected this was what happened.'

Chapter 13

SIBERIA OR THE PACIFIC?

TRIUMPH AT THE ELEVENTH HOUR

'This phrase, permanent expansion, is my own invention. It came to me from Trotsky's phrase "permanent revolution".' SORGE TO THE JUDGE

From the outbreak of the European War (September 1939)
to the return of Matsuoka from Europe (April 1941)

WITH the outbreak of the war in Europe at the beginning of September 1939, Sorge became for the first time formally associated with the German Embassy. He took over the editing of the news bulletin compiled from the official news services cabled from Berlin, and established a daily routine unaffected by late nights in the bars of Tokyo. He was given a small office on the second floor of the old Chancery building adjacent to the DNB (the official German News Agency) monitoring room. Sorge would arrive at six o'clock every morning and stay until ten. 'The first thing I did was to sort out the incoming cables. I chose the more important items for the eyes of the senior members of the Embassy. I then prepared extracts for release to German residents in Japan, and "handouts" for the Japanese press.'

He was paid for this task, but had no official status in the Embassy. He had refused on a number of occasions, according to his account, to become a member of the staff. 'The Foreign Office in Berlin [from 1939 onwards] pressed Ott to take me on in a fairly high position, in charge of information and press relations. But I continued to refuse. Ott became rather offended in the end, so I promised him that I would continue in my rôle of private adviser.'

Sorge had one special reason for avoiding any formal attachment to the Embassy. He not only felt that 'official duties would interfere with my work for Moscow. I also feared that details of my past would be uncovered by the inevitable security investigations before I was accepted as a member of the diplomatic body.'

In any event, Sorge's relations with the Ambassador and the senior members of the Embassy were of a special if indefinable nature. The outbreak of hostilities in Europe led naturally to an increasing intimacy and frequency of discussion of daily developments in Japan and on the European scene. Sorge was undoubtedly an exceptionally valuable source of information to the German Embassy. It was known to Ott that Sorge had special connections with the circle of advisers round Prince Konoye and that he made a particular study of Soviet affairs.

As Sorge later put it:

I believe that I had no small attraction for them because I did not want any status in the Embassy, and because I had a sharp knowledge and judgment of political, economic and military problems. I was well versed also in history and philosophy. I was perhaps the only German close to the Embassy who took an interest in the serious academic books often sent to the Embassy from Germany. I used to borrow them, and take them home to read.

This impressed the Ambassador and his wife.

Sorge claimed that his views were constantly sought by the senior Embassy officials. 'For example, they would tell me that they had such and such information: had I heard of it, and what were my views?' From time to time the Ambassador would show Sorge a draft telegram, and ask him to suggest alterations. 'Thus I came to know the contents of many important cables and dispatches. Sometimes my views would provoke a discussion, during which further information would be revealed.'

During his visit to Moscow in 1935, Sorge had been instructed to concentrate on gaining the confidence of the German Embassy in Tokyo, and had received permission to pass a certain amount of information to them.* The stage had therefore already been set to exploit to the full Sorge's penetration of German Embassy circles, after a long period of careful preparation.

The Moscow Centre, however, seems to have shown little understanding of the practical and technical difficulties involved in this preliminary task, and with the opening of the war crisis in Europe Sorge's superiors displayed a note of unreasonable haste in their need for high-level intelligence from the Sorge ring.

On September 1, 1939, Sorge received the following message from Moscow:

* See p. 155 above.

Your information on current military and political problems has gradually deteriorated in quality during the summer. During this period Japan has taken important steps preparatory to fighting the Soviet Union, but we have received no significant information from you. Since the German Embassy is well informed on the subject, kindly obtain information from it and report it to us by W/T without delay. As you are experienced in the work and your standing at the embassy is extremely high, we ask and expect ample up-to-date information from you on military and political problems. But you have remained aloof, sending us information of negligible value.

My dear Ramsay, I call on you once again to change your method of collecting information. . . . Thus and only thus will your residence in Japan be of any value to our work. In order to obtain better information, the capabilities of Joe [Miyagi], Miki [Koshiro]* and Otto [Ozaki] should be utilized fully. Pay them whenever they have accomplished their work. You must consider the importance of your work . . . we believe that you have infinite trust in your motherland. We anticipate a change for the better in your work. Please acknowledge receipt.

On the same day another message arrived.

Two months ago I pointed out that your most immediate and important problem was to engage services of a few Japanese army officers, but to date I have received no reply. . . . I regard this work as vital to the solution of the problem. Kindly wire observations and prospects. I believe that you will succeed in doing this.

Both messages were signed 'Director' which meant they came personally from the head of the Fourth Bureau.†

There is no trace of Sorge's answer to this reflection on his mission. He had already warned his superiors that it would take time to set up a fully operative intelligence ring in Japan. It had already required five years' experimenting to establish reliable radio communications with Klausen's set. But Sorge was now ready, and needed no such prodding.

During the months prior to September 1939, the central point of interest, in terms of the political intelligence which was Sorge's

* One of Miyagi's sub-agents. See p. 283 below.
† Both messages were intercepted by the Japanese Ministry of Communications listening station in Korea. It is not clear at what stage they were decoded, probably by Klausen in prison.

primary mission, was the course of the Japanese-German negotiations directed towards a political and military alliance. Talks had been initiated on the German side, but progress had been slow. Japan was not ready to go to war with countries other than China, and the prime intention of the German proposals during these months was to commit Japan to action against Britain in the Far East.

As Sorge described these implications:

In proposing an alliance, the German government had war with Britain in mind. But there was another reason why Germany wanted to make Britain the target of the proposed alliance ... Germany was already making top secret approaches to the Soviet Union. Ott hinted to me that this approach could lead not merely to a Neutrality Pact, but also to a German-Soviet military alliance.

The refusal of the Japanese Cabinet at this stage to consider a pact with Germany aimed at Britain directly influenced the decision, in August 1939, to negotiate the Nazi-Soviet Pact.

The Russians showed a natural and anxious interest in these Japanese-German negotiations. If the proposed alliance were directed against the Soviet Union, 'the Russians would have called off their secret talks with the Germans. But the Soviet Union was informed by me that the object of the proposed alliance was Britain—not the Soviet Union. So the Russians concluded their pact with Germany.'

Over a period of some months Sorge frequently heard from Ott about the German-Japanese talks, and he reported on them to Moscow 'every time I was given some information'.

With the opening of the European war, the German Embassy began a systematic study of Japanese reactions 'at every level of the nation and every shade of political opinion'. Ott sent numerous reports on his own talks with members of the Japanese Government, and on information from other sources which was assembled in the Embassy by his senior officials. Sorge claimed that he was shown these reports and passed on summaries 'several times' by radio.

From his subsequent interrogations, this material appears to have been very general and unsubstantial. It was clear that Japanese political and military circles were divided in their reactions, that the Nazi-Soviet pact had made a sharp and negative impression and had strengthened pro-British and pro-American influence in Tokyo, and

that there was little support in high circles for intervention in the
European war.

The close interrelation of Japan's military strength and the course of
her foreign policy was an obvious and central source of study by the
Sorge group. Ever since the China Incident of 1937, the German
Embassy had conducted a systematic study of the organization and
military capacity of the Japanese army. Every time that a battle was
fought in China, a detailed military appreciation was drafted in the
Embassy, and a report sent every month by courier to Berlin, after a
regular meeting between Ott and the acting military attaché, Scholl,
at which Sorge claimed that he was also present. Sorge photographed
these documents and sent the film to Moscow. They also covered the
reorganization of the Japanese army started in 1938.

This 'Embassy study group' seems to have remained in being until
the end of 1939 or early 1940, when Scholl returned to Germany. His
close relations with Sorge, based on their service in the same regiment
in the First World War, were an essential aspect of the latter's penetration of the military work of the Embassy. In this early period Sorge
would check such military information as he received from Miyagi by
producing it at the study group, but when this informal body ceased
to meet, there appears to have been a temporary hiatus in Sorge's
reporting, which did not pass unnoticed in Moscow.

In February and March 1940 radio messages reached Sorge requesting detailed information on military and naval arsenals and on war
production in armaments factories. On May 25 came a further implicit
criticism of the work of the ring.

Your secondary mission, which is next in importance to your primary
mission, is to satisfy the following requirements: We need documents,
material, and information concerning the reorganization of the Japanese
army. What are the units which make up the new organization? What are
the original units which have been inactivated and reorganized? What are
the names of the new units? Who are their commanders? We are anxious
to have detailed information concerning changes in Japanese foreign policy.
Reports following events are not enough. We must have advance information.

During these early months of 1940, Sorge transferred the main
burden of gathering military intelligence to Ozaki and Miyagi, and,

after Scholl's departure, was able to rely less—at least temporarily—
on German Embassy sources.

The appointment of Matsuoka as Foreign Minister in the second
Konoye Cabinet in July 1940 symbolized a new and positive stage in
the direction of a formal alliance with Germany. After preliminary
exchanges in Tokyo with Ott and talks between the German Government and Oshima in Berlin, Ribbentrop's special adviser on Far
Eastern matters, Heinrich Georg Stahmer, came out to Tokyo in
early September to conduct the negotiations. After four weeks of
discussion, the Tripartite Pact, which included Italy, was signed in
Tokyo. The essence of the transaction was that the alliance was to be
directed against England and would apply to the United States in
the event of the latter entering the war against Germany.

Sorge learnt of the gist of these negotiations from both Ott and
Stahmer, and emphasized in transmitting the evidence to Moscow
that the target of the new alliance was, in the first instance, Britain
alone.

The main task of Germany was henceforward to bring Japan into the
war against Britain. After the initial failure to invade the British Isles,
it was only through the opening of hostilities in the Far East that the
stalemate in Europe could be broken. As Sorge described the position:
'The Germans believed that a Japanese attack on Singapore would
reduce British naval forces in the Mediterranean and Atlantic, and so
make it possible for Germany to invade England itself.'

Ott received formal instructions from Berlin to urge the Japanese
Government to launch such an assault. For a whole week he and his
service attachés met every day in the Embassy to study, with a sand
table and models, the operations involved in an attack on Singapore.
Sorge stated that he was not present at these meetings, although there
is eye-witness evidence that at least on one occasion he inspected the
model and discussed the plan with the Ambassador.

The conclusions of this study were taken by the German service
attachés to the Japanese Army and Navy Staff Headquarters, but
'they were greeted only with smiles; and they were unable to obtain
any definite answer'.

Sorge surmised from these activities 'that the German situation must be such as to require, as a matter of particular urgency, Japan's participation in the war against Britain. I found out later that Germany had already decided on war with Russia and could not afford to give Britain a breathing space.'

At the time of the signing of the Tripartite Pact Ribbentrop had extended an invitation, during an exchange of greetings by radio telephone, to Matsuoka to visit Europe. The Japanese Cabinet and service chiefs were divided in their attitude to such a visit, and it was only after a series of government conferences that Matsuoka left for Berlin in March 1941, followed by Ott a few days later, and furnished with categorical and limiting instructions.

Ozaki was closely informed by his friend Saionji Kinkazu of the discussions in Cabinet circles leading up to Matsuoka's brief for his trip. Konoye's circle expected little to emerge from this enterprise. Saionji, who was a member of the delegation, told Ozaki, 'The best we can hope for is that this visit, by increasing Matsuoka's knowledge of the European situation, may contribute to the right choice of foreign policy in the future.'

Matsuoka was instructed to sign no formal treaty in Germany or Italy, and to undertake no commitments on Japan's behalf. He was to study the European situation as a private individual, and listen to German and Italian aspirations. On the return journey via Moscow he was authorized to enter into talks with a view to a treaty which might restore friendly relations with the Soviet Union. Ribbentrop, however, was hoping to impress Matsuoka and win him over to the Singapore operation and, in the event of a deterioration of German-Soviet relations, to bring Japan over to the German side. According to Ott, the Embassy felt that any talks which might take place in Moscow would be ephemeral and concerned only with economic matters.

In the event, Matsuoka made no commitments in his talks with Hitler and Ribbentrop and kept rigidly to his instructions. Hitler had hinted to him that German-Soviet relations might worsen, and Matsuoka revealed in return that Japan might open talks with the Soviet government to relieve existing tensions between the two countries.

The results of Matsuoka's visit to Moscow, however, were both startling and unexpected. On April 13 a Japanese-Russian Neutrality Pact was signed by him, putting an end to frontier problems in

Manchukuo and Mongolia, and containing an exchange of notes on future talks on trade and fisheries and the settlement of the dispute over the island of Sakhalin. Permission to sign this surprise agreement, which had been worked out in twenty-four hours between Matsuoka and Molotov, was cabled from Tokyo and later ratified by the Privy Council. It seemed that Stalin was convinced that there would be no break between Russia and Germany and that ultimately Japan would move southwards.

Both the German Government and Ambassador Ott, on his return to Tokyo, were taken completely by surprise. Ott told Sorge of the general course of the talks in Berlin and added that 'in signing the Neutrality Pact he [Matsuoka] did something which Germany neither desired nor expected'. Matsuoka, however, went out of his way on various occasions after his return from Moscow to assure Ott that, in the event of war between Germany and Russia, the Japanese-Soviet Neutrality Pact would be repealed, and 'that he would do his best to secure Japanese denunciation of the Pact which he himself had concluded'.

This was a curious interpretation. When interrogated in November 1942 by the preliminary judge conducting the Sorge case, Matsuoka denied that he had spoken to Ott in Tokyo on his return from Moscow. He said that he had told Hitler, and Mussolini (whom he had visited briefly in Rome) that he 'would enter into negotiations with the Soviet Union. There was no reason for Ott to be worried. However, I did not mention the matter to Ambassador Oshima while I was in Germany.'

Matsuoka also denied, in the following words, that he had told Ott that the Moscow talks would not nullify the Tripartite Pact of September 1940 or that Japan would join Germany in event of a German-Soviet conflict.

I did not say this. The Tripartite Pact was serving the major purpose of preventing America from entering the war. The Pact did not oblige Japan to enter a German-Soviet conflict, and this conflict did not nullify the Japanese-Soviet neutrality pact. The Tripartite Pact was, however, the central plank of Japan's foreign policy, and in certain circumstances Japan would not be bound by the Neutrality Pact. Stalin and Molotov were clearly aware that Japan did not conclude the Neutrality Pact in order to nullify the Tripartite Alliance.

Matsuoka was being less than candid. On at least one occasion, on

May 6, he had told Ott that Japan could not remain neutral in event of war between Germany and Russia.

But German diplomacy had suffered a general reverse. Talks had already begun in April between Tokyo and Washington, and the idea of an attack on Singapore had disappeared without trace. When Ozaki asked Konoye at this time 'What about Singapore?' the Japanese Premier answered, 'That was Ott's one man play.'[*]

These developments were, as Sorge put it, 'of the utmost interest to the Soviet Union. I reported on them to the Moscow Centre by radio and in written accounts (by courier).' His superiors by now could not have failed to appreciate the quality of at least the political intelligence emanating from the Sorge ring since the outbreak of the European war. But although Sorge, Ozaki, and their friends were rejoicing at the Japanese-Russian neutrality treaty, they were dubious about the possibility of Japanese neutrality in the event of war between Germany and the Soviet Union. Both Sorge and Ozaki, like Ott, had been taken by surprise at the news of this agreement. Ozaki made a study of the general reactions in Tokyo and told Sorge that

the political parties welcomed the pact, as evidenced by the fact that Konoye himself met Matsuoka upon his return and took him to the Premier's official residence for a toast. The general public likewise welcomed the treaty, as could be seen from Matsuoka's popularity after his return to Tokyo. If the army disapproved a policy, it was customary for them to make a statement; the army's silence signified tacit approval. . . .

In short, the treaty was supported by the nation in general. . . . With regard to the relationship between the Tripartite Pact and the Non-Aggression Pact, the pro-Axis elements maintained that the former treaty had priority over the latter because it was concluded according to an Imperial Rescript. On the other hand, I gathered from conversations in the Foreign Ministry, the South Manchuria Railway and the Breakfast Club[†] that these cliques considered that the neutrality treaty clearly made an exception of Soviet Russia and re-emphasized Japan's responsibility as a neutral. Personally I did not think that the treaty made the Russo-Japanese relationship safe.

Sorge and Ozaki conferred together and in the ensuing weeks were to concentrate in particular on studying Japanese military preparations in the north.

[*] In his examination in the rôle of witness by the preliminary judge on November 18, 1942, in connection with the Sorge Case, Konoye denied this incident. 'This is a complete lie.'

† See p. 293 below.

At the end of 1940 or the beginning of 1941, Sorge had instructions from Moscow to send a report, as detailed as possible, on the Japanese Army order of battle—the number and enumeration of divisions; their location; and the names of divisional commanders and leading officers.

Sorge, Ozaki and Miyagi, working together and collating all the information they could obtain, were able to produce a rough chart on these lines—which was drawn by the artist, Miyagi. 'On investigating this chart,' said Sorge, 'we found that some fifty divisions had been organized. With the chart as a basis to work on we proceeded to collect further information. Eventually, after various amendments we came near to a perfect order of battle based on the situation in May and June 1941. I photographed it and sent it to Moscow. This chart was the best product of our group. I do not think it would have been possible to have produced a better one. The Moscow Centre appeared to be satisfied with it, and no further instructions on the subject were sent to us.'

The production of a comprehensive order of battle, covering the infantry divisions of the Japanese Army, represented a considerable technical achievement. During the early stages of the Pacific War it was discovered by the Allied Forces that the Soviet Union possessed the most reliable information on the Japanese order of battle. This may have been due, in substantial part, to the work of the Sorge ring during the winter of 1940 to 1941.

In addition to this military intelligence target, there was the immediate political interest in developments in the relations between Tokyo and Washington taking place at the time of Matsuoka's return from Europe. The Japanese army and navy, and nationalist circles in Japan, had opposed stubbornly and consistently any withdrawal from China or political concessions to collaborationist elements in Nanking. This attitude hardened further when the United States made it known, in April 1941, that she would offer to mediate between Japan and Chiang Kai-shek.

In May 1941 Sorge decided to visit Shanghai to study the attitude of the Japanese authorities in China towards any American mediation. He was asked to undertake this 'political mission' by the German Ambassador in Tokyo 'as Japanese reactions in China could not be studied in Japan'. Sorge travelled as an Embassy courier with a special diplomatic pass from the Japanese Foreign Ministry and carrying dispatches to the German Consul-General in Shanghai. Here he met not only German observers, but the Japanese Consul-General, senior army and navy officers, and the head of the 'Special Bureau'.* 'About 90 per cent of them were absolutely opposed to the idea of arbitration. I was told that if Konoye and Matsuoka pressed on with this line they would encounter most vehement opposition. On hearing this, I formed the impression that the Japanese-American talks would fail.'

Sorge claimed that he sent reports in cipher to Ambassador Ott 'who relayed them to the German Government without alteration'.

On his return to Tokyo Sorge sent the same material by radio to Moscow.

From the preparation of the German attack on Russia to the crisis in the Japanese-American negotiations (March–October 1941)

During the months of April and May 1941, couriers travelling from Europe to the German Embassy in Tokyo, and their escorting officers from the War Ministry in Berlin, began to mention in passing—but with increasing frequency—the movement of German army units from the West towards the Soviet frontier. 'It was also reported that German fortifications on the eastern border had been completed.'†

As the atmosphere tightened, Sorge strained to catch every hint of an impending move by Germany against the Soviet Union. The signs accumulated with each week. The German military attaché in Japan, Colonel Kretschmer,‡ received instructions at this time to inform the Japanese War Ministry that Germany was obliged to take measures against Soviet troop concentrations on the eastern frontier. 'These instructions were very detailed and included a map of Soviet military

* The Japanese Army Intelligence and propaganda organization in China. See p. 150 above.

† On April 24, 1941, the German naval attaché in Moscow telegraphed Berlin: '1. Rumours current here speak of alleged danger of war between Germany and the Soviet Union and are being fed by travellers passing through from Germany. 2. According to the Counsellor of the Italian Embassy, the British Ambassador predicts June 22 as the day of the outbreak of war. 3. May 20th is set by others. 4. I am endeavouring to counteract the rumours, which are manifestly absurd.' This message requires no comment. 'Nazi-Soviet Relations 1939-41', p. 330 (Department of State, Washington 1948).

‡ Colonel Kretschmer was German military attaché in Tokyo from the winter of 1940 until 1942.

dispositions.' Sorge later claimed that he talked to Kretschmer, and learnt from him that

although it was uncertain whether or not the situation would lead to actual hostilities, Germany had completed her preparations on a very large scale; and I understood (from Kretschmer) that, with her concentrations of military forces, Germany would be able to induce the Soviet Union to acquiesce in her hitherto unspecified demands. I also learnt that the decision on peace or war depended solely on Hitler's will, and was quite irrespective of the Russian attitude.

In May, a special envoy from the German War Ministry, Colonel Ritter von Niedermayer, arrived in Tokyo. He brought with him a letter of introduction to Sorge from Dr. Herbert von Dirksen, the previous German Ambassador in Japan.

'From talking to Niedermayer, I found that war against the Soviet Union had already been decided.' Germany intended to occupy the granary of the Ukraine, to exploit one or two million Russian prisoners of war to meet Germany's labour shortage. Only by attacking Russia was Hitler sure that the threat to the Eastern frontier could be removed. 'To put it another way, Hitler believed that it was high time to fight the Soviet Union, and that it would be impossible to force the German people to fight Russia once the war with Britain had ended.'*

These reports were the subject of eager and sombre debate between Sorge and Ozaki. As Ozaki stated:

Sorge had pointed out, as much as three months before the German attack, that there was danger of such an assault. Almost immediately before the outbreak I said to Sorge, 'If Germany is demanding oil from the Caucasus and grain from the Ukraine, the Soviet Union should avoid war even at the cost of drastic economic concessions.' Sorge replied, 'Russia would yield if Germany made such demands. What we fear is a sudden German attack without the forewarning of such demands.' He emphasized that there was a great possibility of a Russo-German war.

On the accuracy of their information might well depend the fate of the Soviet Union. The perils of their daily activities were at last supremely justified and their talents fully mobilized.

---

* This statement to the Japanese procurator is somewhat contradicted by a summary of another Sorge message sent to Moscow in May 1941. 'At the time of the Hess affair, Sorge learned from the German Embassy that Hitler had sent Hess to Britain as a last means of reaching a peaceful settlement with the British before waging war against the Soviet Union. Thus Sorge knew that, in spite of the Non-Aggression Pact, a German attack on the Soviet Union was inevitable.' ('Information collected by Sorge and reported by him to the Soviet Union'. Japanese Police publication, 1957.)

Shortly after Colonel von Niedermayer's visit to Japan, another German Staff Officer arrived from Berlin with conclusive and dramatic evidence. He was Sorge's friend, Scholl. He brought with him, according to Sorge, top secret instructions to the German Ambassador in Tokyo 'on the necessary measures to be taken in connection with war between Germany and the Soviet Union which had now definitely been decided upon.'

Scholl gave me a detailed account. The attack would begin on June 20; there might be a two or three days' delay, but preparations were complete. 170–190 German divisions were massed on the Eastern frontier. There would be no ultimatum or declaration of war. The Red Army would collapse, and the Soviet régime would fall within two months.

Sorge emphasized, in his later interrogation, that he had learnt nothing from General Ott, this information having been obtained on May 20 only from Scholl himself in confidence over drinks. The latter was on his way to take up the post of German military attaché in Bangkok. 'He invited me to visit him in the autumn, as there would be work there with which I could help him.'

Sorge sent all this 'invaluable information', culminating in Scholl's disclosures,* to Moscow 'between the latter part of April and the outbreak of the war, and I drew the attention of the Moscow Centre to the exceptionally serious nature of this intelligence'.

These advance reports from Sorge warning of the German attack on the Soviet Union constitute one of the most dramatic achievements of the ring. In addition to the material assembled by the Japanese during the ultimate trials, recent articles in the Soviet and East German press reveal some further details. On March 5, 1941, for instance, Sorge is said to have transmitted to Moscow a microfilm containing telegrams from Ribbentrop to Ott which gave the date of the German attack as the middle of June; and on May 15 Sorge radioed the exact day—June 22.

This vital and historic message was transmitted from Klausen's house, where Sorge, and possibly Ozaki, gathered in an excited group. Klausen recently described the scene.

We were awaiting every hour further information, confirmation, and above all news of the diplomatic and military reactions of the Soviet

* This evidence was apparently sent by W/T between the end of April and mid-June.

Government. We were aware of the importance of the message, but nevertheless we never got an answer. When war really broke out, Richard was furious. He asked in a puzzled way, 'Why has Stalin not reacted?'

Sorge himself later told his Japanese interrogators that 'the Moscow Centre sent me a radio message of grateful appreciation. This was quite exceptional.'*

Advance intelligence of German plans to invade Russia had, of course, reached Stalin from a number of sources, including Prague and the British Government in London. His reactions to these messages still remain a matter of speculation. But for Sorge and his group in Tokyo the days and weeks following the German assault were of momentous importance. The very fate of Russia was tightly bound up with the immediate intentions of Japanese policy, and the Sorge group alone was in a position to keep Moscow informed of this situation.

On the day after the German invasion of Russia—June 23—in a message summarizing snatches of talk among senior members of the German Embassy, Sorge radioed that General Ott had instructed all German officials in Japan to exert pressure in favour of Japanese intervention against the Soviet Union. Military sources in Japan considered that she might go to war with Russia within one or two months, and the Japanese Foreign Minister, Matsuoka, had told Ott that, despite the Japanese-Russian Neutrality Pact, Japan would attack the Soviet Union. But the German naval attaché, Admiral Wenneker, told Sorge that this would never happen. The interest of the Japanese navy lay firmly in the south. Sorge also agreed with this interpretation.

On June 27 a radio message was received from the Moscow Centre. 'Notify us as to what decisions were made by the Japanese government in regard to our country and the German-Soviet war. Also notify us concerning troop movements towards our border. [signed] Organizer.'†

The material collected in answer to this questionnaire in the ensuing weeks represents an outstanding achievement in the history of espionage.

Japanese political circles were divided in their analysis of the Russo-German war. The first reactions from the Japanese army leaders were

* Procurator's Examination of Sorge, No. 41. The message has not survived.

† 'Organizer' was the code name of the head of the Far Eastern section of the Fourth Bureau.

optimistic. Ozaki recorded: 'First we were anxious to know how the Japanese army expected the war to turn out. I tried to collect data at various meetings which I attended, and from the South Manchurian Railway. My findings indicated that the Japanese government and army expected a speedy Russian defeat followed by the collapse of the Stalin régime.'

There was much talk about this at the Breakfast Club, where most of Konoye's inner circle felt that Russia would collapse. The younger experts in the offices of the South Manchurian Railway were more pessimistic. Ozaki himself, basing his analysis on his knowledge of Prince Konoye's views, and checking them with Saionji, was sure from the outset that Japan would not move.

Soon after the outbreak of the Russo-German war, I told Sorge that Japan had no intention of attacking Russia. Konoye had said that Japan had its hands full with the China Incident. Since he did not know how negotiations with America would turn out, he did not want a war with Russia.

On July 2, 1941, an Imperial Conference was held in the presence of the Emperor at which momentous decisions of policy were authorized. A new plan of operations had been drawn up by the army and navy to co-ordinate planning on both the Northern Front on the Siberian border, and the Southern Front in China and the Pacific. If the negotiations with America broke down, Japan would go to war in the south. According to Ozaki,* three main decisions were taken at the Imperial Conference:

1. Japan would endeavour to obtain a satisfactory solution of the China Incident, but at the same time would prepare for any emergency in the north or the south by carrying out a general mobilization which would make possible the dispatch of troops in either direction.

2. Japan would remain neutral both toward Germany and toward Russia.

3. The policy of neutrality toward Germany and Russia had been definitely decided.

After consulting Saionji, Ozaki reported the findings to Sorge, adding that the Japanese government expected the collapse of the Soviet Union, as could be guessed from the talk of men close to Konoye. That the army held the same opinion could be gathered from reports from the South Manchurian Railway.

* His main source was Tanaka Shinjiro of the *Asahi* newspaper.

About a week after the conference, Ott received a brief account of its decisions from Matsuoka. According to the latter, Japan would increase her military preparations in the north, and would be ready 'to set about the elimination of Bolshevism in the areas adjacent to her territory. At the same time she would continue active expansion in the south.'

The German Ambassador interpreted this statement to mean that Japan's real intention was to mobilize in the north and attack Siberia, while maintaining a holding position in the south. Sorge, in comparing Ott's view as expressed to him with Ozaki's report on the conference, preferred the latter version. 'I gained the impression that Japan would take measures to protect her position in the north without engaging in an actual attack on the Soviet Union, and that the decision had been taken to start active operations in the south, namely in Indo-China.' On July 5 or 6 Ozaki confirmed to Sorge that the decision had been taken to send an expeditionary force to Saigon by the end of the month.

Sorge cabled the Moscow Centre in this sense, adding that Ozaki's account of the Imperial Conference of July 2 was the more reliable.

The final interpretation of Japanese intentions, however, depended on the accurate analysis of Japanese mobilization plans. All the resources of the ring were now concentrated on this end.

It has been suggested that the advance warning sent by Sorge to Moscow, after the Imperial Conference of July 2, 1941, of Japan's intention to strike south into the Pacific and remain neutral on the Siberian border, enabled Stalin to move divisions from the Soviet Far Eastern Army to the Western Front. Thanks to Sorge's intelligence these reinforcements saved Moscow from the Germans.

The latest evidence shows that the Russian High Command gave their first order to move formations (as distinct from isolated units) from the Far East on May 26, 1941, when the Sixteenth Army was transferred from Trans-Baikal to the west. Between October and November eleven rifle divisions were also moved. This operation involved some 250,000 men.*

The official Soviet historians, on the other hand, tend to ignore these measures or to minimize their historical significance. One

---

* The authors are much indebted to Dr. John Erickson of the Department of Government at the University of Manchester, who undertook to make a special study of this point.

Soviet work,* for example, emphasizes the importance which such a strategic move, if it had been made, would have been for the conduct of the war in the west, and also stresses the underlying aggressive intentions of Japan, in spite of her open decision to move southwards. This Russian interpretation of Japanese aims is contrary to Sorge's analysis, with Ozaki's help, of the decisions of the Conference of July 2, which are quoted as:

1. Japan will not enter the war against the Soviet Union. Only when the war takes a favourable turn from the Japanese point of view will she take to arms.

2. Until that point is reached, Japan will camouflage her moves with diplomatic talks with the Soviet Union, and under the protection of this camouflage will arm secretly against the Soviet Union.

This Soviet analysis follows significantly that of Ott rather than Sorge and it is therefore probably derived from Russian interception of German messages from Tokyo at the time, or the post-war capture of German diplomatic documents. In any event, Sorge's telegrams on this subject may have been ignored in the same manner as those which warned of the original German attack on Russia.

In stressing still further the consistently hostile intentions of Japan towards the Soviet Union, the same Soviet historian quotes from evidence by a Japanese general at the post-war trial of Ataman Semjonow, who was the leader of the White Russian colony in Manchukuo, and was captured by the Russians in 1945 after being a leading agent of the Japanese Military Intelligence and source on the Soviet order of battle in the Far East.

The general, Tominaga, claims that the Japanese operational plan for attacking the Soviet Union under the code name 'Kan-Toku-en' was brought up to date in mid-1941. 'We assumed that the Soviet Union would transfer its troops in the Far East to the Western Front, and Japan would gain control of the Far East without appreciable losses.' This operational plan was in fact drawn up in July 1941, but Japan's concentration on the Pacific War—as all reliable evidence shows—was a genuine strategic move and the Kwantung Army in Manchukuo received orders to remain strictly on the defensive along the Siberian frontier.

On June 26 Moscow had radioed a request to the Sorge group for a

* B. S. Telpuchowski: *Die sowjetische Geschichte des Grossen Vaterländischen Krieges 1941–45*, edited and translated into German by A. Hillgruber and H. A. Jacobsen (1961), pp. 511–12.

report on 'the mobilization and transfer to the continent of Japanese troops in connection with the Russo-German war'. The German Government in Berlin was equally pressing Ott and his staff both for similar information and for every effort to be made to bring Japan into the Russian war.

The German service attachés even drew up plans for a Japanese attack on Siberia and Vladivostok, stressing the imminent collapse of the Red armies on the European front. They were told, however, that it would take two months for the Japanese army to mobilize and that Japan would not move before then, or enter the war until Germany had occupied Moscow and reached the Volga.

'Colonel Kretschmer, in his efforts at persuasion, put it about that most of the Siberian armies had been transferred to the West . . . but the Japanese Army . . . discounted Kretschmer's information.'

Ott could only await the results of the Japanese mobilization in the hope that after two months the attack on Russia would follow.

In the meantime Ozaki and Miyagi concentrated feverishly on their key intelligence task. The former was to establish a broad picture showing the numbers of troops to be sent to Manchukuo and the scale of preparations in that province for any attack on the Soviet Union. Details of the mobilization plans were to be provided by Miyagi and assembled by his sub-agents.

The information reached Sorge in piecemeal fashion. When put together it revealed that mobilization 'was on a very large scale indeed'. The army authorities had taken complete independent responsibility and Prince Konoye himself was surprised at the extent of the operation.

The first reports of Ozaki were vague and exaggerated. 'It was not difficult to ascertain that soldiers were being sent both to the north and south, but I could not find out in what proportions. Rumours in Osaka said that the army was buying ice-boxes and mosquito nets. This seemed convincing. So I told Sorge that some units were going south.

During an eel party at the Owada restaurant in Azabu, Kazami* said that 5,000,000 men were affected by the mobilization. I remember repeating this to Miyagi. When I met Oda, the vice-chief of Mitsui Bussan [the well-known trading company] at the end of July, I hinted that the army meant to

---

* Kazami was the Chief Cabinet Secretary in the First Konoye Cabinet and, for a time, Minister of Justice in the Second Cabinet. See also p. 192 above.

strike somewhere in the north. Although Oda did not contradict me altogether, he replied, 'The news I get indicates that more soldiers are going
south than north.'

Other indications, from Miyagi, reinforced this view. In early
August a radio message transmitted by Klausen to Moscow gave the
following detail:

A unique feature – e.g. the Fourteenth Division – is that recruits are
organized in small groups; winter clothing is issued to some, summer to
others; then they are assigned to units already activated. 'Miki' [Koshiro],*
who has been conscripted, contends that all garrison troops in Japan are
to be attached to units stationed in Asia. Ozaki and Miyagi hear that most
will be sent to south China because of further U.S.–Japanese complications.
Possibility of operations against the Dutch East Indies. To be confirmed.

Sorge was tensely occupied in constructing a general pattern. The
mobilization was being carried out in three phases, the last to be
completed by August 15. 1,300,000 men in all were to be called up.
By the end of July a million tons of merchant shipping were to be
requisitioned for the army.

I myself, Ozaki and the Moscow Centre were tormented by the fear that
the Japanese government would accept this grand-scale mobilization as a
fait accompli, and that the mobilization itself might lead to war with the
Soviet Union. Another question of great concern to us was the destination
of the mobilized divisions. Here Ozaki did his best to find out what was
happening.

The group soon noticed that the process of mobilization was slow-
ing down and would not be completed by August 15. As Ozaki stated:

When the German Army struck (on August 7) at Smolensk, and the
relationship between Japan and America worsened because of the Japanese
advance into French Indo-China (on July 24), I heard that some of those
who agreed to the general mobilization in the expectation of a Soviet
collapse were hesitant about making an attack upon Russia.

By mid-July Prince Konoye had formed his third Cabinet, re-
placing Matsuoka as Foreign Minister by the cautious Admiral
Toyoda. His main purpose was 'to find some solution to the question
of Japanese-American relations' which reached a crisis with the
declaration of July 26 freezing Japanese assets abroad.

At this point Ambassador Ott seems to have abandoned any hope

* One of Miyagi's sub-agents. See p. 283 below.

of early Japanese intervention in the Russian war, but his military attaché, Colonel Kretschmer, continued to remain optimistic, and Ribbentrop was pressing in almost daily telegrams from Berlin. The German study of Japanese policy and plans followed unconsciously the lines of Sorge's own enquiry, and was influenced by selected items of intelligence leaked by him to the German Embassy. Sorge was thus able to supplement and correct his own assessments from the German side.

In early August Sorge reported to Moscow that

Ott has been ordered to submit date and conclusions as to whether or not Japan could launch an operation during the winter season. . . . The fact that Moscow was not captured last Sunday, as has been promised Oshima by the highest German authorities, had tended to cool Japanese enthusiasm. Even the Army feels that the Soviet-German war is developing into another China Incident, and that the Germans are repeating the errors committed by it in China . . .

Kretschmer made a last attempt to substantiate his analysis that Japan would be at war by September 1, and set off on a tour of Manchukuo. On his return to Tokyo, he discussed with Sorge his impressions, which were summarized in a radio message to Moscow:

Six divisions have already arrived in Korea. Plans for possible attack on Vladivostok. Manchukuo being reinforced by four new divisions. Japan intends to increase strength in Manchukuo and Korea to thirty divisions. According to Kretschmer, no decision to launch offensive taken yet. First objective would be Vladivostok. Only three divisions sent to Blagoveschensk area.

It was clear, even to Kretschmer, that no immediate Japanese assault on the Siberian front could be expected.

Ozaki's information showed that the Japanese concentration in the north was even less formidable than Kretschmer suggested. Originally one third of the total forces mobilized were to be assigned to Manchukuo, but by mid-August this figure had been reduced to 300,000 men—or about fifteen divisions. A recent Japanese study on the Pacific War confirms Ozaki's estimate.

In spite of pressures from Berlin, Ott and his advisers at the German Embassy were now compelled to accept the view that Japan had no immediate intention of coming to the military support of Germany in her Russian campaign.

About August 15 Sorge was able to report to Moscow a summary of information from German Embassy circles in Tokyo.

As a result of conversations with Generals Doihara and Okamura, however, Ott is convinced that Japan will wait until the Red Army is crippled so badly that a Japanese offensive will be absolutely safe. Doihara points out that Japan cannot engage in a protracted struggle, and that, because her petroleum supply* is badly depleted, she will not start a war unless she is sure that it will be a short one.

The Japanese Foreign Ministry is scheming to use the mobilization as a bluff to intimidate Russia into ceding Sakhalin. Ott believes it highly probable that Japan will carry on such negotiations and avoid going to war this year. He further believes that Japan expects Russia to hold out this winter.

Wenneker disclosed to Sorge the following secret information from Japanese naval authorities, that the navy and government have decided not to go to war during the year, but that Japan, adopting the same methods used in French Indo-China, will probably take the strategic areas of Thailand in October in preparation for the future occupation of Borneo. The same source informed Wenneker that the Japanese army is completely dissatisfied with the above decision . . . but it is not likely that the army will disregard both the will of the government and the navy and start a war against Russia.

The foregoing attitude of the government and navy is based on the following conclusions; that an unpredictable war against the Soviet Union before the winter season would exert an excessive strain on the Japanese economy; that even if the northern [*sic*] areas were captured they would be of little assistance to the Japanese economy [whereas the southern areas are much more important]; and that, in the event of a German victory over Russia, Japan could gain desired objectives by the following year without suffering any losses.

Unlike Wenneker, Ott does not believe that this information is absolutely reliable but . . . the situation may be moving in that direction. Ott told Sorge that he had had a talk with 'Mak's' successor [Matsuoka's successor, Admiral Toyoda], but that it had done little to clarify Japanese policy. Toyoda told Ott about the current negotiations with Russia with respect to Sakhalin. . . . He stressed the point that, in general, Russia's attitude on these matters is quite justified and said that Japan has assured Russia that she will adhere strictly to the Neutrality Pact.

Ott reported to Richard [Ribbentrop] on the above conversation adding

---

* Sorge had already reported, on information from the naval attaché, Admiral Wenneker, that Japanese oil reserves amounted to two years' supply for the navy, six months for the army, and six months for civilian use.

that, as Japan is still undecided as to what steps to take, it would be easy to break up the negotiations but that there is no indication that she will declare war against Russia.

On August 20–23, 1941, a conference of the Japanese High Command was held in Tokyo to discuss the issue of war with the Soviet Union. Ozaki was able to report on this to Sorge, who excitedly transmitted this intelligence by radio to Moscow.

The conference decided not to declare war this year repeat decided not to declare war this year against the Soviet Union. The following reservation was made: this decision may be changed in event of unforeseen developments in the Russo-German war situation of such a nature as to cause grave repercussions in the Siberian area. If such a war situation . . . [Illegible] by September 15 at the latest, it is probable that the question of war against Soviet Russia will be left as decided until next season. Units to be dispatched to Manchukuo will probably spend the winter there if the situation suggests the possibility of an offensive against Russia next spring.

According to information obtained by Ozaki from military sources, the Army will begin to fight when the following two conditions obtain:

    1. When the troop strength of the Kwantung Army becomes three times that of the Red Army;

    2. When there are positive signs of an internal collapse in the Siberian Army.

Ozaki reports further that reinforcements dispatched to Manchukuo have been withdrawn to the rear from the front lines. In view of this turn of events, Sorge has sent Ozaki to Manchukuo to make a first-hand study of the situation. Ozaki will return on the 15th of this month.

Sorge's information from local German sources confirmed this news. Early in September he radioed the Moscow Centre:

After careful consideration of the matter, it is the judgment of Kretschmer, Wenneker, and Ott that there can be no doubt whatsoever that the possibility of a Japanese attack has ceased to exist at least till the winter is over. Japan will attack only when your country withdraws large forces from Siberia, and when internal political disturbances occur there.

The final stage in Sorge's remarkably detailed and accurate enquiry into Japanese policy and plans regarding war with Russia was now reached. His intelligence operation had been a model of thoroughness, and cross-checking of each item from Ozaki's intimate sources in the Konoye circle, to Miyagi's military contacts, and daily discussions between Sorge and the senior officials in the German Embassy. Intermittent leakages of high-level policy decisions from the Imperial Conference of July 2 to the meeting of the Japanese High Command on August 20–23 were carefully analysed in the light of a co-ordinated system of further inquiries.

In the case of the background to this August meeting Ozaki describes such an example.

About the middle of August I heard from someone in the South Manchurian Railway that a representative of the Kwantung Army had come to Tokyo to consult high-ranking officers in the War Ministry as to whether or not an attack should be launched against Russia. To check this rumour I said to Saionji, 'Have they decided to do it?' Saionji replied, '*They decided against the move last week.*' When I repeated this to Sorge I added on my own account that if the Russian war with Germany took an unexpected turn and disturbance should arise in Siberia, Japan might again consider attacking Russia. Despite my prudent warning Sorge was much relieved.

But this dialogue produced but one clue. Miyagi was able to report the following month (around September 20) that

the 3rd, 4th, 5th and 6th Regiments of the Imperial Guards Division are preparing to leave Tokyo. Since they are wearing summer uniforms, and since other Imperial Guards regiments are already stationed in French Indo-China, it is believed that they will be sent to the southern area. . . .

Finally, Ozaki's report on his return from Manchukuo completed this investigation of this group to Sorge's satisfaction. Late in September or early in October 1941 he radioed, in some detail, the substance of Ozaki's mission.

According to what Invest [Ozaki] has learned from the [South Manchurian] Railway, approximately 400,000 troops have arrived during the last two months, and the strength of the Kwantung Army has reached 700,000 including troops already stationed there. A few units have returned to Japan because of the decision against war with the Soviet Union this year; one instance of this is the arrival in Tokyo of one regiment of the Utsunomiya 14 Divisional District. Other newly arrived units have been withdrawn from the front lines, and stationed in various types of newly constructed barracks in Dairen and Mukden. The main force is still concentrated in the eastern border area against Voroshilorsk and Vladivostok.

The railway was ordered last month to construct a secret road and connecting line to Ou-pu opposite Ushman station on the Tsitsihar–Amur line in order to make it possible to utilize the district as a base of attack if developments in the Russo-German war permit the launching of an offensive against the U.S.S.R., around March of next year. No troop movements from north China to Manchukuo—except trucks.

During the first week of mobilization, in preparation for an attack on the Red Army, the Kwantung Army ordered the railroad to furnish 3,000 railway workers for purpose of taking over the Siberian railway network. Number later reduced to 1,500 and army is at present asking for only 50 railway workers to operate its transport organization. *The railway (SMR) interprets this move as definite proof that the offensive against the Soviet Union has been suspended for the time being.*

The Sorge ring had been operating at extended and unremitting pressure since the spring of 1941 against the tense background of the struggle as between peace or war in the Far East. After years of frustration and political preparation, when the crisis came they were able to fulfil impeccably the tasks set originally by Moscow, or adopted as circumstances directed by the course of events in Tokyo.

With the completion of the study of Japanese mobilization in the summer and autumn of 1941, which revealed conclusively that the Soviet Union was in no immediate danger of a Japanese attack in Siberia before early 1942, the resources of the Sorge ring were switched without respite to penetrating Japanese intentions regarding the United States and the issue of peace or war in the south, in Asia and the Pacific. This was to be their last, and perhaps most significant, achievement.

The formation of the third Konoye Cabinet in mid-July 1941 marked a new stage in the long-drawn-out negotiations for a Far Eastern settlement between Japan and the United States. Although the removal of the pro-Axis Foreign Minister, Matsuoka, was an essential obstacle out of the way towards the renewal of talks, the economic blockade of Japan by the United States, the British Commonwealth and the Netherlands on July 26, 1941, in answer to the Japanese advance into French Indo-China while negotiations with the U.S.A. were still pending, provoked a major political crisis in Tokyo.

Ozaki analysed the situation in retrospect as follows: 'Japan was panic-stricken because she did not expect to be boycotted. The new situation was a question of life or death for Japan. In my own opinion there were only two ways open. The first was for Japan to give in entirely to America and Britain and to find a way out of her difficulties by economic negotiations. The second was war with America and Britain to obtain the natural resources of the south, especially oil. I considered this was unavoidable because the negotiations with America must fail for the following reasons:

1. In spite of common interests there was a great disparity in the demands of Japan on the one hand and of America and Britain on the other. There was no hope that they would agree.

2. The upper strata of political and financial circles were anxious to avoid war, but the Japanese people, as a result of propaganda since the outbreak of the China Incident, were confident that they could successfully carry out their 'holy war' and were opposed to a compromise with America and Britain. Pro-Axis groups had the support of the general masses.

3. The economic situation of Japan as a whole was extremely bad, but the fighting forces, especially the navy, had never been so well equipped.

'I drew my conclusions concerning the economic blockade from conversations overheard at the South Manchurian Railway. I drew my conclusions concerning the attitude of the Japanese people from my lecture tours throughout the country.'

Towards the end of August Ozaki told Sorge that 'the Konoye Cabinet had decided to make a fresh start in the negotiations with America because of the extremely difficult economic situation. The Japanese government had notified the United States that the Prince himself would take charge in future.'

Ozaki predicted that the talks would be based, on the Japanese side, on the following conditions: the restoration of economic relations, especially the resumption of petroleum and iron ore exports to Japan; the assistance of the United States in clearing up the China Incident; and American help in obtaining raw materials from South-East Asia. On the American side, Japan would be required to abandon the Axis alliance, to withdraw from China, and suspend her advance to the south.

In spite of the optimism prevalent during these late August days in Prince Konoye's entourage, Ozaki from the outset did not expect a satisfactory conclusion to these talks. The gulf between the demands of the two countries was too great. 'I reasoned as follows: I knew that Konoye had had a secret meeting with his personal advisers at his private villa to ascertain their opinions. The meeting between Roosevelt and Churchill about that time gave me a hint that Konoye wished to conduct the negotiations personally. I asked Saionji about it in a casual manner from time to time. For instance I said "The economic blockade is strangling life from Japan. It is not reasonable to negotiate with a man who grips your throat. The first move is to get free. Then start negotiations." To this Saionji replied, "The economic blockade is their trump card. It is only natural for them to say that they must wait until an understanding is reached before they lift the blockade." Again I said, "What America really wants is Japan's separation from the Axis, is it not?" To this Saionji answered, "Of course, but that is quite out of the question." Another time I remarked, "What will happen if Chiang Kai-shek refused to accept the Japanese proposals? It is possible, even with American mediation, that China may refuse to accede to Japan's demands." Saionji countered, "There will be no point if America cannot make China listen to reason." Thus I gathered my information piecemeal.'

Prince Konoye was questioned in hospital as a witness by the Japanese preliminary judge on November 18, 1942, on Ozaki's reference to this meeting, and in particular on Saionji's relations with Ozaki. Konoye admitted that Ozaki knew his two private secretaries well and came from time to time to his private villa, and also that Saionji was given the tasks of assembling the draft plans of the different ministries on talks with the U.S.A. 'All the documents which I had on the Japanese-American negotiations were handed over to Saionji.'

On August 31 Saionji was invited by Konoye to his villa. In his subsequent interrogation by the Japanese procurator* Saionji described the meeting, and the Prime Minister's request for a written summary of the views expressed during their talks that day. In the end, Saionji's draft was withdrawn, but he kept his own copy.

During the latter half of September, Ozaki returned from his trip to Manchukuo and telephoned to Saionji. On the night of September 20, the two men dined together at the Machiai Kuwana and talked about the Japanese-American negotiations. According to Saionji 'Ozaki took a pessimistic view. I said that, thanks to the European war, the United States would try to avoid a war on two fronts. I said

* On March 30, 1942.

that America, in the name of the principles which they held, would attempt to check Japan but the Americans were not mentally prepared to fight Japan. I was confident, therefore, that the negotiations would be successful.'

Four days later Ozaki telephoned again to Saionji at the Prime Minister's official residence, and suggested a meeting over a glass of beer at the 'Asia' Restaurant in the South Manchurian Railway building. The two men met briefly in another restaurant where Saionji was expecting guests. 'We sat in chairs on the veranda, drinking *saké* or beer. I produced my draft from my bag and showed it to Ozaki, saying: "This is the plan I mentioned the other day."

Ozaki read it page by page, leaning back in his chair. Before he had finished I pressed him for an opinion. But he only said: 'Mm, mm.' He made a more or less pessimistic gesture, shaking his head. Then a maid came and told us my guests were arriving. Ozaki quickly finished reading the paper. He gave it back to me and left the room as the guests came in.

Ozaki reported this episode to Sorge and told him from memory the essential contents of Saionji's draft. 'When Sorge asked me who had shown me the document I said that it was someone close to Konoye.'

The early stages of the negotiations dragged on, and tension mounted in Japanese military and political circles in Tokyo. On October 4 Sorge reported to Moscow that Ozaki had heard that

the main demand to be presented by the U.S. in the Japanese-American negotiations will be withdrawal of Japanese Army from central and southern China; that the current talks are preliminary and informal, although there is a possibility that formal meetings will be held soon; that hope for a successful conference is extremely slight; and that even if Japan decides to thrust southward it will probably be difficult for her to do so at the end of this year.

Ozaki was by now convinced that the talks would fail, and was strengthened in this view by the successful pressure exerted by the army and navy leaders on Konoye to observe the limit already set to the talks at an Imperial Conference on September 6.

Sorge was able to inform the Moscow Centre, early in October, that

Otto [Ozaki] saw the message sent to the U.S. It did not contain any concrete proposals, but was concerned merely with general problems to be discussed during the Japanese-American negotiations. Otto pointed out that up to the present the U.S. has not taken the Japanese proposal seriously and that she has received with indifference Japan's intimation that Konoye is ready to meet Roosevelt.

Contrary to expectation, the general situation has become tense because of the time limit imposed upon Konoye by the army and navy with respect to the negotiations. *According to information obtained by Otto from a person* (two words illegible in Roman script) *close to Konoye, the deadline is set for the end of October. It is likely that the Navy will act in the southern area at once if the negotiations end in failure before then.* Otto has learnt from naval sources that the time limit is set very short, and that, if no satisfactory reply is received from the U.S. by the first week in October, the navy will act.

Otto is certain that both the navy and the government will be forced to act during October if the U.S. does not give a satisfactory answer to the Japanese proposal, although neither the ranking members of the navy nor the government wish to precipitate an incident.

About this time Ozaki told Miyagi that the group had until the end of the month to decide whether Japan would embark on a military campaign in the south. He told Sorge that the navy calculated that the negotiations with America would break down by the beginning of October. It would be politically impossible for the army to withdraw from central and southern China.

There is no evidence to show the reactions of the Moscow Centre to the reassuring reports from the Sorge ring on the impending breakdown of the Japanese-American talks, and the likelihood of a major Japanese threat to the south. At the end of September a solitary message from Moscow requested the following precise technical details:

What are the names of the islands near Kobe on which oil reservoirs and docks are located?

How many new tank units have been organized in Japan?

How many 18-ton tanks does Japan possess? Where is the Tokyo Air Defence Command located? Where are the other projected A/A commands to be located? What units compose a divisional HQ under the new organization?

I have received information concerning army's reorganization and modernization of equipment in 1940–41.

(*a*) Obtain information on government measures to increase production of new equipment.

(*b*) Analyse in concrete detail the characteristics of all types and units.

(*c*) Clarify the strength and scale of units.

Such military intelligence would be essential to the Russians in the event of large-scale hostilities with Japan.

On September 20 Miyagi produced a Japanese Tank Manual and a map, drawn by him, of the anti-aircraft sites in the Tokyo area.

This was to be his last assignment.

Ambassador Ott was still trying to obtain from the Japanese Government a clarification of their attitude to the Tripartite Pact in view of their negotiations with Washington. He was only able to obtain a general statement from the Foreign Minister, Toyoda, that the Pact would not be affected by the present talks. As Sorge reported to Moscow, 'Relations between the two are now rather tense.'

Some time during the first week of October Ozaki and Sorge compiled their final summary and appreciation of the Japanese political scene.

According to information obtained from various Japanese official sources, if no satisfactory reply is received from the U.S. to Japan's request for negotiations by the 15th or 16th of this month, there will either be a general resignation or a drastic reorganization of the Japanese Government. *In either event . . . there will be war with the U.S. this month or next month.* The sole hope of the Japanese authorities is that Ambassador Grew* will present some sort of eleventh-hour proposal through which negotiations can be opened.

With respect to the Soviet Union, top-ranking elements are generally agreed that, if Germany wins, Japan can take over her gains in the Far East in the future and that therefore it is unnecessary for Japan to fight Russia. They feel that if Germany proves unable to destroy the Soviet Government and force it out of Moscow, Japan should bide her time until next spring. In any event, the American issue and the question of the advance to the south are far more important than the northern problem.

This telegram was compiled after a long discussion between Sorge,

* The American Ambassador to Japan.

Ozaki and Klausen, probably on October 4. With the final appreciation that a Russo-Japanese war was unlikely and that Japan would initiate hostilities against the United States within the following weeks, the group felt that their mission to Japan as outlined in the directives of the Moscow Centre had been completed.

Chapter 14

THE BEGINNING OF THE END

'A squad of procurators descended upon us.' OZAKI

IN November 1939 the Special Higher Police (the *Tokko*), in a periodic drive to disrupt the reconstruction of the clandestine Japanese Communist Party, arrested one of the members of a newly formed preparatory committee named Ito Ritsu. He was already known to the authorities and had first come to their attention in December 1932 when at the age of nineteen he was expelled from the First High School in Tokyo as a member of the Japanese League of Communist Youth. For this offence he served a prison sentence, and was released after two years on an undertaking to lead a new life.

In August 1939, on the establishment of the Tokyo research branch of the South Manchurian Railway, Ito was employed as a specialist on agricultural problems. This mammoth organization of Japanese railway, industrial, mining and shipping interests in Manchukuo worked closely with the Kwantung Army in mobilizing and developing the considerable resources of the 'puppet' state, and extended into China with the spreading military occupation, setting up offices in the main Chinese cities. The research department of the South Manchurian Railway had acquired many of the attributes of a civilian intelligence agency. One of its functions was to carry out a detailed and continuous analysis of the economic resources of Manchukuo and China, and the military requirements of the Kwantung Army and, in time, of the Japanese army in China. Although this was a sensitive post in national security terms and a known target for Communist penetration, the police interrogation of Ito concentrated on his rôle in the rebuilding of the Japanese Communist Party. On his re-arrest he was classified by them as a case of 'feigned conversion'.

By this time the Japanese police were aware of Comintern links with Japan via the United States. This Pacific route had been the main channel for agents, couriers and funds since 1935. Miyagi had travelled this way and under these auspices to join the Sorge ring.* It is more than probable that one of the questions put to Ito concerned the Japanese section of the American Communist Party and the identity of any of its members. In the course of interrogation Ito, after resisting for several months, betrayed to the police the name of Kitabayashi Tomo, the former landlady of Miyagi in Los Angeles. She had come back to Japan in December 1936 and was now one of his minor agents.

Ito knew her years before in Los Angeles, and met her by chance on her return. It has been said that he attempted to recruit her for party work and that she rebuffed him.

At the time of his arrest, Ito was suffering from tuberculosis, and understandably dreaded a long term of imprisonment. 'The severe but considerate attitude of the police, however, led him to renounce Communism and confess his crimes.' The revelation of Kitabayashi's name might have seemed a trivial indiscretion. The evidence that he did concede this information is not unequivocal, although the police inspector, who interrogated him in 1939, categorically confirmed this allegation after the war.

Ito was released on parole in August 1940, and returned to his former post in the research department of the South Manchurian Railway. It seems impossible that he could have been reinstated in an organization dealing with highly sensitive military and political data without the active connivance of the police, who would also keep a continuous plain clothes watch on him. There is therefore a strong suspicion that Ito was henceforward acting as a police informer on probation.

Since August 1939 Ozaki had been an unofficial adviser to the Tokyo office of the same research branch of the South Manchurian Railway, and editor of its monthly report. He knew Ito well. They both came from Gifu Prefecture and had been at the same High School in Tokyo. They were now in frequent contact as fellow workers for the South Manchurian Railway. Ozaki was particularly interested in Japan's economic relationship with the tropical regions of South East Asia. and Ito was asked by him to furnish memoranda on this and allied subjects for the monthly report of the Tokyo office.

* The Pacific network was linked to the headquarters of the American Communist Party in New York, and through it to the 'liaison office of the Comintern at 39 East 12 Street, New York City'. See Swearingen and Langer, *Red Flag in Japan*, p. 62 note.

Ito was also Ozaki's main source on wartime agriculture in Japan. He attended meetings of the research staff at which Ozaki would elicit information on specific topics. In September 1941, for instance, a study was initiated into the oil stocks of the Japanese army since the beginning of the China Incident, and in the same month, at a conference held at the head office of the Railway in Dairen valuable data was assembled by Ito on the steel industries there and given to Ozaki.

In mid-September 1941 Kawai saw Ito at Ozaki's house. The two men were clearly on intimate terms. Ozaki described Ito as 'like a right arm to me,' and also as 'a leftist out on parole'.

It is inconceivable that Ozaki himself was not under police surveillance at this time, but the police were interested exclusively in the suppression of Communist organizations, and as yet there was no trace or hint of espionage. Ozaki's high connections would preclude active sanctions, but imperceptibly the net was closing.

Following up the information given by Ito, the Japanese police traced Kitabayashi Tomo to the secluded countryside of Wakayama Prefecture, her husband's birthplace, where she was living quietly. For at least a year the couple were kept under a close police surveillance, which yielded no result.

Sometime in September 1941, however, the police detained Ito's housekeeper, or common law wife, Aoyagi Kikuyo. She was a young worker in a munitions factory, and a member of a clandestine female party cell. The arrest of another member of this cell had led to her. She was also, and more significantly, the niece of Kitabayashi Tomo. It was through her that Ito had learned of Kitabayashi's connections with the Japanese section of the American Communist Party, and probably also of her return to Japan.

In her statement to the police, Aoyagi also spoke of Kitabayashi, and made the disquieting remark that 'the main effort of the Japanese Communist Party is to gather information on Japan's military forces, and all this information is being sent to the Soviet Union through the American Communist Party'.

On September 28, 1941,* Kitabayashi Tomo was suddenly arrested

---

* The day following the arrest of the Kitabayashi couple, on September 29, Ito was again taken into police custody. The episode has not been clarified and he does not seem to have been formally interrogated for at least a year.

together with her husband* and brought to Tokyo. This obscure little dressmaker proved to be the first unwitting clue in the explosive drama which unfolded. She was interrogated on her contacts with Japanese members of the American Communist Party in a police station near the new hideout of Miyagi, and she seems to have naïvely assumed that he too had already been arrested, and mentioned his name to her interrogator. Miyagi was unknown to the Japanese police. The value of her modest fragments of gossip were sadly noted later by him.

After she returned to her part of Japan, I visited her only twice a year. If I obtained some information from her it was haphazard, concerning small things that she had observed by chance, such as: soldiers recalled to the colours; a rumour that the army was digging a tunnel behind the Soviet forces; Air Raid Precaution exercises; the rice crop; living conditions of families where a man had been called up; rice rationing; or the reluctance of farmers to increase their rice crop in preference to growing more profitable things such as oranges or pears.

This low-level informant, whom Miyagi always remembered kindly as his landlady in Los Angeles fourteen years before, was fated to be the first weak link in the chain which was to destroy the whole Sorge ring.

Pursuing their round-up of Communist suspects, the police arrested Miyagi at his house on October 11. They probably hoped to uncover links between subversive groups in Japan and the Japanese section of the American Communist Party. On searching his house the police were astonished to find, among other documents translated into English, a confidential memorandum from the offices of the South Manchurian Railway. As the chief procurator remarked later, 'We thought it strange that an artist should possess a document of this kind.'

In the hours following his arrest, and under ruthless interrogation, Miyagi refused to admit that he was a spy. But he was frail in health, suffering from tuberculosis, and highly strung. During the course of the first day, Miyagi flung himself into the street from a second-floor window of the Tsukiji police station in Tokyo. He fell into the upper branches of a tree and broke a leg. The police jumped after

---

* He was released shortly afterwards.

him, and he was carried back. The questioning continued. On the morning of the following day, October 12, he made a 'voluntary statement'. The procurator recorded later, 'He had calmed down sufficiently to give a coherent account of the details of his crime, and I was able to ascertain that everything which he said was true.'

Miyagi admitted to being a member of a spy ring, operating in Tokyo, which consisted of Sorge, Vukelic, Klausen, Ozaki, and Kawai. A police watch of Miyagi's house after his arrest led to the detention on October 13 of his translator, Akiyama, and a female sub-agent of Miyagi's, Kutsumi Fusako.

The procurator in charge of Miyagi's case reported at once the results of his findings to the Foreign Section of the Special Higher Police, and obtained for inspection the previously prepared confidential dossier on Sorge and the other foreigners involved. The Foreign Section commented that Sorge was an influential assistant to the German Ambassador Ott on matters relating to information, and that it was incredible that he could be a Soviet spy. They did not believe in the case against him, and opposed Sorge's arrest in particular on account of his intimacy with Ott, and the damage it would be likely to inflict on German-Japanese relations. It was therefore decided to detain only Ozaki and the other Japanese mentioned by Miyagi 'and to let future developments determine whether or not the aliens should be taken into custody'.

As Ozaki wrote in prison,

On the morning of October 15, 1941, a squad of procurators descended upon us. I had had an uneasy premonition for several days, and on that morning I knew that the final hour of reckoning had come. Making certain that Yoko had left for school, for I was anxious that my daughter should not be present, I left the house without looking at my wife and without any farewell speech. I felt that, with my arrest, everything had ended; that it was all over.

When I was interrogated that afternoon, it was – as I had expected – on the subject of my relationship with Sorge; I realized that the whole network was being exposed, and I said to myself that everything had ended.

Ozaki made a statement on the day of his arrest identical to that of Miyagi. It appeared clearly, and in detail, that the group was a Soviet spy ring, and by the evening of October 15 a case against Sorge had been established. The procurators then examined Ozaki and Miyagi 'with primary reference to the chain of command of the

Sorge organization' and submitted to their office a case for the arrest of Sorge, Klausen and Vukelic.

The Home Ministry at first opposed this action for diplomatic reasons, but on the following day, October 16, Prince Konoye resigned as Prime Minister. One of the first appointments made in the new Cabinet of General Tojo was the Minister of Justice, Iwamura Michio, who had held the same post in the previous government. The Procurator's Office now submitted to him a summary of the statements made by Ozaki and Miyagi together with a request for the arrest of Sorge. The important sections of the memorandum were underlined in red pencil; for Iwamura was known, as a rule, to read only those portions of a report which were underlined in red. The Minister was in a good humour at his re-appointment, and agreed to the arrests without considering the significance of the case.

On the evening of Tuesday, October 14, Sorge had arranged a customary meeting with Ozaki at the Asia Restaurant in the South Manchurian Railway building. He kept the appointment in vain. Miyagi was due to come to Sorge's house two days later, but failed to appear. On Friday, October 17, Klausen and Vukelic called on Sorge, by prior arrangement, in an atmosphere of mounting disquiet. Vukelic telephoned to Ozaki's office at the South Manchurian Railway and received no answer.

Klausen describes the final meeting of the European members of the group.

Around 7 p.m. on October 17 I went to visit Sorge, who was in bed at the time, to talk about our secret work. He was drinking with Vukelic when I arrived and I joined the circle, opening the bottle of saké which I had brought. The atmosphere was heavy, and Sorge said gravely – as if our fate were sealed – 'Neither Joe nor Otto showed up to meet us. They must have been arrested by the police.'

I was gripped with a strange fear and left after ten minutes. We did not discuss what we would do if we were arrested.

For the first time Klausen was told by Sorge that 'Otto' was Ozaki and learnt the real identity of the 'Joe' of the telegrams.

About 5 a.m. on the morning of Saturday, October 18, Detective Ohashi of the Special Higher Police came on duty at the Toriizaka

Police Station in Tokyo, which was situated in sight of Sorge's home about two hundred yards away. At this early hour a German Embassy car was stationary in front of the house. The presence of a German official* caused temporary embarrassment to the police and the waiting group of procurators, led by Yoshikawa Mitsusada. When the car left, the party burst into the house. Ohashi shouted in some confusion, 'We have come to see you about your recent motor-cycle accident', and without further interchanges Sorge, who was in pyjamas and slippers, was bundled into a police car, protesting loudly that his arrest was illegal.

The party drove to the Toriizaka Police Station, but, in order to avoid any indiscreet enquiries from prowling journalists, Sorge was briskly removed to Sugamo remand prison.

On leaving Sorge's house the previous evening, Klausen had run into detectives from the police station near his home, with whom he had had routine dealings as a foreigner over many months. He was aware and uneasy that he was being closely shadowed, and more so than usual.

Early the following morning one of the same police officers entered his house and his bedroom. He was told: 'We would like you to come to the police station to answer some questions about that car accident you had the other day.'

Recalling what I had heard the previous night, I had a premonition that something more serious than a mere car accident was in the wind. I hurried through my breakfast and made my preparations to leave absentmindedly, incapable of reasoning clearly, and left the house under escort. Out in the street a car was waiting with two plain-clothes men inside.

As the car rocked on its way, not to the Toriisaka Station but in another direction, I resigned myself to my fate. I was detained at the Mita Police Station.

With the simultaneous arrest of Vukelic in the early hours of October 18, the capture of the European members of the Sorge ring

---

* This was Wilhelm Schulze, a close journalist colleague of Sorge's and the head of the official German News Agency in Tokyo. Ohashi, the police inspector conducting Sorge's arrest, stated later that he was watching the house and thought that the presence of this visitor was probably connected with the fall of the Konoye Cabinet two days previously, and that he had come 'to collect a report from Sorge on this'.

was completed, except for Anna Klausen, who was detained only on November 19.

The Japanese police, with bureaucratic thoroughness, made an inventory of items seized at Sorge's house. These bare objects—the physical tools of espionage—were to form the first grim and material skeleton in the chain of proof to be forged against him in the coming months. They included three cameras, one copying camera with accessories, three photo lenses (one telescopic), developing equipment, one black leather wallet containing $1,782, sixteen notebooks with details of contacts with agents and with finance, Sorge's Nazi party card and a list of party members in Japan, two volumes of the German Statistical Year Book (the source of decoding and encoding tables), seven pages of reports and charts in English; and, lastly and fatally, two pages of a typewritten draft, also in English, of the final message of achievement compiled to be sent to Moscow on October 15. In Klausen's house a copy of the same message was found, half encoded, thus producing the starting point for the long drawn-out drama of the interrogations ahead.*

In moving contradiction and contrast to these material revelations of illegal activities, the police noticed the extensive and scholarly library fitting to the work of an innocent specialist and writer on Japanese history and literature, and containing over a thousand volumes. On the table by his bed lay an open volume of the verses of a sixteenth-century Japanese poet. The police also found a manuscript of three hundred pages, the first draft of a book on modern Japan, which it was Sorge's pertinacious and illusory ambition to complete.

During those October days the stresses and strains of undercover work, with the mounting risks of detection after so long a period of operating, had begun to tell on the Sorge ring.

Klausen, in addition to transmitting and receiving radio messages, was responsible for encoding and decoding and keeping the accounts, and at times acting as a courier and keeping in contact with Zaitsev in the Soviet Embassy.† His commercial affairs had prospered, and a tinge of capitalist complacency began to affect his keenness. This attitude turned to marked irritation when the Moscow Centre, at

* See p. 259–60 below.
† Klausen was due to see Zaitsev on November 20.

the end of 1940, sent him this curt message: 'You will use part of the profits of Klausen & Co. as funds for the ring.'

Apart from these frustrations, he was under continuous emotional stress on account of his wife's hatred of his conspiratorial work for the Soviet Union. Her private loyalties were permanently taxed to the limit. He became increasingly slack. He had not made up the accounts of the group for 1941 'because I had lost all confidence in our success and abandoned my duties'. He was behindhand in transmitting radio messages to the Moscow Centre, and the texts en clair began to accumulate on his desk. Ten of these were found there, written in English, on his arrest.

Vukelic was in a similar mood. He had never established fully harmonious relations with Sorge. 'Sorge regarded me as an outsider so far as his group was concerned. Until the very end I could not escape this impression. . . . The first view which he formed of me was not a favourable one; and it is probable that he considered that I was not very serious in my work.'

Feminine influences also, as in the case of Klausen, played a determining part in Vukelic's 'illegal' activities. His marriage to Edith had finally collapsed and ended in divorce. She also had been a reluctant and unreliable witness of the activities of the ring. As she had therefore become a security risk to the group, Sorge sought permission from Moscow to finance her departure from Japan. According to Klausen, writing his prison notes, Vukelic was trying to persuade Edith to leave with their son for Moscow. 'But since my wife (Anna) had told Edith about things there, she was afraid to go. Vukelic was angry about this, and told Sorge. Edith later decided to go to Australia, and Vukelic was satisfied.'

In August or September 1941 Sorge cabled the Moscow Centre:

Gigolo's (Vukelic's) divorced wife and child have been invited by her younger sister to Australia and under the present circumstances it is almost impossible for us to prevent her going. Although Fritz (Klausen) has been using her home as one of our bases of operations, he thinks he can work without her. At any rate her departure probably will result in a reduction of our monthly expenses. A special grant of $400 is requested for her journey through your subordinate man [i.e. Zaitsev at the Soviet Embassy] and also that you send us permission to let her go.*

In September he received instructions to pay her fare to Australia, and she sailed at the end of the month to the general relief of everyone.

* The text of the reply from Moscow was found by the police in Klausen's house.

Vukelic had remarried in January 1940. His second wife was Japanese and she was unaware of her husband's secret work. Since May 1935 he had held a satisfactory and legitimate job as a journalist with the French Havas News Agency. He was happy in his new home, and after the birth of a son, and in constant fear that his wife would discover the real nature of his activities, he was increasingly reluctant to continue to expose himself to the daily risks incurred by the ring. He became idle and elusive. Klausen wrote of him: 'When I first came to Tokyo, he did a great deal of work for the spy ring, but towards the last he was always doing something else when he was supposed to be working for Sorge. . . . I am sure that at the end he was falling away. At times, when Sorge wanted to see him, he kept out of sight for a whole week. Sorge got very angry, but I did not tell him why Vukelic failed to appear. The reason why I understood Vukelic so well was that I too was breaking with Communism.'

Sorge could not have been unaware of this atmosphere around him. But the very nature of his position as leader of the ring limited his personal relations with his collaborators, and his mask of noisy and alcoholic exhibitionism isolated him still further from them. With Klausen and his inferiority complex in the company of intelligent people, and with Vukelic with his vague lack of concentration, Sorge had few personal bonds. Ozaki was, however, his intellectual equal, and the gentle artist Miyagi worked harmoniously with him.

It was with Miyagi that Sorge had the most frequent contacts, drafting and analysing—after translation into English—material and oral reports from Ozaki, and intelligence assembled by Miyagi himself. And it was from Ozaki, his closest collaborator, that Sorge obtained —apart from his own German Embassy sources—the most triumphantly valuable intelligence ever sent by the ring. 'I knew that Ozaki was a reliable man. I knew how far I could question him, and I could ask no more. So if Ozaki said that he had obtained data from someone close to Konoye I took his word for it. And that was that.'

Vukelic later sketched in firm and vivid outline the climate of Sorge's leadership of the little group.

The general atmosphere surrounding our work is one indication that our organization was essentially Communist in character. We held political meetings in a comradely spirit. These meetings were quite untouched by any suggestion of formal discipline. Sorge made it a rule not to become involved in theoretical controversies on political issues. I assume this was in order to avoid the emergence of Trotskyite heresies. Sorge never gave us orders. He only explained what our urgent duty might be; what each of us must do. He would hint to one or two of us what might be the best means of achieving the tasks before us. Or, sometimes, he would say: 'How about taking such and such a course?' Klausen and I, as a matter of fact, were awkward customers, and we behaved in undisciplined ways. Nevertheless, Sorge through all these nine years, except once or twice when he was offended, never adopted an official manner. And even when he was offended, he only appealed to our political conscience and, above all, to the ties of friendship. He never appealed to other motives. He never threatened us; and he never did anything that might be construed as threatening, or as arising from the requirements of official discipline.

This is the most eloquent proof that our group did not possess a military character. The whole atmosphere much resembled that of the Marxist Club to which I had belonged in Yugoslavia. This was thanks in part, of course, to Sorge's personal character. The atmosphere was comradely, quite devoid of military discipline, and of both the good and the bad sides of a military organization.

Among Sorge's many statements to the Japanese police after his arrest, there is no hint of disillusionment with his Moscow superiors during the last months of activity in Tokyo, no admission of searching doubts, which must have occurred to him during his Russian visit in 1935, as to the juggernaut progress of the Stalinist terror in the Soviet Union which was beginning to move. He preserved until the end a monolithic and petrified front of confidence in the future of International Communism in face of his Japanese interrogators.

The only hint of his own weariness and depression comes from recent alleged quotations from his Moscow file in the post-Stalinist Soviet press. 'He did not know that General Berzin who had recruited him in 1929 (if not earlier) as a Soviet intelligence officer, and his immediate superior in the Fourth Bureau, "Alex" Borovich, had been executed in the purges but he could not help sensing the change'. In a letter sent to 'Director' of the Moscow Centre, which from internal evidence must be dated in October 1940, he wrote:

Max [Klausen] is unfortunately so seriously ill that a return of his former working capacity cannot be counted on. He has been working here five years, and the conditions here would undermine the strongest constitution. I am learning his job now, and will take his work on myself.

As for me, I have already told you that, while the European war is still in progress, I shall remain at my post. But since the Germans here say that

the war will soon be over, I must know what is to become of me. May I
count on being able to return home at the end of the war? I have just turned
forty-five, and have been on this assignment for eleven years. It is time for
me to settle down, put an end to this nomad existence, and utilize the vast
experience which I have accumulated. I beg you not to forget that I have
been living here without a break, and – unlike other 'respectable foreigners'
– have not taken a holiday every three or four years. That would look
suspicious.

We remain, with health undermined, it is true, always your true comrades
and fellow workers.

This missive, written clearly in a passing gust of depression, vividly
reveals the sense of isolation and the insecurity of 'illegal' work and
of a double existence in a remote and hostile land.*

Almost exactly a year later, after the undeniable if as yet unrecognized triumphs of the ring, Sorge returned to the same theme, but
this time with a sense of fulfilment. On October 15, 1941 – unknown
to him, the day of Ozaki's arrest – Sorge drafted a telegram to Moscow
in the following terms.

We are deeply moved, and closely attentive to your nation's valiant
struggle against Germany. We greatly regret that we must stay here where
we are rendering no important service or assistance to you.

Fritz [Klausen] and Fix [Sorge] would like to know whether it would
not be wise to have them return home or go to Germany to embark on new
activities. They realize that either of these moves would be extremely
difficult, but we are familiar with the work, and believe that by crossing the
border and serving under you, or by going to Germany to engage in new
activities, we will be able to do something of use. We await your reply.

When questioned later by the Japanese preliminary judge in charge
of his case whether at this moment he had asked Moscow for his recall
because he 'felt dangers drawing near', Sorge replied: 'Not particularly. It was rather because I had completed my task in Japan,
and I wanted to continue my work in Moscow or in Europe. When I
speak of "my task as having been completed" I mean that I had confirmed that Japan would not enter the war against the Soviet Union.'

* It seems that Sorge had remained in intermittent touch with his former wife, Christiane, who had settled in New York. Early in 1941 Frau Ott, the wife of the German
Ambassador in Tokyo, had visited her and brought money and greetings. Christiane
obtained a visa to visit Japan, shortly before traffic between the United States and the
Far East was cut off. She cabled Sorge, but received no reply. Shortly afterwards he was
arrested.

There is nevertheless an air of tired unreality about this message. After discussion with Klausen, it was decided to wait a few days before dispatching it. In the event, the text remained on Sorge's desk and was never sent.

The net had closed in on the Sorge group from separate and uncoordinated directions. The actual arrests were the work of the Special Higher Police, who were subordinate to the Home Ministry and whose special function was to deal with left-wing suspects. It was in pursuit of this particular task that the trail led from Ito Ritsu to Kitabayashi Tomo, and through her to Miyagi. It was a matter of embarrassment and disquiet to the Home Ministry when a European spy ring was unearthed at the end of the trail.

Cases of espionage came within the province of the Military Police (*Kempei*). Competitive clashes of jurisdiction between these civil and military organizations were notorious and frequent, and the Sorge affair provides further illustrations of these rivalries. After the arrests, one of the civilian procurators in charge of the case was summoned to the Military Affairs Bureau of the War Ministry, which was responsible for the *Kempei*, and told: 'We have been sniffing round Sorge's heels. In fact the army has been looking into his activities secretly. But in the end we were dished by outsiders.'

The existence of a spy ring working in Japan was known to the Military Intelligence. Since 1938 radio messages had been intercepted by listening stations of the Ministry of Communications both in Korea and on the Japanese mainland. The first of these dated from July of that year, but neither the exact location of the transmitting set nor the identity of the group seems to have been established by the military police before the arrest of Sorge and his collaborators by the Special Higher Police. As the latter maintained control of the case, the Japanese military authorities never revealed to their civilian counterparts whatever investigations they had pursued in attempting to track down a ring whose existence was known to them.

The Gestapo attaché in Tokyo, Colonel Meisinger, however, claimed later that during such preliminary investigations of Sorge's activities, the Japanese Military Intelligence not only intercepted some of Klausen's radio messages, but did not disturb the set, as they wished to trace the source of the data—much of which could only have been supplied by senior Japanese government officials. The Japanese authorites also boasted to Meisinger that they had intercepted a message from Moscow thanking Sorge for the timely transmission of information on the German attack on Russia.

It seems that during the months prior to the arrests in October 1941 Sorge was the subject of more marked police surveillance than would be normal even in the case of a prominent European resident, and that his close associations with the German Embassy were arousing suspicion. As the police officer who arrested him described it,

> The reason why Sorge was being watched by the sharp eye of the authorities as a suspicious person was that, although his position was solely that of special correspondent of the *Frankfurter Zeitung*, he enjoyed the absolute confidence of the German Ambassador, Ott, and he could come and go as he wished so far as access to the Embassy was concerned. Furthermore, he had the reputation of being a man 'who knew everything'. The Foreign Section of the *Tokko* (the Special Higher Police) had a strong hunch that he was not just a newspaper correspondent.

In August Hanako-san was summoned to the police station and urged to break off her relations with Sorge. The latter's sardonic reaction to this move was to invite the local police chief to dinner.

It has also been suggested that the suspicions of the Japanese police regarding Sorge had been aroused through an indiscretion by Colonel Meisinger, whose task it was to report on German nationals living in Japan and to maintain liaison with the Japanese authorities on suspect individuals. Before his departure for Tokyo, Meisinger had been ordered by his superiors in Berlin to investigate Sorge's activities, and although his report was favourable he is said to have discussed the matter with the Japanese police, who were thus prompted to pursue their own enquiries.

The arrests of Ozaki and Miyagi revealed at once not only the existence of Sorge's ring, but also the alarming high-level leakages from Prince Konoye's circle of the Japanese-American talks. It was probably these disclosures, obtained from Ozaki and Miyagi which led the Procurator's Office to press for the immediate apprehension of Sorge and his European collaborators.

The Japanese police claimed also to have discovered that Sorge was due to leave Japan by ship for Shanghai, but this evidence is not confirmed. It is only clear that, on the eve of his arrest, Sorge had regarded his mission as completed; which was the case.

PART III

Chapter 15

TOKYO DETENTION HOUSE

'I wish I could fly with the sparrows to the skies of Siberia.'

HISTORICALLY, criminal procedure in Japan was profoundly influenced, during the Meiji era (1867–1912), by the legal system of France. Later, during the first half of the twentieth century, until the reforms of the Occupation period, the influence of German law became general. The Penal Code of 1907 and the Code of Criminal Procedure (in force from 1923 to 1948) were based on the corresponding German codes, and they embodied what has been called 'a semi-accusatorial principle'.

In other words, a suspect in police custody could look forward to a long inquisition—how long would depend upon the gravity and complexity of the alleged offence. In serious cases the questioning of the accused could last for well over a year. The trial itself was often little more than a formality, the presiding judge and his colleagues asking further questions, of a confirmatory nature, and permitting small latitude to counsel for the defence.

When grave charges were involved, the inquisition of the suspect, before he was brought to trial, occupied three successive stages — interrogation by the police, interrogation by the procurator, and examination by the preliminary judge. As a rule the first stage took place in a police station, the second in the detention house (or remand prison), the third at the district court. The first stage might overlap the second; but the third—the examination by the preliminary judge —could not begin until the procurator had completed his investigation.

The key figure in the whole process, from arrest to final verdict, was the procurator. Interrogation by the police was supposed to be under his direction; and it was he who decided whether or not the case should go before the preliminary judge. The latter's examination was in large measure a recapitulation of earlier questioning. Like the

263

procurator, the preliminary judge investigated not only the facts of the case, but also — as one authority has written — 'those subjective and psychological elements of a crime that often can be definitely proven only by the defendant's statement of them'. But the preliminary judge, when examining the accused, worked from a brief provided by the procurator; and during the trial the procurator occupied a position, sitting above the defendant and his lawyer, that seemed to place him virtually on level terms with the presiding judge.

Indeed, the status of a procurator was scarcely lower than that of a judge. They were on the same salary scale, and it was the procurator who had the better chance of promotion. The number of highly paid positions was about the same in both branches of the legal profession, but there were more judges than procurators.

As for private lawyers, they were regarded on the whole as decidedly inferior to procurators and judges. In a criminal case the defence lawyer had no powers during the long process of investigation. His functions were very restricted. It was rare for him to probe into a case, beyond questioning the defendant on the facts. He would also interview the defendant's relatives and friends for information to be submitted at the trial in mitigation of the crime. In nearly all cases the aim of defence counsel was to obtain for his client a lenient sentence or, at best, a sentence with stay of execution.

The procurator directly responsible for the interrogation of Sorge was Yoshikawa Mitsusada of the Thought Department of the Tokyo District Court Procurators' Bureau.* Procurator Yoshikawa was thirty-four — twelve years younger than Sorge. For a Japanese he had a formidable physique, being large-boned and slightly above average in height. His long face with its firm mouth and angular jaw suggested an independent and determined character.

Yoshikawa had an extensive knowledge of current political and economic thought, including Marxism. It was rumoured that he had been a Marxist himself when he was a student at Tokyo Imperial University. Soon after graduating from the university, he had written a comprehensive study of the Rice Riots of 1918.

Professor Ikoma, who taught German at the Tokyo Foreign

---

* The procurator in general charge of the case was Tamazawa Mitsusaburo; and he interrogated Ozaki.

Language School, was interpreter during most of the procurator's interrogations of Sorge. Writing of Yoshikawa at that time, Ikoma refers to his youthful appearance but adds: 'He had already acquired many of the characteristics of a Thought Procurator, and in his questioning he mingled the hard and soft approach with great skill. Sorge himself seemed to have some admiration for him.'

As we have seen, Sorge was held for only a short time at the Toriizaka Police Station. The first stage of the investigation — interrogation by the police — began at the Detention House, the remand prison that was part of Sugamo Jail, in the northern suburbs of Tokyo.

For the first few days the Special Higher Police, under the direction of Yoshikawa and other procurators, failed to extract from Sorge any admission that he had been working for the Soviet Union or the Comintern. He acknowledged from the outset that he had been collecting secret information. But he insisted that he had been working for the German Ambassador, not for the Russians. He demanded, again and again, permission to see General Ott.

The claim that he had been spying for Ott was ingenious. It was not, after all, wholly implausible. Sorge could perhaps cherish a slender, dwindling, hope that his claim might be accepted. If so, his position would still be vulnerable, but no longer desperate. He knew that war in the Pacific was near. There was the virtual certainty that Japan would soon be fighting side by side with Germany against the British and Dutch. But if, as seemed likely, Japan took up arms not only against Britain and the Netherlands, but also against the United States, would Hitler and Mussolini honour their obligations under the Tripartite Axis Pact? Would they declare war on America? This was the important question that the Japanese were asking themselves and their Axis allies.

The thought must have occurred to Sorge that the Japanese, at a moment when their relations with America were close to breaking point, would not be so foolish as to risk offending the German Embassy. To arrest a senior German correspondent, holding a semi-official post in the German Embassy, was one thing; to deny the Embassy all contact with him, quite another.

Sorge was arrested on the morning of October 18, which was a Saturday. When Monday arrived, with no hint that he was to be allowed to see Ott or anyone else from the Embassy, the tormenting probability grew with every hour that his interrogators were speaking the truth when they said they had damning evidence against him. Whatever Miyagi and Ozaki had admitted, and such documentary material as had been found in their homes, could be acknowledged in terms of intelligence collected for Ambassador Ott. The weak links, from Sorge's point of view, were Klausen and Vukelic—particularly the former. Much depended on whether Klausen's transmitting set had been discovered and, if so, where. According to one source, he began to confess on the day of his arrest, October 18. But Yoshikawa's recollection is that Klausen confessed 'three or four days after his arrest'*—in other words, on Tuesday, October 21, or Wednesday, October 22.

In a statement prepared after his police interrogation had been completed, Klausen, writing about Sorge, remarked of the latter that 'he was a man who could not bear up under certain conditions'.

I say this since it appears that he told everything after his arrest. If at the time of his arrest he had remained a firm Communist he would have held his tongue and not told everything.

No doubt the police assured Klausen, as an inducement to tell all, that Sorge had confessed everything as soon as he was arrested. But it seems unlikely that even Max Klausen would have had the hardihood to volunteer those remarks, unless he himself had put up more than a token resistance to his inquisitors in the period immediately following his arrest. It is possible, then, that he did not give way until October 22 or 23. As for Vukelic, the meagre evidence suggests that he confessed after Klausen.

The procurators wanted to obtain a confession from Sorge, of whose guilt they felt reasonably sure, before he was allowed to meet General Ott. Indeed they had done their best to prevent any such meeting ever taking place. But they were overruled. Facing a crisis of the first magnitude with the United States, the new Prime Minister, Lt.-General Tojo, when approached directly by the German Ambassador, felt obliged to insist that the Ministry of Justice should permit Ott to visit Sorge.

Tojo, though never a dictator, had at this time exceptional power; for in October 1941 he was Home Minister and Minister of War as well as Premier. But the officials of the Japanese judiciary, including, of course, the bureaux of procurators, had built up, from the end of

---

* Yoshikawa, when interviewed by one of the authors.

the nineteenth century, a tradition of sturdy independence. They were notoriously not amenable to political pressure.*

The unyielding professional independence of the judiciary was a factor gravely underrated by Sorge, if he calculated that diplomatic considerations would force the authorities to accept Ott's intervention on his behalf. The Justice Ministry in Tokyo never bowed its head to the Ministry of Foreign Affairs.

When the reluctant procurators therefore came to make arrangements for Ott's visit to Sorge they made sure that the meeting should be so brief and so hedged about by formality as to be almost meaningless.

Procurator Yoshikawa has described the inhibiting restrictions that were imposed:

I laid down certain conditions for the meeting.
(1) No mention must be made of the case under investigation.
(2) I must be present at the meeting.
(3) The meeting must be limited to five minutes' duration.
(4) Ott must speak first, to Sorge. His words would then be translated into Japanese by an interpreter. If I approved them, then I would raise my hand, and Sorge would be permitted to reply.

In evidence to the Un-American Activities Committee in Washington, in August 1951, and when interviewed in Japan ten years later, Yoshikawa maintained that Sorge finally confessed that he was a Communist agent on Saturday, October 25—just a week after his arrest. Moreover Yoshikawa declared that this happened before the meeting with Ott took place. Yoshikawa's senior colleague, Tamazawa, also stated that Sorge made his first confession ('to Yoshikawa and myself') on 'a Saturday afternoon five or six days after his arrest'.

But Ott's first telegram to Berlin on the Sorge affair, dated October 23, includes this sentence: 'So far it has only been possible to pay

---

* This tradition is generally considered to have been established through the famous Otsu case of 1891. At Otsu, near Kyoto, the Russian Tsarevitch, later Tsar Nicholas II, was attacked and wounded by a Japanese policeman. The Japanese Penal Code laid down that an attempt on the life of a member of the Japanese imperial family was punishable by death, but that the maximum penalty for any other murder attempt was life imprisonment. The Japanese Government, however, believed that the Otsu policeman should be given a capital sentence and put pressure on the judiciary accordingly. This pressure, however, was successfully resisted.

When the Head of the Press Section of the Berlin Foreign Office met Oshima at the end of October, to discuss the matter of Sorge's arrest, Oshima, in pointing out that the courts were independent and responsible only to the Emperor, made a reference to the Otsu Affair.

a short formal visit to Sorge'. And this was the visit that was described by the Japanese 'as a special and unique favour only conceded because of Japan's friendly relations with Germany'.

It is clear from this that Ott's meeting with Sorge occurred on, or before, Thursday, October 23. If it is correct that Sorge did not confess until the 25th, then Yoshikawa's memory is at fault when he asserts that Sorge's resistance collapsed before Ott arrived at Sugamo. To quote Yoshikawa:

The Minister of Justice was told by Tojo that he must allow Ott to meet Sorge. Now this happened at a crucial moment. It was the crisis of the investigation. I wanted to have Sorge's confession before Ott saw him. In fact Sorge did confess before they met.

Whether or not Sorge had confessed by the 23rd, the meeting between himself and Ott was necessarily a strained and painful episode. General Ott recalls that Sorge was reticent, declining to answer certain questions that were put to him. When the short interview came to an end Sorge asked that his good wishes be given to Frau Ott and the family.

Yoshikawa's narrative of the meeting between Sorge and Ott is worth recounting in his own words.

When the meeting took place Sorge looked completely exhausted, and his expression was one of extreme gravity; and as soon as Ott saw his face he appreciated at once the seriousness of the situation.

Ott said, 'Well, how are you?'
Sorge replied: 'I am well.'
Ott: 'How about the food you are getting?'
Sorge: 'It is sufficient.'
Ott: 'Is there anything you need?'
Sorge: 'No thank you.'
Then Sorge said: 'This is our last meeting.' Whereupon Ott was visibly moved. He was in uniform, and he saluted Sorge in soldierly Prussian style and then left the room.

According to Yoshikawa, Sorge — having confessed — was reluctant to meet the Ambassador. He pointed out that, after all, he and Ott were good friends, though their political opinions were different. But Yoshikawa told him that he ought to see Ott. 'A Japanese in this kind of situation would see him to say a last farewell.'*

* When interviewed, Yoshikawa recollected that he said to Sorge: 'Well, as for us Japanese, we would have a last meeting, as human beings, even if ideology made us enemies.' ('*Ware ware Nihonjin nara, shugi no ue de teki mikata ni nattemo, ningen toshite saigo wakure wo suru.*')

For Sorge the breaking point came when statements by Klausen, and the others, were shown to him, and when Yoshikawa made the following characteristically Japanese appeal:

What about your obligations as a human being? Your followers, who have risked their lives to work with you, have confessed and may hope thereby to secure some mitigation, however slight, of their sentences.

*Are you, as their leader, going to abandon them to their fate? If I were in your place I would confess.**

The interrogation was taking place in the Buddhist chaplain's room at Sugamo, the chief inquisitor on the police side being Detective-Inspector Ohashi Hideo of the *Tokko*.

Unexpectedly, Sorge asked for paper and a pencil. He wrote down, in German: 'I have been an International Communist since 1925'. He then screwed the paper into a ball and threw it across the room. He rose to his feet and began walking round the room. Suddenly he burst into tears. 'I am defeated,' he cried. 'For the first time in my life I am defeated.'

In the spring of 1949 American Military Intelligence in Tokyo obtained statements on oath, from judicial officials who had dealt with the case, claiming that Sorge, Klausen, Ozaki and Vukelic had not been subjected to abuse or coercion during their period of confinement up to and including their trial by Tokyo District Criminal Court. Among those who made sworn statements to this effect were Procurators Tamazawa and Yoshikawa, the preliminary judge who examined Sorge and Ozaki, and the two surviving judges of the three who tried Sorge in the District Court. An affidavit on similar lines was sworn by the lawyer who had represented Sorge, the Klausens and Vukelic.†

If we feel bound to give little weight to such statements, this is by no means to accuse the officials concerned of deliberate mendacity, although it is not unlikely that a procurator, for example, might

* Specialists may care to know Yoshikawa's actual words: *Ningen toshite do suru ka? Kimi to kimi no tomodachi wa inochi wo kakete issho ni hataraite kita. Tokoro ga kimi no tomodachi wa minna jihaku shite sukoshi demo tsumi no karu karan koto negaite iru. Kimi wa 'leader' toshite buka wo migoroshi ni suru no ka? Washi nara jihaku suru.*

† The affidavits were obtained in order to meet claims by Agnes Smedley and her friends that statements about her made by Sorge, Ozaki and others were valueless, since they were made under interrogation by the Japanese and were therefore extracted under duress.

succeed in forgetting occasions of police brutality—assuming the improbable contingency that these took place in his presence.

During the feudal period in Japan, as in Europe, torture was a recognized part of the investigation of suspects, and of the punishment of those convicted of heinous crimes. In a passage of the recantation that he addressed to the District Court, in the summer of 1943, Ozaki wrote: 'If it had been the feudal era I would probably have been summarily broken on the wheel or hanged on the gallows as guilty of a political crime against the state and condemned to eternal damnation.' He was not exaggerating. Men still living could remember those days. Japan's feudal past was not remote.

The Japanese police before the war had a universal and deserved reputation for severity. The treatment of those accused of ideological offences was apt to be particularly harsh, especially for those who refused to abandon or modify their beliefs. There was more than one instance between the wars of suspects dying in police hands as a result of the treatment they received.* And we have seen what Kawai endured in the cellars of Hsinking.

Foreigners were not necessarily immune from police violence, although in general they were treated more humanely than many, perhaps most, Japanese suspects. But a very few disagreeable or tragic episodes, involving foreigners in custody, had already occurred before the outbreak of war in December, 1941.† On the day of Pearl Harbour a number of American and British nationals were held for questioning as suspected spies. The observations on the police made by the American and British Ambassadors, in their memoirs, are not unfair. 'The stupidity of those Japanese police,' wrote Grew, 'was only surpassed by their utter cruelty.' Sir Robert Craigie's comment reads: 'I made a point of seeing all who had suffered imprisonment. . . . There were many cases of inexcusable harshness and even physical cruelty.'

Two of those arrested—Otto D. Tolischus of the *New York Times*, and a British journalist, Phyllis Argall of *Japan News-Week*—wrote accounts of the process of investigation by police and procurators,

---

* Two notorious cases occurred in 1933. In February the left-wing novelist, Kobayashi Takiji, was murdered by the police. At the end of the year Noro Eitaro, a well-known Marxist, died in police custody.

† Two instances may be cited. A New Zealander, W. M. Bickerton, was badly beaten under interrogation by the Special Higher Police in 1934. In 1940 Melville Cox, Reuter's correspondent, jumped or fell to his death, while under interrogation, from a window of *Kempeitai* headquarters in Tokyo.

ending in the farce of the District Court trial. The recorded experiences of the two journalists provide a glimpse behind the closed doors of Sugamo, where Sorge and his confederates were detained.

Tolischus was questioned by the Special Higher Police at Sugamo on at least thirty-eight days between January 3 and March 11, 1942, the average duration of each session being four hours. In five of the early interrogations he was the object of violence amounting to torture.* But after the second week in January he was not physically ill-treated. His chief inquisitor celebrated the end of the police investigation by inviting Tolischus to a *tête à tête*, in the examining room, over coffee, cigarettes and a newspaper, begging off him a pair of shoes as a farewell gift.

Phyllis Argall's experience of police procedure was more agreeable. While in Sugamo she was not exposed to violence or the threat of it. She became, she says, quite friendly with her interrogators.†

Otto Tolischus and Phyllis Argall were not brought before the procurator until the police had finished with them. In the case of Sorge, as we shall see, the two stages overlapped.

The procurator's record of his interrogation of Tolischus, which lasted only three weeks, was not translated until Tolischus had been made to put his signature and thumb-print to the Japanese text. When Tolischus objected to several statements attributed to him, the procurator sternly refused to change them, and he cautioned Tolischus against trying to challenge the document in court.‡

The procurator's opening gambit in her examination, writes Phyllis Argall, will always remain in her memory 'as a prize example of supreme inanity'.

However friendly we may be personally our countries are at war, and we are actually enemies. Hence you must tell me the truth. I want you to confide in me as fully and frankly as you would in your own mother.§

Phyllis Argall does not say whether her procurator compelled her to sign a report against her will. But she has some revealing comments

---

* On these five occasions Tolischus was compelled to remain in a kneeling position, in formal Japanese style, while three detectives struck him repeatedly, stamped their feet on his knees, or twisted his head and arms in a judo hold.

† Her account suggests that she may have been arrested by the *Kempei* (she refers to 'the gendarmerie'). The single instance of violence in her case occurred on the day of her arrest, when a police, or *Kempei*, officer struck her on the face.

‡ 'If you dare,' said the procurator, 'to challenge this report in court, you will be punished very severely.'

§ She goes on, however, to point out that the man 'was nobody's fool'. 'His legal mind soon had me tying knots in my own statements.'

to make on the way the police in general prepared their interrogation records.

> They were by no means required to record everything we said. . . . They also had the privilege of omitting any part of an argument, or stringing statements together with no regard to their unified sequence or relevancy. . . . All these statements had to be signed with a thumb-print at the end of the day's interrogation. If we refused to sign, the thumb was forcibly pressed on the ink pad and applied to the paper.

Otto Tolischus and Phyllis Argall were fortunate. They were spared the tedious ordeal of examination by a preliminary judge; and after an extremely short, cursory trial by the District Court they were given suspended sentences of eighteen months' imprisonment. This meant that they could be repatriated on an exchange ship. If their arrest was unconnected with the Sorge affair, this must nevertheless have greatly inflamed long-standing police suspicions of Western correspondents.

It will scarcely be denied, then, that the Special Higher Police could be brutal and capricious in their handling of suspects. The procurators — better educated and much more sophisticated than the police — remained as a rule in the background, out of sight, while the accused was undergoing the rigours of the first stage of investigation.

There is no reliable evidence to show whether or not Sorge was tortured before he agreed to confess. It is known that he faced a relentless interrogation during the first days at Sugamo, from early morning to late at night. A passage in Yoshikawa's testimony to the Un-American Activities Committee underlines the fact that this was a harsh ordeal. (The reference is to the situation shortly before Sorge broke down.)

> About 4 o'clock my colleague, prosecutor Tamazawa, and a policeman went to see if his health would stand any further investigation.

Nevertheless, leaving aside all self-exculpatory disclaimers by Yoshikawa, Inspector Ohashi and others, the general view of those in Japan who have studied the case or were close to members of the ring is that Sorge was not subjected to physical torture. On such matters the truth sometimes tended to emerge after the war, when political prisoners were released and the habit of free speech took hold.*

Because of the exceptional gravity of the case, Yoshikawa was present at many, probably most, of the first interrogations by Inspector Ohashi and the police. Yoshikawa claims that at the outset he and his colleagues had to discover the answers to three questions. Was Sorge in fact a German spy (as he claimed), who had been making use of Communist contacts in Japan? Was he a double agent, working for Moscow as well as Berlin? Or was he really a spy for Moscow who pretended to be a Nazi?

As soon as it was established, following Sorge's dramatic admission, that they were dealing with a Communist spy, Yoshikawa and the police set out to clarify other basic questions. Was Sorge simply a Communist spy, or was he also a 'Roosevelt spy'? And as a Communist spy did he work for the Fourth Bureau of the Red Army or for the Comintern?

The first point, presumably, was cleared up without much difficulty, although instinctive suspicion may have made the police hesitate for a long time before they finally accepted that Sorge was working only for the Russians. The second main question was more complicated. By this time Klausen had confessed that he had been sent to Japan by the Fourth Bureau of the Red Army. But apparently Vukelic had told his inquisitors that Sorge was working for the Comintern. And in his answers to the police, and indeed to the procurator, Sorge deliberately blurred the issue. As he was to admit later to the preliminary judge, he was 'intentionally imprecise' in the written confession he submitted to Yoshikawa.

Sorge in fact underplayed the rôle of the Fourth Bureau so far as he was concerned, implying that his links with it were technical and organizational only—as though the Bureau were little more than a forwarding office for reports destined to reach the leadership of the Comintern and of the Communist Party of the Soviet Union. The interrogators and himself seem to have agreed on the somewhat loose term 'Moscow Centre' to describe the organization that directed his activities. Not until his examination by the preliminary judge— when he had the benefit of some advice from a defence lawyer—did

* Ishii Hanako, for example, does not believe Sorge was tortured; and she has been in constant touch since the war with persons such as Kawai Teikichi, Ozaki's half-brother, Ozaki's son-in-law, and others who have studied the case and whose natural bias is certainly not favourable to the pre-war police. Equally, the accepted view is that Vukelic (as well as Miyagi) was tortured. On the treatment of Ozaki and Klausen opinions differ.

Sorge acknowledge that all his information was sent to the Fourth Bureau, as the only organization with which he had contact.

His reluctance to make this clear to the police was due to his belief that, once it was realized that he belonged to a military apparatus, he would be handed over to the *Kempei* and shot out of hand.

Once he had agreed to confess, Sorge asked that he should be interrogated only by Yoshikawa. But the police phase of the investigation could not be omitted. Thus Sorge was examined by the police in the morning, and by Yoshikawa in the afternoon and evening until late at night. It seems that at first Yoshikawa questioned Sorge without an interpreter. For Yoshikawa knew a little German as well as some English. The interpreter who served Inspector Ohashi of the *Tokko* police earned Sorge's contempt; and there can be no doubt that until the police had completed their part of the investigation, in early March 1942, the forenoon was for Sorge the most trying part of the day.* The Special Higher Police permitted him no respite, except on two occasions—namely December 8, 1941, when Japan fell upon her enemies, and New Year's Day, 1942, when even the *Tokko* took a holiday.

The police interrogations lasted for some eighteen weeks—a good deal longer than impatient procurators had expected. An official with the forbidding title of Chief of the Thought Department of the Tokyo District Criminal Court Procurators' Bureau had ordered the Metropolitan Police Board to complete their report on the Sorge case within the year 1941. But he encountered strong opposition.

Although the Procurators' Bureau had undoubted authority to direct the scope—if not the method—of police inquiries, the exercise of this authority could be thwarted by departmental jealousy. All divisions of the civil police came under the Home Ministry. But the procuracy was a branch of the Ministry of Justice. There was often friction, muted but unmistakable, between police and procurators.

The Chief of the Special Higher Police was not prepared to have his men hurried by the Procurators' Bureau. Evidently he had no intention of complying with instructions from the Ministry of Justice to have everything finished, so far as the police were concerned, by December 31, 1941. He met complaints with the tart

---

* It is just possible that the police interpreter concerned with Otto Tolischus, and the most unpleasant of his tormentors, may have taken some part in the police interrogation of Sorge. This creature (whom Tolischus nicknamed 'the Snake') shouted at Tolischus: 'I asked the *Frankfurter Zeitung* man, and he told me you were a spy.'

observation that 'it passed his comprehension' why, in the most dramatic case they had ever handled, the police should be told to work with greater speed. They were accustomed, he said, to spend a full year, or a year and a half, on 'ordinary left-wing cases'; so in the matter of Sorge and the others the police 'must be given every latitude to carry out a thorough investigation'.

Yoshikawa's formal interrogation of Sorge, then, started well before the police had finished their own investigation. Procurator Yoshikawa began his official questioning in December, and he now called in an interpreter, in the person of Professor Ikoma of the Tokyo Foreign Language School.* Ikoma recalls that he happened to be extremely busy on work of his own at that period.

The times that were convenient for the procurator and for myself rarely coincided. So we would keep in touch by telephone. A taxi would be sent for me, to take me to Sugamo; and the interrogations would have to take place at any free time, irrespective of whether it was day or night.

Professor Ikoma was also required to make a Japanese translation of a typewritten autobiographical statement, or confession, composed by Sorge under the general supervision of Yoshikawa. This document amounted eventually to some 50,000 words. It had grown week by week on the basis of Yoshikawa's early interrogations when, for the most part, he had seen Sorge alone. At intervals of a few days Sorge, using his own machine, would type a statement, going over the ground that had been covered. Yoshikawa would read it carefully with the help of a dictionary; and he often made Sorge amend or clarify certain passages. Thus the final document shows us the range and sequence of subjects on which he was first examined by Yoshikawa — the Comintern, the Shanghai ring, the Tokyo ring, general activities undertaken by Sorge and the ring in Japan, Sorge's 'contacts with the central authorities while in Moscow', and his 'past history as a German Communist'.

This document is one that would hardly have satisfied a European interrogator; for it deals only in cursory fashion with Sorge's early career. The precise nature of his activities in the nineteen-twenties

---

* Ikoma was asked to undertake this duty by the Education Ministry, which had been approached by the Ministry of Justice. He recalls: 'There were of course suitable interpreters in the Foreign Ministry; but because of the latter's connections with the German Embassy, the Ministry of Justice wanted the Foreign Ministry to be kept out of the case as far as possible. . . . I had to accept the invitation whether I wanted to or not.'

is left obscure. Even on Shanghai, where Yoshikawa did press for some further elucidation, Sorge's own story suggests that he was successfully evasive. Why was Sorge able to blur so many issues? Why did the procurator accept a statement or confession that fell short of the whole truth?

Two reasons suggest themselves. In the first place, Yoshikawa, was primarily concerned to investigate Sorge's activities in Japan over the previous eight years. What happened before 1933 was of less immediate interest. Secondly, it is probable that in volunteering to write his own story, Sorge's purpose was to obtain a small but not insignificant tactical advantage over his interrogator. From his knowledge of Japanese psychology Sorge was aware that a procurator, when dealing with an ideological offender, always looked for some change of heart or 'conversion' that would entitle the accused, after the purgatory of investigation and trial, to be re-admitted to society as a loyal Japanese subject. A foreigner could not be expected to undergo this kind of conversion. Sorge indeed never recanted, in the sense of renouncing allegiance to Moscow. But his apparent eagerness to co-operate, once he had admitted that he was 'an International Communist', no doubt impressed the procurator. This is not to imply that the sophisticated Yoshikawa was disarmed by Sorge's readiness to talk; but it may be that at the very moment when Yoshikawa believed he had won a decisive moral victory the initiative, in a sense, passed to Sorge.

At all events Sorge was able to keep out of the record the names of those, in Europe and possibly in Asia, who might suffer for their past association with him. And it was Sorge's luck that the Japanese would not allow anyone from the German Embassy to take part in the investigations.

Yoshikawa himself seems to realize that he met his match in Sorge. Any other interpretation makes his fulsome praise of Sorge somewhat difficult to understand. 'In my whole life', Yoshikawa has declared, 'I have never met anyone as great as he was.'*

Inspector Ohashi of the Special Higher Police, interviewed in 1961 by a Tokyo magazine, has also professed a warm regard for Sorge, even claiming that his amicable relations with Sorge at Sugamo

---

* Interview with Yoshikawa by one of the authors. His words, in Japanese, were '*I-sho ni anna rippa na ningen atta koto ga nai.*'

earned him the disfavour of his superiors and delayed his subsequent promotion in the *Tokko*.* He says that, in return for Sorge's co-operation, he brought the newspaper to Sugamo every day, together with a supply of Sorge's own tea. They would drink this together while Ohashi explained, through the interpreter, what was happening outside the gates of the Detention House — 'covering', as Ohashi put it, 'the whole paper, in a rough way, from the social page to the advertisements.'

At least some of the anecdotes related by Ohashi seem credible. On one occasion Sorge suggested that in spite of early victories Japan would probably lose the war; and then, with a touch of characteristic bravado, the kind of bravado that would impress a policeman, though not a procurator, Sorge said: 'When conditions become desperate the Japanese Government will want to avail itself of my services. Should this occur I pray that I may do my best for Japan.'

According to Ohashi, Sorge never imagined for a moment that he might be given a capital sentence. But one day he said to Ohashi, jokingly; 'If I am sentenced to death, Ohashi-san, I shall become a ghost and haunt you.'†

On March 7, 1942, when at last the police interrogation was completed, Ohashi bought some fruit and tea and gave what he described as a 'farewell party' for Sorge. Perhaps, like the *Tokko* man who interrogated Tolischus, Ohashi begged a farewell gift off Sorge; or it may be that Sorge acted spontaneously. But on that day he gave Ohashi a note, written in English in his own handwriting, that may have accompanied a photograph of himself or some other memento. The note speaks of Sorge's gratitude to Ohashi for 'his most profound and most kindly investigation of my case during the winter of 1941–42'. 'I will never forget,' writes Sorge, 'his kindness during the most difficult time of my eventful life.'

Only the ingenuous would accept this as sound evidence that Sorge was throughout well treated by the *Tokko*. Ohashi's own memory certainly played him false in one particular. He recalls that when, as was his duty, he had to recommend the punishment to be imposed on Sorge, he wrote simply: 'I request a penalty suitable to the offence in

---

* Ohashi was in fact an Assistant-Inspector, and he does not seem to have risen above this rank.

† Ohashi says that he replied to Sorge: 'Do you mean to tell me that you — a materialist — believe in ghosts!' Whereupon Sorge burst into a roar of laughter.

question.' He did not feel that Japan had suffered actual harm from Sorge's activities.

But Ohashi's report on the case, dated March 11, 1942, ended with these words immediately over his signature: '. . . the harm sustained by our country is enormous and terrifying in its implications. Accordingly, it is recommended that the crime be punished by the imposition of the death penalty.'

There is some discrepancy, then, between the facts and Ohashi's recollection of them twenty years later.

By the time the police had completed their questioning of Sorge, Yoshikawa was drawing near to the end of his own investigation of the case. His last official interrogation—the forty-seventh—took place on March 27, 1942.

Like the police, Yoshikawa had covered a lot of ground. He had paid particular attention to Sorge's activities in the German Embassy, his association with General Ott, and the items of intelligence that Sorge had obtained from German sources. As one would expect, the questions became more searching when the investigation turned to the events of 1941—German reactions to Matsuoka's European tour, and to the Japanese-Soviet Pact; the German attack on Russia; and, above all, Japanese plans in the summer of 1941.

Yoshikawa also investigated in detail the information Sorge received from Ozaki and Miyagi. Moreover, he devoted one period of interrogation entirely to the issue of Sorge's political activity—as distinct from espionage—in other words the extent to which Sorge had tried to influence opinion in the German Embassy. And Yoshikawa asked a question of considerable significance to the Japanese. *'What political activity did you undertake in order to influence, through Ozaki, the Konoye circle in 1941, after the German-Soviet hostilities had broken out?'*

Sorge's reply was that he had told Ozaki—whose opinion was identical with his own—that the Soviet Union was no menace to Japan, that Japan's economic and political interests lay not in the north, but in the south. 'Surely it was more profitable for Japan to acquire the tin and rubber of the south than to engage in a very hard campaign in Siberia.'

This was the expected answer. But the question of the influence exerted, indirectly, on Prince Konoye by Ozaki and, even, by Sorge himself—through Ozaki—was one that the procurators refrained from pursuing very thoroughly.

It is possible that after 1945, chastened by defeat, many Japanese saw in Ozaki—as one under the baleful influence of the formidable Sorge—a scapegoat on whom to place part of the blame for Pearl Harbour. It was not suggested, by anyone well-informed, that Ozaki could directly sway Konoye's outlook on affairs. Ozaki was not on intimate terms with Konoye. But he was of course on close terms with some of Konoye's own intimates.

Thus after the war the procurator who interrogated Ozaki made the following statement on oath:

Sorge's special relationship to Ambassador Ott, Ozaki's ties with Prime Minister Konoye and others, the social positions of the defendants, and similar considerations made it reasonable to suspect them of having engaged in political activities; and during the course of our investigation we found ample justification for such a suspicion, both Sorge and Ozaki confessing that following the outbreak of the Russo-German war, when a northward thrust had seemed imminent, they had started a political movement aimed at diverting Japan's energies southward against England and the United States.

By the time we investigated this political plot angle, however, the Pacific War had started, and we were afraid to delve too deeply into it, *lest, by proving that the war was provoked by the Communists, we invite internal conflict. We deliberately refrained from making a thorough investigation, and, in consequence, the statements of the defendants on the point were far from conclusive.*

The editor of *Zoruge Jiken* (*The Sorge Affair*), the three-volume collection of Japanese documents relating to the case, attaches weight to the theory that the procurators failed to probe deeply into the purely political influence consciously exerted by Sorge and Ozaki. For, it is argued, if this had been thoroughly investigated 'the Japanese leaders would have been placed in an awkward position.'

It would have looked as though their 'Holy War' had been intended and directed by spies .ⁿ. every care was taken so far as possible not to touch either Konoye's circle or the army and navy. No persons connected with the army or navy were touched (i.e. questioned as witnesses). For the principal actors in the drama of the 'Holy War' could not be arraigned for interrogation.

However, at a time when Japan's 'southern advance' seemed amply justified by its initial success, the procurators were not interested — whatever their views after the war — in this question.

Yoshikawa ended his formal interrogation of Sorge by asking him for his views on the current situation of the world. Sorge's reply took the form of a synoptic prediction, only partly fulfilled by later events. He declared that the British Empire would collapse — irrespective of whether or not the Axis won the war. 'Britain,' he declared, 'is like a man made immobile by surplus fat.' But Sorge went on to state with assurance that Britain would not surrender. The British, he said, might not offer very resolute resistance against attacks on their colonies, but they were fighting tenaciously to defend their own country and the Suez Canal.

Sorge predicted a stalemate as the probable outcome of the Pacific War, and stated that he had no confidence in Japanese claims to be able to solve the economic problems afflicting China and South-east Asia. As a dogmatic Marxist, he forecast revolution in the United States; and as one who was half-Russian, he believed that the Germans would be driven from Soviet territory; and 'Nazi power, unable to crush the Soviet Union, must of necessity decline'.

Two more sessions of interrogation terminated the proceedings by the end of March, 1942. Sorge now awaited the third stage — the examination by the preliminary judge.

Meanwhile, his direct associates, and many others, were undergoing varied ordeals. They formed the several branches, major and minor, that constituted the ramifications of the Sorge case.

Chapter 16

RAMIFICATIONS OF THE SORGE CASE

'I was doubly astonished to learn that Japanese intellectuals were involved.' THE VICE-PRESIDENT OF THE OTARU BRANCH OF THE RESERVISTS' ASSOCIATION, on reading the announcement of the arrests of all concerned.

OVER a period of eight and a half months, from September 28, 1941, when Mrs. Kitabayashi was taken into custody, to June 8, 1942, the Japanese police arrested and interrogated thirty-five men and women in connection with the Sorge case. The figure includes Sorge and his four confederates, Ozaki, Klausen, Miyagi and Vukelic. It also includes eighteen persons adjudged innocent of a conscious breach of the law.

The compact size of the Sorge ring and its sub-agents is illustrated by the fact that the number of sub-agents arrested by the authorities, who conducted an exhaustive investigation of the whole affair, did not exceed eleven. Seven of these belonged to Miyagi's subsidiary ring, four to Ozaki's.

Even so, from the point of view of safety and efficiency, there were too many of them. Miyagi took what proved to be a fatal risk, when, for reasons of sentiment, he got in touch with Mrs. Kitabayashi and sought her co-operation. And, however convenient it may have been to have the help of a competent translator, it was also rash of Miyagi to have enlisted the services of Akiyama Koji.*

A more legitimate risk was incurred when, at the beginning of 1936, Miyagi met and confided in a middle-aged woman with a Communist past. This was Kutsumi Fusako, who had been a member of the Hokkaido District Committee of the Japanese Communist Party. Towards the end of a four years' sentence of imprisonment, awarded in 1929 for violation of the Peace Preservation Law, she had made a formal recantation of her political faith. When she moved south to Tokyo, after her release from jail, Kutsumi Fusako must have been known to the police as a lapsed Communist.

Whether or not her apostasy in prison was genuine, Kutsumi's

* See p. 146 above.

allegiance to the Communist cause was firm when she met Miyagi, at the beginning of 1936. She agreed to work for him. For a time at least they met once a week, and Miyagi gave her a small allowance to cover expenses. She collected information about the February Mutiny and thereafter on the left-wing movement in general.

Kutsumi Fusako introduced Miyagi to a friend of hers, Yamana Masami. He too had been sentenced to imprisonment by the same court in Hokkaido for Communist activities. Yamana, the son of a farmer and a man of little formal education, had for years taken part in the left-wing agrarian movement in Hokkaido. Miyagi says that at first he did not think of enlisting Yamana's help but that, from the spring of 1936, he came to use him as a source of information on agricultural conditions. Yamana did a good deal of travelling—in 1939, for example, he went to Manchukuo—but the nature of his occupation is not clear, although for a time he was employed in Tokyo by the Farmers' Union, and also by an ultra-nationalist society, the *Tohokai*.

Miyagi financed several of Yamana's journeys, including a trip to south Sakhalin, and it was his practice to meet Yamana at regular intervals, to be given verbal reports on economic conditions in various parts of the country, on troop movements, popular morale, and on other matters of general interest—the kind of miscellaneous intelligence that a man might gather from gossip in railway trains, country buses and provincial inns.

Neither Kutsumi nor Yamana met Sorge, who indeed never heard of them by name. Kutsumi was detained for questioning when she walked up to Miyagi's front-door three days after he himself had been arrested. Yamana, on the other hand, was not arrested until the middle of December, two months later.

It was Yamana who introduced Miyagi in November 1939 to another Hokkaido man, Taguchi Ugenta. As an intelligence agent the latter was more valuable than Yamana. According to Miyagi, Yamana 'lost his sense of integrity from about 1938 and tended to think only in terms of money'. Miyagi was almost equally disparaging about Taguchi. He declared that Kutsumi Fusako warned him against the man, whom she had known in Hokkaido. Like herself and Yamana, Taguchi had been imprisoned as a Communist. She told Miyagi that Taguchi was 'stubborn and obstinate' and would not be helpful. Miyagi implies that she was right.

But Miyagi was rarely complimentary about his sub-agents. It is conceivable that his remarks did not reflect his true feelings. He may have tried to protect his accomplices by underrating the help they gave him.

Unlike Yamana, Taguchi was a man of some substance, being the son of a wealthy landowner in the bleak Abashiri region of northern Hokkaido. In spite of his past as an active Communist and his prison record, he was an energetic entrepreneur, concerned with many ventures, such as peat-cutting in Manchukuo and lumbering in Hokkaido.

Taguchi provided Miyagi with information on military preparations in Manchukuo in the summer of 1940. But most of his information was supplied in 1941, when—in the words of the *Tokko*—'he spied on military preparations in Sakhalin and Hokkaido'. Taguchi's address at the time of his arrest, on October 29, 1941, was in Yotsuya, Tokyo; and the records give his occupation as 'dealer in rope manufacturing materials'. Business, however, took him frequently to Hokkaido and Sakhalin. After the outbreak of the German-Russian war Miyagi visited Taguchi at least twice a month, sometimes more often. This suggests that the information supplied was by no means negligible. Sorge, who heard of Taguchi only as 'a man from Hokkaido', states that the latter 'provided much detailed information'.

The only member of Miyagi's group known personally to Sorge was Koshiro Yoshinobu, whom Miyagi met in the late spring of 1939. Koshiro had just been discharged from the Japanese army. He had served in Manchukuo, north China, and Korea, and had risen to the rank of corporal. He was a graduate of Meiji University, Tokyo; and it was during his university days that he became interested in Marxism, through the influence of a man who lived next door. It was this neighbour who, years later, introduced Koshiro to Miyagi.*

Koshiro was a godsend to Miyagi. For the Sorge ring had always lacked adequate military information direct from Japanese sources. As Sorge told the police, were it not for the fact that he had ready access to the German Embassy he would have had to cultivate sources within the Japanese armed forces; 'and this would have been very difficult'.

To pick up scraps of military information, Miyagi had to spend many a night in the cafés and bars of Tokyo; and he often complained

---

* This neighbour, a man named Kiotake, probably died before the Sorge ring was uncovered. Otherwise he would certainly have been arrested, and his name would have appeared in the records of the case.

to Sorge about the amount he had to drink in order to learn a few trivial facts. Koshiro had been no more than a corporal. But as an educated and intelligent man he had been in a position, despite his modest rank, to discover things unknown to civilians.

It may be significant that Miyagi asked Koshiro to help him in May 1939. It was during the summer of 1939 that Sorge received instructions from the Fourth Bureau to enlist a Japanese army officer in the espionage ring. Obedience to an order of this kind raised formidable problems; and it seems certain that in ex-Corporal Koshiro Sorge felt he had the answer to the instructions from Moscow. For, having met Koshiro and sized him up, Sorge sent his *curriculum vitae* to the Bureau; and Koshiro's code name, 'Miki', was duly registered.

Koshiro agreed to collect information from friends and acquaintances who had served with him in the army. From May 1939 to July 1941—when he was recalled to the colours—he supplied much valuable intelligence on the distribution and equipment of troops, the organization of new units, defence arrangements in Manchukuo, the Nomonhan battle, the scale and quality of new artillery and tanks. He also obtained for Miyagi classified military manuals. The Sorge ring, through Miyagi, paid him a small monthly allowance.

Miyagi asserted that Koshiro was a liberal rather than a true Marxist.

I did in fact educate Koshiro in Communist ideology [Miyagi told the preliminary judge]. But he has not progressed far enough to realize a sense of responsibility as a Communist. In that sense I think that he has still not moved beyond the threshold of liberalism.*

Koshiro was with his unit in south China when the Sorge ring was exposed. He was arrested there by the *Kempei* on April 11, 1942. He was not handed over to the Special Higher Police for nearly a year.

The seventh member of Miyagi's subsidiary ring, and the last to be arrested (June 8, 1942), was a doctor of medicine, of known left-wing views, Yasuda Tokutaro. Miyagi had visited him as a patient at the beginning of 1935. When he did so, he may have known that Dr. Yasuda had been arrested two years earlier as a Communist sympathizer, although he was soon released. Kutsumi Fusako also visited

---

* Here again, in Miyagi's comment, one seems to detect the note of calculated disparagement.

Dr. Yasuda, and it was through her that he learned that Miyagi was a Communist agent. This was in March 1936 soon after she became Miyagi's accomplice.

However, it was not until September 1937, after heavy fighting had begun in China, that Miyagi asked Dr. Yasuda to help him. Either on that occasion or earlier, Miyagi said to Yasuda: 'Friends have told me that one can consult you not only in case of illness.'

Dr. Yasuda agreed to answer Miyagi's questions on such matters as medical and food supplies, and to pass on any military information that he might happen to learn from his patients. In return, Miyagi gave him at least one of his paintings.

It is difficult to assess the value of the information supplied by Yasuda. But probably it was not great. It may be that his most important service to the ring was his provision of a sulpha drug for Sorge when the latter suffered from a sudden and dangerous attack of pneumonia. He never met Sorge; and the sulpha drug was doubtless given to Miyagi to take to an unknown foreigner. But if a recent statement by Dr. Yasuda is to be believed, the Special Higher Police were not unaware of the medical help he had, indirectly, given to Sorge. Yasuda declares that while he was being beaten by the *Tokko*, during the police interrogation, one inquisitor said to another: 'This is the swine who cured Sorge and saved him from certain death.'

Dr. Yasuda, however, was the only one of Miyagi's group of sub-agents to receive lenient treatment by the District Criminal Court. He was sentenced to two years' imprisonment, with five years' suspension; which meant that he was released from custody.

The other six members of the group fared worse. Koshiro, the ex-corporal, was given the stiffest sentence, fifteen years. Taguchi was sent to prison for thirteen years, Yamana for twelve. Kutsumi Fusako was sentenced to eight years, and Akiyama, Miyagi's translator, to seven. Mrs. Kitabayashi was sentenced to five years. She died in January 1945 soon after her release. The others were liberated after the Occupation began in the late summer of 1945.

Ozaki's four sub-agents were Kawai Teikichi, Mizuno Shigeru, Kawamura Yoshio and Funakoshi Hisao. From the time of his release from custody in Hsinking in the summer of 1936 until September 1940, Kawai remained on the continent, chiefly in north China. At first he was active in promoting an organization called the China

Problems Research Institute, at Tientsin, his chief collaborator in this venture being Funakoshi Hisao, the manager of the Tientsin branch of the newspaper *Yomiuri Shimbun*, an old friend of Ozaki's and a former member of Sorge's Shanghai ring. The aim of the Institute— as its title suggests—was to study the political and economic situation in north China. This was a period of intensive Japanese penetration, economic, political and military, of the whole region centred on Peking and Tientsin. The China Problems Research Institute, therefore, was the kind of organization, much in fashion in those days, that could be sure of support from Japanese officials in north China. It also provided excellent protective cover for Communists.

In 1938, however, Funakoshi was appointed an unofficial adviser (*shokutaku*) to the Japanese forces in Hankow, in the same year. Kawai Teikichi dabbled in what we might describe as the 'puppet-making politics' of the Japanese North China Army.* This work— of which coercion, bribes and intrigue were the main constituents— was one with which Kawai was already familiar. It seems to have suited his adventurous temperament. It gave him, at the same time, a good deal of insight into what was going on behind the scenes; and once or twice he was able to visit Japan and report his observations to Ozaki.

In September 1940, Kawai returned to Japan for good. Ozaki asked Miyagi to look after him; but it seems that Miyagi and Kawai were now on unfriendly terms. Miyagi asked Kawai to carry out an intelligence task in the Nagoya area—an assignment that Kawai, through indolence or ignorance, failed to fulfil—and, in the end, it was Ozaki who found him work in a paper company in May 1941.

For this reason, and because he cherished an immense personal admiration for Ozaki, the Japanese police and procurators listed Kawai as one of Ozaki's sub-agents, rather than Miyagi's.

It is hard to believe that after 1940, when he came back to Tokyo, Kawai was of much use to the Sorge ring. He was arrested on October 22, 1941, and was sentenced to ten years in jail.

Mizuno Shigeru—described by Sorge as 'more of a scholar than a political spy'—had entered the East Asia Common Script School in Shanghai in 1929, at the age of nineteen. While at the school he met Ozaki. Later he was introduced to Sorge by the Communist

---

* Kawai as a member of the Osako Special Service Organ took part in the abortive effort to persuade the former warlord, Wu Pei-fu, to come forward as a Japanese-sponsored political leader.

apparatchnik, Kito Ginichi;* and he became a member of Sorge's Shanghai group.

Mizuno and other left-wing students of the school were arrested by the consular police for distributing pacifist leaflets, concealed inside match-boxes, among Japanese naval cadets visiting Shanghai. Mizuno was fortunate to suffer nothing worse from the police than ten days in their custody. But he was expelled from the Common Script School. He now became involved in clandestine work with the Chinese Communist Party. Eventually this led to his arrest, and deportation to Japan.

Back in Japan, Mizuno – thanks to Ozaki's help – joined the staff of a well-known private research institute in Osaka. In 1936, however, he was arrested for taking part in the secret reconstruction of the banned Japanese Communist Party. His rôle in this may have been relatively inactive and unimportant, for the authorities soon released him. He then moved to Tokyo, no doubt at the suggestion of Ozaki, who always took a considerable interest in Mizuno and thought highly of him.

Indeed Ozaki was to tell the police: 'I had great faith in Mizuno and regarded him as my successor.' There was always the possibility that Ozaki might be appointed to an *Asahi* post in China, and if this happened he wanted a reliable protégé to take his own place in the Sorge ring. The fact that he considered Mizuno for this rôle is of some interest. It implies that Mizuno possessed staunch conspiratorial abilities as well as a quick intellect, and an acute understanding of the political situation in Japan.

Ozaki saw to it that Mizuno obtained successive employment in a number of scholarly organizations in Tokyo. Mizuno appears to have met Sorge only on one occasion in Japan.

For a time, at least, Ozaki used Mizuno as a kind of secretary or personal assistant, and he used to ask him to prepare written reports on broad political and economic issues. These were designed specifically to provide Moscow with background material. Ozaki would pass Mizuno's reports to Miyagi, who then gave them to Sorge; for it is evident that the prudent Ozaki was always reluctant to pass written information direct to Sorge.

Mizuno, like Miyagi, was often ill; and there is some evidence that partly for this reason Ozaki came to have second thoughts about his suitability as an intelligence agent. Nevertheless, in addition to general

* See p. 74 above.

background information, Mizuno was able to provide some useful intelligence on military matters in a particular area—namely Kyoto. This ancient city was his home, to which he would retire for convalescence after a bout of illness. He reported on the destination of large troop movements from the Kyoto area in 1939, when the Nomonhan fighting was at its height, and in 1941, when Sorge and Ozaki were acutely concerned to assess Japanese reactions to the German-Russian war and to the growing crisis with the United States.

Mizuno was arrested on October 17, 1941. He was sentenced to imprisonment for thirteen years. His weak health could not survive this ordeal. He died in prison on March 22, 1945.

Kawamura Yoshio, Ozaki's third sub-agent, also died in custody. Little is known about him. He died soon after he had been brought to Tokyo following his arrest in Shanghai on March 31, 1942. Kawamura was a journalist, the Shanghai correspondent of the *Manshu Nichi Nichi* ('Manchukuo Daily News'). He and Mizuno had been in the same class at the Common Script School in Shanghai. He left the school before completing the course—perhaps he was expelled, like Mizuno—and obtained work as a journalist in Manchukuo. But he was certainly in north China, too, for Kawai introduced him in 1933 to Agnes Smedley in Peking. In the previous year Kawai had recruited Kawamura as a fellow-worker in his own secret activities on behalf of the Chinese Communists; an arrangement approved by Ozaki, after he had called on Kawamura in Dairen and 'quietly looked him over'. He became in due course Ozaki's Shanghai sub-agent. It has been claimed that Sorge knew of him and regarded him as a member of the ring.

The fourth member of Ozaki's own group, Funakoshi Hisao, is a less mysterious figure than Kawamura. He was the son of a sauce manufacturer in Okayama Prefecture and was brought up—so the police say—'in a strict home environment'. After graduating from Waseda University, Tokyo, in 1925 he went to China, first to Tsingtao and then to Shanghai, where he became a reporter for a local Japanese daily paper. He met Ozaki and they became close friends.

Funakoshi, it seems, was attracted to Marxism as a result of his study of domestic Chinese politics; and he was soon ready to translate academic interest into active work. He was drawn into Sorge's Shanghai ring by Ozaki and Kawai, and he had frequent meetings with Sorge, who, before returning to Moscow in 1932, made sure that his European successor, 'Paul', met Funakoshi. Indeed the latter, some time after Ozaki's return to Japan, became the leading Japanese member of the Shanghai ring. He was in constant touch with Sorge's successor, 'Paul', and with Agnes Smedley. He also collected subscriptions for the Chinese Communist Party from Japanese sympathizers in Shanghai, including at least one member of the teaching staff at the Common Script School.*

Funakoshi left Shanghai, however, early in 1933. He went to Hankow as representative of the Rengo News Agency. Nearly a year later he was transferred to Tientsin, where he resumed contact with Kawai; and when Kawai wanted to go to Japan Funakoshi paid his travel expenses.

As we have seen, it was Funakoshi who found Kawai a place in the China Problems Research Institute at Tientsin after his release from imprisonment. It must have been with considerable relief that Funakoshi learned that Kawai had divulged nothing to the police about the Sorge ring in Shanghai or its successor in Tokyo. For Funakoshi was still in touch with Ozaki and would continue to see him from time to time over the next few years. Ozaki indeed took an active interest in Funakoshi's Research Institute, which became a kind of Trojan horse for Japanese Communist writers and scholars resident in north China.

From October 1938 to May 1941, Funakoshi was an adviser—as member of the Hankow Special Service Organ—to Japanese-sponsored Chinese political leaders in the Wuhan area. This instance of successful Communist penetration must have appeared particularly alarming to the Special Higher Police in Tokyo, into whose hands Funakoshi was delivered, following his arrest in north China on January 4, 1942. The *Tokko* Report on Funakoshi ends:

> Despite the fact that the suspect has gradually repented his conduct in the course of the present case and has given evidence of an unmistakable change of heart, it is believed that, in view of the heinous nature of his offence, his rehabilitation should be assured by imposition of the maximum penalty.

Funakoshi was sentenced to ten years. But he died in prison on February 27, 1945.

On May 17, 1942, the Ministry of Justice issued the first official announcement on the Sorge case—a bald statement giving the names

* This was Nozawa Fusaji. See page 93.

of those arrested. No doubt to test public opinion, the police made a record of the way various persons, representing different organizations and opinions, reacted to the news all over Japan.

The reactions, as one would expect, were indignant, and reflect both astonishment and horror. The country was at war; and appeals to patriotism and a sense of national purpose had reached a crescendo. No wonder that those who had heard no rumours of the affair were astounded to read that not only foreigners—that caused no particular surprise—but also Japanese in high official circles had been arrested as secret agents of the Comintern.

In many of the reported comments there is more than a note of class feeling. 'The upper class should take this opportunity for unsparing self-criticism,' says a reserve lieutenant in Saitama. 'Upper-class intellectuals who handle state secrets should know better,' thunders a retired major in Miyagi.

But a Commander of the Imperial Japanese Navy (retd.) voiced what thousands believed, when he declared: 'I take it for granted that Konoye has been put in custody, and that the announcement is being withheld in view of its international repercussions.'

The general suspicion that Prince Konoye had been or would be arrested did not arise from the fact that Ozaki was personally known to him, and had served for a time as unofficial adviser to his first cabinet. The doubts about Konoye's position, the widening slur on his reputation and the whispers that spread through Japan and beyond, to troops and civilians overseas—these sprang from the news that the Procurators' Bureau in Tokyo had indicted Inukai Ken and Saionji Kinkazu.

Inukai Ken, born in 1896, was the eldest son of Inukai Tsuyoshi the Prime Minister assassinated by ultra-nationalist fanatics on May 15, 1932. When still a young man he achieved some distinction as a novelist, but in his thirties he turned to politics, and he was elected to the Diet. He had a deep interest in Chinese affairs, a subject on which his father, who had befriended many Chinese nationalists before 1911, was an expert. In 1929 father and son attended the ceremonial reinterment of Sun Yat-sen at Nanking, and it was here that Inukai Ken first met Ozaki. The acquaintance soon ripened into friendship.

The bond between them was China. But it must be emphasized that Inukai's contacts and sympathies were with members of the Kuomintang. This made him, inevitably, a critic—a secret opponent indeed—

of the methods and pretensions of the Japanese army in China from 1937 onwards. In a word, he was a liberal, at a time when to confess the fact in public was not only unfashionable but also perilous.

He regarded me [Ozaki said of Inukai] as a trustworthy friend; and he had a high regard for my expert opinion on Chinese affairs. Because of this special relationship I have had a lot of information from him on the situation in China. But this information was, for the most part, fragmentary; and I do not recall the exact details.

In claiming that he could not recall the details of Inukai's 'fragmentary' information on China, Ozaki was being neither evasive nor disingenuous. It seems definite that Inukai never consciously divulged to his friend information classified as secret. Thorough investigation by the procurators narrowed Inukai's possible breach of the law to a single indiscretion.

At the beginning of 1940 he had allowed Saionji to make a copy of the draft treaty negotiated between the Japanese and Wang Ching-wei, the Kuomintang leader who had defected from the Nationalist Government in Chungking. Inukai himself had been the prime architect of this agreement. It was to form the basis of the relationship between Japan and Wang Ching-wei's administration at Nanking, which Tokyo was to recognize – not without secret misgivings – as the legitimate government of China.

The first paragraph of the procuratorial indictment of Saionji clarifies the nature and consequences of Inukai's indiscretion.

Saionji Kinkazu was shown by his friend, Inukai Ken, documents containing the so-called Interim Agreement between Japan and China, of December 30, 1939, concerning the distribution of the Japanese army and of naval vessels in the area of China. He retained a copy of this material, and some days later he lent this copy to Ozaki Hotsumi. Thus he revealed a military secret that came to his knowledge by accident.

Ozaki, in his turn, made a copy of the document lent him by Saionji. Miyagi visited Ozaki, translated Ozaki's copy into English and gave it to Sorge.

The material which reached Sorge, and then Moscow, in this way was of strategic significance, politically and militarily, for it revealed Japanese long-term intentions and defence commitments. As Sorge remarked to Yoshikawa: 'It goes without saying that the whole subject was of importance to the Soviet Union.'

Inukai was arrested on April 4, 1942. He was charged with violating the Military Secrets Protection Law. The case reached the Supreme Court, which gave a verdict of Not Guilty. But the judiciary felt unable to find Saionji innocent of breaking the same law.* Recognizing, however, that his offence arose from carelessness rather than ill intent, the Court was merciful and awarded Saionji a suspended sentence of eighteen months' imprisonment. Thus he was spared the shame and hardships of a Japanese jail.

The nature of Saionji's careless talk—the information on Japan's attitude and intentions towards Russia, and on the Japanese-American negotiations—has already been described.† Saionji's indiscretions were serious and damaging. His temperament seems to have lacked the balance and self-control that saved Inukai, with his considerable experience of public life, from committing the same kind of error.

Yet, thanks to these very defects, Saionji seems a more sympathetic figure than Inukai. In part perhaps this is because Saionji composed, for the procurators, an autobiographical statement that shows us rather clearly the kind of man that he was. For example, the statement describes his reactions to the European scene, to England in particular, when he came from Japan, in the nineteen-twenties, to enter Oxford University. First, he spent some time at a private school in Bournemouth, preparing for Responsions. Eventually he was admitted to New College, where, as he puts it, 'there was an atmosphere of ageless calm, which seemed appropriate for study'.

A vivid and amusing series of recollections of undergraduate life‡ is followed by an account of Saionji's return to Japan, of his activities in journalism and as an unofficial consultant (*shokutaku*) at the Foreign Office, of his journey to the conference of the Institute of Pacific Relations at Yosemite, and of how he met Ozaki and of the way their friendship developed.

Saionji was younger than Ozaki, whereas Inukai was older. There is something of what the Japanese call a '*botchan*'—a spoiled boy— about Saionji as a young man. Yet his upbringing, though sheltered, had not been soft. In many respects his training, until he went to Europe, was Spartan. His father, the son of the aged Prince Saionji,

---

* Saionji was also charged with violating the National Defence Security Law, in particular Clause 6 of this Law, dealing with 'leakage of information to others'.

† See p. 243 above.

‡ For example, 'On the whole, Oxford undergraduates worked very hard. But there were some who romped around in conspicuous fashion, in their own groups; and a certain number of these left Oxford without completing their course.'

was determined that the boy should understand that the privileges of high birth imposed corresponding obligations and responsibilities. So the young Saionji was always eager 'to do something for Japan'. He was not prepared to live a life of private enjoyment. It was this civic spirit, together with his personal connections, that made him acceptable as a Foreign Office consultant and, in the summer of 1941, as *shokutaku* to Konoye's Third Cabinet.

The fact that Ozaki had held a similar position would make it all the more natural for Saionji to place no particular guard on his tongue when talking to his friend about confidential matters affecting high policy.

In the course of his interrogation by the procurator Saionji expressed his remorse at what had occurred, and he made a plea on behalf of Ozaki.

I can find no words to express to my friends my apologies for the blunder I committed. Ozaki has committed a public crime, which is to be condemned. I have been terribly deceived by him. Here I blame myself, rather than Ozaki, for my own blindness. Apart from the crime he has committed I still appreciate Ozaki for his good nature and ability. I sincerely hope that in future I shall be able to correct Ozaki's ways and so reform him as to turn him into a true Japanese in the service of the State.

Both Saionji and Inukai were members of the *Asameshikai*, 'the Breakfast Club', founded in 1938 by Konoye's two private secretaries, Ushiba and Kishi Dozo, and Ozaki himself, then a Cabinet consultant. The Breakfast Club was made up of Konoye's friends. It was given its title because its meetings were held over breakfast at about eight in the morning. The purpose of these gatherings, said Ozaki, 'was to be of some help to the Konoye Cabinet, through the medium of the secretaries, by an expression of various views'. The meetings took place twice a month and they were not discontinued when the Konoye Cabinet resigned in January 1939. In fact the group began to meet every Wednesday. Hence it was later known as 'the Wednesday Club'.

Konoye himself rarely attended these meetings. But the relatively small circle of writers, scholars, and officials—popularly known as Konoye's 'brains trust'—found the Breakfast Club an ideal forum for a confidential, frank, exchange of views. They were anxious men, out of step with the times and, for all the influence they had on Konoye, largely out of touch with the most important source of political power—namely the inner sanctum of the Japanese army.

When it became public knowledge, in 1942, that, apart from Ozaki, two leading figures in the charmed circle round Konoye – of which the Breakfast Club was a collective symbol – had been arrested, Konoye's enemies rejoiced and his admirers quailed. Senator McCarthy himself could not have improved upon the more extreme views of Konoye's opponents. On this interpretation, Konoye and his friends were all traitors, corrupted by liberalism if not actually in the pay of foreign agents. The opposing view, in its extreme form, was that the Sorge case had been engineered by the army to secure Konoye's downfall and discredit him for ever.

The Japanese police rounded up many others suspected of guilty traffic, directly or indirectly, with the Sorge ring, in China as well as in Japan.

The owner of a small foundry at Osaka was arrested, interrogated first by the police and then by a procurator, and was finally found not guilty. This verdict, on the face of it, is surprising. For the accused – Shinozuka Torao – in fact admitted that he had provided Ozaki and Miyagi with items of military information. Shinozuka's father and Ozaki's had been friends, and when Ozaki entered the First High School he shared lodgings with Shinozuka.

Although, according to Ozaki, Shinozuka had shown interest in socialism when he was a student, the evidence suggests that in adult life he had no particular left-wing sympathies. His association with Ozaki was not based on a shared ideology.

But when Ozaki and Miyagi, as early as 1935, were wondering how to overcome their shortage of intelligence from military sources, Ozaki remembered his boyhood friend, Shinozuka. He recalled that Shinozuka had been keenly interested in weapons and all kinds of machinery. Ozaki's approach to him was to say that, as a writer, he needed to know something about military affairs and would therefore be grateful for Shinozuka's expert help. For friendship's sake the latter agreed to this proposition. Ozaki's exploitation of Shinozuka makes a squalid little tale. He did not even take the trouble to see him on some occasions. He left this to Miyagi, whom he had introduced to Shinozuka as an artist particularly interested in painting scenes of warfare or pictures of weapons.

Thus over meals in various Tokyo restaurants the ingenuous Shinozuka, drawing on the knowledge that his hobby provided, told Miyagi

—and sometimes Ozaki also—about the organization of the army air force and the location of airfields, about aircraft factories, and the distribution of infantry divisions.

Ozaki always spoke to Sorge of Shinozuka as 'a specialist'. But Sorge has one or two unkind remarks to make in this connection:

> Lastly, I must mention a certain specialist. He was an old friend of Ozaki's who was brought into our work soon after I arrived in Japan, but who turned out to be far from what we had expected. Instead of a military expert, as we all had thought at the beginning, he gradually turned into a 'money expert'.

Among those arrested and indicted, or questioned without being held in custody, or interrogated as witnesses by judicial officials, were most of the members of the Konoye circle—including Konoye himself—leading persons on the *Asahi*, members of the *Showa Kenkyukai*, and a number of people connected with, or employed by, the South Manchurian Railway in Tokyo, Shanghai and Manchukuo. Some of these arrests—like those of Kawamura and Dr. Yasuda—occurred many months after the Sorge ring was unearthed in October 1941.

In June 1942, the Japanese authorities in Shanghai, acting on information from the Tokyo police, arrested nearly a hundred people on suspicion of supplying information to the Chinese Communists. Of these some twenty were held for prosecution. Among them was Nakanishi Ko—famous since the Second World War as a Communist writer, journalist, and member of the Upper House of the Diet.

Nakanishi Ko had been a student at the East Asia Common Script School in Shanghai in the same class as Mizuno Shigeru and Kawamuro Yoshio. He was an active member of Funakoshi's Institute in north China. But he was not a member of the Sorge ring, in China or Japan. However, he worked for the Chinese Communists; and, at the time of his arrest, he was in the Investigation Department of the South Manchurian Railway, in their Shanghai office. It was the uncovering of the Sorge ring, although he had no active links with it, that led to Nakanishi's arrest and prosecution. The stages of criminal procedure were not, it would seem, hastened in his case. For he did not come before Tokyo District Court until September 1945, when American troops were already in Japan. Nakanishi was sentenced to life imprisonment. But twelve days later, with the general order for the release of political prisoners, he walked out of jail a free man.

A curious episode, which occurred before the first arrests in the

Sorge case, was the so-called 'Planning Board Affair'. The police discovered that several officials in the Cabinet Planning Board were Marxists or Communist sympathizers. These officials were not charged with espionage, but with plotting to seize every opportunity, by the exercise of their influence on governmental policy, to transform Japan into a Socialist state. The Special Higher Police, ever alert to uncover a conspiracy, believed that there was a deliberate plot by the Communist underground in Japan to infiltrate key organs of the government, such as the Planning Board. Some colour was given to this interpretation by the admission, on the part of some of the accused, that the move towards a planned economy—induced by the demands of the China war—seemed to offer a chance for crypto-Marxists in the government to destroy the capitalist system in Japan.

While there was no known direct link between the Sorge ring and those arrested in the Planning Board case, it is certain that the evidence of Communist penetration of government, which the police believed they had found, sharpened the watch that the authorities were already keeping on Ozaki Hotsumi.

One other incident—involving a European—may be mentioned as a last example of the almost hysterical zeal shown by the police, once the character of the Sorge ring began to unfold. Nobody, perhaps, will ever know to what extent the Sorge case influenced police action in arresting a number of British and American journalists as soon as the Pacific War began. But no doubt such arrests would have been fewer, and the treatment of foreign suspects less harsh, if Sorge and his accomplices had remained undetected in wrongdoing.

On the morning of Monday, December 8, 1941, a posse of *Tokko* police endeavoured to lay their hands on the chief of the Information Department of the British Embassy, Mr. Vere Redman. One of his duties at the Embassy was similar to those performed, after the outbreak of war in Europe, by Sorge at the German Embassy. His task, in other words, was to edit the daily British news bulletin. And for this purpose Redman—like Sorge—arose early each day. Indeed he was usually at work even before Sorge, his practice being to reach the British Embassy shortly after 5 a.m.

Thus when the police arrived at his house they found that Redman was no longer there. They were not prepared, however, to let matters rest. Mr. Redman was now within his own Embassy, and it seemed improbable that the Japanese authorities would attempt to take him by force. But this they were ready to do.

Sir Robert Craigie, the British Ambassador, has described how the Tokyo Foreign Office, making use at first of the Argentine *chargé d'affaires* as a go-between, tried to persuade him to surrender Redman. Craigie told the Foreign Office representative that he believed Redman to be the victim of some German intrigue.

The day after this interview Craigie was informed that the Japanese Government had decided to take Redman by force. Some sixty plain-clothes police occupied the Embassy buildings and grounds, and over the Ambassador's vigorous protests Redman was taken into custody.

It was Craigie's view that the Germans were the prime movers in this unpleasant affair, and there is no reason to doubt that this was so. But, affected by the current xenophobia, the police and judicial authorities—perceiving the range of Sorge's activities and knowing that Vukelic had contacts in the British Embassy—certainly suspected that Redman might have been in touch with the Sorge ring.

Thanks to this particular episode, the ramifications of the Sorge case may be said to have extended as far as Brixton Remand Prison in the southern suburbs of London. For as a reprisal for the arbitrary and unjustified incarceration of Redman, the British Government removed from internment and placed in a cell at Brixton, a press attaché of the Japanese Embassy in London, Matsumoto Kaoru.*

But it was certain members of the German community in the Far East who were to suffer some of the most disagreeable consequences arising from the Sorge Affair.

---

* Mr. Redman (now Sir Vere Redman, c.m.g., o.b.e.) and Mr. Matsumoto returned with their Embassy colleagues to their respective countries in 1942.

Chapter 17

THE REVENGE OF COLONEL MEISINGER

'No, there is no such thing as a desperate situation.' HITLER

COLONEL Josef Meisinger had arrived in Tokyo as police liaison attaché at the German Embassy in May 1941. His previous career had been a model example of the police system of the Third Reich. He had fought with the Freikorps, the independent commando units organized in the troubled years after 1920, both for the defence of the eastern frontiers against the Poles, and in suppressing Communist revolution inside Germany. Like Sorge, he had won the Iron Cross (Second Class) as a young man at the front. In 1922 he joined the Bavarian police and, at about the same time, the early Nazi Party. He seems to have belonged to a Storm Troop before Hitler's abortive Munich *putsch* of 1923. His formal party record dates from May 1933, and his promotion in the police and the S.S. advanced simultaneously and smoothly. His zeal in pursuing homosexuals and abortionists, and in recruiting them, earned him a special reputation.

In 1934 Meisinger served briefly at Gestapo Headquarters in Berlin, and shortly afterwards took part in Himmler's descent on Bavaria and the liquidation of Roehm and the Brown Shirts. In 1938 he saw service in Vienna during the Nazi take-over in Austria, and was then appointed director of the 'Internal Party Archives', again at the Gestapo in Berlin. In October 1939 he was sent as commander of the Security Police to Warsaw, holding at the same time the rank of colonel in the S.S.

His long record of brutality, culminating in his activities in Poland, was frowned on even by his hardened superiors, and his police mission to the Far East in 1941 seems to have been a form of banishment.

Meisinger's new post in Japan had been created under the terms of the German-Japanese Anti-Comintern Agreement of 1936, but was not on the diplomatic list. On paper, the duties of the holder were far-ranging: close liaison with the Japanese police in combating Communist activities, exchange of information about Comintern and Soviet espionage, surveillance of German exiles in Japan and Manchuria, and German nationals generally in the Far East; the enforcement of German race laws within the German community, and the handling of security questions in the German Embassy in Tokyo, including the political scrutiny of members of the mission.

In practice, the police liaison attaché had little to do. The Japanese authorities showed scant interest in general collaboration and exchange of information. The work of surveillance and, in some cases, of denunciation of German nationals, could be limited or expanded according to the energy and character of the attaché himself; Meisinger's predecessor had found himself employed, in order to fill in time, in the decoration of the Embassy for formal receptions and official occasions.

Meisinger had arrived in the Far East with no special training for his assignment. He was dependent on the Embassy interpreter, Hamel, for his personal contacts with the Japanese authorities, and the early months of his new assignment passed in a climate of bewildered isolation. His relations with his Ambassador were polite but distant, and one of his few convivial acquaintances was the distinguished German foreign correspondent, Richard Sorge.

The new police attaché had apparently received instructions from his superiors in Germany to investigate Sorge's activities, but the latter's high standing with the German Embassy and the community in Tokyo, together with his sardonic charm as a boon companion, disarmed the policeman.

In October 1941 Meisinger was on an official trip to Shanghai, and was suddenly recalled to Tokyo when the German Embassy learnt of the action taken by the Japanese police against the Sorge ring. They had at no stage indicated to Meisinger, as the liaison officer attached to them, their intentions to take into custody a leading German national, together with Max Klausen and his wife. They had not even informed the Embassy after the arrests had taken place.

The measure of Meisinger's personal and official standing was further lowered when his attempts to secure Sorge's release, or even visit him in prison, were unsuccessful, and when his Japanese colleague refused to furnish any evidence relating to the case.

The post of German police liaison attaché in Tokyo appeared to be of the utmost insignificance, and the manner in which the Sorge affair had broken brutally underlined the position.

The arrest of Sorge and his associates not only brought confusion into the circles of the German Embassy in Tokyo, but also anxiety as to the possible espionage activities among other German nationals in the Far East and its implications on German-Japanese relations. It spurred the malevolent interest of Meisinger in the activities of his compatriots, and gave rise to a witch hunt on his part to distract attention from his own short-comings in relation to his misjudgment of Sorge. Awkward incidents were by the nature of things an operational risk, but a series of minor affairs increased Meisinger's alarm and was to drive him to initiate, or at least exacerbate, further 'cases' to prove, by unmasking them, his own technical efficiency.

The first episode concerned a young German exchange student, Klaus Lenz. He had been unmasked in November 1941 while attempting to suborn an Embassy courier, who was at the same time an agent of the German Military Intelligence, to attempt to build a clandestine radio transmitter inside the German Embassy compound. It was not clear on whose behalf this action was attempted. Meisinger had arranged to have Lenz abducted aboard a German blockade runner which had arrived in Japanese waters in mid-March and was now bound for Europe. The enterprising young man had however managed to escape ashore and spend three evenings with his mistress, Stella Kasprick, who was the wife of a former Polish assistant attaché in Tokyo, and to give her information about the ship.

Lenz was again taken in custody on board and dispatched to Germany. The Japanese police then hinted that he might have been in touch with the Russian Intelligence Service, and also that the day before he was taken on board the German vessel he had met, through his Polish mistress, a member of the British Embassy.

Meisinger was at a loss how to interpret the significance of the case of Klaus Lenz, which suggested in vague terms the existence of certain moves by the Soviet, and possibly British, services on the edge of the Sorge affair. Meisinger reported: 'Request urgent instructions on further handling of the affair as the Japanese police are *very* interested.'

The latter had already asked Meisinger the previous year to secure the return of Lenz to Japan for interrogation, and inevitably a link had been established between Sorge and Lenz 'who had had an office together'. Sorge himself was questioned about Lenz. 'I wondered whether he was not crazy.'

This odd young man had worked for the official German News Agency. His duties consisted of monitoring the press cables every night in the Embassy office where Sorge also worked. The two men had no direct contact, meeting only when Lenz came off duty early in the morning and when Sorge arrived to draft the daily news bulletin.

On his return to Germany Lenz had been called up into the army. Through lack of administrative co-ordination, it took many months to trace him, and he was not arrested and interrogated until December 1943. He stated—which was accurate—that his only relationship with Sorge was strictly 'as a colleague'. With these statements Lenz vanishes from the scene.

But worse was to come.

In March 1942 Meisinger's colleague in the Far East and his predecessor in Tokyo, Franz Huber, the German police attaché in Bangkok, had drawn the attention of the German security authorities in Berlin to the suspicious activities of an Austrian press photographer and journalist, Karl Hofmeier.

The German security services in Berlin ordered an enquiry, which was held by Meisinger in July in Tokyo, where Hofmeier had been apprehended. The preliminary results of this political investigation were as disquieting as the Sorge case. Hofmeier had been educated at a Jesuit College in Austria and joined the Communist Party in Vienna in 1931. During the following year he taught Marxist theory in party cells and was an Agitprop leader, writing occasional articles for the party paper *The Red Flag*. On two occasions he had been arrested by the Austrian police.

In January 1933 Hofmeier went to Turkey on an 'educational visit'. Here he was recruited by the Soviet counter-intelligence, and given the general assignment of uncovering Polish agents who had been sent into the Soviet Union.

In the spring of 1934 he joined, on instructions, the local Istanbul branch of the German Nazi Party, in order to give him the same cover as Sorge had acquired in Tokyo and at the same period.

Hofmeier's party card, like that of Sorge, is on record. To the local Nazi leader in Turkey, Hofmeier passed himself off as a patriotic German student, anxious to work for the cause, and he built up with financial support from Nazi funds an 'information service', under close Soviet control, which recruited Polish and other counter-revolutionary agents who were sent on bogus missions into Russia, where they were 'put out of the way'. He wrote articles for the official Nazi paper, the *Völkischer Beobachter*, but these were, in the first instance, censored by the Soviet Intelligence.

In 1936 he was in danger of arrest by the Turkish police, and, after another hasty 'educational visit' to Kurdistan, he was ordered by the Russians first to Prague and then via Switzerland to Paris. His relations with the Soviet Intelligence, according to his version, became somewhat intermittent, though he apparently received funds to study at the university.

In the summer of 1937 he travelled to Turkey and Iran, and was then arrested and expelled on his way back to Istanbul by the Turkish police. He appeared in Moscow, where he 'was received by the OGPU with cool impartiality. My work in Turkey was praised. For the rest there was no explanation and my request for a visa to travel to central Asia was refused.' He returned to Paris after a short trip to London, and contacted the French Communist Party. Without receiving any definite Russian orders he left for Japan as the correspondent of the *Völkischer Beobachter* and an illustrated German paper. He made repeated journeys to China, reported the Japanese campaign in Malaya, and was attached to the Japanese army in Thailand as a photographer.

Hofmeier kept away from his German colleagues in the Far East, and it was his close relations with the Japanese military authorities which first aroused the suspicions of the German officials in Bangkok. He was the only foreigner allowed to visit the Malayan front, and Meisinger reported the suspicion that Hofmeier might be working for the Japanese Intelligence. The gist of this preliminary investigation of Hofmeier was passed to the Japanese police, and he was arrested by them on July 15, 1942.

The case was compared with that of Sorge in the final and personal report on the enquiry into the latter's case sent by Himmler to Ribbentrop in December of that year. From the security point of view, the case of Hofmeier had disturbing similarities to that of Sorge. Both men had succeeded in joining the Nazi party through its overseas branches, one in Istanbul and the other in Tokyo, and without any check as to their political past; both had obtained impeccable cover as journalists, and were thus able to operate with impunity as Soviet agents for many years.

Hofmeier was eventually handed over by the Japanese authorities to the German Embassy in Tokyo. He was placed on a German blockade-runner whose captain was given strict instructions, if intercepted, to dispose summarily of his prisoner. In August 1944 Meisinger received a laconic signal from Gestapo headquarters in Berlin. Hofmeier was a prisoner on the blockade-runner *Burgenland* which had been stopped by an Allied warship on the high seas off the east coast of South America. The captain had scuttled his ship; the crew were in a Brazilian prison. Five people were missing. 'Hofmeier must certainly be among the latter.'

Two months later the German naval attaché in Tokyo informed Meisinger, who reported to Berlin, that, when the ship was sunk, Hofmeier had been shot.

Both professional zeal and genuine panic spurred Meisinger and the Japanese police in their search for traces of Soviet espionage in the Far East. The ramifications of the Sorge case in Japanese society had assumed alarming proportions. The German and European aspects of the affair and the involvement of German nationals in Japan and Manchukuo in such activities had already been substantiated in some degree in the case of Lenz, and particularly in that of Hofmeier.

An unsolicited intrusion from an unexpected quarter into the Sorge affair threatened further and more substantial damage. On March 23, 1942, a telegram dispatched through the German Legation in Hsinking, Manchukuo, was received in Berlin.

The author of this message was the local representative of the German Military Intelligence, who had been in the habit of using Foreign Office radio channels to transmit his reports to his superiors. It was signed 'Lissner'. The document did not, however, fall into the usual series of intelligence reports. It was a startling and distorted summary of the sinister implications of the Sorge case, aimed at the German Ambassador in Tokyo, but revealing some inside knowledge of the affair. Lissner's sources must have been local Japanese contacts in Harbin, and the information had been passed to him, as he stated, 'under seal of secrecy'.

This message, addressed to Lissner's superiors in the German Military Intelligence, would normally have been sent from the Far East by special courier, but after the German attack on Russia the overland route was blocked and the only link was by the Legation W/T transmitter in Hsinking. The implications of his Embassy telegram were clear. Owing to Sorge's intimate relations with General Ott and the staff of the German Embassy in Tokyo, a major leak of vital intelligence to the Russians had taken place.

When the official on duty in the Foreign Office in Berlin received the deciphered message on his desk, its significance was at once alarmingly clear. The hitherto smooth routine enquiries into the Sorge case were brutally shaken up. A copy of the Lissner telegram was transmitted to Ribbentrop's private office, and the reaction was immediate and explosive.

A personal telegram from the German Foreign Minister to Ambassador Ott was sent on March 27, 1942, asking for an explanation of Lissner's insinuations. In his reply Ott firmly denied the accuracy of the report, and the implications of the Sorge case as suggested by Lissner's insinuations. In his reply Ott firmly denied the accuracy of Ambassador in Tokyo in Ribbentrop's eyes, and was largely instrumental in Ott's ultimate dismissal. Its immediate effect, however, was to focus unwelcome light on Lissner's own activities, and on the tensions and rivalries of the German agencies and their representatives in the Far East. This personal initiative was to prove nearly fatal to Lissner himself.

According to the enquiries of the German Foreign Office, Ivar Lissner had represented several German newspapers in the Far East in the late 1930s, and in particular the *Völkischer Beobachter* in Tokyo. In 1938 he was one of the accredited foreign correspondents invited to witness the fighting during the Changkufeng Incident on the Korean-Soviet border.* On the outbreak of war in Europe, he had been taken on by the German Embassy in its propaganda service. He was in effect a predecessor of Sorge in such work.

In January 1940 the Berlin office of the *Völkischer Beobachter*

---

* The authors are indebted to Mr. John Chapman of St. Antony's College, Oxford, for this and certain other details in this chapter, and which are contained in his forthcoming book on German-Japanese relations during the Second World War.

informed the Tokyo Embassy that Lissner was of non-Aryan descent and that they had dispensed with his services. Instructions were therefore sought from the Foreign Office as to the extension of his contract with the Embassy. This was done as a temporary measure, although his relations with the Ambassador, General Ott, were strained and there were elements of sharp personal friction which lent a shrill note to the later accusations of Lissner with regard to the Sorge case.

Lissner was sent on an information tour in Manchukuo, and received payments for a series of articles which were placed in the Japanese press. The last sum was paid to him in April, 1940. He never returned to Tokyo. According to a German Foreign Office minute of March 31, 1942, he 'took up another type of employment in Manchukuo'. He was not, however, stationed as a regular representative of the German Military Intelligence in Hsinking, but was a valuable 'V-Mann', or informant, and had been working for them presumably in liaison with the German security services for a period unknown to the Foreign Office.

The harsh consequences of his personal intrusion into the Sorge affair were, however, not to be visited on Lissner at this juncture.

On August 16, 1942, however, in a cable to the head of the Gestapo, Colonel Meisinger reported that Lissner 'claimed to be the local Nazi leader for Manchukuo . . . that he was not an honorary Aryan, but recognized personally by the Fuehrer as of Aryan stock'. He was, according to Meisinger, under continuous Japanese police observation 'for unreliable activities', but no action had been taken against him 'as he was thought to have powerful German friends'. He also had enemies among the German colony in Manchukuo, who reported on him to Tokyo.

Lissner was now Meisinger's main target in his purge of the Nazi party organization in the Far East, and in his vengeful search to uncover treasonable activities among German nationals in these regions. But his enquiry was tenaciously blocked by the German Military Intelligence, and regarded by the German Foreign Office as a distasteful Gestapo manœuvre. His superiors were, indeed, able to secure for Lissner a military decoration for his services in the Far East.

Two months later, the new German Ambassador in Tokyo, Dr. Heinrich Georg Stahmer, who had succeeded General Ott in May

1943,* was informed in confidence of the Fuehrer decree certifying that Lissner was of Aryan stock, but instructing the embassy not to give Meisinger any details. This remarkable legislative act was in recognition of Lissner's 'special services'.

It now seemed that the affair would lapse and that Lissner would be left undisturbed in Harbin. In March 1943 the German military attaché in Tokyo, Colonel Kretschmer, reported that in conversation with the head of the Japanese military mission in Harbin Lissner's name was not mentioned, and that 'at present the Japanese have no further serious suspicions'.

In May however, 'at the repeated request of the Japanese military police', Meisinger travelled to Harbin. Lissner had been claiming, according to them, to be the Gestapo chief in Manchukuo. They also suspected that he was working for the Russians.

Meisinger, on his return, assembled a series of hectic and distorted charges; that Lissner was systematically collecting intelligence from Japan, China and Manchukuo; that he had obtained marked maps of Manchukuo from a deceased German mining engineer; that he had contacts with Soviet representatives, and that the information which he obtained was seventy-five per cent correct and therefore, although the Russians clearly knew of his German connections, they must value his work.

According to Meisinger, the Japanese police would not act because of Lissner's claim to supreme protection in the highest circles in Germany. Not only did he hint that he was the Gestapo chief of the region, but also that he was employed by the Hsinking Legation on important duties, and a special envoy of the Fuehrer with direct access to him. The Japanese police would, however, appreciate his immediate removal, and would prefer not to embarrass the Legation by arresting him.

The German Ambassador in Tokyo seemed convinced, and added to Meisinger's telegram of May 25 his personal view that

since suspicion exists in Japanese circles of Lissner's activities on behalf of the Soviet Union, I urgently recommend his recall to Tokyo and later dispatch home. . . . A danger exists of a second Sorge case, whereby

---

* Stahmer was earlier on the staff of Ribbentrop's special private office and the liaison officer with Oshima, the Japanese Ambassador in Berlin. Stahmer negotiated the Tripartite Pact in Tokyo in 1940 on direct and personal instructions from the German Foreign Minister. See p. 223 above.

Japanese-German relations, which have not yet quite recovered, would be again severely impaired.

Meisinger now found an unexpected ally at the summit. On May 30, 1943, the German Foreign Office liaison officer attached to Hitler's staff sent the following note to Ribbentrop: 'I have submitted the Tokyo telegram on Ivar Lissner to the Fuehrer. The name is unknown to the Fuehrer, and he naturally agrees to Lissner's immediate recall. With the Fuehrer's well-known antipathy to such so-called agents he has criticized the use of such people. In skimming through the second part of the telegram, which contains Lissner's statements that he was a member of the Fuehrer's staff and had been given corresponding positions of authority, he said that the best thing would be to shoot such people straight away.'

The ripples of this local affair abruptly extended, and the varying implications of a potential case of espionage in the Far East were the subject of comment and tensions in the highest circles.

On the day following the Fuehrer's picturesque comments, the head of the German Military Intelligence himself, Admiral Canaris, set out his personal views on the Lissner affair in a note to the Foreign Office.

After thorough investigation of his personal relationships and intelligence work, the War Ministry is not of the opinion that the charges of the Japanese military police against Lissner of working for Soviet Russia are valid. He is not a bearer of military secrets. Any contact between Lissner and Soviet Russian circles is to be seen as desirable in the interests of his intelligence work.

Lissner has hitherto refused to reveal his work to the Japanese in exchange for their making intelligence material available to him, in view of the peculiar attitude of the Japanese authorities. This agent is the Foreign Intelligence Office's only source supplying extensive reports on the area of Asiatic Russia and the border area Manchukuo/Russia. The reports received, particularly recent ones, are extremely comprehensive and constitute our only reconnaissance information on the reserves, new formations, etc., particularly of the Soviet Air Force in Siberia. Japan's offer of an exchange of information through military attachés would not, in the light of previous experiences, be a satisfactory equivalent.

The War Ministry has instructed the Armed Forces Attaché, Admiral Wenneker, to intervene very strongly with the Japanese military authorities in Lissner's favour on the above-mentioned grounds, emphasizing that in the opinion of this office it could only be agreeable for Japan if the representative of the Intelligence Service against Soviet Russia is a German and not a Japanese.

In the present circumstances, the Japanese could only be offered a full share in the intelligence material supplied by Lissner on Russia on condition that he can continue his work unhindered. Since he did not send his reports via Tokyo, their value cannot be estimated from there.

I would be particularly grateful if, for the Foreign Office, the Ambassador [Stahmer] would also indicate the extreme military importance of the continued activity of this source of information, and also support the intervention of the Armed Forces Attaché in this sense.

Meisinger's pursuit of this affair exacerbated the already delicate relations between the German Minister in Hsinking, Dr. Wagner, and the Embassy in Tokyo. The main element behind these manœuvres was the catastrophic effect in Tokyo of Lissner's damaging intervention in the Sorge case in the previous year.

Wagner's indignant rejection of the aspersions against Lissner is similar to that of Ott in regard to Sorge. On June 3 Wagner, who was on a visit to Tokyo in order to confront his colleague, Stahmer, on the Lissner affair, telegraphed the Foreign Office: 'The charges against Lissner are largely identical with the nonsensical rumours circulating in Harbin.' It was quite untrue that Lissner had received any funds from the Legation. There was no concrete evidence that he was working for the Russians, and as to the allegations of his close connections with the Legation, he was treated as 'a deserving writer' so as to give a normal impression in line with precise instructions from Berlin that his work must not be disturbed.

But Ambassador Stahmer had already, as the senior diplomatic representative in the Far East, summoned Lissner to Tokyo, and had warned Wagner that he would be arrested on arrival.

On June 3 Stahmer telegraphed to Berlin:

The alleged 'nonsensical rumours' are in my opinion really unofficial warnings by the Japanese military police to the German consulate in Harbin. According to material at hand, the police are aware of all the communications from the Russians to Lissner.

The latter had apparently been advised by the Counsellor of the German Legation in Hsinking not to obey the summons to Tokyo. The Japanese military police, therefore, according to Stahmer, would be forced to make 'a sensational arrest' of Lissner. 'The evaluation of the case is complicated by the fact that the Sorge trial has now begun and has therefore reopened the whole situation.'

Wagner loyally defended his Legation, and indirectly Lissner's position, even to the point of a mild counter-attack on his irrepressible Tokyo colleagues. In a cable of June 19, Wagner stated that one could not talk of 'a new Sorge case'. It had not so far been shown that Lissner had been spying on behalf of the Soviet Union. He was a recognized 'liaison officer' and as such it was the duty of the Legation to support him in his work. His relations with German officials 'were essentially different to those of Sorge with the Tokyo Embassy where, to the best of my knowledge, Sorge had a post in the Embassy itself (editing the news-sheet), and went in and out daily'.

On June 5, 1943, Lissner was arrested by the *Kempei* and brought to Tokyo. Stahmer now took the opportunity to propose to Berlin that in future the Hsinking Legation should be brought under the supervisory control of the Embassy in Tokyo. 'The Japanese are drawing an incorrect comparison between the Sorge case, as they consider Lissner was also spying on behalf of the Soviet Union, and just as Sorge in Tokyo, Lissner in Hsinking had particularly close contacts with the German official representatives.'

At the time of Lissner's arrest, Werner Crome, a leading German journalist in Tokyo, together with his secretary Ursula Schwarz and a Japanese assistant, was also detained. Meisinger reported: 'Further arrests of Germans and foreigners are expected.'

On June 5 he sent to the German security services, without comment, the following list of German nationals under arrest in Japan on charges of spying for the Soviet Union:

1. Richard Sorge	5. Dr. Hermann Grauert
2. Max Klausen	6. Waldemar Bartels
3. Karl Raimund Hofmeier	7. Willi Förster
4. Dr. Ivar Lissner	8. Stefanie Kacarova

The first four names require no comment. The others had been subject to political checking by Meisinger with the Gestapo in Berlin, and their cases brought to his attention by the Japanese police.

Dr. Hermann Grauert had been arrested in May 1942 on suspicion of spying activities. Meisinger had reported cryptically to his superiors within a few weeks that a conviction could almost certainly be expected. Grauert had been born in Japan, and was at one time the German Consulate doctor in Yokohama. Police enquiries in Germany showed that he had certain charges pending against him for illegal export of currency, and was about to be deprived of his German citizenship. Little further light has been thrown on his case which, like the others, was presumably based on espionage activities on behalf of the Soviet Union.

The arrest of Waldemar Bartels was more unsettling to the Germans. In July 1942 Meisinger had sent to Berlin a list of over twenty German nationals in Japan, most of them journalists, for political checking in the Gestapo records 'in connection with the cases of Sorge and Hofmeier'. With two exceptions, and the details were of minor importance, they were all cleared – including Bartels.* He was however arrested towards the end of the year, and Meisinger reported that he was closely involved with Max Klausen. The charge against Bartels was that he had been reporting on the movements of German ships in Yokohama, and he confessed to the Japanese police that he was working for the Russians.

There is some evidence to show that Bartels was connected with an independent Soviet ring functioning in Japan and not directly connected in any way with Sorge. According to the Japanese police, Bartels was working under the instructions of a Swiss citizen named by them as Schweitzer [sic], a former German national, who was also arrested. This man was allegedly in touch with a member of the Soviet embassy in Tokyo known as 'Ivanov'. The German security authorities in Berlin showed a special and alarmed interest in the Bartels affair, and requested a detailed report from Meisinger.†

Shadows closed round this case. Bartels died later in prison.

Willi Förster was a well-known figure in the German colony in Japan. He owned an aircraft propeller factory, and his house was the scene of many parties attended by leading German and European residents, including both the Ambassador and Sorge. His office was a meeting place for anti-Axis foreigners, and under surveillance by the Japanese police.

* A further list of German residents in Japan was also sent to Berlin by Meisinger in August 1942, with similar results.

† There is no trace of such a communication in the German records.

Meisinger had initiated a police check in Germany on Förster, and in collaboration with the Japanese had spent a year building up a case against him. Förster was arrested in May 1943. The charges against him are not known, although it was specifically mentioned that he was in some way connected with Sorge.

His previous career, as established by the German security authorities, needed some clarification. According to their records, Förster had left Germany for Moscow in 1928, and had worked as an aircraft mechanic in the Soviet Union until 1931. He was thought to have been a member of the German Communist Party at one time, and was the subject of reports by the German Embassy in Moscow. He had arrived in Japan in the middle thirties, and came to the attention of the German National Socialist Party branch in Tokyo as an anti-Nazi. He was vaguely suspected by them of being a Comintern agent.

Förster survived his detention in prison, and returned to Germany after the war.

Stefanie Kacarova remains a more mysterious figure, and the evidence about her case has vanished. She was already under arrest in September 1941, before the capture of the Sorge ring, and Meisinger had reported laconically at the time that suspicions about her were justified. She was suspected of being involved with a large spy ring in which as yet no German was implicated.

The telegram drafted by Meisinger, listing names* of the eight Germans under arrest in Tokyo for spying on behalf of Russia, attracted the personal attention of Ribbentrop, who cabled on June 10 to the German Ambassador, Stahmer:

> The German Foreign Minister begs you to ask the Japanese in an amicable manner for a more detailed explanation of the reasons for the arrest of Lissner and the other German nationals. So far, reports do not give a clear picture. For your own information: if the Japanese give valid reasons for the arrests, it is intended to do nothing further in favour of the arrested men, so as to avoid straining German-Japanese relations.

The German Foreign Office was alarmed by the repercussions of the arrests of further German nationals in Japan on accusations of

---

* For an unexplained reason, Werner Crome and his secretary Ursula Schwarz are not included in the list.

pro-Soviet espionage. In none of these cases had the arrests by the Japanese police been the direct result of any action by Meisinger. They appear to form part of a general and intensified drive to uncover the existence of Soviet espionage groups operating independently of the Sorge ring, but occasioned by its unmasking. In the case of Lissner, however, neither the German Military Intelligence, nor the Security Services, believed the charges against him. The German Foreign Office officials took the view that Wagner had been correct in supporting a valuable intelligence agent. 'The Japanese were more likely to be seeking an excuse to liquidate the German Intelligence set-up in the Far East, which is known to the Japanese Military Intelligence, but being uncontrolled by them is a source of disquiet.'

At the beginning of August, the Japanese military police had handed to Meisinger a memorandum entitled 'Survey of the Lissner Espionage Affair', summarizing the results of their interrogations to date of Lissner, Crome and the latter's secretary. In reporting the contents of this document to Berlin on August 12, Stahmer stressed that the other German nationals, who had been listed by Meisinger in June as under arrest, had no connection with Lissner, but were merely suspected of spying for the Russians. Stahmer had expressed his interest in the Lissner case to the Japanese Foreign Minister and did not propose to raise the subject again. 'After the Sorge case, which has not yet been completed, Lissner will be handled strictly on a criminal not a political basis in order to avoid any further strain on German-Japanese relations.'

On August 19, 1943, Meisinger summarized the Japanese report on the Lissner case in a telegram to the head of the Gestapo, General Mueller. Lissner had allegedly been working as a double agent in Harbin since 1940, in contact with the Soviet Consulate. Crome had confessed to receiving intelligence tasks from Lissner and to being aware of the latter's activities on behalf of the Soviet Union. Crome had collected material on Japanese policy and military affairs and transmitted 'decisive information' to Lissner. In a further interrogation Lissner declared that he was instructed by his German superiors to learn about conditions in Japan and that he had instructed Crome to send him such reports.

Meisinger, and the official interpreter of the German Embassy, Hamel, interrogated Lissner on three occasions at the invitation of the Japanese military police, and without any Japanese being present. In talking to Meisinger, Lissner confirmed Crome's statement, but denied having given him any concrete tasks. The reports on conditions in Japan were, however, compiled on specific instructions from Berlin.

The military attaché in Tokyo, Colonel Kretschmer, commented in a telegram to Berlin some weeks later that Japanese military circles were impressed by

the fact that not only is a German again conducting espionage in Japan on behalf of the Soviet Union, but also that a German should be collecting secret Japanese material on instructions from the German War Ministry.

With the conclusion of the case against Sorge with the death penalty, and with proceedings pending against other Germans, there has arisen in intelligent Japanese military circles serious mistrust of the German colony in East Asia, which has in no small way been increased by the instructions of the German War Ministry to Lissner on Japanese intelligence. When speaking to Japanese officers I have clearly explained that Lissner could only be lying . . . and that he was only collecting Russian information. Any intended intervention of the German Military Intelligence in favour of Lissner would be misunderstood by the Japanese, and politically delicate.

The German Ambassador added his own pompous comment to the telegram. 'I very much regret that Lissner by his own behaviour made impossible any attempt to clear the affair openly, and has given further nourishment to Japanese chatter about alleged German espionage activities.'

The 'confession' of Lissner could only have catastrophic repercussions on the technical relations of the Japanese and German Intelligence Services. With his arrest, the Germans had lost their one vital source of intelligence on the Soviet order of battle in the Far East.

As Colonel Kretschmer had gloomily and accurately reported in mid-September:

After the espionage case of Sorge who was connected with the German Embassy, and now the accusation of spying against Lissner who was working for the German War Ministry, and also against Crome, the Japanese General Staff is extraordinarily suspicious of any form of German collection of intelligence. This is possibly bound up with Japanese determination not to have their policy of neutrality towards Russia upset by foreign 'clumsiness.

It was also vain for Meisinger to tell the Japanese police—as he did—that Lissner was lying when he claimed that he was reporting on Japanese political and military conditions. Such reports had frequently been passed through the German Legation in Hsinking and signed formally by the Minister. Even if he had not had specific instructions to do so, there is no evidence to show that Lissner's superiors in Berlin either ordered him to cease such operations or did not value such information.

The particularly hostile reaction of the German officials in Tokyo to this aspect of the Lissner affair was natural. Such reporting was a direct and impertinent invasion of their own functions as specialists on the Japanese political and military scene, and the suppression of a competitive and rival outpost beyond their control, especially in view of the sharp increase in Japanese suspicions of German intelligence activities in the Far East, stemming from the Sorge case, seemed more than justified. But Lissner's rôle in exacerbating the Sorge affair was the main contributory factor in the attitude first of Ott and then of Stahmer and his staff towards him.

No move on behalf of Lissner was made by the German Embassy to the Japanese authorities on his behalf. He was released, however, early in 1945 as the Japanese could find no case against him. He had suffered during his long confinement such ill-treatment that his health was seriously impaired. His superior, Admiral Canaris, was already under arrest in Germany for his part in the July Plot, and Lissener remained in precarious isolation in Japan.

The zealous and brutal pursuit of 'suspects' in the German community in Japan, which Meisinger had conducted since 1941, according to the methods if not the resources of the Gestapo, may have patched up his personal reputation as a police expert. But it was in another, and far more grim, connection that he was to be called to account.

At the close of the war Meisinger was taken into custody in Tokyo, along with the members of the German Embassy, by the American occupation authorities. After interrogation in Europe, he was extradited to Poland to stand trial for his responsibilities as commander of the German Security Police in Warsaw in 1940. He was sentenced to death by the Supreme National Tribunal of the Polish People's Republic on March 3, 1947, and hanged.

Chapter 18

THE LAST ACT

'I am just a leaf on a big tree. When I have played out my role I shall
fall to the ground.' VUKELIC, writing to his wife from prison

ON May 15, 1942, General Ott telegraphed Berlin that the Japanese
Foreign Ministry had informed him

that the charge against the Communist group, in which the Germans Sorge
and Klausen are implicated, will be read the day after tomorrow. . . . As well
as Prince Konoye's intimate associate Ozaki and other Japanese, Saionji
the grandson of the last Genro Prince and Inukai, the son of the Minister
President murdered in 1932, will also be charged. Indictment charges the
accused with having carried on espionage for the Communist International.
Saionji and Inukai are charged with passing on state secrets to Ozaki,
although not aware of his role.

Charge includes a short personal description of Sorge and his statements
about known Communist connections in Europe. Sorge, who came to China
in 1930 and afterwards to Japan, is said to be the Comintern's contact man
for the Japanese group and to have handed over its instructions.

The chief assistant to the Ministry of Justice had informed Minister
Kordt that all mention of Sorge's belonging to the Nazi party would be
avoided in the wording of the indictment. Japanese justice regards him
purely as an international Communist. The head of the European division
of the Foreign Ministry added that announcement had become necessary
because the Cabinet was interested in people involved. Further releases not
intended. The Press will only carry the Ministry of Justice release. He
hopes German government will understand the circumstances of the release.
In Japanese view the incident will not disturb German-Japanese relations.

The Japanese Ambassador in Berlin, General Oshima, called on
Ribbentrop on the day of this press release in order to point out even
more carefully: 'Tokyo found this publication to be necessary, as
several high-placed Japanese personalities were involved and this was
generally known. If nothing were published, this would lead to unpleasant and dangerous rumours. Naturally nothing was mentioned
in the communiqué of any connection whatsoever between the

German Communists Sorge and Klausen and official German agencies in Tokyo.'

The German authorities in Tokyo had awaited with concern the actual terms of this first and only official statement by the Japanese on the Sorge affair. It appears that the Ambassador and the senior members of his staff were also closely shadowed by the Japanese police on the eve of this press release.

On the evening of May 16 the office of the German News Service burst into life. The two Japanese assistants on night duty were asked to prepare an urgent memorandum on the personal histories of Saionji and Inukai. There was much coming and going between the office and the Ambassador's residence. 'It seems that the Embassy was sending a report to Germany on the announcement of the Sorge Incident.'

General Ott and his wife spent the following day, Sunday, May 17, at their villa in the country, returning in the evening to dine with friends in Tokyo. 'The Otts displayed no particular emotion. But it seems that Ott has ordered the Germans in the Embassy not to discuss the case in any way.'

This official release by the Japanese Ministry of Justice to the Press had been drafted and redrafted with minute care, in close consultation with the Foreign Ministry and the Supreme Court.

The main reason for the statement had been the inescapable decision to arrest Inukai and Saionji, and the disturbing extent of the ramifications of the Sorge case in Japanese political circles. This aspect of the affair was, however, carefully played down. Although the guilt of the principal accused was stressed, there was no hint of either the importance or the sources of their information, collected from Japanese and German officials. There was therefore no reference in the release either to 'high political figures' in Japan or to the German Embassy.

The Sorge group was described very deliberately as 'a Red spy ring under the orders of Comintern headquarters'. All mention of Sorge's real mission as an intelligence officer of the Fourth Bureau of the Russian Army was suppressed. By referring only to the Comintern, and by creating the fiction that Sorge and his associates were essentially members of an international Communist organization, the Ministry of Justice could at one and the same time take the view that the Soviet Union, with whom Japan had a valid treaty of non-aggression, was not involved in the affair as a national government, and that, as members of a Communist party, the accused could be tried for violation of the Peace Preservation Law, which came within the purview of the Ministry of Justice and not under the National Defence Security Law which, it could be argued, might have to be applied by the military authorities.

The next step, after the public announcement of the arraignment of the accused, was to conduct the preliminary judicial examination of the principal accused, Sorge and Ozaki; and then, with special caution in view of their high political associations, that of Saionji and Inukai.

Now that leading Japanese politicians seemed to be implicated, even if loosely, in the affair, the task of proceeding to the preliminary examination of all the leading figures called for care.

The accused were examined in court throughout the summer and autumn of 1942. The proceedings were held in camera.

At first the journeys from Sugamo to the court provided a welcome break to the monotony of the Detention House. It was the rule that prisoners awaiting trial must wear large basket-like hats over their heads. The prisoner could view the world through slits in this head-dress, while his own features could not be seen.

Through his vizor Sorge studied the streets and crowds as the car bumped its way across the city; and in court he would sometimes create a small diversion by reproducing the ideographs of shop signs and advertisements which he had noted on the journey from Sugamo.

Professor Ikoma, interpreter for Judge Nakamura as well as for the procurator, was conscious that he was 'in a kind of mediating position between Nakamura and Sorge', and he found it useful to talk to Sorge about the progress of the German-Russian war. Stalingrad was under siege, and Sorge, who perceived that this was the crisis of the war, took great interest in news of how the battle was going. He would ask Ikoma, when he met him at the court, to give him the latest information.

He used to ask me in a whisper about the Stalingrad battle [says Ikoma] when the judge was talking to his clerk. I could only reply in an undertone, but I would tell him the general situation. The preliminary judge knew what was going on, but he did not stop us.

Ikoma remembers that when the situation changed dramatically in favour of the Russians, Sorge was delighted and 'his stern face became a mass of smiles'.

There is another vignette of Sorge at this particular moment. Kawai Teikichi, following prolonged interrogations in a police station, was transferred to Sugamo in the autumn of 1942. Sorge was in Cell No. 20 on the first floor of No. 2 Building. (Ozaki was in Cell 11 of the same building.) Kawai happened to be locked up in the same block. He chanced to see Sorge's enthusiastic reaction to the news that Stalingrad was saved. Watching through the peephole of his cell, Kawai saw Sorge take off his basket hat in the corridor and dance with joy, patting a warder affectionately on the shoulder.

Ikoma declares that Preliminary Judge Nakamura's examination of Sorge was stricter than Yoshikawa's. During the procurator's interrogations there was always time for some small talk. According to Yoshikawa, 'only about two-thirds of those months of my interrogation were taken up by actual investigation; a third of the time was occupied in general talk, mostly on the German-Russian war — Sorge was always saying what he would do if he were a Russian army commander.'

But the atmosphere of the preliminary judge's examination seemed to prohibit random, personal, talk between the prisoner and his interpreter. Ikoma did not find it easy to translate legal Japanese into German. Yoshikawa's report, the basis of Judge Nakamura's examination, presented many difficulties.

The document was very long and difficult, couched in legal phraseology, without punctuation. I kept breaking into a cold sweat with the effort of translating it into the sort of language a German would understand.

But I managed it somehow, because I knew fairly well the contents of the report.

This time Sorge could make no jokes. He had to listen to the translation, pointing out errors from time to time. On occasions he would protest quite strongly. It must have been very boring for him.

When Judge Nakamura argued with him in an unpleasant way or asked some particularly sharp question, Sorge would often utter very vigorous retorts or not answer at all.

The preliminary judge's examination dragged on into the winter. Long before that, says Ikoma, 'all of us — accuser, accused, and interpreter — were very exhausted.'

Very often it was already dark by the time we had finished the business — at 7 or 8 p.m. after a long summer day — of letting the accused listen to all that was read out, and obtaining his agreement to what he was reported to have said.

Sometimes the servants of the court, being weary and wanting to go home, would put the lights out, in spite of the fact that the court was still sitting. This was done to annoy the preliminary judge; and when this happened, Judge Nakamura — who reminded one of an English-type gentleman — would loudly reprimand the staff.

It was all most tedious.

At last, on December 5, 1942, Judge Nakamura closed his investigation of Sorge and Ozaki, and ten days later he decided in favour of a formal trial in both cases.*

The accused remained at Sugamo until the next stage in the procedure — trial in court — began the following April. Each man stood trial separately in the Tokyo District Criminal Court, the public being barred from access. The hearings began with the trial of Ozaki in April 1943, followed by that of Sorge in May, and continued through the month of August.

The interpreter on this occasion was an academic colleague of Ikoma's, Professor Ueda Toshiro. Ikoma tells us that he felt much relieved at being spared the duty of interpreting at the trial.

The evidence against Sorge was assembled from the previous interrogations by the procurator and the preliminary judge, together with Sorge's own confession. Sorge's Japanese lawyer, Asanuma Sumiji, was allowed to consult this evidence in court only with the permission of the president of the court. The charges in the indictment against Sorge were classified pedantically according to the series of security laws promulgated in Japan between 1937 and 1941. In spite of the original intentions of the Ministry of Justice at the time of the press release in May 1942, the final indictment concentrated on offences committed after the passing of the National Security Law on May 10, 1941, and in direct connection with its provisions.

The crux of the case against Sorge, apart from a general conspiracy with Ozaki, Klausen, Vukelic and Miyagi, to secure information in Tokyo and other areas and supply it to a foreign power 'in the full knowledge that it might be employed against the interests of our national defence', was the passing on of state secrets, 'the gravest of the crimes perpetrated by the accused'.

* The same procedure was applied to Saionji and Inukai on December 7, 1942.

The two secrets upon which the trial concentrated were the leakages conveyed by Ozaki to Sorge of the decisions of the Imperial Conference of July 2, 1941, and of the Japanese 'Draft Proposal to the United States'. Under the National Security Law such action made the accused liable to the death penalty.

There was no reference in the trial to Sorge's links with the Fourth Bureau of the Red Army, and only a brief mention that Sorge had obtained certain documents of military value from General Matsky, the military attaché at the German Embassy in Tokyo. The significance of the whole case was therefore concentrated on the activities of the Sorge ring in the summer and autumn of 1941 and in direct connection with the historic decision of the Tojo government to strike south into the Pacific and against the United States rather than into Siberia against the Soviet Union.

The investigation of this particular achievement of Sorge and Ozaki revealed to the Japanese authorities and government, to their alarm, the disquieting effects on Japanese politics of the affair and occasioned not only the arrest of Saionji and Inukai, but also the suppression of Sorge and Ozaki themselves.

Both men had been hoping that they would be tried on the Peace Preservation Law as members of an international Communist organization, as such a charge did not carry with it the death penalty. But once they appeared in court the change in the tactics of the Ministry of Justice was grimly clear. Sorge, in particular, attempted a final defence in his statement: 'It must be remembered that the negotiations between the Japanese and the Americans were no secret. The matter was discussed in Japanese as well as American papers. It was well known that the American Ambassador Grew was active behind the scenes. . . . I myself received orders from the *Frankfurter Zeitung* to report fully, with particular regard to the prospect of American mediation between Japan and China. I sent long telegrams. None of them were censored.'

Such other information, which Sorge had dispatched to the Soviet Union, had been collected voluntarily and more or less openly. Sorge summed up his defence as follows:

'Japanese laws are subject to interpretation, either broadly or according to the strict letter of the text. Although leakages of information may, strictly speaking, be punishable by law, in practice the Japanese social system is not amenable to the keeping of secrets— I consider that in the drawing up of the indictment insufficient consideration was given to our activity and to the nature of the information which we obtained. Data which Vukelic supplied was neither secret nor important; he brought in only news which was well known to every press correspondent. The same may be said of Miyagi, who was in no position to obtain state secrets. What may be termed political information was procured by Ozaki and by me.

'I obtained my information from the German Embassy, but here again I consider that little if any of it could be termed "state secret". It was given to me voluntarily. To obtain it I resorted to no strategy for which I should be punished. I never used deceit or force. Ambassador Ott and Colonel Scholl asked me to help them write reports — especially Scholl, who put much confidence in me and asked me to read all of his own reports before he sent them to Germany. As for me, I placed much trust in this information, because it was compiled and evaluated by competent military and naval attachés for the use of the German General Staff. I believe that the Japanese government, in giving data to the German Embassy, expected some of it to leak out.

'Ozaki obtained much of his news from the Breakfast Club. But the Breakfast Club was not an official organization. Such information as was exchanged within the club must have been discussed by other similar cliques, of which there were many in Tokyo in those days. Even such data as Ozaki considered important and secret was actually no longer so, because he had procured it indirectly after it had left its secret source.'

Such a plea was vain. On September 29, 1943, the Tokyo District Court brought in a sentence of death on Richard Sorge. Certain items in his possession at the time of his arrest were confiscated, the visible signs of his activities: two drafts of intelligence reports written in English; seven other similar documents; three cameras and accessories; and $1,782 in cash.

The trial of Ozaki followed a similar course.

Both men appealed to the Japanese Supreme Court. Sorge's plea was dismissed on January 20, 1944, on the grounds that it had not been made within 'the legally declared time limit'. Ozaki made a final statement to the Supreme Court, together with his appeal, on the pressing advice of his lawyers. In a long decision this statement was also rejected by the Court on April 5, and the death sentence confirmed.

Of the other main accused, Klausen and Vukelic were sentenced to life imprisonment. Anna Klausen received three years.

On the morning of November 7, 1944, Ozaki was engaged in writing a card to his wife. He was anxious about his father, who was about to leave his home village to return to Formosa, broken by the trial and sentence of his son. Ozaki was wrapped in the chill monotony of his cell, unaware that, in the next few minutes, he would receive a visitor. The door opened and the Governor of Sugamo Prison entered. He asked, with bleak and ritual formality, the name, age and domicile of the condemned man, and after identification announced that, by order of the Minister of Justice, Ozaki would be taken to execution that morning.

Ozaki listened with outward calm, and bowed formally to the Governor. He changed into clean garments, already set aside for this last moment, and took his place in the procession of court officials and witnesses — handcuffed, and with a straw hat on his head. The small group crossed the prison courtyard, and entered a concrete building with high walls. Here Ozaki was received by the prison chaplain in an anteroom lit by the tapers of a Buddhist altar. The chaplain enquired of Ozaki regarding his will and last wishes, and offered him tea and cakes. After ritual prayers, he was led behind the altar to an adjoining room, bare and without windows, with a gallows erected in the middle. He took his place on the trap, and the noose was placed round his neck. As he was reciting the Buddhist prayer of comfort, the trap was sprung. It was 9.33. Eighteen minutes later the prison doctor formally certified that Ozaki Hotsumi, aged forty-three years, was dead.

Within a few minutes, after the removal of Ozaki's body, the Prison Governor and his escort visited the cell of Richard Sorge. He too was not expecting such a visit on that day. The same formalities were repeated, and Sorge was asked if he wished to say anything. He answered 'No, nothing else', and he thanked the chaplain and the prison staff for their kindnesses.

According to the bare official record, 'Sorge proceeded with composure to the place of execution'. He was escorted through the anteroom, without pausing before the Buddhist altar, to the gallows.

He gave no word or sign.* The trap was sprung at 10.20, and sixteen minutes later he was pronounced dead. He was forty-nine years of age.

A legend arose that Sorge had never been hanged, but had been mysteriously exchanged and removed to the Soviet Union. The subsequent report of the executioner is, however, grimly conclusive. 'I watched Richard Sorge as he took his exercise from the time he was in prison. Therefore I can swear that he was he and no other person.'

Ozaki's wife and his lawyers came later that day to collect his body. They found it, and, beside the coffin, another such box awaiting burial.

November 7, 1944, was the twenty-seventh anniversary of the Russian Revolution.

The following day a brief telegram from the German Ambassador in Tokyo closed the case of Richard Sorge in Berlin.

The German journalist Richard Sorge who, as previously reported, had been condemned to death for espionage on behalf of the Soviet Union, was, according to a communication from the Foreign Ministry, hanged on November 7. The list of questions drawn up by the Embassy concerning Sorge's earlier Communist activity against Germany will be answered by the Japanese State Prosecutor on the basis of available documentary material.

One morning Klausen, in his cell at Sugamo, heard footsteps in the corridor. As the party passed by—in Japanese prisons there is a gap between the floor and the bottom of the door—he recognized a pair of feet. It was Sorge being taken down to the interrogation room. This was the last link between the two men. Later Klausen learnt of Sorge's execution from a Japanese prisoner in the baths.

Klausen himself was nearly burned to death during an American air-raid on Tokyo. Blazing fragments of wood crashed through the window of his cell and set fire to the sleeping mats, and Klausen was overcome by smoke. He was soon afterwards transferred to Akita

* The Japanese records make no mention that he shouted 'Long live the Communist Party, the Soviet Union and the Red Army', as claimed in the Soviet press.

prison, where he was liberated by American troops on October 8, 1945. His physical condition was so fragile that he was taken at once to a local American army hospital. At the time of his arrest in October 1941 Klausen weighed 176 lbs.; on his transfer to Akita his weight was only 99 lbs.

After a brief recovery Klausen was brought under American escort in a military train to Tokyo. As in the case of other survivors of the Sorge ring, the American authorities were oblivious of their existence.* This was not the case with the Soviet Embassy in Japan. As soon as Klausen, with the help of a Japanese lawyer, had been reunited with Anna, who had also been released from prison – 'we looked like old people' Klausen wrote recently – and had settled the recovery of his modest personal effects from a former domestic servant, Soviet officials took brisk charge of the couple. They were flown in a Soviet military aircraft to Vladivostok, where Klausen, who was suffering from an unsterilized injection for a liver complaint, was placed in a naval hospital.

Max and Anna left on the Trans-Siberian railway, on the same train on which they had travelled eastwards to their fate in Japan sixteen years before, and reached Moscow 'where they had a warm reception from their friends'.

The rapid action of the Soviet Embassy officials in Tokyo spirited the Klausens out of range of the American authorities in 1945. From that time all trace of them vanished, except to the Russian authorities, until the Supreme Soviet, for motives which excite speculation, decorated Richard Sorge posthumously as a Hero of the Soviet Union on November 6, 1964, after a prepared series of press releases on the Sorge case.

The East German Government were not to be outdone, and indeed stole a march on Moscow. After their sojourn in the Soviet Union, and presumably exhaustive interrogations by the intelligence authorities, the Klausens had come to East Berlin, where they were allowed to rebuild their existence 'quietly and modestly'. They changed their name and joined the East German Communist Party. In 1953 Max was working on a building site in the Moderson Strasse in East Berlin 'helping in the reconstruction of democratic new

---

* The U.S. Army authorities had merely recorded Klausen's release from Akita prison on October 9, 1945. See Willoughby, *Shanghai Conspiracy*, p. 131.

Germany'. A photograph of him appeared in the newspapers at the time.* He became a party instructor in the Kopenick shipyard and the East German Inland Shipping Company.

He had thus returned, after the strains of years of underground work which had begun with his admission into the original German Communist Party in 1927, to the fraternity of seafaring men. But the routine obscurity of these post-war years was suddenly invaded. At the beginning of October 1964 General Erich Mielke, Minister for State Security of the German Democratic Republic, in a public ceremony conferred on Max and Anna Klausen the Service Medal in Gold of the National Popular Army.

After years of illegal work and prison and two decades of obscurity the Klausens have received public recognition for their very special services as agents of one of the most successful rings ever organized by the Soviet Military Intelligence. They can now take their allotted place in the history of the Sorge Affair.

As for Miyagi, the most courageous member of the ring, he died in prison – before he was sentenced – in August 1943.

The fate of Branko Vukelic ended in tragedy. All the members of the ring who were under arrest were tried separately in camera. In September 1943, together with Klausen, Vukelic had been sentenced to life imprisonment. He remained for a time in Sugamo prison, where his Japanese wife Yamasaki Yoshiko was able to visit him and bring clothing, books and money to buy food. In April 1944, after the rejection by the Supreme Court of all the appeals of the accused, the prison régime permitted only monthly visits.

In July 1944, Vukelic was transferred to the grim Abashiri prison in Hokkaido in the harsh and forbidding climate of north Japan. Yoshiko was allowed to bring her baby son for a last brief reunion with her husband thirty minutes before he was taken away. He looked thin and exhausted after nearly three years of confinement and severe interrogation, and was suffering from chronic dysentery. Vukelic refused to allow his wife to move to Hokkaido in winter with a small baby. 'He smiled his optimistic smile and consoled me as he always did.' Perhaps she might join him in the spring.

* Reproduced in the *Neues Deutschland* article of November 2, 1964.

On January 15, 1945, Yoshiko received a telegram from the prison authorities at Abashiri. 'Will you take charge of the body or shall we take the necessary steps?' Vukelic had not survived the savage climate and prison conditions in Hokkaido. He had died of pneumonia two days previously.

In a letter written to her mother-in-law, Vilma Vukelic, in Zagreb on December 15, 1946, Yoshiko wrote: 'I found him already in his coffin at the prison. He was wrapped in white as is the custom in Japan. He was so thin, frozen and stiff. They sent a horse-drawn hearse for him, and he was taken to the crematorium where I attended the cremation.'* The odyssey of the young Marxist student from Zagreb had ended.

In January 1965 Yoshiko, and her son by Vukelic, were received by the President of the Soviet Union, Anastas Mikoyan and presented with the 'Order of the Patriotic War, First Class' in posthumous recognition.

Hanako-san had been held for questioning by the *Tokko* soon after Sorge's arrest. But she was not brought before the procurator. Sorge convinced Yoshikawa that the girl knew nothing of his secret work. 'She will marry a school-teacher in the end,' said Sorge. 'Please don't do anything to her.'

But in August 1943 she was again taken into custody—this time by the *Kempei*. They interrogated her with insulting severity, abusing her as a spy and an enemy of her own country. After five days of this she was allowed to leave, and she was not molested again.

After the war Hanako decided to recover Sorge's remains, for she had read the following item of news in a magazine: 'Sorge's body was buried in Zoshigaya Cemetery by the Sugamo authorities. For there was nobody to take charge of it. A humble wooden grave-post was erected, but someone has taken it away—to meet the fuel shortage perhaps. And now there is no trace of the grave.'

She got in touch with Asanuma Sumiji, the lawyer who defended Sorge, and she enlisted the help of Ozaki's younger half-brother, Hotsuki. For two years she pestered the prison authorities and those

---

* Quoted in *Review*, a Yugoslav monthly magazine published in Belgrade, October 1964.

The Yugoslav press, following the example of their Russian and East German colleagues, have also paid their tribute to their own national implicated in the Sorge case.

in charge of the dismal cemetery at Zoshigaya. And at last she was successful.

The coffin was discovered in a part of the cemetery reserved for homeless vagrants. Decomposition was far advanced, and only a skeleton remained.

Hanako-san was satisfied that her quest had ended. The large skull and the bones were those of a foreigner; and there were clear marks of damage to the bones of one leg — the lasting result of Sorge's war wounds. Hanako recognized the teeth from their gold fillings.

She has described her feelings on that day, in November 1949, five years after Sorge's execution.

I grasped two very long and robust bones in my hands and examined them intently. One bone was split vertically in the centre and had set unevenly. The part where the join occurred was larger and stronger than the rest. This bone was over a centimetre shorter than the other.

'Was he injured?' the young man beside me asked in a quiet tone.

'Yes, I have heard so. I think this is a wound from the first world war.'

In a comment on this scene, Ozaki's half-brother — almost certainly the young man by Hanako's side at Zoshigaya — has written: 'Sorge, who was raised in a season of war and died in a season of war, carried on his bones, even in his final resting place, the marks of the battle-field.' Hanako-san had a ring made from the gold fillings in the teeth. She has worn this ever since.

She had the coffin removed to the quiet Tama Graveyard, just outside the city. There it was reinterred beside the remains of Ozaki Hotsumi and Miyagi Yutoku.*

---

* In the early summer of 1965 Hanako-san was invited to visit the Soviet Union. According to the Japanese press, Russian papers described her as Sorge's 'closest friend, who shared the courageous agent's woes and joys'. At the Black Sea resort of Sochi, she saw a performance of *Press Attaché in Tokyo*, a Russian play dealing with Sorge's career in Japan (*Mainichi Daily News*, Tokyo, June 12, 1965).

LEGEND AND REALITY

'Eternally a stranger, fleeing from himself.'
FROM A POEM BY RICHARD SORGE. Kiel 1918

SOME time after his arrest, Sorge requested his police interrogator to approach the Soviet Embassy in the hope that they would negotiate his exchange through diplomatic channels. He was in an exalted and sleepless state during these first days in the nightmarish unreality of his cell. His abrupt and unexpected arrest was a supreme irony following within a few days of the fulfilment of his Japanese mission— his message that Japan would strike southward and that there would be no war with the Soviet Union. He had changed the course of history. Moscow could now look forward to months of tranquil negotiation with Tokyo. With his unique knowledge of the Japanese political scene, and after such an achievement in his intelligence assignment, surely his superiors in Moscow would take every step to secure his immediate release or exchange. Sorge also knew that his old friend from Russian days, Solomon Lozovsky, was Vice-Commissar for Foreign Affairs in the Soviet Government. He had appreciated Sorge's qualities, and it might well be that Sorge could still play a key political role in future Russian-Japanese negotiations.

The mood of euphoria passed in the following days. The Japanese had told Sorge that they would not contact the Soviet Embassy, but during the long months of detention in Sugamo Sorge returned again and again to this mirage of an exchange, explaining to his interrogators that the time would come when they too would need his services as a negotiator with the Russians, and when the 'inevitable defeat of Japan' would draw near.

Sorge consistently and haughtily denied that he was a common spy. As he stated in his final words to the preliminary judge, 'Normal espionage means searching for the weak points in a nation's structure. My aim, however, was to preserve peace between Japan and the Soviet Union. Therefore I do not consider that my activities were contrary to the national interests of Japan.'

His confidence in his Soviet superiors survived. On occasions, he reverted to the case of Noulens, whom he had known as the head of the Comintern apparat in Shanghai, and who had been successfully exchanged in June 1932, only a year after his arrest, after a world-wide campaign of protest organized from Moscow.* This precedent seemed directly relevant to his own case, and he clung to it tenaciously.

The arrest of Sorge was an embarrassment to the Japanese authorities in their relations not only with Nazi Germany but also with the Soviet Union. It was for this reason that at almost every stage of the case Sorge was treated purely as a Comintern agent, without reference either to his membership of the Nazi party and his standing with the German Embassy, or to his links with Soviet Military Intelligence.

During the intricate Japanese-Soviet negotiations to maintain Soviet neutrality in the Pacific War, which coincided in time with the detention of Sorge and his associates, it is probable that at some stage the Japanese prepared the exchange of Sorge for agents of the Kwantung Army caught in Siberia. The existence of such a move has been seriously hinted at on several occasions, particularly in German Embassy circles in Tokyo and even by Ambassador Stahmer himself. If such a negotiation took place it would have been handled by the Japanese Embassy in Moscow. But no firm evidence has as yet come to light.

A persistent legend nourished by feverish rumours and gossip in Tokyo towards the end of the war, however, has grown up that such an exchange took place. According to this version certain staff officers in the Kwantung Army felt that the execution of Sorge, whose importance as a Comintern agent had been magnified by himself in the hopes of his ultimate release, might endanger Soviet-Japanese relations; and it is claimed that on November 7, 1944, Sorge was taken by General Doihara to Macao where he was exchanged by secret agreement with Soviet representatives for a group of Japanese agents of the Kwantung Army.† Several Europeans later claimed that they saw Sorge alive in this Portuguese colony at the time.

The discovery and identification of Sorge's body by Hanako-san, disposes of this absurd invention.

The stark fact of the executions and their timing, has also given

---

* See p. 94 above.

† The legend features in particular in Hans Otto Meissner's book *The Man with Three Faces*, which in its version as a novel has appeared in Soviet translation under the title of *The Sorge Case*.

rise to further conjecture. It has been suggested that they were carried out in retaliation for the breakdown of the Japanese-Soviet negotiations in Moscow. It is, however, more probable that Sorge and Ozaki were sent to their deaths for other reasons. It was necessary to destroy rumours circulating in Tokyo of imminent peace moves, in which Sorge might have featured as an intermediary with Moscow, and to discourage any support for Ozaki's plans for social reform in Japan. The date of the executions was therefore fixed with grim and symbolic meaning on the anniversary of the Russian Revolution of 1917.

THE GERMANS AND SORGE

The enquiry of the German security services into the identity and past activities of Sorge revealed his long and successful evasion of official scrutiny and suspicion. His close personal relationship with senior German diplomats and officials in the Far East had directly led to his appointment as Japan correspondent of the *Frankfurter Zeitung*, his admission to the Nazi party and Association of Journalists. At no time had there been any check into his police record, and his perfunctory entry in the party file bears no mark or comment.

The German investigation of the case terminated with a personal letter from Himmler to Ribbentrop on October 27, 1942, in a tone of smug and wounding superiority. After outlining the results of the police enquiries 'which were now made for the first time, but which, had they been requested and carried out earlier, would have produced the same results', Himmler wrote: 'Since Sorge constantly obtained his information about Axis policy and its future plans from the best German sources, the Sorge spy case represents great political dangers.'

The German report thus accepted the general thesis that the German Ambassador in Tokyo, General Ott, and senior members of his staff had shown negligence in their dealings with Sorge.

On November 23, 1942, Ribbentrop telegraphed to Ott, having considered Himmler's letter, that

various indications point to the fact that the Sorge affair has left the Japanese authorities with an impression which reflects unfavourably on your personal position in regard to those authorities. After considerable thought, the Fuehrer has therefore decided to act on my suggestion, and to make a change at the head of your Embassy, and to summon you for other employment in the Foreign Office.

But owing to the difficulties of arranging a safe conduct to Germany, Ott was told to remain in the Far East as a private individual for the time being. He made an urgent request to be allowed to return by blockade-runner to Europe and join the army. Hitler refused, and Ott and his family moved to Peking and were ultimately detained by the American authorities in China at the end of the war.

The unmasking of Sorge had ruined the career of Ott on evidence almost exclusively produced by Sorge himself in his 'confession' under interrogation, and in certain intercepted messages sent to Moscow. Sorge went into impressive detail in describing his penetration of the German Embassy, and his close relations with its members, and these 'admissions' produce a prima facie case involving Ott's discretion and judgment on security matters.

The German Foreign Office enquiry perfunctorily covered the questioning of former members of the Tokyo Embassy during the period under review. The exposure of the Sorge case had been received in the Foreign Office in Berlin in an atmosphere of hushed concern. Those diplomats who had been in China or Japan sensed the danger of being personally compromised, and there was a natural tendency for these officials and their colleagues investigating the affair to play it down. Lissner's accusations against Ott in April 1942, however, provoked a special official enquiry among past members of the German diplomatic service in Japan. Certain of them denied any recollection of Sorge; others ventured an interpretation of his relations with the German Ambassador. One of them describes Sorge

as a gifted person, sociable and with good Japanese connections, who had suffered somewhat from being thrown from a motor-cycle. He kept up lively relations with the staff of the Embassy, and received many invitations. . . . Ott, even before he was Ambassador, took an interest in Sorge and saw a good deal of him socially, as is customary between a member of the Embassy staff and a useful and well-informed German journalist.

This witness thought, however, that Ott 'cultivated Sorge exclusively for the purpose of making use of his reports and knowledge. . . . It is quite out of the question that any material deemed confidential or secret should have reached Sorge through Ambassador Ott.'

Another witness stated that 'Sorge was repeatedly asked by the Embassy to prepare political reports, largely on internal matters', and that the assitant military attaché, Major Scholl, entered into an intimate exchange of ideas with Sorge.

Ott himself has never made any public statement on his relations with Sorge. He firmly denied being responsible for any leakage of secret material to Sorge or of any verbal indiscretions, and this is, with certain exceptions, the general view of his diplomatic subordinates and colleagues at the time.

The successive military, naval and air attachés have not openly recorded their comments on Sorge's allegations. Sorge's accounts of his own relations with the Embassy, and his activities there, are extant in circumstantial detail; and he estimated that material and information obtained from this source represented sixty per cent of his total achievement as a Soviet intelligence agent. It was, however, essential to the creation of his own personal legend, in confronting his Japanese interrogators, that he should exploit to the limit—and even beyond— his standing with Ott and the Tokyo Embassy.

The written evidence, in particular his intercepted telegrams to Moscow, shows that he had many private conversations with Ott on current issues affecting German-Japanese relations, in particular on the progress of the European war, and as a fellow German and responsible journalist Sorge exchanged with him ideas and general information on Japanese politics, on the China Incident, and allied subjects. With the outbreak of war in 1939 a closer and more intimate series of consultations, as might seem natural among compatriots in a foreign land, seems to have taken place on military subjects such as the strength of the Japanese armed forces, and speculation on Japan's strategic aims. In this hothouse climate of war-time, Sorge's professional skill as a journalist may well have enabled him to elicit details of interest to him as a spy which would in other circumstances have been concealed from him.

The most significant leakages which occurred are linked with the assistant military attaché, Major Scholl. There is no doubt that Sorge obtained from him the report of the interrogation of the Soviet defector Lyushkov, and vital prior information regarding German plans to attack the Soviet Union in the spring of 1941. It is also clear that Sorge had access to, and filmed, documents of varying confidential and secret rating on the Japanese economy and war industries, originating from various sections of the Embassy. Certain of these papers were found in his house on his arrest and were a special feature in the indictment against him. This material was used by Sorge in a typically ingenious manner—to compile reports, amplified with carefully selected material from his own Japanese sources, for the German Embassy, overtly as a patriotic duty; to send details hitherto unknown to him to the 'Moscow Centre', and to form the basis of articles sent by him to the *Frankfurter Zeitung* and to the *Zeitschrift für Geopolitik*.

Sorge undoubtedly had become a personal friend and, within limits, which on the evidence it would be invidious to define, the confidant of Ott, and he abused this special relationship to the best of his considerable abilities in the interests of his secret work as a Soviet agent.

Equally, there is no doubt that Sorge's reputation and high standing with Ott, and with the German Embassy officials, was derived not only from his talents as an experienced foreign correspondent with a remarkable understanding of Japanese affairs and wide contacts in Tokyo, but also because of his special sources of information from high political circles in the entourage of Prince Konoye, of which Ott was aware, and from other links—unidentified by the Embassy—with Japanese military quarters. Sorge played back to Ott carefully censored items of intelligence, gathered in the course of his espionage activities through Ozaki and Miyagi, and thereby increased the chances of provoking disclosures of confidential material from the German side.

The question inevitably arises as to whether Sorge was at any time working for the Germans as well as the Russians. The head of the German security service, Walter Schellenberg, in his posthumous memoirs, categorically insists that Sorge sent intelligence reports to Berlin, and that in 1940 the German security authorities protected him from 'difficult' and inquisitive investigation by the Nazi Party because of the value of this intelligence material, which ostensibly came through the channel of the official German News Agency, whose head Wilhelm von Ritgen was passing Sorge's information to Schellenberg.

Thus another Sorge legend emerges—that of the double agent. The credibility of this plausible theory, like other facets of Sorge's activities, cannot, in light of existing evidence, be established or disproved. It is, however, evident that any foreign correspondents in war-time are liable to be connected in varying degrees of informal commitment with the intelligence services of their own country. It is also true that Sorge did replace on occasion the local head of the German News Agency in Tokyo, when the latter, Dr. Rudolf Weise, was on leave, and in this capacity he would be reporting to Ritgen in Berlin. There is also evidence to show that Weise himself had connections with the German Intelligence Services.

If, however, Sorge were directly employed in this way, it seems likely that it would have emerged in some form during the enquiry initiated by the security services into Sorge's past after his arrest, as happened in the case of Lissner—unless it was considered more advisable to liquidate an expended agent without comment. But the real assumptions behind Schellenberg's statements are merely that Sorge was suspected of working for the Russians, that he was sending valuable information on Japanese intentions and British and American policy in the Far East, that he must therefore be preserved and protected as a source, reporting through normal channels, and under surveillance. For this latter purpose Colonel Meisinger, as the police attaché in Tokyo was, according to Schellenberg, instructed to carry out such an assignment. Meisinger reported favourably on Sorge, but for some reason clumsily indicated to the Japanese police that he had orders to watch his compatriot. This blunder came to the knowledge of Schellenberg, to his shocked surprise, from a visiting Japanese police mission to Berlin in the spring of 1941.

Sorge's intelligence material grew more and more important to us, for in 1941 we were very keen to know more about Japan's plans concerning the United States. . . . And after the beginning of our campaign in Russia, he warned us that in no circumstances would Japan denounce her non-aggression pact with the Soviet Union.

Schellenberg's thesis, however, does not directly imply that Sorge was a professional agent of the German Intelligence Service, but at most an indispensable source of highly valuable information. One explanation may well be that Sorge, who carefully stressed the importance of his self-appointed 'political' mission in striving to influence, through the German Embassy in Tokyo, German policy-making in Berlin in certain directions beneficial to the Soviet Union, was in fact sending such reports designed to have precisely this effect. If he could persuade the Germans in this manner that Japan would not attack the Soviet Union, then his real mission was indeed doubly fulfilled. It is probable, therefore, that such reports were transmitted by Sorge to Berlin, on his own initiative, and with this intention. There is no conclusive evidence, apart from Schellenberg's account, that throws any further light on the theory that Sorge was technically a double agent. The nature of his press work in the Embassy, or even his occasional services as an official courier, do not in themselves lend weight to this line of enquiry.

There is, however, one fact later elicited from Meisinger which provokes a tantalizing and final speculation. Among the papers of Franz Huber, Meisinger's predecessor as police attaché in Tokyo, Meisinger found a receipt signed by Sorge for certain funds paid to him. This could be explained on the grounds that, on some occasion, it might have been convenient and profitable to Sorge to render a particular service of an intelligence nature to Huber, but this single small clue is perhaps just sufficient to lend a flicker of life to the double agent legend, which is among the others which have grown around Sorge. That the possibility of such a theory also occurred to the Japanese is indirectly confirmed by the procurator, Yoshikawa, who interrogated Sorge.

We were wondering whether Sorge was really a spy for Germany, and using the Communists in Japan, but actually spying for the Nazi régime. That was one question. The second question was whether Sorge was a double agent for both Berlin and Moscow. The third question was whether he was really a spy for Moscow, pretending to be a Nazi. Therefore, we examined Sorge without preconceived opinion. We took a very cautious attitude.

This 'cautious attitude' of Yoshikawa must also be that of the historian.

THE AMERICANS AND SORGE

In October 1945 the American occupation authorities in Japan rescinded the Peace Preservation Law, under which political prisoners had been detained in war-time, and some five hundred men and women held in various prisons throughout the country were promptly released. They included eight persons connected with the Sorge case.

Military Intelligence (G.2) branch of the American administration, under the direction of Major-General Charles A. Willoughby, had only been set up in the previous month, and amid the urgent and stupendous task of dismantling the Japanese war machine of over five million men in the home country and overseas, and establishing an occupation authority. Any investigation of the background of the small group of political prisoners who had just been liberated was inevitably a low priority. As far as the Sorge case was concerned, apart from brief and unrewarding reports from various press agencies during the war, no prior information was available on the significance and ramifications of the affair.

According to General Willoughby, the first clue came from 'an excited Japanese official who advised me that the release list of political prisoners, contained foreign espionage agents, the remnants of the Sorge espionage ring—in particular, one Max Klausen'.

Klausen, who had been taken to an American army hospital on his release from prison and by military plane to Tokyo after medical treatment, was living quietly in the Japanese capital until the spring of 1946. But as soon as he noticed that he was under surveillance by the Americans, he abruptly vanished, with the connivance of the Soviet Embassy, to the Soviet Union.*

No further action was taken except to assemble, on the working level, various materials relating to the Sorge Case, which were acquired from the Japanese court records and the police files. The basic source emerged as the Japanese Police Year Book (1942), and the 'Sorge Material Parts 1 and 2' which had been published by the Japanese Ministry of Justice as a top secret document with restricted circulation in April of that year. These contained the basic 'confession' of Sorge himself. On the personal instructions of General Willoughby, an initial report was compiled from this evidence by Lt.-Colonel T. P. Davis of the CIS (Civil Intelligence Service) and forwarded to Washington early in 1946. This document had a professional and historical interest as an example of intelligence technique.

The explosion of the Canadian Espionage Case in February 1946, in which Igor Guzenko revealed the first detailed account of a Soviet espionage network operating in time of peace in a friendly country and war-time ally, produced a profound psychological shock on Western public opinion. In the United States a similar and more marked impression was produced by the Hiss affair. Were these cases isolated, if regrettable, examples of the clandestine operations of the Soviet intelligence services, or did these services operate a wider network of penetration throughout the Western world? General Willoughby was not slow to appreciate the actual significance of the Sorge Case in this broad context. His first step was to instruct Dr. H. T. Noble, another member of the Civil Intelligence Service and a trained historian, to redraft the Davis Report, and this revised version was sent to Washington in December 1947 with a recommendation that it should

* See p. 324.

be used in military training schools 'as instructional material in view of the apprehensions aroused by the Canadian espionage case'.

General Willoughby was opposed, at this early stage, to releasing any of this material to the press, on the grounds that it contained sensitive intelligence relating to the workings of an espionage ring. Certain enterprising American journalists in Tokyo were, however, already on the trail of the Sorge affair, which had in any case been the subject of attention in the Japanese press,* and the secret became increasingly difficult to preserve.

On June 25, 1948, the War Department in Washington cabled Willoughby that the State Department wished to release the Sorge material at the request of the American Ambassador in Moscow, General Bedell Smith, as a counter-measure against continued Soviet charges of espionage by members of the American embassy in Russia.

A see-saw battle between G.2 Tokyo and the War Department continued until the end of the year. During these months General Willoughby's staff began actively to substantiate and supplement the original evidence contained in the Japanese records by interrogating the survivors—in particular Kawai—and the prosecutors and police officials connected with the case. Willoughby himself had realized, and come to accept and welcome, the inevitability of publication. After certain, probably inspired, leakages to the press, the Sorge material, as summarized in the section of the CIS Periodical Summary No. 23 of December 16, 1947 (the final version of the Davis-Noble Report), was cleared by the War Department and released to the press in Tokyo on February 10, 1949.

The first version of the Sorge Case became public knowledge as the result of a deliberate decision on the part of the American Intelligence authorities in Tokyo, with the express clearance of the Secretary of the Army, to stir American public opinion to a realization of the extent of a world Communist conspiracy directed by the intelligence services of the Soviet Union against the Western democracies, in particular the United States, and of its continuous existence since the creation of the Soviet State. All other aspects of the Sorge affair were obliterated in the ensuing political storm whipped up in the United States by this Tokyo press release.

The publication of the Sorge report was essentially an episode in the campaign in the United States, organized by certain groups to discredit all those elements in American public life, in government

* See p. 343 below.

service, in the armed forces, in the liberal professions, in journalism and academic institutions, who had championed the alliance with the Soviet Union in war-time, and subsequently co-operation with the Communist bloc in peace. This agitation, fed in public opinion by a mounting disillusionment at Soviet tactics in the international field, lay at the heart of the cold war in foreign affairs, and the successive attacks on the home front on the loyalties of certain leading citizens of the American left.

Evidence contained in the Sorge material became valuable ammunition in the fray. There were new clues revealing the subversive activities of the American Communist Party, especially among the Japanese migrants in California where Miyagi had been recruited. Former and present members of the party, such as Earl Browder with his international Communist activities in Shanghai, and foreign Communists like Gerhart Eisler received unwelcome publicity. 'Eighteen names of American Communist agitators, agents and suspects were reported as connected with the Sorge case.' Public organizations such as the Institute of Pacific Relations were shown to have invited to their meetings Sorge's main associate Ozaki and the latter's friend and chief source of information, if an unconscious one, Saionji.

Behind a façade of well-meaning liberalism in certain circles in the States seemed to lie an army of fellow travellers, and within its ranks a hard core of secret agents under Soviet orders.

Two figures in particular were singled out, as a direct result of the disclosures regarding the Sorge ring. They were the journalists, the American Agnes Smedley and the naturalized Englishman Gunther Stein.

The initial evidence in the Sorge Case showed that at least Agnes Smedley had been of direct assistance to the ring in Shanghai, owing to her close connection with the Chinese Communists, and that there was a suspicion that she had some links with the Russian intelligence service. Gunther Stein, who had also connections with the Institute of Pacific Relations, featured in Sorge's notebook in which were listed members and helpers of the ring in Japan, and appeared as acting as a courier for the group between Tokyo and Shanghai. On the day of the publication of the Sorge report, Stein was in New York. Shortly afterwards he surfaced in Paris. Agnes Smedley's reactions to the disclosures were violent and prompt. She declared that she would call on General MacArthur himself to waive his official immunity and that she would consider action for libel.

This action is of considerable importance in the story of the Sorge Case, as it forced Willoughby to pursue his researches into the affair in order to meet such eventual charges, even if to the detriment of a sober historical analysis of the case. To him the real nature of Sorge's activities as a Soviet agent, and the significance of his work in Japan, were secondary to the theory of a world Communist conspiracy linking both espionage rings, and world-wide front organizations organized from Moscow, with the main centre outside Moscow in Shanghai.

The proof, if any, of Smedley's connections with Communist espionage lay in this Chinese city, and it was this threat of legal action against him that pressed Willoughby to concentrate the resources of his organization here. As he wrote:

An epic search began, to get access to the Shanghai Municipal Police Records. I exploited my friendship with the Chinese Ambassador in Tokyo. . . . I interviewed former Shanghai police officials. . . . We tracked down invoices and shipments from Chinese warehouses. . . . Finally a series of dossiers, not all complete, were assembled and shipped to Tokyo.

In addition, the procurators, police officers, and other witnesses were interrogated by Willoughby's officers with specific reference to links between the Sorge ring and Smedley and Stein.

It appeared that the Japanese authorities would have arrested both of them, if they had been in Japan at the time. The police had even considered picking up Stein in Hong Kong. Yoshikawa was later obliged to give evidence on the whole case before the Un-American Activities Committee which marked the culmination of the campaign against 'the fellow travellers' in the United States in 1951. He stated that he realized that both Smedley and Stein were key figures in the ring and would have been detained if available.

But the intention to arrest was hardly evidence of guilt, and this laborious enquiry by G.2 Tokyo led to no positive result although it revealed grounds for suspicion. In the event, Agnes Smedley did not press her action for alleged libel. On being summoned to appear before the Un-American Activities Committee, she left peacefully for Europe and died suddenly in the Radcliffe Infirmary in Oxford in 1950.*

Gunther Stein remained out of sight, also in Europe, until his death.

---

* Not in a London nursing home, as stated by Willoughby.

Whatever Agnes Smedley's covert status was with the relevant Soviet agencies, her services to the Sorge mission in China were of central importance. The very functioning of the group largely depended on her constant co-operation. It was in her flat in the International Settlement in Shanghai that Sorge would most frequently meet his close associates; it was Agnes Smedley who maintained direct contact with the Zeitgeist Bookshop, and its manager Mrs. Wiedemeyer, where documentary material was at times received and meetings arranged with informants. Whatever links, if any, existed between the ring and the Chinese Communists passed through this passionate dedicated woman. It was she who introduced the first Chinese associates to Sorge and, most vital of all, she produced Ozaki Hotsumi.

She may have been recruited by the Russians as an agent during her stay in the Soviet Union. The Shanghai Police reported, shortly after her arrival in the city in May 1929 on an American passport in the name of Mrs. Petroikos, that she was in the direct service of the Far Eastern Bureau of the Comintern and under the orders of its Executive Committee. She was kept under surveillance, but no connection was ever established between her and Sorge. Her real status is not clarified by Sorge's own statements, although her name is mentioned twelve times in two interrogations alone. He denied that she had been sent by Moscow to join him in China. He did not admit whether or not he had met her previously, but stated that he had an introduction to her from the *Frankfurter Zeitung*.

In his 'confession' he stated that 'she was used by me as a direct member of my group. She worked for me very competently. She stayed in Shanghai after I returned to Moscow.' In fact she was in Russia within a few months of Sorge's own arrival.

On another occasion Sorge stated: 'I enlisted her as a member, and made her a member of the Comintern Headquarters staff [*sic*].' If she were registered, there is no trace of a code name being allotted to her. When questioned, he did not know whether or not Agnes Smedley was a member of the American Communist Party.

Her energetic and direct participation in setting up an intelligence group in northern China in 1932–3, which seems to have been more connected with the Chinese Communists than the Russians, suggests that she had some independent or even self-appointed role, and that her co-operation with Sorge was a separate compartment of her life.

The role of Gunther Stein in the Sorge affair is equally baffling, and again the only evidence of any link comes from statements by Sorge and the other members of the ring.

Stein, like Smedley, was a well-known and established journalist of progressive views. Sorge first met him, as a fellow European news-paperman working in Japan, at a Foreign Ministry Press Conference in the spring of 1935. Stein was of a certain interest as an open source of information from the American and, especially, British Embassies, where he was regarded as a well-informed economic journalist of left-wing but not Communist views. Sorge reported to Moscow several items of news derived from these contacts of Stein, who was allotted a code name ('Gustav') in these communications.

According to Sorge, he hinted to his colleague the true nature of his activities, and Stein agreed to contact Ozaki on an occasion when Sorge was ill. Stein's house in Tokyo was later used as a meeting place for Sorge and Klausen. The latter, according to his later statements, used Stein's house intermittently as a base for radio transmitting for nearly two years. This was a helpful and additional precaution against detection by the direction-finding units of the Japanese authorities. Klausen also stated that Stein confessed to him that he was a Com-munist sympathizer since his work in Moscow as a correspondent of the *Berliner Tageblatt* prior to 1933.

Stein left Japan in 1938 for Hong Kong where he started an English-language news sheet, financed by the Chinese Nationalist authorities, and seems to have had some meetings with Sorge during his visits to the British Colony. Klausen, on the other hand, ventured the theory that it was after Stein had left Japan that 'he became a member of the ring'.

Sorge, as in all his statements relating to associates who might be in danger of eventual detention by the Japanese authorities, was guarded and confused in his references to Stein. He admitted that Stein was aware of the activities of the ring, that he had acted as a contact with Miyagi and Ozaki, and had carried microfilms as a courier to Hong Kong; and that he had allowed his house to be used by Klausen for radio transmitting. The Japanese police alleged that Stein's name featured as a member of the ring in the notebook found in Sorge's house, but that this evidence was subsequently burned.

Sorge told the police that Stein was 'more than a sympathizer', and in the amended notes to his 'confession' he described Stein as 'having taken a lively part in the work of my group . . . as a sympathetic member'. He added that he asked Moscow to recognize him as a member of the ring but received a 'negative answer'. The assumption, from this statement, would be that Stein was already engaged in similar but strictly separate activities—and this would be confirmed by the suggestion that Sorge was ordered to discontinue any association with Stein when the latter left for Hong Kong in 1938.

The case of Gunther Stein, however, like that of Agnes Smedley, remains unproven for lack of decisive evidence.

The motives of General Willoughby in releasing the original Sorge material, and pursuing his researches into international Communist activities in Shanghai in an effort to prove the subversive activities of leading American fellow travellers and Communists, have led to a distortion of the historical significance of the Sorge Case. The affair was thus highlighted as one episode in a conspiracy, whose ramifications were intertwined with the operation of Soviet agents and stooges within the United States. But the publication by Willoughby of the *Report on the Sorge Case* had equally startling repercussions in Japan.

THE JAPANESE AND SORGE

The political and ideological implications of the Sorge affair in Japanese terms became apparent with the liberation by the Americans of the surviving members of the group, and the feverish public interest in the alleged 'treason' of Ozaki which followed a series of early disclosures in the Tokyo press. In October 1945, Ozaki's own paper, the *Asahi Shimbun*, had published an article on the case, followed by similar reports in other leading newspapers. The figure of Ozaki, the martyr, rapidly emerged as a resistance leader and symbol of the opposition in high circles to the catastrophic entry of Japan into the war, and as the main victim of Japanese 'fascism'. The publication in 1946 of his letters written in prison to his wife with the title *Love is Like a Falling Star* became the leading best-seller for the next two years, and opened an organized campaign by Ozaki's surviving friends to eliminate the official image of him as the traitor to the Fatherland, and to replace it with the picture of the man as the prophet of the new progressive and patriotic Japan which was turning its back on the militaristic imperialism of the past.

This group of Ozaki's supporters hoped to extend their activities to include the publication of the records of the Sorge Case. It was at first believed that all the evidence had been destroyed during American air-raids on Tokyo, and an early attempt was made to compile instead a biography of Ozaki. In 1948, however, 'a Society for the Disclosure of the Facts about the Ozaki-Sorge Case' was formed, and actively supported by the main Japanese survivor of the ring, Kawai Teikichi. The publication by General Willoughby in February 1949 of the *Report of the Sorge Case* electrified Japanese opinion, and transformed the whole issue. Just as the effect in the United States was to divert any study of the affair into immediate American cold-war controversies and into insinuations of acts of disloyalty and treason by alleged associates of the ring—in particular Smedley and Stein—so in Tokyo the immediate repercussions to the publication of the G.2 report centred on the exposure in that document of the alleged role of Ito Ritsu in the betrayal of Sorge, Ozaki and the others to the Japanese police. The immediate significance of the Sorge Case in Japan was at once to stimulate controversy and debate on the integrity of Ito, who was now a member of the Politburo of the central committee of the Japanese Communist Party, which was already licensed by the American occupation authorities as a legal political organization. Beside the resurrected figure of Ozaki 'the patriot' appeared the 'traitor' Ito. The release of this news caused not only a major upheaval in the leadership of the Japanese Communist Party, but also widespread repercussions on public opinion.

The first reaction in party circles was a statement that, on the basis of their own investigations, the Sorge Case was the invention of the militarist government of the day, and that Ito was in no way involved. This attitude bears a striking resemblance to the similar position adopted by the Soviet Embassy in Tokyo at the time of the announcement of the arrests of members of the ring.

Officials of the Ministry of Justice, procurators and police, were not unwillingly drawn into the fray. Their own interest in discrediting a leading figure in the nascent Japanese Communist Party needed no subtle explanation. Their 'revelations' to the press lent weight to the rumours now circulating widely of Ito's betrayal of the ring.

Ozaki's half-brother, Ozaki Hotsuki, aided by Kawai and a progressive body called the 'Free Lawyers Association' now took a leading part in pursuing the affair.* It seems that a delegation called at the

---

* This account is largely based on Ozaki Hotsuki, *Zoruge Jiken.*

Metropolitan Police Board, and demanded the handing over of the records of the Sorge Case. They left with two lorry loads of documents. In a moment of naïvety, one of the lawyers took this material to the headquarters of the Japanese Communist Party to seek advice on how to handle the matter. An official obligingly took charge of the material which disappeared without trace. There is no means of checking the veracity of this version.

The G.2 disclosures in February 1949 did not outwardly shake Ito's position in the Communist Party, and the first sharp reaction of its central committee was to secure by oblique pressure the dissolution of the 'Society for the Disclosure of the Facts about the Ozaki-Sorge Case'. It was one thing to exploit the myth of Ozaki 'the Patriot Communist', and another to question the integrity of a living member of the Politburo of the party.

The Japanese party leadership had, however, its own troubles and factions, which had no connection with 'the Sorge revelations', and Ito—after going underground at the time of the purge of certain leaders in June 1950—was formally expelled from the Politburo in October the following year, and from the party itself in September 1953. His present domicile is unknown but rumour has it that he is living in Peking.

Whether or not Ito betrayed Kitabayashi Tomo as the first step in the discovery of the Sorge ring has not been proved beyond doubt, and is likely to remain as a police mystery and a subject of recrimination in Japan.*

The main influence of the Sorge Case in Japan has been to create around the group a cult of Ozaki and his associates, Japanese and European, who had fought and sacrificed themselves for a revolutionary 'New Order in Asia' which would finally lead to the emancipation of the nations of the Far East.

In 1956 a 'Society for the relief of those sacrificed in the Ozaki Case' was founded in Tokyo to keep alive the memory of this group of martyrs in the cause of peace. It was this society which raised funds for Sorge's gravestone upon which the inscription reads: 'Here sleeps a brave warrior who devoted his life to opposing war, and to the struggle for the peace of the world.'

---

* For a careful and balanced discussion of this subject see Chalmers Johnson, *op. cit.*

THE SOVIET UNION AND THE SORGE CASE

The only public reaction in Moscow to the arrest of Sorge and his associates in October 1941 had been the radio announcement a few days later that a certain Branko Vukelic had been detained in Tokyo. The charges were not specified.

The Japanese authorities themselves, apart from a bald and reluctant notification to the German Embassy, maintained total silence on the affair; and there was no press release until the following May. Apart from vague and sinister rumours in diplomatic and newspaper circles, nothing was known of the development and implications of the Sorge Case, although it was common gossip, until the publication of this careful public statement issued by the Japanese Ministry of Justice. The police were nervously anxious to discover the reactions of the foreign colony in Tokyo to this belated admission of the arrests, and by direct interviews by detectives, interrogations of Japanese nationals in touch with foreigners, and discreet surveillance, they gained certain impressions.

Senior officials of the Soviet Embassy in Tokyo, in answer to such enquiries, were unanimous in denying any knowledge of the affair. As the First Secretary put it, after dining with a Japanese acquaintance at a draughts party on May 15 (two days before the release), 'We did not expect to hear any talk about the case, but Takamori [his host] spoke to me about the Sorge affair. Our comment was that, although it is said that the Comintern in Moscow is concerned, the fact is that the whole affair was planned by a Gestapo Fifth Column. So the authorities in Moscow know nothing about it.' And the Tass correspondent, Kisiliev, commented: 'The German Ambassador in Tokyo must know all about the Sorge affair, and if he has said nothing about it he must be anti-Hitler. This fact proves that there are two opposing forces within Hitler's government. The question now is to watch, with eager attention, what attitude the Japanese Government is going to adopt. Neither the Soviet Government nor the Soviet Embassy has had any connection with the case.'

Both the Soviet and the Japanese authorities had a mutual interest in endeavouring to conceal Sorge's links with Moscow, and to limit any damage to the lengthy negotiations in progress between the two governments aimed at maintaining a neutral *status quo* on the borders of Manchukuo and Siberia.

The presence in the Soviet Embassy of the local representative of 'the Moscow Centre', the Second Secretary and Consul, Zaitsev, who had been the link with the ring, was now delicate and embarrassing. Zaitsev was unobtrusively and speedily withdrawn from Tokyo.

During one sitting of the International Military Tribunal for the Far East in Tokyo after the war, Mr. Cunningham, the defence counsel of General Oshima, the former Japanese Ambassador in Berlin, attempted repeatedly to introduce the name of Richard Sorge into the case against his client. On each occasion he met with violent opposition from the Soviet prosecutor, General Vasiliev and was finally ruled out of court by the President of the Tribunal.*

Mr. Cunningham attempted to interrogate a prosecution witness, Colonel von Petersdorf, who had succeeded Colonel Scholl as Assistant German Military Attaché in Tokyo in December 1938, and remained in this post until January 1943. The American lawyer was intending to prove that Sorge had obtained much of his intelligence, which he transmitted to Moscow, from the German Embassy. In a sworn affidavit, Colonel Petersdorf—who had been captured by the Russians on the Eastern Front and interrogated in detail by the Soviet security authorities in Moscow on the Sorge Case—had stated that Sorge was a main source for the German Embassy on the order of battle of the Japanese Kwantung Army in Manchukuo and North China; and that through him the Germans learnt of matters not passed to them by the Japanese General Staff. It was therefore through Sorge in particular that such vital military information on Japan reached Berlin rather than from Japanese sources, such as Cunningham's client, General Oshima.

The following extracts from the dialogue in court present an illuminating picture.

Mr. Cunningham (in cross-examination): In your search for information you suggest that, in addition to the Japanese General Staff, you received information about the strength of the Kwantung Army in different periods from the German correspondent Richard Sorge. Is that right?

General Vasiliev: Mr. Cunningham knows well that this part of the

---

* Chief Justice Webb of Australia.

affidavit [by Colonel Petersdorf] has been stricken out, and therefore I object to the question . . .

The President then ruled that the parts of this document, struck out on Soviet insistence, was not in evidence.

Mr. Cunningham (referring to a previous statement by Colonel Petersdorf): Now, concerning the German correspondent Richard Sorge, from whom you received 'exact data as to the number of Kwantung Army divisions and some of their numbers': What position did he hold in the German Embassy at any time?

General Vasiliev (again objected to the question): We submit that the data which the witness has, concerning the strength of the Kwantung Army is so incomplete and unreliable that we decided to strike out this part of the affidavit, because this data, which he had, would bring no help to the Tribunal.

The motives of the Soviet prosecutor were not obscure. This information passed by Sorge to the German Embassy was the direct fruit of espionage collected by Ozaki and Miyagi, given to the German Embassy with the consent of the 'Moscow Centre', who also received the same reports. Further questioning of Petersdorf might well reveal the whole story of the ring.

The tone of this verbal duel between Cunningham and Vasiliev heightened.

Mr. Cunningham: I would like to show, if I can have the opportunity, that Richard Sorge, through whom this witness was getting his information and through whom Ambassador Ott was getting all his information, to whom Ambassador Ott was showing his telegrams from Germany and from whom Ambassador Ott was getting advice, was the most notorious spy – one of them – in Russian history.

The President submitted that such a line of questioning was a waste of time, as it was unlikely that the witness would be shaken into any such admission.

Cunningham now attempted a rapid change of attack, asking Petersdorf if he had known Crome 'the newspaperman and associate of Sorge'.* This question was allowed, but nothing emerged from Petersdorf.

Cunningham then made another move to inveigle Petersdorf into throwing light on Sorge's sources of information, which would have led to the heart of the matter. The question was again disallowed.

* See p. 309 above.

The dialogue ended in a final frustrating clash between the American and Soviet lawyers.

Mr. Cunningham (to the witness): When did you discover that Richard Sorge, from whom you had been receiving exact data, was a Russian spy?

Petersdorf was heard to mutter something unintelligible in English, and was told by the President of the Tribunal not to say any more.

General Vasiliev categorically objected to the question: 'In its form it is an attempt to attack the country which is represented in this Tribunal. . . . The Tribunal has not as yet established the fact whether Sorge was a Russian spy, or some other sort of spy, and therefore Defence Counsel Cunningham has no right to state that.' The President wavered on the issue of alleged insult, but doubted whether the defence counsel was in a position to prove his statement. Cunningham hastily interjected that no gratuitous offence was intended but that 'the fate of three nations rested, to a great extent, upon the information which Richard Sorge was sending out of the German Embassy'.

In a last effort to hang on to the implications arising out of the activities of the Sorge ring, Cunningham provoked deliberately the final ruling of the Court. He presented for further cross-examination questions as to the association of Petersdorf with Ozaki, Vukelic and Miyagi. The Court was adjourned to enable the Tribunal to give a majority decision.

The result was inevitable. Petersdorf's affidavit was only evidence in so far as it showed co-operation between Japan and Germany and 'any cross-examination of collateral matters' was disallowed. The discussion was closed.

General Vasiliev had succeeded in suppressing any questions or evidence relating to the Sorge case during the proceedings of the International Military Tribunal for the Far East. Even the suggestion that one of the three members of the victorious Great Alliance against the Axis should have organized a spy ring in an enemy country in time of war, and one of decisive influence, was regarded in 1947 as an insult. Nearly twenty years later, however, the Soviet authorities were to make public their own triumphant version—this 'collateral matter'—of the case of Richard Sorge.

On November 7, 1944, the anniversary of the Russian Revolution of

1917, was celebrated in the Soviet Union with marked jubilation. The Russian armies had expelled the Nazi invaders from the Western Soviet republics and were driving into Germany. A special tribute was paid in the newspapers to the contribution of the Intelligence Services to this decisive military victory. On that morning, the names of certain secret agents were revealed to the Russian public on the occasion of their receiving the decoration of Hero of the Soviet Union. At the same moment, in the Sugamo Prison in Tokyo, Richard Sorge walked to his execution, in lonely isolation, unrecognized by his Moscow superiors, but with his mission fulfilled.

On November 5, 1964, in anticipation of the same celebrations of the anniversary of the 1917 Revolution, and also of his execution, Richard Sorge was awarded the supreme decoration of Hero of the Soviet Union—posthumously. The occasion was marked by a series of tributes in the Soviet press by leading journalists to his contribution to victory in the Second World War, which both reveal certain hitherto unknown historical details of his career, and refrain from mentioning others. A street in Moscow was named after Sorge, and more recently a tanker. In the spring of 1965, the Soviet authorities issued a postage stamp, to the value of 4 kopecks, in his honour. The commemorative stamp shows Sorge full face on a scarlet background, together with a reproduction of the medal of Hero of the Soviet Union.

What is the true significance of the timing of this abrupt and tardy rehabilitation of one of the outstanding Soviet secret agents of the war? As the *Pravda* correspondent has written with marked caution, even after Stalin, 'In subsequent years a number of considerations did not make it possible to inform the people of this heroic intelligence officer. Only after twenty years were there favourable conditions for telling the truth about Sorge.'*

The immediate background to these 'revelations' is the recent detailed discussion in the Soviet Union of the events immediately following the German attack on Russia in June 1941, and the criticism directed at Stalin for his failure to anticipate this disaster and for the faults displayed in his direction of the war.

In the centre of the controversy lies the failure of Stalin to heed warnings from several quarters of the impending Nazi assault. This

---

* For a detailed provisional list of the articles which have appeared in the Soviet, East German and Yugoslav press on Sorge and his associates, see the Bibliography, p. 356 below.

eccentricity highlights Sorge's cardinal achievement, and has been the starting point of a belated act of justice. Sorge's reports from Tokyo on German intentions were apparently filed under the heading 'Doubtful and misleading information'.

But this neglect by Stalin of reliable intelligence from one secret source was only an element in his general rejection, and lack of appreciation, of the strategic planning of the Soviet High Command and the ancillary contributions of the military intelligence activities of the Fourth Bureau. Behind the lonely figure of Sorge now emerge the ghosts of his superiors, General Berzin and Colonel 'Alex' Borovich, both shot in the purges and rehabilitated in 1964. They were accorded posthumous recognition for their war-time services.

In sketching the public image of Sorge, an unprecedented recognition is also made of his profession. 'A spy is above all a man of politics, who must be able to grasp, analyse and connect in his mind events which seemingly have no connection. He must have the breadth of thought of a strategist, and meticulous powers of observation. Espionage is a continuous and demanding labour which never ceases.' And again, 'Least of all was Sorge like those secret agents whom certain Western authors have created. He did not force open safes in order to steal documents; the documents were shown to him by their very owners. He did not fire his pistol to penetrate the places which he had to penetrate: the doors were graciously opened to him by the guardians of the secret.'

The Soviet agent, in contrast to his Western counterpart, is alleged to be a master mind of outstanding intellectual quality and erudition. The concept of the sneaking shadowy spy has no place in the gallery. Sorge was a legendary 'Soviet Intelligence Officer', a dedicated 'International Communist', whose ideology and technical skill were in themselves a practical and decisive contribution to the cause of peace.

This recent Soviet portrait of Sorge has certain attributes of a patriotic cult. The figure has set in a rigid and adulatory mould; the personality already fixed in the selected attitudes of a legend. It has been the intention of this book to present a more rounded and human impression of the man.

(I) SELECT BIBLIOGRAPHY

(A) Primary Sources

1. JAPANESE: Obi Toshito (Editor), *Gendai-shi Shiryo, Zoruge Jiken* (Materials on Modern History, The Sorge Incident), Tokyo, Misuzu Shobo, 3 vols. 1962.
2. GERMAN: Foreign Office Archives. State Secretary Files, Japan. (1941–1944) Special files on the Sorge and Lissner Cases.
3. *International Military Tribunal of Far East: Proceedings.* Tokyo 1946–1948.
4. *U.S. House of Representatives, 82nd Congress, First Session: Un-American Activities Committee.* Hearings on Un-American Aspects of the Richard Sorge Spy Case. Washington Government Printing Office, 1951.

(B) General Works

(i) ENGLISH

Argall, Phyllis, *Prisoner in Japan* (Geoffrey Bles, London 1945).

Butow, Robert J. C., *Tojo and the Coming of the War* (Princeton University Press, 1961).

Carr, E. H., *A History of Soviet Russia. Socialism in One Country 1924–1926* (Macmillan, 1964).

Chambers, Whittaker, *Witness* (Random House, New York 1952).

Craigie, Sir Robert, *Behind the Japanese Mask* (Hutchinson, London 1946).

Dallin, David, *Soviet Espionage* (Yale University Press, 1955).

Degras, Jane, *The Communist International, Selected Documents 1919–1928* (2 vols. Oxford University Press, 1960).

Fleisher, Wilfrid, *Volcanic Isle* (Cape, London 1942).

Grew, Joseph C., *Ten Years in Japan* (Hammond, London 1944).

Jones, F. C., *Japan's New Order in East Asia* (Oxford University Press, 1954).

Kublin, Hyman, *Sun Yat-sen: Asian Revolutionary* (Princeton University Press 1964).

Liu, F. F., *A Military History of Modern China 1924–49* (Princeton University Press: Oxford University Press 1956).

Massing, Hede, *This Deception* (Duell, Sloan and Pearce, New York 1951).

Nollau, G., *International Communism and World Revolution: History and Methods* (London 1961).

North, R. C., *Kuomintang and Chinese Communist Elites* (Stanford University Press 1952).

Presseisen, Ernst L., *Germany and Japan 1933–41* (Nijhoff, Den Haag 1958).

Schellenberg, Walter, *The Schellenberg Memoirs* (André Deutsch, 1956).

Swearingen, Rodger, and Paul Langer, *Red Flag in Japan* (Harvard University Press 1951).

Taylor von Mehren, Arthur (Editor), *Law in Japan* (Harvard University Press 1963).

Tolischus, Otto, *Tokyo Record* (Hamish Hamilton, London 1943).

Ypsilon, *Pattern for World Revolution* (Ziff Davis, Chicago 1947).

(ii) JAPANESE

Mitamura Takeo, *Senso to Kyosanshugi* (War and Communism). (Minshu Seido Fukyu Kai, Tokyo 1950).

Nihon Kokusai Seiji Gakkai (Editors), *Taiheiyo E No Michi* (The Road to the Pacific War), 7 vols. (Asahi Shimbun Sha, Tokyo 1963).

Yabe Teiji (Editor), *Konoye Fumimaro*, 2 vols. (Kobundo, Tokyo 1952).

(iii) GERMAN

Boveri, Margret, *Der Verrat im XX Jahrhundert* (Rowohlt 1957).

Dirksen, Herbert von, *Moskau, London, Tokyo* (W. Kohlhammer 1949).

Kordt, Erich, *Nicht aus die Akten* (Deutsche Verlagsanstalt, 1950).

Lupke, Hubertus, *Japans Russlandpolitik von 1939 bis 1941* (Alfred Metzner Verlag 1962).

Sommer, Theo, *Deutschland und Japan zwischen den Mächten 1935–40* (J. C. B. Mohr [Paul Siebeck], Tübingen 1962).

Telpuchowski, B. S., *Die sowjetische Geschichte des Grossen Vaterländischen Krieges 1941–1945*. (German edition with critical notes by A. Hillgruber and H. A. Jacobsen) (Bernard Graefe 1961).

Wollenberg, Erich, *Der Apparat* (Bundesministerium für gesamtdeutsche Fragen, Bonn) (no date).

(C) Works Connected with the Sorge Case

(i) ENGLISH

Johnson, Chalmers, *An Instance of Treason: Ozaki Hotsumi and the Sorge Spy Ring* (Stanford University Press 1964).

Meissner, Hans Otto, *The Man with Three Faces* (Pan Books 1957). [*Der Fall Sorge* (in fiction form) (Wilhelm Andermann Verlag 1958)].

Willoughby, Charles A., *Shanghai Conspiracy: The Sorge Spy Ring* (E. P. Dullin and Company Inc., New York 1952).

(ii) JAPANESE

Ishii Hanako, *Ai wo subete Ningen Zoruge* (All My Love for the Man Sorge) (Masu Shobo, Tokyo 1951).

Kawai Teikichi, *Aru Kakumeika No Kaiso* (Memoirs of a Revolutionary) (Nihon Shuppan Kyokai, Tokyo 1953).

Kazama Michitaro, *Aru Hangyaku* (A Case of Treason) (Shinseido, Tokyo 1959).

Ozaki Hotsuki, *Zoruge Jiken* (The Sorge Affair) (Chuo Koron Sha, Tokyo 1963).

(iii) RUSSIAN

Dement'yeva, I.; Agayants, N. and Yakolev, Ye, *Tovaritch Sorge* (*Sovietskaya Rossiya*, Moscow 1965).

(iv) FRENCH

Chatel, Nicole; and Guérin, Alain, *Camarade Sorge* (Julliard, 1965).

(D) Articles

(i) JAPANESE

Ikoma Yoshitoshi, 'Zoruge Kaiso' (Recollections of Sorge), *Misuzu*, March 1962.

Lyushkov, General G. S., 'The Far Eastern Red Army', *Contemporary Japan*, Vol. VIII No. 8, October 1939.

Matsumoto Shinichi, 'Nihon Teikokushugi to Ozaki Hotsumi' (Japanese Imperialism and Ozaki Hotsumi), *Sekai*, December 1946.

Ohashi Hideo, 'Watakushi wa Zoruge o Toraeta' (I Arrested Sorge), *Sunday Mainichi*, July 2, 1961.

(ii) WEST GERMAN AND SWISS

Freund, Michael, 'Das Märchen von Dr. Sorge', *Die Gegenwart*, January 11, 1958.

Massing, Hede, 'Richard Sorge', *Deutsche Rundschau*, April 1953.

Sorge, Christiane, 'Mein Mann—Richard Sorge', *Die Weltwoche*, December 11, 1964.

Series of articles on the Sorge Case: *Der Spiegel* (June 13 to October 3, 1951).

(iii) SOVIET

Budkevich, S., 'The Credo of Richard Sorge', *New Times* No. 43, October 28, 1964.

Chernyavsky, V., 'The Feat of Richard Sorge', *Pravda*, November 6, 1964.

Dementieva, I., and Agayants, N., 'Richard Sorge, Soviet Intelligence Officer', *Sovietskaya Rossiya*, September 5–6, 1964.

Geller, 'On the Seventieth Birthday of S. P. Uritsky' (*The Red Star*, March 2, 1965).

Gorev, Ya, 'I Knew Sorge', *Komsomolskaya Pravda*, October 8–9–10, 1964.

Maevskii, Viktor, 'Comrade Richard Sorge', *Pravda*, September 4, 1964.

Pekel'nik, N., 'The Exploits of Richard Sorge: The Story of a Soviet Spy's Heroism', *Izvestiya*, September 4, 1964.

Petrov, V., 'There was nothing else I could do . . .' (Richard Sorge's letters to his wife, Yekaterina Aleksandrovska Maksimova), *Komsomolskaya Pravda*, January 1, 1965.

(iv) EAST GERMAN

Eisler, Professor Dr. Gerhart, 'Erinnerungen an Richard Sorge', *Neues Deutschland*, November 2, 1964.

Krahl, Dr. Franz (Correspondent in Moscow), 'Aus dem Schatten getreten'. Uber das ungewöhliche Leben und den Heldentod unseres Genossen Richard Sorge. *Neues Deutschland* (official organ of the East German Communist Party), October 18, 1964.

Wolf, Dieter, 'Der Funker des Senders "Ramsai"': Wie Max und Anna Christiansen-Klausen an der Seite Kundschafters Dr. Sorge kämpfen'. *Neues Deutschland*, November 2, 1964.

(v) YUGOSLAV

Cvetic, Dusan, 'Who was Branko Vukelic?' *Review*, October 1964, Belgrade (published in English).

Vukovic, Milan, 'Pogibija Branka Vukelica', *Trideset Dana* No. 73, January 1952.

(vi) DANISH

Moltke, Kai, 'When the Master Spy drank beer in Copenhagen', *Politiken*, December 27, 1964.

Jensen, Richard, 'I saw Sorge last', *Politiken*, December 27, 1964.

(II) WRITINGS OF RICHARD SORGE

(A) Books

1. R. J. Sorge, *Rosa Luxemburg's Akkumulation des Kapitals* (*Bearbeitet für die Arbeiterschaft*). (Rosa Luxemburg's 'Accumulation of Capital'. Presented for the workers). Druck und Verlag. Genossenschafts—Buchdruckerei. Solingen 1921.

2. I. K. Sorge, *Das Dawesabkommen und seine Auswirkungen* (1925). (The Dawes Plan and its Effects).

3. R. Sonter, *Der neue deutsche Imperialismus* (The new German Imperialism), Hamburg 1928. (Japanese translation 1929).

(B) Articles

1. Political leading articles in *Die Bergische Arbeitsstime* (The Voice of the Mineworkers), the Communist daily newspaper published in Solingen. Sorge's articles, signed with an 'S', appear in this paper between August 1921 and June 1922.

2. Contributions to the Comintern press. Articles or pamphlets in the *Communist International* under the name of 'I. K. Sorge' or 'R. Sonter' between 1925 and 1929.

3. *Frankfurter Zeitung.* Sorge sent articles from Tokyo between April 1936 and October 6, 1941.

4. *Algemeen Handelsblad Amsterdam.* Certain contributions from Tokyo 1934 to January 1940.

5. *Zeitschrift für Geopolitik* (Berlin). Sorge contributed the following special articles between 1935 and 1939:
   'Mandchukuo im Umbau' (June 1935)
   'Die Armeerevolte in Tokyo' (May 1936)
   'Japanische Agrarfragen' (January 1937)
   'Zur Lage in der inneren Mongolie' (May 1937)

'Hongkong und Südwest China im japanischen-chinesischen Konflikt
I' (July 1938)
'Kanton und Sudwest China im japanischen-chinesischen Konflikt II'
(August 1938)
'Die Japanische Wirtschaft im Chinakriege' (February 1939)
'Die japanische Expansion' (August 1939)
6. *Die Wehrmacht* (publication of the German War Ministry), 'Von
Samurai zur Panzertruppe—article on the Japanese army, June 1,
1937.

(III) CODE NAMES OF THE SORGE RING

Richard Sorge	'Robert' (Hamburg)
	'R. Sonter' (Comintern)
	'Johann' (Scandinavian missions)
	'Schmidt' (China)
	'Johnson' (China)
	'Ramsay' (China and Japan)
	'Smith' (Japan)
	'Fix' ⎱ (Japan W/T)
	'Inson' ⎰
Ozaki	'Otto' (China and Japan)
	'Invest' (W/T)
Miyagi	'Joe'
	'Intelli' (W/T)
Klausen	'Fritz' (W/T)
Vukelic	'Gigolo' (W/T)
Koshiro	'Miki'
Shinozuka	'Specialist'
Dr. Voigt (Woidt)	'Kommersant'
Zaitsev	'Serge'
Stein	'Gustav'

Note: Certain W/T code names were used to denote sources of informa-
tion, or leading personalities.
'Marta' (German military attaché, Tokyo); 'Green' (Japan); 'Paula'
(Admiral Wenneker); 'Richard' (Ribbentrop); 'Green Box' (Japanese
Army); 'Mak' (Matsuoka); 'White Bottle' (German Navy).

NOTES

Prologue

Chapter 1

Chapter 2

Chapter 3

Chapter 3, continued

PAGE

78 'Which helped to decide Comintern policy towards the C.C.P.': Japanese Police Report on Sorge.

79 'I was at a crossroads': Police Interrogation of Ozaki, No. 3.

Chapter 4

84 Frölich ('Teo'): Klausen's Notes.

90 Eisler press interview: *Neues Deutschland*, November 2, 1964.

94 Sorge impressed by Noulens exchange: Yoshikawa and Professor Ikoma, interviewed by one of the authors.

Chapter 5

95 Smoliansky's son remembers: *Sovietskaya Rossiya*, October 2, 1964.

97 'I was an independent leader': Preliminary Judge's Examination of Sorge, No. 11.

99–100 'Gorev's' account: Y. 'Gorev', 'I Knew Sorge', *Komsomolskaya Pravda*, October 8, 1964.

100 A Soviet agent at Gestapo files?: C. A. Willoughby, *Shanghai Conspiracy*, p. 39.

100 Schellenberg, *Memoirs*, pp. 175–6.

102 Last letter from Berlin: 'Gorev' in *Komsomolskaya Pravda*, October 9, 1964.

Chapter 6

104 Saito's remark: Wilfrid Fleisher, *Volcanic Isle*, p. 58.

105 Note in Grew's diary: Joseph C. Grew, *Ten Years in Japan*, pp. 93–4.

Chapter 7

116 'Bernhardt'–Vukelic dialogue: Japanese Home Ministry Police Bureau Report, Part IV, Ch. 3 ('Establishment of Japan Organization').

119 Vukelic's report on Yugoslav Army: Vukelic Statement (Procurator's Office, Tokyo District Criminal Court).

121–2 Barbé: David J. Dallin: *Soviet Espionage*, pp. 45–7.

124 Vukelic's last talk with his mother: *Review*, published in Belgrade, October 1964: 'Who was Branko Vukelic?'

126 Bir apparat: Dallin, *op. cit.*, p. 56.

129–30 Dissensions in 'Dawn Society': Note by Miyagi on 'The Communist Party', attached to Procurator's Examination of Miyagi, No. 30.

131 Long Beach arrests: Note attached to Examination No. 30. The same document gives Miyagi Yosaburo as among those who joined the party in 1928 or 1929.

Chapter 8

136–7 'The accused readily agreed': Report by Preliminary Judge, Tokyo District Court, at the conclusion of his examination of Ozaki, December 15, 1942.

139 'Neither Nazi nor Communist': Procurator's Examination of Sorge, No. 34.

139–40 Frau Ott's good influence: Authors' interview with Prince von Urach.

140 'Ott was a fine man': Procurator's Examination of Sorge, No. 34.

143 Sieburg's description of *Fledermaus*: *Der Spiegel*, August 9, 1951; and interview with authors.

143 Urach recalls *Fledermaus*: *Ibid.*, and in conversation with authors.

PAGE

144-5 Grew and Yurenev: Grew, *op. cit.*, p. 116.

145 Miyagi on *Sakurakai:* Procurator's Examination of Miyagi, No. 22.

147 Miyagi on Akiyama: Preliminary Judge's Examination of Miyagi, No. 18.

150 Seiyukai nationalist societies: These were the *Tesshinkai* (Iron Will Society) and the *Seikin Seisha* (Blue Collar Political Society) – Home Ministry Police Bureau Report, Part II (Personal Data, etc. – Kawai Teikichi).

151-2 Ozaki introduces Kawai to Miyagi: Kawai Teikichi, *Aru Kakumeika no Kaiso* (Memoirs of a Revolutionary), p. 255.

153 'Ika had changed visibly': Hede Massing, quoted in *Der Spiegel*, June 27, 1951.

Chapter 9

155 'Absolute freedom': Procurator's Examination of Sorge No. 35 – italics are the authors'.

155 'Sprat to catch mackerel': *Ibid.*, No. 36. In the Japanese text the words are *ebi de tai wo tsuru*, 'to use a prawn to catch a sea-bream'.

160 Moscow influenced destination of Long March?: R. C. North, *Kuomintang and Chinese Communist Elites* (Stanford, Calif., Stanford University Press, 1952), p. 38.

161 Klausen's thoughts on Japan: Klausen's Notes.

161 'Ultimate duty to prevent war': Preliminary Judge's Examination of Sorge, No. 13.

161-2 Uritsky's warning about Japan and Germany: 'Sorge's Own Story'.

162 Hack and Oshima: Ernst L. Presseisen, *Germany and Japan*, p. 83.

162 Willoughby and Junkers flight: Willoughby, *op. cit.*, p. 61.

163-4 Weingarten and Gestapo: *Der Spiegel*, July 18, 1951.

Chapter 10

166-9 Kawai Teikichi: The account of Kawai's arrest and subsequent ordeal comes from his book, *Aru Kakumeika no Kaiso*, *op. cit.*, pp. 275 *et seq.*

169 'If under interrogation ...': *ibid.*, p. 288.

173 'To Dirksen, Ott and Wenneker': Procurator's Examination of Sorge, No. 37.

174 Reference to navy in *Geopolitik: Zeitschrift für Geopolitik*, May 1936.

174 Sorge to Urach on Japanese Communists: Interview with Prince von Urach.

176 'This phrase, *permanent expansion*': Preliminary Judge's Examination of Sorge, No. 16. Italics in original.

176 'I should ... have been a scholar': 'Sorge's Own Story'.

176 'This ability to select material': *Ibid.*

177 Embassy assessment of mutiny reported: Procurator's Examination of Sorge, No. 37.

178 Quotations from Sorge's article: *Zeitschrift für Geopolitik*, May 1936.

179-80 'These fellows laid the bloody head': *Der Spiegel*, July 11, 1951.

Chapter 11

182 Helped Ott to encode telegram: Procurator's Examination of Sorge, No. 37.

183-4 Confidential talks, Berlin knew nothing: Presseisen, *op. cit.*, pp. 98-9.

190 Saionji 'tried to help Konoye': Autobiographical statement by Saionji.

192-3 Ozaki's association with Kazami: Procurator's Examination of Ozaki. No. 22.

195 'Summer house in small garden': Dr. Friedrich Sieburg, interviewed by authors.

Chapter 11, continued

PAGE

195 Visitor recalls Sorge's books: Dr. Margret Boveri, interviewed by authors.

196 Description of Sorge's bathroom: *Der Spiegel*, August 1, 1951.

198 'An almost demoniacal expression': Dr. Friedrich Sieburg, interviewed by authors.

200 Moscow message dated September 5, 1938: Home Ministry Police Bureau Report, Part VII.

Chapter 12

204-6 Communication from the editor of the *Frankfurter Zeitung*: German Foreign Office Archives ('The Sorge Case').

207 The disposal of Bernhardt's set: Klausen's Notes.

209-10 Klausen's journeys to Shanghai in 1936 and 1939: Police Interrogation of Klausen, No. 6.

216 Klausen loses his wallet: Klausen's Notes.

216 Women 'absolutely unfit for espionage work': Sorge's Statement to *Tokko* Police.

217 'I myself was surprised': *Ibid.*

Chapter 13

218 Sorge's refusal of official status: Procurator's Examination of Sorge, No. 34.

219 Sorge shown draft telegrams: *Ibid.*, No. 36.

220 Messages signed 'Director': Home Ministry Police Bureau Report, Part VII.

221 'Germany already making . . . approaches to the Soviet Union': Procurator's Examination of Sorge, No. 36.

222 'Embassy study group': *Ibid.* No. 38.

225 Matsuoka's denial of assurances to Ott: Preliminary Judge's Examination of Witness Matsuoka Yosuke.

225-6 Matsuoka less than candid: Lupke, *Japans Russlandpolitik*, p. 128.

227 Order of battle chart: Procurator's Examination of Sorge, No. 44.

229-30 Niedermayer and Scholl: *Ibid.*, No. 41.

230 Microfilm of Ribbentrop-Ott telegrams: Article in *Pravda*, November 6, 1964. Another article in *Sovietskaya Rossiya* (September 5-6, 1964) gives the date as June 15, not May 15.

231 'Why has not Stalin reacted?': Article in *Neues Deutschland*, October 30, 1964.

231 'Message of grateful appreciation': Procurator's Examination of Sorge, No. 41.

231 Message from 'Organizer': Preliminary Judge's Examination of Sorge, No. 38.

232 Ozaki and Imperial Conference: Procurator's Examination of Sorge, No. 41.

234 The text of the decisions of the Imperial Conference of July 2, 1941, was first published in *Pravda* on October 11, 1946.

235 Kretschmer's 'efforts at persuasion': Procurator's Examination of Sorge, No. 41.

236 Radio message on troops' clothing: Home Ministry Police Bureau Report, Part VII.

236 'Mobilization itself might lead to war': Procurator's Examination of Sorge, No. 43.

236-46 Sorge's messages to Moscow, August-October, 1941: Home Ministry Police Bureau Report, Part VII.

237 Recent Japanese study on the Pacific War: Nihon Kokusai Seiji Gakkai (ed.), *Taiheiyo e no Michi* (The Road to the Pacific War), Vol. 5, p. 320.

PAGE

242 Ozaki's views to Sorge on the American negotiations: Analysis attached to Police Interrogation of Ozaki, No. 10.

243-4 Ozaki and Saionji: *ibid.* and examination of Saionji by the procurator on March 30 and 31, 1942.

243 Konoye questioned in hospital: Preliminary Judge's Examination of Witness Konoye Fumimaro.

Chapter 14

249 'Severe but considerate attitude of the police': Home Ministry Police Bureau Report (Review of Sorge Affair).

250 Ito and Ozaki, oil stocks and steel: Sorge Judgment (Tokyo District Criminal Court) and Preliminary Judge's Examination of Witness Ito Ritsu.

250 Aoyagi's statement to the police: Ozaki Hotsuki, *Zoruge Jiken* (The Sorge Affair), p. 16.

251 Miyagi on information from Kitabayashi: Preliminary Judge's Examination of Miyagi, October 30, 1942.

252 Ozaki's account of his arrest: Written statement by Ozaki, dated June 8, 1943, addressed to Judge Takada Masashi of Tokyo District Criminal Court.

253 Iwamura and the red pencil: Obi Toshito, *Gendai-shi shiryo, Zoruge Jiken* (Materials on Modern History, The Sorge Affair), Vol. 1, 'Historical Background'.

254 Arrest of Sorge: Ohashi Hideo, *Watakushi wa Zoruge o toraeta* (I Arrested Sorge), *Sunday Mainichi*, July 2, 1961.

254 Klausen on final meeting and arrest: Klausen's Notes.

257-8 Vukelic on Sorge's leadership: Vukelic Statement (Procurator's Office, Tokyo District Criminal Court).

258-9 Sorge's letter to 'Director': Article in *Sovietskaya Rossiya*, September 5-6, 1964.

259 Draft telegram requesting recall: Home Ministry Police Bureau Report, Part VII, and Preliminary Judge's Examination of Sorge, No. 43.

260 'We have been sniffing round . . .': Obi, *Zoruge Jiken*, 'Historical Background'.

261 'Reason why Sorge was being watched': Ohashi, 'I Arrested Sorge'.

Chapter 15

263 'A semi-accusatorial principle': A. Taylor von Mehren (ed.), *Law in Japan*, Ryuichi Hirano: 'The Accused in Society', p. 274.

264 'Subjective and psychological elements': *Ibid.*

264 Judges and procurators, comparison: Mehren, *op. cit.*, Takaaki Hattori: 'The Legal Profession in Japan', pp. 125-6.

264 Defence lawyer's function: Mehren, *op. cit.*, Atsushi Nagashima: 'The Accused and Society', pp. 304-5.

265 Ikoma on Yoshikawa: Ikoma Yoshitoshi, *Zoruge Kaiso* (Recollections of Sorge), *Misuzu*, March, 1962.

266 'I say this since it appears . . .': Klausen's Notes.

267 Yoshikawa's 'conditions for the meeting': Yoshikawa interviewed by one of the authors.

267 Yoshikawa on the date of Sorge's confession: Hearings before the Committee on Un-American Activities, House of Representatives; 82nd Congress, First Session, August 9, 1951. (Washington, U.S. Government Printing Office, 1951), p. 1142; and Yoshikawa, when interviewed by one of the authors.

267 Tamazawa's version: Statement by Tamazawa.

Chapter 15, continued

267-8 'A short formal visit': German Foreign Office Documents.

268 'The crisis of the investigation': Yoshikawa interview.

268 Ott's recollection: General Ott, interviewed by the authors.

268 Yoshikawa's narrative of the meeting: Yoshikawa interview.

269 'I am defeated': *Idem*, Committee Hearings (cited); and Ohashi, *op. cit.*

270 'Summarily broken on the wheel': Written Statement by Ozaki Hotsumi to Judge Takada Masashi (cited).

270 Grew's comment: J. C. Grew, *op. cit.*, p. 460.

270 Craigie's comment: Sir Robert Craigie, *Behind the Japanese Mask*, p. 154.

270 Accounts by arrested journalists: Otto D. Tolischus, *Tokyo Record* (London, Hamish Hamilton, 1943). Phyllis Argall, *Prisoner in Japan* (London, Geoffrey Bles, 1945).

272 'If we refused to sign': Argall, p. 223.

272 'About 4 o'clock my colleague': Committee Hearings (cited), p. 1144.

273 The three basic questions: *Ibid.*, p. 1144.

273 Sorge also a 'Roosevelt spy'?: Yoshikawa interview.

273 Fourth Bureau or Comintern?: Committee Hearings, p. 1144.

274 Order from Procurators' Bureau: Judicial Officers (procurators and others) Conference, February 28, 1942, on Sorge Case — Obi, *op. cit.*, Vol. 2, pp. 541-3.

274-5 Police Chief's resistance: *Ibid.*

278 Ohashi recommends the death penalty: Police Report on Sorge.

279 Procurator's statement on oath: Statement by Tamazawa. Authors' italics.

279 *Zoruge Jiken* editor's opinion: Obi, *op. cit.*, Vol. 2, p. 540.

Chapter 16

283 Koshiro: The characters for this man's name can be romanized as 'Kodai' (cf. Chalmers Johnson, *op. cit.*, p. 151), but Koshiro is the more felicitous and acceptable reading.

283 Sorge's remark on 'ready access': Statement to *Tokko* Police (4. 'Personal Views on Espionage Operations').

285 Miyagi's remark to Yasuda: *Izvestiya*, September 7, 1964.

285 'This is the swine . . .': *Ibid.*

287 The research institute in Osaka: This was the Ohara Social Problems Research Institute. A brief description of this organization can be found in Chalmers Johnson, *op. cit.*, pp. 37-8.

289 'Maximum penalty' recommended for Funakoshi: Police Report on Funakoshi.

290 Comments from Saitama and Miyagi prefectures: Home Ministry Police Bureau Report, Part XIV 'Effect of the Public Announcement of the Case'.

290 Comments about Konoye: *Ibid.*

291 Inukai's indiscretion: Procurator's Indictment of Saionji.

292 Saionji's autobiographical statement: Obi, *op. cit.*, Vol. 2, p. 519 *et seq.*

293 Saionji's plea on behalf of Ozaki: Procurator's Examination of Saionji, No. 4.

293 Ozaki on the Breakfast Club: Procurator's Examination of Ozaki, No. 22.

297 Redman taken into custody: Craigie, *op. cit.*, pp. 143-4.

Chapter 17

301 Sorge and Lenz shared office: German Foreign Office Archives, Tokyo telegrams (Meisinger), April 15 and December 17, 1942.

303 Hofmeier placed on the blockade runner: *Ibid.*, Tokyo telegrams (Meisinger), July 1, 1942, and February 13, 1943.

305 Extension of Lissner's contract: *Ibid.*, File on Lissner Case, Draft memorandum, March 31, 1943.

305 Cable on alleged claims by Lissner: *Ibid.*, Tokyo telegram (Meisinger), August 16, 1942.

306 Kretschmer's conversation in Harbin: *Ibid.*, Hsinking telegram, March 17, 1942.

306 'Danger . . . of a second Sorge case': *Ibid.*, Tokyo telegram (Meisinger), May 25, 1943. Significantly Meisinger had been accorded full diplomatic privileges on the German Embassy list by the Japanese authorities four days previously.

307 The Fuehrer's comments: *Ibid.*, German Foreign Office memorandum to Ribbentrop, May 30, 1943.

307-8 Note by Canaris defending Lissner: *Ibid.*, Admiral Canaris, Note to German Security authorities, May 31, 1943.

308 Wagner's telegram from Tokyo: *Ibid.*, Tokyo telegram (Wagner), June 3, 1943.

309 'Sensational arrest' forecast by Stahmer: *Ibid.*, Tokyo telegram (Stahmer), June 3, 1943.

309 Wagner's counter-attack: *Ibid.*, Hsinking telegram (Wagner), June 18, 1943.

309 Stahmer proposes supervision of Hsinking: *Ibid.*, Tokyo telegram (Stahmer), June 24, 1943.

309 List of Germans under arrest: *Ibid.*, Tokyo telegram (Meisinger), June 5, 1943.

311 Ribbentrop seeks 'a more detailed explanation': *Ibid.*, Fuschl telegram (Ribbentrop at his country house), June 10, 1943.

312 Foreign Office support for Wagner: *Ibid.*, German Foreign Office minute, June 28, 1943.

312 Stahmer's comment on Japanese memorandum: *Ibid.*, Tokyo telegram (Stahmer), August 12, 1943.

313 'Intervention of the German Military Intelligence would be misunderstood': *Ibid.*, Tokyo telegram (Kretschmer), October 24, 1943.

313 'Japanese General Staff is extraordinarily suspicious': *Ibid.*, Tokyo telegram (Kretschmer), September 15, 1943.

Chapter 18

315 Ott's telegram on indictment: German Foreign Office Archives, Tokyo telegram (Ott), May 15, 1942.

316 'Otts displayed no particular emotion': Home Ministry Police Bureau Report, Part XIV.

317-18 Sorge in court: Ikoma, 'Recollections' (cited).

318 Kawai sees Sorge's joy: Ozaki Hotsuki, *op. cit.*, pp. 148-9.

318 'A third of the time . . . general talk': Yoshikawa interview.

318 Ikoma's difficulty in translating legal Japanese: Ikoma, 'Recollections' (cited).

319 'Very often it was already dark': *Ibid.*

319 Ikoma not on duty at the trial: *Ibid.*

321 Ozaki's trial: Chalmers Johnson, *op. cit.*, pp. 192 *et seq.*, contains a study of the proceedings against Ozaki.

323 Stahmer reports execution to Berlin: German Foreign Office Archives, Tokyo telegrams (Stahmer), November 8, 1944.

Chapter 18, continued

PAGE

326 Sorge's plea for Hanako-san: Yoshikawa interview.

327 Teeth recognized from the gold fillings: Ishii Hanako, interview.

327 Hanako describes the bones: Ozaki Hotsuki, *op. cit.*, pp. 203–4.

327 Comment by Ozaki Hotsuki: *Ibid.*, p. 204.

Epilogue

331 Himmler's letter and Ribbentrop's telegram: German Foreign Office Archives ('The Sorge Case').

335 Schellenberg's view: *The Schellenberg Memoirs*, p. 176.

337 'Release list . . . contained foreign espionage agents': Willoughby, *The Shanghai Conspiracy*, p. 16.

339 Eighteen Americans allegedly connected with the case: *Ibid.*, p. 279.

340 'An epic search began': *Ibid.*, p. 271.

347–9 Cunningham, Petersdorf, and Vasiliev: Transcript of the International Military Tribunal for the Far East, pp. 38,413 *et seq.*; 38,469; and 38,472.

351 'He did not force open safes': *Izvestiya*, September 4, 1964.

INDEX